P9-CLK-143
ILLINOIS CENTRAL COLLEGE
PR463.K8
STACKS
British Victorian literature;
A12900 392358

British Victorian Literature

BRITISH VICTORIAN LITERATURE

RECENT REVALUATIONS

Edited by
SHIV K. KUMAR

New York • New York University Press
London • University of London Press Limited
1969

Library of Congress Catalog Card Number: 69-16343
Manufactured in the United States of America

Contents

PART IV Prose

PART V Criticism

PART VI Drama

Preface

The period extending from the Reform Act of 1832 until the death of Queen Victoria (1901) has undergone thorough revaluation during recent years. If to the first half of our century the literature of the Victorian age appeared to be conditioned by moral, social, and literary philistinism, during the past decade or so, we have begun to perceive in the Victorian writer a compelling urge to confront the complexities of the human situation. We have now realized the fallacy of interpreting "Victorianism" as a concept synonymous with mere self-complacency, prudery, certitude, pragmatic idealism, and utilitarianism. No longer do we consider Browning, for instance, a poet of sentimental idealism, but a writer whose profound moral insight may be interpreted in terms of existential commitment. The novels of Charlotte and Emily Bronte anticipate the contemporary dichotomy between free expression and repression. And Henry James had prophesied, as early as 1885, that the novel of the future would explore the subliminal layers of human consciousness in an attempt to penetrate the crust of the superficial ego and establish contact with the inner self. In fact, the Victorian age now impresses us with the amazing multiplicity of its points of view, its conflicting ideologues, and its moral fervor to strive, to seek, and to find. Hence, the Victorian age has come to acquire a peculiar contemporary relevance.

British Victorian Literature brings together a set of thirty scholarly and provocative articles, published during the past few years, on what may be described as one of the most seminal epochs in English literary history. T. S. Eliot, Graham Greene, René Wellek, Lionel Trilling, and Herbert Read, to mention only a few of the distinguished critics and writers included here, make this collection of essays truly representative of the best that has been thought and written about this period. Most of these essays have never been anthologized before, and two have been written especially for this volume.

This book is divided into different sections, each dealing with a separate genre (poetry, fiction, prose, criticism, and drama) so as to present a comprehensive survey of this period. A select bibliography at the end suggests items for supplementary reading, both books and articles, on the authors discussed in this volume.

I am indebted to Professor Oscar Cargill and Mr. John Hammond for their help and guidance; to Dr. Hari Singh, Mr. Harry Curtis, Miss Rebecca Moss, and particularly Miss Sherry Van Meter, I am grateful for their invaluable editorial assistance.

Marshall University
Huntington,
West Virginia

Shiv K. Kumar

PART I Victorianism

1. Jerome H. Buckley

"Victorianism"

Oh, so, when modern things are thrust
By death below the coffin lid,
Our liberal sons will spurn our dust
And wonder what it was we did.
—TENNYSON

By the time of Prince Albert's death in 1861, many of the Manchester liberals had come to regard the monarchy as merely the relic of an unprogressive age which had not yet learned the advantages of a complete laissez faire. Five years later, when Victoria had long since retired from public life, John Bright addressed a great rally of British reformers, some of whom were prepared to demand the queen's abdication. As suggested president of the new republic, Bright was earnestly confident of his cause. Still, he felt it only right during the course of his remarks to repudiate the libels that his more zealous followers had passed upon their widowed sovereign. But the mere mention of Victoria's name brought an immediate and not altogether expected response: of one accord the republican audience arose to sing with fervent heart and voice,

God save our gracious Queen,
Long live our noble Queen,
God save the Queen![1]

Victoria indeed outlived most of Bright's republicans by many years. She lived long—long enough to see her name indissolubly linked to a remarkable century's culture. Yet if "Victoria" had once been able to awaken a distinct and uniform impression in the minds of one assembly, the age which bears her name has since been subject to diverse and divided judgment. Already by the 1890's "Victorian" had become a favorite derogatory epithet to a generation which, ironically enough, was spending lavishly of its pounds and poetry to celebrate Victoria's Diamond Jubilee. And into the twentieth century "Victorianism," defined ambiguously if at all, persisted, a shield for the conservative and a target for the modernist.

Any cultural period suffers distortion from a generalized indictment, however speciously formulated. But the outlines of the Victorian era blur beyond recognition in the confusion of contradictory charges. The Victorians, we are told, were "a poor, blind, complacent people";[2] yet they were torn by doubt, spiritually bewildered,[3] lost in a troubled universe. They were crass materialists, wholly absorbed in the present, quite unconcerned "with abstract verities and eternal values";[4] but they were also excessively religious, lamentably idealistic, nostalgic for the past,[5] and ready to forego present delights for the vision of a world beyond. Despite their slavish "conformity,"[6] their purblind respect for convention, they were, we learn, "rugged individualists," given to "doing as one likes,"[7] heedless of culture, careless of a great tradition; the were iconoclasts who worshiped the idols of authority. They were, besides, at once sentimental humanitarians and hard-boiled proponents of free enterprise. Politically, they were governed by narrow insular prejudice, but swayed by dark imperialistic designs. Intellectually and emotionally, they believed in progress, denied original sin, and affirmed the death of the Devil; yet by temperament they were patently Manichaens to whom living was a desperate struggle between the force of good and the power of darkness.[8] While they professed "manliness," they yielded to feminine standards; if they emancipated woman from age-old bondage, they also robbed her of a vital place in society.[9] Though they were sexually inhibited[10] and even failed to consider the existence of physical love, they begat incredibly large families and flaunted in their verses a morbidly overdeveloped erotic sensibility.[11] Their art constitutes a shameless record of both hypocrisy and ingenuousness. And their literature remains too purposeful, propagandistic, didactic, with too palpable a design upon the reader; yet it is clearly so romantic, aesthetic, "escapist," that it carries to posterity but a tale of little meaning.

Since most of such charges represent personal reaction rather than objective analysis, the terms "Victorian" and "Victorianism" have acquired the vaguest of emotional connotations. They have become what Ruskin chose to call "masked words droning and skulking about us." While the social historian[12] of the Victorian age who is able to withhold opinion is forever aware of intrinsic complexities, the critic intent upon cultural evaluation is constantly betrayed into premature judgment. And it is the aggregate of these judgments that obscures definition. Many are agreed that in Victorianism inheres a single tragic flaw which vitiates all its sounder impulses. But to one it is a moral hypocrisy,[13] to another a deliberate sentimentalism,[14] to a third a social snobbery.[15] An eminent debunker[16] laments the total failure of the critical faculty. And a sensitive student of abnormal psychology detects in all Victorian life "a manifestation of the anal complex[17] operating upon the group psyche." Yet all the subtleties of oversimplification merely confuse; "Victorianism" remains obscure; we approach no nearer the Victorian essence.

But whatever its central defect, the age, we gather, must in some hidden way have been deeply pernicious. Apparently so persuaded, not a few essayists have attempted to salvage their favorite Victorian authors from the contamination of an unfortunate background. Lewis Carroll has been recently depicted as a frustrated professor attacking "those jungles of nonsense which were merely the daily life" of cultured adults "in the now legendary reign of Victoria"; and his biographer advises us that we may safely "call the *Alice* books art, and the entire Victorian age a neurosis."[18] From a similar point of view, the Brownings may be commended for having reared their son Pen with intelligence and sympathy, for "neither Robert nor Elizabeth Browning were in any way typical Victorian parents."[19] Even Tennyson, who is somewhat more difficult to dissociate from his milieu, finds an apologist who contends that the Laureate, having resisted the "rigid dogma" of his time, may speak to an inquiring modernity, "in spite of all his Victorianism."[20]

It has been possible to recognize the manifold dissatisfactions and rebellions of Carlyle, Dickens, Ruskin, Morris, Samuel Butler, and at the same time to insist that "the note of revolt is not characteristic of the Victorian Age."[21] By definition, the cultural leader must advance beyond his less gifted contemporaries in grasping the problem of his time, but he can scarcely be considered a leader at all if he stands entirely out of relation to those who lag behind. It is, therefore, by no means clear how reasonably we may dogmatize about the acquiescence of the Victorian era, when many of its most representative and influential writers appear restive or refractory. At any rate, we are hardly to be convinced by criticism like that of the British scholar who, writing in the year of the Munich appeasement, condemns Victorian smugness, with the conviction that Englishmen of 1938 have "scarcely a trace of complacency left."[22]

Whether or not, then, their entire age was spiritually apathetic, the most articulate Victorians were, like wakeful minds in any generation, quite prepared to assail omnipresent stupidity and vicious self-satisfaction. Often, to reinforce their assault on the forts of folly, they resorted to the same sort of oversimplified indictment that has since been turned against them. Almost always, they were able to muster their attack with a vigor of statement compared to which latter-day polemics pale into gentle censure. John Morley, for instance, could ally impassioned eloquence to reasoned principle in his denunciation of Victorian England as

> . . . a community where political forms, from the monarchy down to the popular chamber, are mainly hollow shams disguising the coarse supremacy of wealth, where religion is mainly official and political, and is ever ready to dissever itself alike from the spirit of justice, the spirit of charity, and the spirit of truth, and where literature does not as a rule permit itself to discuss serious subjects frankly and worthily—a community, in short, where the great aim of all classes and orders with power is by dint of rigorous silence, fast shutting of the eyes, and stern stopping of the ears, somehow to keep the social pyramid on its apex, with the fatal result of preserving for England its glorious fame as a paradise for the well-to-do, a purgatory for the able, and a hell for the poor.[23]

If Morley, by reason of his relationship to the positivist radicals of the seventies, seems too clearly biased a witness, we may turn to a comparatively calm early-Victorian chronicler who makes no claim to peculiar insight. Reporting with statistical exactitude on the industrial advance of his generation, George Richardson Porter paused to caution a complacent reader against undue optimism. "It must be owned," he wrote, "that our multiplied abodes of want, of wretchedness, and of crime—our town populations huddled together in ill-ventilated and undrained courts and cellars—our numerous workhouses filled to overflowing with the children of want—and our prisons (scarcely less numerous) overloaded with the votaries of crime, do indeed but too sadly and too strongly attest that all is not as it should be with us as regards this most important branch of human progress."[24] Beside strictures so disillusioned and so vehement, twentieth-century anti-Victorianism seems imaginatively stale and rhetorically flabby. The Victorians are still their own severest critics possessed of an amazing capacity for detachment, a singular command of invective, and, as we shall see, an unequaled talent for parody. "Victorianism" was undoubtedly, at least in part, a monster created by rebellious spirits and bequeathed to a posterity which all too frequently is content to regard the spirits as the monster's children.

Violent and vituperative as it frequently was, Victorian self-criticism found direction in the implicit sense that the faults it assailed were remediable by individual and collective reform. For the Victorians were quite unable to view their long era as a static entity, a unique whole to be described by a single sweeping formula. The doctrine of organic development was so thoroughly diffused throughout nineteenth-century science and philosophy that no serious thinker could escape its implications. Whether or not the thoughts of men were widening with the process of the suns, there were everywhere evidences of continual growth and decay. Wistfully Frederic Harrison looked to the joys of a vanished past; early Victorian life, he felt sure, must have been pleasanter than existence in the seventies, for certainly Dickens and Thackeray "tell us of a livelier, jollier age than that recorded in *Middlemarch* and *Fors Clavigera*."[25] In a more sanguine mood, Walter Besant chronicled the incalculable changes between the accession of Victoria and the Golden Jubilee. He lingered over quaint customs long outmoded, as if contemplating the strangeness of a remote antiquity; for in 1887 he could find scant similarity to early Victorian tastes, no parallel, for instance, to the rules of etiquette acceptable fifty years before:

> Never ask a lady any questions about anything whatever.
>
> If you have drunk wine with every one at the table and wish for more, wait till the cloth is removed.
>
> Never permit the sanctity of the drawing-room to be violated by a boot.[26]

If many changes were wrought by deliberate reformers fighting old prejudices, many also, like the shift in standards of deportment, resulted from the gradual operation of hidden social forces.

All in all, the Victorian period achieved little of the stability we have learned to associate with a semimythical neoclassic culture. It moved from form to form, and nothing stood. Almost every Victorian thesis produced its own antithesis, as a ceaseless dialectic worked out its designs. Throughout the period there were vast differences between rural and urban society; the fields of the agrarian South were, as Mrs. Gaskell suggested, a far cry from the smoky cities of the industrial North. And between the towns themselves sharp distinctions could be drawn; the London of Oscar Wilde had little in common with the Birmingham of Joseph Chamberlain. Besides, the "climate of opinion" varied from year to year, from decade to decade; the seventies was perhaps as distant from the eighties as we imagine the twenties of our own century remote from the thirties. The Victorian age as a whole was forced to adapt itself to new values as old traditions crumbled; and the term "Victorian" is, therefore, egregiously abused when invoked to describe attitudes that the Victorians inherited, modified, or discarded.

Viewed in its long perspective, nineteenth-century culture appears entirely relative to the manifold developments of a changing society. Yet within the Victorian period itself, "Victorianism" may well have been a necessary postulate, a distinct absolute deduced from a vague composite of social and aesthetic values which creative thinkers felt compelled to dismiss, in order to clear the way for radical innovation. And to the Edwardians the fiction may have served an essential purpose in assisting toward fresh objectives, until such a time as those objectives were attained and the generation of Virginia Woolf and James Joyce might devise the myth of "Edwardianism." Ultimately the debunking of things Victorian became an amusing pastime rather than a meaningful criticism; the distortion of a past culture represented little more than the evasion of a present problem. Havelock Ellis, who in 1890 had attacked all that seemed to him false within the Victorian world, lived to find "the gesture that was once a vital reaction to real things" becoming at last "a stale and empty trick."[27]

Now that half a century has elapsed since Victoria's death, facile repudiation of the Victorian era seems, in truth, quite as outmoded as the attitudes we can no longer recapture. But the sentimentalization that in some quarters has replaced it is scarcely more constructive. The interests of modern design are not appreciably furthered by the self-conscious revival of baroque styles or the rediscovery of bric-a-brac which has acquired the charm of the antique. We can understand the significant backgrounds of contemporary thought only by transcending indiscriminate praise or blame. Collective guilt, we have learned, is never easy to determine; and value-judgments are best confined to specific creeds and individual works of art.

Working inductively, distrustful of "masked words" and slanted evidence, the historian might discover the sources of the precise concepts upon which less objective interpreters have based their general indictment. The idea of progress, for instance, an idea which admittedly had considerable currency during the Victorian period, might be related to a broader cultural context. It might be seen as an outgrowth of Cartesian philosophy, receiving its major extension among the *philosophes* of eighteenth-century France, passing with variations through the anarchism of Godwin and the poetry of Shelley towards the socialism of Saint-Simon and the positivism of Comte, until with Herbert Spencer came the assumption that progress and evolution moved consistently in the same direction. Or within the age alone, it might be linked to the Victorian's awareness of his very real social advance. The notion of perfectibility would seem to have some immediate sanction at a time when men were devising a system of education on a broad democratic basis, establishing the rights of free speech and trade unionism, progressively extending the franchise, reshaping their entire legal code, and discovering the principles of a medical science by which the sum of human suffering might be immeasurably reduced.

It might then be debated whether the idea of progress was not as much an incentive to further reform as a cause of stupefying satisfaction with the advances already achieved. Yet a cursory review of Victorian opinion indicates that the idea, whatever its effect upon those who embraced it, was much less widely accepted than we have been led to believe. Huxley who was at least as articulate as Spencer, insisted that evolutionary change not seldom ran counter to ethical improvement. And Tennyson, whose early visions of the future have too readily convicted his generation of blind optimism, attained by 1886 a throughly disillusioned view of the "glooming alleys" where "Progress halts on palsied feet" and a sense of the disaster involved in the failure of social adaptation to keep pace with scientific discovery; if Tennyson held to a modified faith in evolution, he recognized the possibility of regression:

> Forward then, but still remember how the course of time will swerve,
> Crook and turn upon itself in many a backward-streaming curve.[28]

The Victorian temper is thus not to be adequately gauged in terms of a concept which flourished long before 1837 and was subject to important qualification from 1850 onwards.

Many of the specific values associated with the anomaly known as "Victorianism" have, like the idea of progress, partial basis in objective evidence; and the inconsistency of the generalizations itself testifies to the bewildering complexity of the era. It is almost impossible to reduce a culture so various to a common denominator; and conflict, indeed, may emerge as the only unity in a great diversity. Yet it is not difficult to find certain doctrines perhaps opposing each other but recurring with an insistency which suggests the breadth of their influence. Probably the most prominent of these, in the early Victorian period at any rate, are Evangelical religion and Benthamite philosophy, both pre-Victorian in origin and both vigorously questioned throughout the nineteenth century. To the one has been ascribed the sententious hypocrisy of Mr. Podsnap; to the other, the uncompromising factualism of Mr. Gradgrind. But apart from their baneful effects, which are to some extent problematical, each encouraged a sense of social responsibility which did much to mitigate the miseries of an expanding industrialism; each contributed, even to its bitterest enemies, something of its earnestness and fixity of vision.

If hardheaded Benthamism was ultimately undermined by the reservations and subtleties of the greatest utilitarian, its zeal for practical reform infected many who found Mill's hedonistic paradox more ingenious than convincing. And if Evangelical restraints and dogmas slowly dissolved under the scrutiny of critical intelligence, the old thirst for righteousness animated so reluctant a heretic as George Eliot, so willful an agnostic as John Morley. Whether actuated by self-interest or Christian principle, moral duty remained for most a categorical imperative. With all the assurance of his brother's orthodoxy, F. W. Newman the freethinker could insist that "all social action, all national cohesion, all reverence for law, all sanctity in rule, is founded upon man's moral conscience."[29] For a few social purpose seemed at one time effectively to coalesce with ethical premise in the short-lived Religion of Humanity. But even to fervent atheists like Charles Bradlaugh the demand for moral sanction and the claims of social justice seemed inescapable. Craving adjustment amid the peril of change, representative Victorians, at least until the seventies, sought either in the radiance of God or in the dim consciousness of man some spiritual absolute by which to interpret and control their material advance; whatever misdirections they may frequently have followed, their impulse was in essence deeply religious.[30]

Prince Albert, we are told, was much concerned with art, though unfortunately he felt it to lie "somewhere between religion and hygiene."[31] Now, if for "hygiene" we might substitute "the general health of the body politic," Prince Albert's view of art would differ little from the first principles of any considerable mid-Victorian aesthetician. The "morality of art"—its religious content—lay in its relationship to the full experience and its power to speak to mankind in the language of universal emotion. For it was the artist's first duty to communicate, and the substance of his message was necessarily of social and, therefore, moral significance. To Ruskin it was clear that the student of art gained the deepest insight into the totality of human affairs. And to Arnold it seemed natural that the critic of books should be first and last a critic of society. The "moral aesthetic" was by no means a Victorian invention; it rested on the major premises of almost every classical aesthetic theory. Yet it bore special relevance to Victorian needs. Confronted with the unprecedented developments of nineteenth-century culture, an emerging middle class with the meagerest intellectual traditions behind it strove desperately to achieve standards of judgment. The early Victorian poet, sometimes no more certain than his contemporaries, was expected to furnish instruction as well as amusement. He could fulfill his vital function in society only by passing dramatic commentary upon the conflicts of his time. Often like Tennyson he had first to relinquish a personal prejudice for a more disinterested aesthetic. But usually he came in the end to feel his renunciation morally—and socially—essential. At all events, out of his sacrifice was born a considerable didactic literature.

In its many-sided concern with manners and morals, the Victorian era was not unlike the Elizabethan age, when conduct-books, pamphlets, plays, sermons, poems explored the problems of degree in an expanding economy. Both periods brought to the present a deep sense of the national past, based upon high scholarship and eager research. Both shared the excitement of vital education. Far from sinking beneath the weight of its "moral," their art at its best followed new experience beyond the bounds of thought. In the years after 1850 novelists and poets exploited the forgotten "local color" of every English county to produce a kind of nineteenth-century *Poly-Olbion*.[32] Like the Elizabethans, the Victorians embarked on their own voyages of discovery. To the far corners of the unknown traveled "manly" adventurers—Layard to buried Nineveh, Livingstone to the dark heart of Africa, Richard Burton to Brazil and Tanganyika and the Great Salt Lake in a valiant effort to live his unexpurgated Arabian nights.

But whether at home or abroad, many a Victorian captured the almost Elizabethan exuberance that led Hurrell Froude to exclaim on the launching of the Oxford Movement in 1833: "What fun it is living in such times as these! How could one now go back to the times of old Tory humbug!"[33] A tireless emotional energy carried Carlyle through continents of passionate prose, just as a physical stamina impelled the somewhat calmer Leslie Stephen to tramp the fifty miles from Cambridge to London on a hot day.[34] Like the Elizabethans, the high Victorians valued a manifold competence; Ruskin like Bacon took all knowledge to be his province, and whether or not, as Whistler suggested, he failed to master his specific subject, he left his mark on many others. Not without some reason, then, did John Addington Symonds conclude that "the English Renaissance of the sixteenth century became renascent in the nineteenth."[35]

Yet it will not do to press the parallel too far. Symonds himself detected in the Victorian period, whatever its bouyancy and promise, elements of "world fatigue" which were, he felt, quite alien to the Elizabethan temper. Certainly the desperate unbelief that permeates so much of Arnold's verse and wracks so little of his prose arises from distinctly Victorian cultural conditions, a sad contemplation of withering faith and an unprecedented fear of encroaching materialism. The paralysis of doubt that is said to have gripped Arnold's generation is far removed from the divided aims of a disillusioned Hamlet. Even if, as seems likely, both conflicts have been overstated, the very real crosscurrents of Victorian assent and denial are scarcely "Elizabethan" in source or direction.

Victorian society was forever subject to tensions which militated against complete spontaneity and singleness of purpose. It experienced in various forms the self-consciousness that is at once the strange disease of modern life and the genesis of analytic science. It learned to fear its own ardors, to distrust the falsehood of extremes. Whenever artist or philosopher was betrayed by the intensity of his conviction, Victorian parody served to restore a lost perspective; laughter prodded eccentric genius into an awareness of common reality. Despite the resounding clash of individual wills, there was until late in Victoria's reign a desire for cultural synthesis urgent enough to inspire from even the most rebellious many a concession to an established social morality. It was often as if the discords were hushed by a half-heard imperious command, "Hark, the dominant's persistence till it must be answered to!" Again and again the poet dreamed of a remote harmony which might catch up diverse themes into a larger pattern, a meaningful Victorian counterpoint. Tennyson prayed for his whole generation a prayer which might be echoed by Victorians of vastly different intellectual persuasion:

> Let knowledge grow from more to more,
> But more of reverence in us dwell;
> That mind and soul according well,
> May make one music as before.

For all his sharp censure of Victorian culture, even John Morley came to feel that the prayer had been at times richly fulfilled; in the best effort of his age he saw "mind and soul according well." In 1921, nearly fifty years after the first appearance of his essay *On Compromise,* he added a few words by way of epilogue, a Victorian's final answer to a skeptical posterity. "Whatever we may say of Europe between Waterloo and Sedan," he wrote, "in our country at least it was an epoch of hearts uplifted with hope, and brains active with sober and manly reason for the common good. Some ages are marked as sentimental, others stand conspicuous as rational. The Victorian age was happier than most in the flow of both these currents into a common stream of vigorous and effective talent. New truths were welcomed in free minds, and free minds make brave men." Though later critics might charge the Victorians with divorcing intellect and feeling, the liaison was in fact well sustained into the 1870's, and the process of separation was, as we shall see, prolonged and painful. By 1884, when Ruskin sensed a great "storm cloud of the nineteenth century" blotting out the sun and breaking an old "harmony," English culture, heedless of his mid-Victorian warnings, was entering upon a new phase of its development.

Notes

[1] For the anecdote, see Frank Hardie, *The Political Influence of Queen Victoria* (London, 1935), p. 206.

[2] The charge is stated ironically by Arnold Bennett (*The Old Wives' Tale,* Chap. I), but is seriously repeated in various forms; cf. H. H. Asquith, *Some Aspects of the Victorian Age* (Oxford, 1918), p. 6, or an incidental remark by an art critic in the *New Yorker* (January 26, 1946), p. 58.

[3] Cf. H. V. Routh, "The true sign of the times was spiritual isolation" (*Towards the Twentieth Century* [New York, 1937], p. ix); or see W. C. Frierson, *The English Novel in Transition* (Norman, Okla., 1942), p. 36.

[4] H. J. and Hugh Massingham (eds.), *The Great Victorians* (Garden City, 1932), p. 11; or, for a more extravagant judgment, see E. B. Burgum, "Victorianism," *Sewanee Review,* XXXVI (1928), 282, 286.

[5] Cf. Routh, *Towards the Twentieth Century,* p. 45.

[6] Cf. Osbert Sitwell, *Sober Truth* (London, 1930), 22, or A. C. Ward, *Twentieth-Century Literature* (New York, 1940), pp. 2–3.

[7] Arnold's charge freely echoed by the neo-humanists, who often dismiss Arnold himself along with his lost generation.

[8] Contrast Routh, *Towards the Twentieth Century* p. 74, with William Gaunt, *The Aesthetic Adventure* (New York, 1945), p. 237.

[9] Cf. Edith Batho and Bonamy Dobrée, *The Victorians and After* (London, 1938), p. 81; contrast G. M. Trevelyan, *English Social History* (New York, 1942), p. 521: "The last thirty years of Victoria's reign . . . the real period of the 'emancipation of women' in England."

[10] Cf. Batho and Dobrée, *Victorians and After,* p. 37, or Florence B. Lennon, *Victoria through the Looking-Glass* (New York, 1945), *passim.*

[11] See Mario Praz, *The Romantic Agony* (London, 1933).

[12] Observe the wise cautions of Trevelyan, *English Social History,* p. 509, and of G. M. Young, *Victorian England* (London, 1936), p. 150.

[13] See Bonamy Dobrée, "Addison," *Essays in Biography* (London, 1925), p. 206. Addison seems to Dobrée sufficiently hypocritical to merit the title, "the first Victorian."

[14] Lascelles Abercrombie, for instance, in a generally judicious estimate of Tennyson, speaks of "that false emphasis of feeling which is the peculiar vice of the Victorian age"; see *Revaluations* (London, 1931), p. 63

[15] See O. F. Christie, *The Transition from Aristocracy* (London, 1927), p. 108; here the historian indulges in generalization.

[16] Lytton Strachey, still the liveliest of the iconoclasts; see esp. "A Victorian Critic" (Arnold), *Characters and Commentaries* (New York, 1933).

[17] See Anna Kavan (author of the distinguished fiction, *Asylum Piece*), "Back to Victoria," *Horizon,* XIII (1946), 65.

[18] See Lennon, *Victoria through the Looking Glass* p. 5.

[19] Isabel C. Clarke, *Elizabeth Barrett Browning* (London, 1929), p. 241.

[20] See William H. Swift, "Tennyson in the Twentieth Century," *Search Quarterly,* III (1933), 343; cf. also C. H. O. Scaife, *The Poetry of Alfred Tennyson* (London, 1930), p. 96.

[21] See Asquith, *Aspects of Victorian Age,* p. 13.

[22] Batho and Dobrée, *Victorians and After,* p. 36.

[23] See Morley, *Critical Miscellanies* (London, 1923), pp. 74–75.

[24] G. R. Porter, *The Progress of the Nation* (London, 1851), p. 631.

[25] See Harrison, *Autobiographic Memoirs* (2 vols.; London, 1911), II, 313.

[26] Quoted by Walter Besant, *Fifty Years Ago* (New York, n.d.), p. 124.

[27] Havelock Ellis, *The New Spirit* (1890), preface to the 1926 edition (Boston, 1926), p. xii.

[28] Tennyson, "Locksley Hall Sixty Years After" (1886).

[29] F. W. Newman, *Causes of Atheism* (Ramsgate, 1871), p. 12.

[30] Cf. R. C. K. Ensor, *England, 1870–1914* (Oxford, 1936), p. 137.

[31] See Clive Bell, "Victorian Taste," in R. S. Lambert, ed., *Art in England* (Pelican Books, 1938), p. 45.

[32] A comparison suggested by Oliver Elton, *A Survey of English Literature, 1780–1880* (4 vols.; New York, 1920), III, 3.

[33] Quoted by John Henry Overton, *The Church in England* (2 vols.; London, 1897), II, 324–325.

[34] See F. W. Knickerbocker, *Free Minds* (Cambridge: Harvard University Press, 1943), p. 29.

[35] See Symonds, *Essays Speculative and Suggestive* (2 vols.; London, 1890), II, 274.

2.

E. San Juan, Jr.

Toward a Definition of Victorian Activism

The Faustian spirit of endless striving is a recurrent thematic motif which provides the most pervasive psychological atmosphere in Western literature. It appears as a dominant motivation in English romantic literature, assuming the personae of the Byronic heroes Childe Harold and Manfred, the Prometheus of Shelley, and the Hyperion of Keats. In Victorian literature, the spirit of Faust may be seen conditioning the moral impetus and temper of such writers as Carlyle, Browning, Charles Kingsley, Haggard, Newbolt, Blunt, and others who appealed to man's will power for the purpose or reconciling the conflicting interests and desires of a frenzied, "undisciplined age."[1] The distinguishing attitude of such an appeal is a fundamental courage and alertness of heart and intellect which may be called "activism," the meaning of which I hope to define here.

The word "decadence," generally used to characterize the literary and artistic temper of the nineties, seems to me so absolutely pejorative in implication (perhaps because of the sense of "decay") that such aesthetic qualities of complexity and multiple significance are altogether sacrificed in the process of a deterministic evaluation. I concur with the opinion that any actual period suffers distortion from a generalized indictment, however speciously formulated. Arthur Symons, for one, discerns a spiritual and moral perversity ascendant in the nineties. Ac-

Reprinted by permisssion of the author and the editor from *Studies in English Literature,* Vol. 4, No. 4 (Autumn, 1964), pp. 583–600.

cording to Max Nordau, nihilism characterizes the period in such varied manifestations as mysticism, egomania, and realism involving a lot of psychological aberrations: ineptitude for attention, clear thought, and control of emotions; and other abnormalities of the instinct leading to negative, immoral attitudes.[2] "Exhaustion, melancholia and disease" are qualities found in the works of Pater, Wilde, Beardsley, and their French contemporaries, qualities that tend to vitiate whatever positive moral or aesthetic values "decadent art" may have.[3] But the nineties, needless to say, was not all Pater, Wilde, and Beardsley. Indeed, this decade may be more intelligently understood not as an isolated period but as a complex point of view with multiple facets; such a view, it is hoped, should enable us to indicate with a certain precision the vicissitudes of outlook and taste that then prevailed. Otherwise, how, if not through this all-encompassing angle of vision, can one explain the expansive, dynamic upsurge of creative energy in Stevenson's declining years; Henley's "wrackful siege" and its fertility; or Kipling's industry and inventiveness amidst the horrors of heat and death? Within this design of a Victorian dialectic of themes, the thesis of life-for-art's sake inevitably begot its own antithesis: art-for-life's sake, or activism as the self-assertion of the driving force of will against the morbid, sterile introspectiveness of sentimental poseurs. Following the progressive breakup of Victorian equilibrium since the fifties, disquietude about the norms of conduct had increasingly prevailed. As a reaction of vital instinct against the deliquescence of intellectualism, doctrines of action, of moral energy and physical exertion, asserted themselves with urgency to free man's imagination, instincts, and dreams from all the oppressive shackles of social conformity into adventurous, experimental ways. Such doctrines of action served as the main rallying modes of life and thought for Kipling (1865–1936), Henley (1849–1903), and Stevenson (1850–1894).[4]

Toward the end of the nineteenth century, problems involving social amelioration and economic growth became continually less insistent and less immediate as prosperity spread from the upper to the lower classes, population became more mobile and literate, and the parochial attitudes of self-righteous "economic" men more externalized in the form of imperialist agitation.

Thinking of the great "grabbed-up British Empire," Henry James confessed fear of being "too lost in the mere spectacle of any decent morality."[5]

"Spectacular" is surely a fitting epithet to describe the radical, revolutionary mutations wrought by vast industrial expansion. With the growth of urban areas, humanitarian sentiment intensified, initiating numerous movements for reforms to rectify what Carlyle called the "concrete mendacity" of London. Because of improved medical knowledge and practice of hygiene, optimism and buoyancy of spirit increasingly became the predominant mood. The opening of new colonial territories to the commercial market offered unlimited opportunities for the middle and artisan classes to exercise their skill and energies more strenuously than before in the diligent conduct of trade, experimentation with machines, keen study of nature, enhanced scholarship, and mass dissemination of opinions which encompassed in purpose and direction secular and spiritual subjects alike.[6] To G. M. Young, the seeds of internal change lay precisely in the spirit of dissent found during this period in "the greater care for the amenities of life, natural and domestic; and behind this, a far more critical attitude toward the structure of society which few could any longer think of as divinely ordered or logically irrefutable."[7] On the whole, an accelerated pace in all lines of endeavor sustained itself until the beginning of the twentieth century.

At the center of the great Victorian "compromise" stand the theory of laissez faire and the vogue of self-help, both of which derive impetus from Darwin's evolutionary hypothesis, evangelical religion, and Mill's liberal utilitarianism. Samuel Smiles, indeed, represents Victorian activism for the collective: "For the nation is only the aggregate of individual conditions, and civilization itself is but a question of personal improvement,"[8] and so forth. Although not an absolute of Victorian culture, laissez faire undeniably formed an integral part of the Victorian *ethos*. It encouraged new experiments, daring commercial ventures, the dream of "Locksley Hall," Kingsley's "muscular Christianity," Browning's "Prospice," and other poems illustrating spiritual evolution, Barrow's Whitmanesque instinct for the open road, Carlyle's hero worship.

Amid these exciting changes in the social structure, there prevailed the routine monotony of industrial life, which contributed not a little to the marked restlessness of the era. Among the critics of urban squalor, William Morris and John Ruskin discerned that despite the great improvement of their living standards, the workers felt neither pride nor joy in their work: labor gradually became, as Marx analyzed it, a self-alienating influence. To compensate for *tedium vitae*, urban dwellers were led to indulge themselves in sports and in such momentary self-release as could be gained in clubs, dives, and city pubs. During the seventies and the eighties, the need for organized sports manifested itself in competitive archery, cricket, and rugby football, which provided an outlet for the predatory, aggressive urges of post-Darwinian man. In "Mandalay," written in 1890, Kipling articulated the average man's insistent, enormous craving for adventure in answer to the "call of the Blood and the Empire." As usual, the English landed gentry pursued games as recreation: shooting, fishing, hunting, horseracing, etc. At the root of this enthusiasm lies the demand for a stimulus best calculated to evoke the most potently creative variations in life so as to offset the regress toward any kind of Spartan specialization. With the rise of industrialism, Arnold Toynbee remarks, organized games and sports became popular as "one attempt to counter-balance the soul-destroying specialization which the division of labour under industrialism entails."[9] The notion of war as a game where, as in the bullfight, passions are disciplined by the rules and rituals of the fight and thus brought to the state of heightened sensitivity, should in this light vindicate Kipling and Henley, among others, from the false charge of fostering a mystique of cruelty and irrational sadism: "Each man born in the Island entered at youth to the game—As it were almost cricket, not to be mastered in haste, But after trial and labour, by temperance, living chaste . . . Weighed and pondered and worshipped. . . . "[10] Charles Kingsley forecasts Kipling's "Recessional," Ruskin's warrior ethics, and William James's "The Moral Equivalent of War" in speaking of war as a moral force which brings us

> face to face with the realities of life, as it has been in all ages . . . giving us sterner and yet more loving, more human,

> and more divine thoughts about ourselves, and our business here, and the fate of those who are gone, and awakening us out of the luxurious, frivolous, moral dream in which we have been living so long—to trust in a living Father who willeth that none should perish—and therefore has not forgotten or suddenly begun to hate or torment, one single poor soul who is out of this life into some other, on that accursed Crimean soil.[11]

But it was not because of sports and games that H. Rider Haggard, the renowned fabulist of "sanguinary horrors," enjoyed rapid public acclaim, together with Henty, Maryatt, and other prolific purveyors of romance. During the first twelve months, 31,000 copies of *King Solomon's Mines* (1885) were sold, surpassing the phenomenal success of *Treasure Island* (1883).

We can attribute Haggard's and also Kipling's and Stevenson's tremendous popularity to two main factors: first, the "literary" imagination of the audience in the eighties and nineties was conditioned by Scott, Bulwer-Lytton, Reade, and Kingsley to respond to a type of fiction that had easily become formula in the hands of Blackmore, Lang, Hewlett, and Hope; second, the use of the telegraph by war correspondents more and more stimulated public interest in Britain's far-flung colonies.

Ever since the Zulu War of 1878, the annexation of the Transvaal (where Haggard acted as secretary of Shepstone), the defeat at Majuba Hill, the death of Gordon at Khartoum, up to the occupation of Alexandria and the Sudan, Africa constantly occupied the forefront of imperial activity. Upon the discovery of diamonds and gold in the Transvaal in 1886–1887, public interest in Africa once more flared up. Following the romanticized exploits of Livingstone and Stanley, an "African fever" had earlier seized the European imagination: the ordinary citizen fancied himself involved with strange safaries setting out from the Sahara desert toward the African veldt, from lowland wilderness and plains toward the mysterious Mountains of the Moon—England reliving its youth with Burton on the road to Mecca, Livingstone in Africa and Disraeli speaking in the accents of Cromwell and Pitt.[12] In "The New Downing Street" (1850) Carlyle spoke of the "godlike task," the "sublime destiny of thousandfold expanded manfulness" which familiarly echoes Goethe's "romantic" message of industry and ceaseless toil.[13]

At a time when Dickens's multicolored milieu of the philistine had become superseded by an extremely genteel, staid type of urban uniformity in which the worker felt a neurotic desire to flee the brutal facts of his surroundings, Haggard composed his African dream of barbaric tortures, savage warfare, and hair-breadth escapes from death by thirst, hunger, and horrible privations of the body. Far more than *Treasure Island, King Solomon's Mines* immediately proved its worth as an efficacious agent for liberating the habit-constricted mind through vicarious participation in the exciting feats of its heroes. Through his self-identification with such "mana" personalities as Quatermain, Kipling's Strickland, Stevenson's Alan Breck, or even Conrad's Marlow and Tuan Jim in *Lord Jim* (1900), the ordinary citizen was enabled to achieve what may be termed an "empathic" overcoming of the barriers of his status and his personal incapacities. For now his impulses were given free play, and—in Coleridge's words—"carried forward, not merely or chiefly by the mechanical impulse of curiosity, or a restless desire to arrive at the final solution; but by the pleasurable activity of mind excited by the attractions of the journey itself."[14]

To the mid-Victorian of Dickens's time, the Empire aroused no strong emotional response. Although Palmerston sympathized with Europe's oppressed minorities, he did not pay much attention to England's colonies. With the establishment of "organic filaments" through steamer trips to Australia (1852), deep-sea cables (1872, 1879), and the national crisis on the death of Gordon, a resurgence of interest in the Empire burst with enthusiastic energy. Earlier, Kingsley's *Westward Ho!* celebrated the Elizabethan gallants in England's battle against the Spanish Armada. But it was Disraeli who glamorized the Empire in proclaiming Victoria Empress of India. Moreover, the emotional impact of Victoria's two jubilees brought to a head the imperialist themes of John Robert Seeley's *The Expansion of England* (1883) and James Froude's *Oceana,* or *England and Her Colonies* (1886). At last the major European powers—Bismark's Germany, France, Russia, and England—brought their expansionist careers to a culminating stage in the Berlin Conference of 1845–1846.

When the 1890's arrived, England then was at the height of its prosperity. The nation's surplus wealth, transformed into capital for new investments, sought broader fertile grounds abroad. The national wealth was also used to purchase raw materials and raise higher dividends. With the growth of tariffs in Europe and America, there suddenly emerged a nation-wide clamor to annex more territories in order to provide British commerce and industry with the necessary suppliers of raw materials, and buyers for her consumer goods. What made Kipling's Gospel of Empire so attractive to the middle class then was not so much the vogue of romantic pioneering initiated by Disraeli to solve the businessmen's pressing need for markets. To no small extent Kipling owed his popularity more to the stock exchange than to the taste for exotic art or the craving for vicarious excitement—although both conspired to intensify sentiments aroused by Kipling's novels. Those two psychological needs Kipling also satisfied when he furnished his readers picturesque scenes of Simla, Lahore, and the Himalayan plains, creating at the same time a persuasive image of the British Tommy and the Anglo-Indian sahib so devoutly serving the Empire without thought of personal welfare. Upon such idealized images the bored urban dweller could project his unfulfilled longings for action so persistently that later "he came to need these same colonies, not for any consideration of high policy, but in the same instinctive way as the mother needs her child, because their possession as he deems it—fills a void in his own being."[15]

Like Cecil Rhodes, the fabulous builder of Empire, Kipling appeared in the nineties a man with a mission: to preach the gospel of duty and active service to the Law. In this context the idea of the Law signified that ordered arrangement of life which afforded man the maximum opportunity for the full exercise of his native talents, for the full realization of his possibilities. Duty to the Empire for him denoted the defense of civilization, the "age's slow-bought gain," against the anarchy of barbarism and its destructive steel, fire, and stone.[16] Ultimately the Empire assumed, to Kipling, a mystical import which he felt so strongly, impelling him to the task of communicating to the average citizen, who earlier took the Empire for granted, an awareness of its transcendent reality, its grandeur, and the weight of responsibility associated with its goods. Such a notion and feeling of responsibility he typified in characters like Kim, Strickland,

Mulvaney, and others. His heroes generally act as defenders of civilized society against the incursions of irrational forces, whether from within or from without. Or else they function as representatives of the civilized mind sustained by historical tradition and nature. Doubtless Kipling proved himself a confirmed authoritarian in his belief in the strong man governing alone a society ordered according to a heirarchy of talent and ability.[17] In stories like "The Bridge Builders" (1893), "His Chance in Life" (1887), or in *The Light That Failed* (1891), he dramatized vividly the need for a ruling class who would impose the Law upon the brute and the degenerate. The Law demands obedience; consequently, animals submit to man, man follows "his station and his duties." Although highly repellent in its anti-democratic implications, Kipling's fixed principle that the job belongs to the man who can do it can nevertheless be understood within the framework of his conception of human nature. Even his contradictions become intelligible if interpreted within the context of his whole achievement. Consequently, his "crude, vulgar, drumbeating jingoism" should be duly qualified, particularly on account of his critical attacks against the easy, ruthless optimism of irreponsible colonialists. Alarmed by the materialistic complacency shown by the British during the Diamond Jubilee of 1897, Kipling in "Recessional" called for scrutiny of conscience, stressing heavily the rational, crusading purpose of "the white man's burden." While it is probable that in certain cases Kipling's Law regresses into mere "law of the jungle," the Mowgli fables of *Jungle Book* (1894) nonetheless affirm the value of hierarchy when panther and bear submit to their human master. Seen from this perspective of the artistic integration of man's impulses, action then acquires a complex pragmatic significance as a strategy in life.

The peculiar circumstances of Kipling's life inevitably led him to identify the meaning of his actions with a cause of cosmic dimension. To a certain extent, the fact of Empire for him became a myth (unconsciously held), that is, a value-system and picture of the world, which infused moral content into routine behavior by associating it with impersonal, collective ends for the total apocalyptic transformation of the world. The highest good thus turns out to be the heroic, aggressive action performed with a sense of impersonal consecration to the ends of a particular race bound together in fervent solidarity and impelled by a passionate confidence in its role of being God's elect. According to Niebuhr:

> The ability of the self to envisage a wider world than its immediate environment is the occasion for the rise of imperialism long before it leads to the establishment of any universal concord between particular interests. It is always through some particular center of power that the human community is organized; or from some particular viewpoint that meaning is given to the course of history.[18]

The case for Stevenson is quite different. His Calvinist inheritance, formed by a Tolstoyan ethic of charity, drove him to help improve the lot of Mataafa's warriors in the squalid prisons of Samoa, and bring happiness to the lepers of Molokai. Only once before, in 1887, did Stevenson display any gesture of political revolt when he thought of committing himself to the cause of the Land Leaguers in Ireland. Although he had sought to promote the well-being of others, his basic moral axiom remains a simple imaginative respect for oneself: "Justice is no right of a man's own but a thing like the King's tribute, which shall never be his, but which he should strive to see rendered to another."[19] Addressing the chiefs of the Samoan tribes in 1884, Stevenson display a political attitude in the spirit of Ecclesiastes and the later Faust:

> There is a time to fight and a time to dig. You Samoans may fight, you may conquer twenty times, and thirty times, and all will be in vain. There is but one way to defend Samoa. Hear it before it is too late. It is to make roads, and gardens, and care for your trees, and sell their produce wisely, and, in one word, to occupy and use your country. If you do not, others will. . . . Because all things in a country band together like the links of the anchor cables, one by another: but the anchor itself is industry.[20]

Like Stevenson, Henley was not born a "political man." At the start of the nineties, however, Henley's individualism began to acquire a political orientation that it never had before. His association with Kipling, whose *Barrack Room Ballads* (1892) he first published in the *National Observer,* and with Walter Blaikie, a staunch imperialist and member of Henley's famed "Regatta," resulted in his awareness of the larger world of political affairs. In this world he came to recognize the need for involvement: the "unconquerable soul," in yielding to an active participation in the broader enterprise of serving the Empire, attains universal identity. According to George Herbert Mead, "Only in social situations does the self arise—the individual becomes an object to himself."[21] In adopting an attitude of political conservatism, he was simply elevating personal prejudices to the level of rational propositions. Averse to that "conspiracy of bad public breeding and individual prurience called popular culture," he took the stand of an "elite" class: thus, he extolled Disraeli as the "Uncommonplace incarnate" since he could "slaughter an opponent, butcher a measure, or crumple up a throng. . . ." (Note how the verbs betray a martial pugnacity of spirit.) Temperamentally, Hensley subscribed to the doctrine of personal freedom within the framework of a democratic, open society which would insure the free, full flowering of the individual's potentialities. Confronted by the petty partisan squabbles of his day, he longed for an escape into the "sunny-eyed heroic age" of Homer when the individual, challenged by superhuman odds, becomes himself superhuman. For "the age is great as we see it, and man grows in accordance with the greatness of the age."[22] Henley expressed his historical "archaism" thus:

> It is relief unspeakable to turn from the dust and din and clatter of modern life with its growing trade in heroes and its poverty of men, its innumerable regrets and ambitions and desires, to this immense tranquillity, this candid and shining calm. They had no Irish question then, you can reflect, nor was theology invented. Men were not afraid of life, nor ashamed of death; and you could be heroic without a dread of clever editors, and hospitable without fear of rogues, and dutiful for no hope of illuminated scrolls.[23]

And so "the vital—the imperial—quality of politics" now emerged as a compelling interest, and a unified British empire became a religious ideal in the midst of the national crisis brought about by the Jameson raid (1895), the Fashoda incident (1898), and the Boer War (1899). It then seemed that the liberty to form and express opinions, together with the freedom to exercise one's creative talent, could only be safeguarded against the forces of anarchy by the massive strength of national corporate unity. Ultimately the cause of the Empire became, to Henley and Kipling, an inner call of conscience, for the Empire involved the whole cultural heritage of England, the fabric of man's total accomplishment which they had inherited from England's glorious past: "For beyond working class unrest and parliamentary debate stretched the British tradition of 'beef, beer, horses,' Moll Flanders, and the Church of England, the King, and the Newgate Calendar."[24] In the names of those sacred institutions and hallowed practices, Oscar Wilde also exalted the Empire and the "spears of crimson-suited war" in his early verse "Ave Imperatrix" (1882). Like Kipling, Henley committed himself to the Empire insofar as it stood for freedom, life, creativity.

Social historians of the nineties have noted that the phenomenal rise of imperialist sentiment practically coincided with the fast decline of interest in theological disputes and religious discussions. Although Spencer still provoked churchmen to heated controversies now and then, the tumultuous days of the Tractarians and the *Essays and Reviews,* Huxley and Wilberforce, were all gone. Through the speculative minds of Browning, Tennyson, Carlyle, Ruskin, Mill, and Arnold, religious issues underwent a radical sea-change until in Pater's *Studies in The Renaissance* (1873) and *Marius the Epicurean* (1885), secular relativism became the ruling order of the day. T. S. Eliot describes the status of religious belief in the nineties thus:

> The dissolution of thought in that age, the isolation of art, philosophy, religion, ethics and literature is interrupted by various chimerical attempts to effect imperfect syntheses. Religion became morals, religion became art, religion became science or philosophy; various blundering attempts were made at alliances between various branches of thought.[25]

Especially during the last decade, a fanatic faith in the collective destiny of the English people absorbed much of the emotional energy once spent on the fanfares of the mid-Victorian Protestantism.

Under the shadow of the Empire, a national and racial absolute seems to have grown to such a commanding height of political and social importance that people were then increasingly led to project those feelings and affections attached by customary practice to evangelical religion upon a messianic myth. This Anglo-Saxon myth, fostered by Kingsley, Kipling, Pearson, Newbolt, and Hyndman, exerted so great an influence that, once transformed into the "mystique" of the Empire, it virtually became a religion. And so we find Kipling and Henley constantly addressing the "Virgin of the Sword," the "Red Angel of the War," "the Lord God of Battles," and the "Lord of the far-flung battle line." In "England My England" (1892), we encounter biblically charged phrases: "The Lord whispering terrible things"/"You whose mailed hand keeps the keys/Of such teeming destinies. . . . " The struggle between two forces representing opposite values has since Bunyan's *Holy War* adopted liturgical or apocalyptic emblems in an effort to bestow the transcendent value of an ideal to the temporality and finitude of historical events.[26] Between Henley's

> England, my own
> Chosen Daughter of the Lord,
> Spouse-in-Chief of the Ancient Sword,
> There's the menace of the Word
> In the Song of your bugles blown . . .

and St. Paul's *To the Ephesians* (VI.16-17) to cite one instance: "Above all, taking the Shield of Faith, wherewith ye shall be able to quench all the fiery darts of the wicked. And take the Helmet of Salvation, and the Sword of the Spirit, which is the word of God," there is an unquestionable affinity of tone, imagery and rhythm.

In this connection, the poems of Henry Newbolt exemplify a consistent elaboration of this technique. He exploits the messianic function of the Island Race, and the religious spirit associated with the mystique of the Empire. Newbolt, essentially a hero-worshipper, exalts heroic men of action, like Drake, Nelson, Gordon, and then surrounds them with a divine aura:

> Drake nor devil nor Spaniard feared,
> Their cities he put to the sack;
> He singed his Catholic Majesty's beard,
> And harried his ships to wrack.
> He was playing at Plymouth a game of bowls
> When the great Armada came,
> But he said, "They must wait their turn, good souls,"
> And he stopped, and finished the game.

Such a popular legend, crystallizing a particular scene, a decisive moment, and a heroic man of action playing a part in the historical process, figures as a leitmotif in Newbolt's verse. There are also the familiar themes of Duty ("Quarter Gunner's Yarn"), the Nelson touch (Minora Sidera"), and Kipling's Law, as shown in "A Ballad of John Nicholson": "When the strong command, obedience is best," which suggests Newbolt's authoritarian temper.

Moreover (to return to Kipling) in reading "Recessional," for example, the reader catches at once the tone of evangelical exhortation behind the conventional rhetoric of "secular prayer." This feature is not at all unusual. In the published speeches of prime ministers and cabinet members during this period, one frequently detects the subtle presence of a submerged religious vocabulary. It would seem that although the original religious impulse had entirely vanished, the highly connotative language of the rituals which served as a vehicle of emotion remained alive in the recesses of the ordinary mind, responsive still to external happenings. Thus Arnold proposed poetry as a surrogate to religion.

Religion assumes above all that the spiritual dimension penetrates the mundane life and thus transfigures it for participation in a transcendent realm. Kipling's "Recessional" and Henley's "Song of the Sword" (1891) are examples of the manner in which the material, finite realm of human ends has been brought to the level of, and identified with, the transcendent ideal, such that all action in this world becomes imbued with an eternal significance, and thus functions for an apocalyptic goal. This will explain too Western man's mystique of history; that is, the "conviction that the ideal is not only immanent in history but has actually been materialized, at least in part, in particular myth-events."[27] From both historical thought and religious attitudes, imperialism in the nineties drew its vitalizing potential.

And yet what value, what psychological function other than that of illusion-fulfillment could be assigned to such poems as "Recessional" and Newbolt's "Hymn in Time of War and Tumult"? To clarify in part the causes why activism of the imperialist orientation appealed to a supra-natural Providence for guidance, I should like to quote Toynbee:

> To call in God cannot be denounced as infantile escapism if, at the same time, the human actor withdraws his *libido* from his previous mundane aim. And, conversely, if the act of invocation does produce so great and so good a spiritual effect as this in the human soul that performs it, that would appear, *prima facie,* to give ground for a belief that the Power which has been invoked is not a mere fragment of the human imagination. . . . Through the disappointment of a mundane hope we have been admitted to an apocalypse of reality which has been there all the time behind the scenes of a narrow man-made stage.[28]

I began this exposition of some ideas and attitudes which may be said to characterize "activism" with the working assumption that Western man, under a Christian framework, strives for union with the transcendent absolute over and against nature. This is not meant, however, to deny the supreme importance of the material world to man's life here and now. To be sure, Henley, Kipling, and Stevenson shaped and tested their individual visions of truth with constant reference to the sphere of subjective experience. Uttering only what they had perceived through their senses, despite the curse of physical infirmity, they struggled to achieve a condition of complete expressiveness and inclusiveness, disclosing the essences of objects, capturing and reproducing the diversity and complexity of existence. Nature still reigns supreme, since the creative process is a living force implanted in the soul of man. And

> the unborn work in the soul of the artist is a force of nature that effects its purpose either with tyrannical might or with that subtle cunning which nature brings to the achievement of her end, quite regardless of the personal weal or woe of the man who is the vehicle of the creative force. The creative energy lives and waxes in man as a tree in the earth from which it takes its nourishment.[29]

Nature receives her just desert when, according to Browning, "a soul declares itself—to wit, by its fruit, the thing it does." What I should like to call attention to are the basic Christian presuppositions which give universality to the works of the Victorian activists; and these are: the unique worth of the immortal soul of man—strongly emphasized by Kingsley, the early exponent of the strenuous life set against the "Lotus-eaters"; the aspiration for self-transcendence—a Nietzschean ethic present in Carlyle's *Sartor Resartus,* Henley's "Invictus," Kipling's Law; and lastly, the gospel of work for one's fellow-men—vigorously espoused by Stevenson.[30] In the context of Victorian society, we find these general presuppositions at the basis of laissez faire, utilitarianism, "doing as one likes," and imperialism. There is then a constant tension in the paradox of the self striving for something permanent and eternal, just as there is a continuing tension between the ideal structure of art and the finitude of the experience it seeks to preserve. Such an ambiguity may be said to exist between the lives of the Victorian activists treated here and the total achievement that has survived them.

Activism is fundamentally romantic in spirit and substance. Sharing Chateaubriand's passion ("I was overwhelmed with a superabundance of life") , Henley, Kipling, and Stevenson manifested to the utmost a herculean and robust capacity for inclusiveness and openness of mind and heart. Their inspiration was Goethe's axiom: "In the Beginning was the Deed." To them energy was not a cult but a fact. With Byron and Rousseau, they considered not happiness, but activity as the goal of life;

for their shibboleth was *streben.* Surmounting great physical hardships, Stevenson harnessed all his resources in an effort to integrate the chaos of his experiences into some intelligible form. And so he willed a life of danger, exposing his frail body to the hazards of arduous journeys. Kipling, on the other hand, lived amidst surroundings of deadly squalor and heat, breathing the stench of corpses and fighting against tropical fever, fatigue, and the threat of blindness, while he wrote the stories in *Plain Tales from the Hills* (1888). It is common knowledge that Henley struggled against the crippling pain of disease, but instead of paralyzing his will to create, his enormous difficulties challenged him to fiercer toil and more frenzied production. If we take bulk as a measure of vitality, certainly the sum-total of the works of Henley, Stevenson, and Kipling would not be far behind that of Goethe, Byron, and Hugo.

Since the value of any feeling lies in its discharge into constructive action, either by changing the world or the self, we may judge the activist writers as belonging to the dynamic strain of the romantic tradition whose chief representative is Goethe's composite image of Faustian man. For the activist, action, which acts upon feeling, serves as the touchstone of the life-enhancing value art is supposed to give. Henley, Kipling, and Stevenson strove against all forms of opposition from within or without, rejoicing in the risks and dangers, in the depth and intensity, of experience which the adventures of life entailed. In their total effort to create harmony out of the discontinuity of sensory impressions, they understood that experience has no value unless the individual creates the value. And because activism was at bottom an outlook on life founded on personal strivings, the work of Henley, Kipling, and Stevenson should be properly judged according to how far they were able to transform suffering and decay into acts of affirmation.

Virtù is the Renaissance word for doing and excelling. The Victorian activists recognized the worth of *virtù* in their quest for self-mastery. Knowing that the besetting temptation of the human psyche is the infantile desire to escape from reality, the activists summoned each one to the challenge, essentially romantic and existential, of Stein in *Lord Jim*: "To the destructive element submit yourself, and with the exertion of your hands and feet in the water make the deep, deep sea keep you up." Napoleon spoke of "careers open to talent"; and to this call Henley, Kipling, and Stevenson responded in their various commitments. Through the aesthetic patterns and prospects they offered to their audience, they renewed the meaning of existence as "presence, being there, always some experience of seeing, hearing, smelling, tasting, touching, acting on, feeling." Activism holds that man's eternal role is not merely to "measure" a world fixed and dead, but rather to create and re-create it. As Bergson counseled: "One makes one's road as one goes along." Juxtapose, for emphasis, Stevenson's idea in *Pulvis et Umbra*: "Let it be enough for faith, that the whole creation groans in mortal frailty, strives with unconquerable constancy," with Emerson's challenge to the American scholar:

> Action is with the scholar subordinate, but it is essential. Without it he is not yet man. Without it thought can never ripen into truth. . . . Inaction is cowardice, but there can be no scholar without the heroic mind. The preamble of thought, the transition through which it passes from the unconscious to the conscious, is action. Only so much do I know, as I have lived.[31]

Open in its full novelty and richness, the universe then ceases to be an abstraction or an absolute, and begins to manifest its inexhaustible wealth of appearances, its chaos, its symmetry, its disorder. And life as it moves on carries—to William James, whose pragmatism is the philosophical formulation of literary activism—an "air of being, or at least of involving a muddle and a struggle, with an ever 'not quite' to all our formulas, and novelty and possibility forever leaking in."[32]

Although activism fundamentally defines itself in the direct confrontation of the lives and works of Henley, Kipling, and Stevenson (I have limited myself to describing a few salient traits), may I nevertheless venture a provisional definition of activism? Within the tradition of Western literature, the activism of Henley, Stevenson, and Kipling may be defined as the vital, heroic attitude to life which consists in (1) the realistic acceptance of the human condition as both finite in body and infinite in spirit; (2) the affirmation of life as process and perpetual becoming; and (3) the energetic, if fated, pursuit of integral selfhood, or style in character, as a harmonious pattern of experience—a result of involvement in a world of trials and possibilities. Man's primary task lies, therefore, in self-development: the ultimate goal of the person is to exhibit his humanity.

Notes

[1] Emile Legouis and Louis Cazamian, *A History of English Literature* (London, 1948), p. 1293.

[2] See Max Nordau, *Degeneration* (New York, 1895), pp. 536, 553.

[3] More intelligent appraisals have been written, e.g., Graham Hough, *The Last Romantics* (London, 1947); Frank Kermode, *Romantic Image* (London, 1957).

[4] Besides Madeleine Cazamian's book *Le Roman et les Idées en Angleterre* (Paris, 1955), and Professor Jerome H. Buckley's *William Ernest Henley* (Princeton, 1945), which attempts to define counter-decadence from Henley's standpoint, there exist only appraisals of individual writers; and in them activism does not even figure as a dominant concept. For example, Sister Mary Joan Reinehr, *The Writings of Wilfred Scawen Blunt* (Wisconsin, 1940).

[5] Quoted by G. D. Klingopulos, "Notes on the Victorian Scene," *From Dickens to Hardy,* ed. Boris Ford (Penguin Books, 1958), p. 48.

[6] See R. C. K. Ensor, *England 1870–1914* (Oxford, 1949), pp. 269-340; G. M. Trevelyan, *History of England,* III (New York, 1952); David Thomson, *England in the 19th Century* (Penguin Books, 1950).

[7] G. M. Young, *Victorian England: Portrait of An Age* (London, 1960), p. 166.

[8] Quoted by Crane Brinton, *The Shaping of the Modern Mind* (New York, 1959), p. 165.

[9] Arnold Townbee, *A Study of History* (New York, 1946), p. 305. See Raymond Williams, *Culture and Society* (New York, 1960), pp. 174–212; Walter E. Houghton, *The Victorian Frame of Mind* (New Haven, 1957), pp. 196–217; and, in general, Jerome H. Buckley, *The Victorian Temper* (Cambridge, Mass., 1952).

[10] A. E. Rodway, "The Last Phase," *From Dickens to Hardy,* p. 393, quoting Kipling.

[11] Guy Kendall, *Charles Kingsley and His Ideas* (London, n. d.), p. 86.

[12] For the wider context of this attitude, see Mario Praz, "The Victorian Mood: A Reappraisal," *The Nineteenth Century World,* ed. Guy Métraux and F. Crouzet (New York, 1963), pp. 19–42. Consult also the concise account of imperialism in the nineties in Geoffrey Bruun, "The Fruits of Industrialism and Imperialism," *Nineteenth-Century European Civilization* (New York, 1960).

[13] On the ideology of organism, see Alfred North Whitehead, *Science & The Modern World* (New York, 1925), pp. 75–95; Stephen Pepper, *World Hypotheses* (Berkeley, 1961), pp. 280–315.

[14] *Biographia Literaria,* II, 2.

[15] Esmé Wingfield-Stratford, *The Victorian Sunset* (New York, 1932), p. 271.

[16] For the theoretical basis of nineteenth-century racism, see Richard Hofstadter, *Social Darwinism in American Thought* (Boston, 1955), pp. 170–200.

[17] Cf. George Orwell, *Dickens, Dali and Others* (New York, 1946), pp. 141–58. See also Bonamy Dobrée, *Rudyard Kipling* (London, 1951); T. S. Eliot, "Rudyard Kipling," *On Poetry & Poets* (New York, 1961), pp. 265–94.

[18] Reinhold Niebuhr, *Faith and History* (New York, 1951), p. 94. See also his *An Interpretation of Christian Ethics* (New York, 1935), pp. 84–85.

[19] Quoted by J. C. Furnas, *Voyage to Windward* (New York, 1951), pp. 233–34.

[20] Quoted by Furnas, p. 34.

[21] George Herbert Mead, *The Philosophy of the Act* (Chicago, 1953), p. 450.

[22] Carl Jung, *Psychological Reflections* (New York, 1953), p. 264.

[23] Buckley, quoting Henley, pp. 109–110.

[24] *Ibid.,* p. 317.

[25] T. S. Eliot, "Arnold and Pater," *Victorian Literature,* p. 247.

[26] For this idea, cf. John T. Marcus, "The World Impact of the West: The Mystique and the Sense of Participation in History," *Myth and Myth-Making* (New York, 1960), pp. 221–35.

[27] *Ibid.* p. 222.

[28] Toynbee, pp. 524–25.

[29] Jung, p. 175.

[30] Cf. Vivian de Sola Pinto, *Crisis in English Poetry, 1880–1940* (London, 1951). pp. 31 ff.

[31] *The Selected Writings of Ralph Waldo Emerson* (New York, 1950), pp. 52.

[32] *The American Pragmatists,* ed. Milton Konvitz and Gail Kennedy (New York, 1960), p. 28.

PART II Poetry

3.

Kingsley Amis

Communication and the Victorian Poet

Above all ideal personalities with which the poet must learn to identify himself, there is one supremely real which is the most imperative of all; namely, that of his reader. And the practical watchfulness needed for such assimilation is as much a gift and instinct as is the creative grasp of alien character. It is a spiritual contact hardly conscious yet ever renewed, and which must be a part of the very act of production.

—D. G. Rossetti

The aim of this article is to see what light, if any, can be thrown on the "communication" *imbroglio* by investigating the attitudes and practice of particular poets. Less modestly and more precariously, it seeks to suggest that a poet who is concerned to communicate with an audience is more likely than one who is not to produce work which will survive the passing of its original readers.

The poets chosen for investigation are some of the more prominent mid- and late-Victorians. They are suitable, firstly, because their careers are comparatively well documented, and, secondly, because their attitudes to the communication problem were heterogeneous.

The relevant attitude will, with any given poet, show itself most clearly in his dealings with his inner audience, that circle of intimates for whom, if for anybody besides himself, his poetry will be written in the first instance.[1] These poets can be divided, though not neatly, into a group that set some store by the opinion of qualified intimates, and a group that tended to ignore or not to canvas such opinion. Since assertion seems to be traditional in this topic, it may not be out of place to assert at this point that the practice of this first group was normal, that of the second

Reprinted by permission of the author and the editor from *Essays in Criticism,* Vol. 4, No. 4 (October, 1954), pp. 386–99.

abnormal. It was abnormal in the sense that it was, at the period under discussion, of comparatively recent growth, and is now already on the way out. It is an adjunct, not of Romanticism proper, but of Romanticism in decline. No less than assertion, some passing of personal judgments of the poets' work seems hard to avoid. It is hoped nevertheless that those who would not agree that the alleged defects in Morris' work, for example, are at all decisive would still grant that they are real, and that the suggested explanation of them is therefore still worth consideration.

The poets belonging to the first of the two groups mentioned above are conveniently headed by Rossetti. The circumstances of his life, in combination with his temperament, made him heavily reliant on the advice of others once a poem was approaching its final form, and again when it looked like going into a book. His adolescence had been almost absurdly literary, and had been marked by energetic verse-writing, by no means entirely of the round-game sort, in concert with William and Christina. Long before *The Early Italian Poets* (1861) was being prepared for publication Rosetti had formed the habit of making William, though apparently not Christina, his regular poetic adviser. Apart from general biographical statements, the best indication of this is the group of letters written on Rossetti's trip to Paris in 1849. The sending to William of fourteen sonnets in ten days may indicate a desire to inflate an envelope, but makes it at least likely that work written at home was also regularly proffered. It was William who supplied notes and helped with the proofs for *The Early Italian Poets,* which was also overhauled in detail by Allingham and Patmore.

In 1869, Rossetti, now planning the 1870 volume of *Poems,* was engaged in two very detailed exchanges of views on the texts of these poems: with William, especially over the *House of Life* sonnets, which he had seen "almost as soon as they were written"; and with Swinburne, whose task was to "pitch into" Rossetti when he needed it. Between them, Swinburne and Rossetti anatomized *Jenny, Troy Town* and *Sister Helen.* This can be studied in T. J. Wise's *The Ashley Library*[2] and in Hake and Compton-Rickett's *The Letters of Algernon Charles Swinburne.*[3]

The tempo and minuteness of these exchanges can perhaps be gauged from the following postcard:

> Dear Swinburne,
> I fancy I've hit it—
> "Marked his arrow's burning crest"
> One line, please, by return, and pardon these babyish bulletins.
> D. G. R.
>
> This is better I believe than
> 'Knew his shaft its rambling quest'

To these two consultants Rossetti added a third, William Bell Scott, whose habitual wonderment at "what it is those fellows seem to see in Gabriel," allied with his heavily documented stodginess, was at least a corrective against any unduly favorable bias shown by the other two. By 1873, however, all three men had yielded their status to Theodore Watts, who now became "the friend to whose judgment [Rossetti's] poetry was always submitted." Watts's judgment was to prove a notoriously inefficient faculty when applied to Swinburne's poems, and the relative poverty of Rossetti's later work might partly be traced to him. It should be remembered, on the other hand, that Watts was capable of showing toward Rossetti a critical severity that Swinburne never saw, and that, if Hall Caine's account is trustworthy, it was Watts's ingenious encouragements which induced Rossetti to break his vow of poetic silence after the "Fleshly School" attacks launched by Robert Buchanan. For all his apparent self-sufficiency, Rossetti, throughout his career, needed encouragement, which is perhaps as true an explanation as any for his habit of reading new poems aloud to a group of friends; and that need is as relevant here as the need for advice shown in his dealings with William, Swinburne, and the others. Yet others could be mentioned: Ruskin, Browning, Hall Caine, Sharp, Morris, Burne-Jones; and such a roll call may at least suggest how difficult it was to know Rossetti without somehow becoming involved in his poetry writing.

Such was Rossetti's practice in this matter. The handful of reviews which comprise his only critical writing preach what he practiced. The views put forward and developed in them are unusual in a Victorian. The degree of success in communication was to be a primary test of poetry, and the poet must perpetually maintain "a self-examination and self-confronting with the reader." Whether this was "a part of the very act of production" with Rossetti is unknowable; but William Sharp, who knew his methods of work, said that such was Rossetti's sincere aim even if he sometimes failed to live up to it. As far as the visible part of the process is concerned, Rossetti's intentions are obvious, and his concern with the problems of communication was accompanied by an accurate gauging of his audience and of the effect of his work upon it. "The Blessed Damozel" he singled out as likely to be "pretty generally admired"—a view which was officially confirmed thirty years later when Quiller-Couch, editing the *Oxford Book of English Verse,* represented him by that poem alone—"but," Rossetti went on to say, " . . . the greater portion of my poetry is suited only to distinctly poetic readers." It was not his "vocation" to "get within hail of general readers" by "rude aiming at the sort of popular view that Tennyson perhaps alone succeeds in taking." This again was accurate: at this time (1871) Tennyson was the only living poet read by the general public; sales of *The Earthly Paradise* were not yet above the 2,000 mark. In general, no Victorian poet understood more clearly than Rossetti the task of working to reach an audience, and the fuss he made over the physical form of his books, the care taken to lobby a favorable critical reception, even the hysteria at the repetition of Buchanan's attack (which stopped him from writing as well as from publishing), whatever else they may signify, are all aspects of that understanding.

Like Rossetti, Hopkins saw the poet's task as one of communication, but, unlike him, he wrote in circumstances peculiarly uncongenial to that task. Beginning with "The Wreck of the Deutschland" (1876) he formed the habit of sending copies of new poems to Bridges for comment, and it is quite clear that he regarded Bridges as his special, indeed his only, audience: "you are my public," "a poet is a public in himself," and so on. Bridges provided the comment with conscientious persistence, but it was not the sort of comment that Hopkins needed or the poems deserved. The tale is familiar enough: Bridges went resolutely on accusing Hopkins of being affected, of being obscure, of being like Walt Whitman; Hopkins summed up his criticisms as "only a protest memorializing me against my whole policy and proceedings," and more shortly, nine months later, as "water of the lower Isis." Whatever Bridges' merits as a friend, as an audience for a poet like Hopkins he was unsatisfactory. Nevertheless, Hopkins remained dependent on him, even after Richard Watson (by now Canon) Dixon had shown himself a more understanding and more encouraging audience. Encouragement was a deep need of Hopkins's nature; it is established that the "rain" petitioned for in the last line of the "Thou art indeed just, Lord" sonnet refers partly to such encouragement as Bridges failed to provide. Patmore, with his Bridges-like objection to "obscuring novelty," failed too. It may be heretical to suggest that there are places in Hopkins's work where that objection is valid, and that more understanding and encouragement would have been the prelude to the removal of such "novelty"; but if so Hopkins shared that heresy himself. In a letter to Bridges, discussing his work in verse and music, he sums up one point by saying: "To return to composition for a moment: what I want there, to be more intelligible, smoother, and less singular, is an audience."

By this time (September, 1888) Hopkins must long have estimated the true value of what poetic audience he had. This estimation, although Hopkins's attitude to his poetry writing is admittedly a complicated question, was surely one of the causes of the increased melancholy and decreased output of his later years. Another of the same kind was the unsolved conflict between his religious objections to being published and the view advanced in a letter to Bridges of 1886:

> What are the works of art for? to educate, to be standards. Education is meant for the many, standards are for public use. To produce is of little use unless what we produce is known, if known widely known, the wider known the better, for it is by being known it works, it does its duty, it does good. We must then try to be known, aim at it, take means to it.[4]

The hope that the degree to which poetical consultation is practiced might show any straightforward correlation with poetical merit receives a partial check at Christina Rossetti. Almost alone among the Victorians, her status has never been seriously impugned, nor is it proposed to impugn it now. The facts are that although she shared Gabriel's early literary environment, Christina was poetically far more self-reliant than he, although her attitude changed a little when publication was approaching. According to William, who had the best chance of knowing, "she consulted nobody, and solicited no advice," and "in the course of her work, invited [no] hint, counsel, or cooperation." However, Gabriel, who had been acting, with unequal success, as her literary agent since 1854, selected and arranged the contents of *Goblin Market* (1862) and did a good deal more for *The Prince's Progress* (1866). The eponymous poem was an expansion made at his suggestion from "a brief dirge-song" she had written. When completed it and other poems were offered to him for emendation, and he was finally given a free hand not only to select what poems he wished from her manuscripts, but to make small alterations in proof without consulting her at all. After 1866, there is nothing to record until 1877, when Gabriel was once more consulted, this time over half a dozen poems he was to get into *The Athenaeum* for her; Watts, then on the staff of the paper, was to assist him. Neither of them liked the poems, and Gabriel wrote to say so, adding briefly that she "had better buckle to at once and write another poem." This she did to his and Watts's satisfaction. Gabriel was not consulted at any stage over *A Pageant and other poems* (1881), the last of his sister's volumes to be published in his lifetime. All the evidence suggests that Christina regarded Gabriel as a conveniently available and articulate specimen of the outside public, who could be dispensed with once he had discharged his function of introducing her work to its audience in the form they would find most acceptable, a task she was unable to perform for herself. This is confirmed by her apparent ignorance of, or lack of interest in, the nature of her audience, at least as far as her "secular" poems were concerned. With her "secular" readers (it is not unjust to distinguish between them and readers of her religious work) she had virtually no contact at all; with "religious" readers she had some, mainly via the S.P.C.K., who sponsored her religious volumes. Her attitude to her religious poems—they were comfort offered to those in need of it—was comparatively definite; but, as regards her secular poems, her few utterances on the subject leave her motives for publication obscure, doubly so in view of her morbid vigilance against any conceivable form of vanity.

The point of view set out in this article is, I repeat, intended only as a hypothesis, a possible addition to the current set of critical tools. Even the best tools will not do for every job, and it seems more practical to admit that the work of Christina Rossetti resists, to a large degree, the application of this one. If information about her were more complete, study along the present lines might be more profitable. All that can be offered at this stage, however, is the suggestion that there are poets whose "self-examination and self-confronting with the reader" can be effected without the specimem reader's presence being more than occasionally necessary. The evidently deep humility of Christina's nature, too, was the best of protections against that arrogance which is the trap of the solitary poet, who is inclined to dismiss as irrelevant the painful tasks of revision and clarification (cf. the remarks on Morris and Swinburne below). The picture clears again when the second group of poets is examined, those who display a perceptible indifference to the problem of communication. Before turning to them, however, a brief illustration of the effects of complete artistic solitude may be provided.

James Thomson is an example, in as pure a form as is likely to be found, of the poet working in an isolation not deliberately chosen. "Writing simply for my own pleasure," he said in a letter to William Rossetti written two years before his death, "I enjoyed the writing," and a glance at the records of his life makes it clear that until 1874, with *The City of Dreadful Night* already behind him, there was nobody else's pleasure to write for. When at last he had acquired the handful of intimates who might have formed the small audience he needed, when some little recognition had come his way, he was, as Roden Noel put it "quite above, or below, caring either for approbation or contempt"; Bertram Dobell, the friend who became Thomson's biographer, traces his lack of concern with poetry between 1874 and 1881, not to the effects of vice, but to "the want of encouragement and appreciation he had met with." This may be disingenuous, but the fact of the seven years' sterility goes some little way, at least, to refute the false Romantic notions that suffering and frustration help a poet's work by hurting the poet, that "if it's in you it's bound to come out." More often, as Mr. Cyril Connolly has observed, "it stays in and goes bad." It is not claimed, of course, that this sort of isolation is necessarily fatal, nor that Thomson's ruin was not largely due to temperamental weaknesses; the tougher Meredith wrote his way through the indifference of others; the more self-assured Browning was contentedly indifferent to it. Philip Bourke Marston, a friend of Thomson's, noted of him that he belonged to "no special community or brotherhood in art." Marston, as Rossetti's devoted camp-follower, no doubt exaggerated the importance of artistic brotherhoods; but one is tempted to think that membership of such a circle might have lent Thomson the confidence and resolution he could not supply for himself. And, if a critical remark may be ventured, some of Thomson's poetical crudities might have been removed if someone had had the chance to "pitch into" him.

The group of poets comparatively unconcerned to communicate through their work is conveniently headed by Meredith. Born in the same year as Rossetti, he too became the central figure of a circle; but where Rossetti's was vehemently artistic, Meredith's, with its scholars, innumerable journalists, and three different editors of *Punch*, was not the sort to provide a qualified inner audience for his poetry. The potentially fruitful, but never close, association with the Rossetti circle was broken after a couple of years; Stevenson and Thomson confined their attention to Meredith's novels; Bridges, Leslie Stephen, and others seem to have been no more than acquaintances. Despite a large group of associates, Meredith lived in some seclusion and had almost no close friends. The great friendship of his life was with Frederick Maxse, a naval officer of literary leanings and fervid eccentricities, and it was nearly always in correspondence with him that Meredith discussed such problems as his failure to find acceptance as a poet. But in all their exchanges, which stretch over forty years, all that can be found of actual poetical consultation is a reference (in 1862) to Meredith sending Maxse part of *Modern Love* in proof, asking for "the honest judgment," and (in 1883) an implication, no more, that Maxse was to see the proofs of *Poems and Lyrics of the Joy of Earth.* Poems are rarely even mentioned by name at any time; no secrets are divulged before publication, and after it there is a corresponding refusal to do more than generalize. There is one instance on record of Meredith's responding to outside opinion of his verse: the writing of an expanded *Love in the Valley,* published in the *Poems and Lyrics,* because the first version, in *Poems* 1851, had sometimes been singled out for praise among Meredith's acquaintances. But his general disposition to keep other people away from his verse is clear, and is abundantly confirmed by his many utterances on the subject of its reception.

Beginning with the legitimate hope of gaining, on the strength of the 1851 volume, "a certain position among those who best appreciate good poetry," Meredith went on to deny any justifiable "hope for general esteem" to the poet who (like himself) "follows out vagaries of his own brain" (1864); to "aim only at satisfying [his] own taste" (1871); to define his audience as "the bull, the donkey and the barking cur" (1878); to "scorn" at his "folly" in retaining "a remainder of esteem for our public" when he could "get no audience" (1883); to feel "disdainful of an English public" (1888); and finally, long after the esteem and support of the nineties poets, of whom Richard le Gallienne was the most active, had brought Meredith a devoted audience of something like a thousand readers, he was complaining that he was still an unaccepted poet (1908). His obsession with the subject makes it obvious that he always wanted an audience, but his early failure to achieve one, linking perhaps with an innate secretiveness, bred in him a baffled determination to write for himself alone. Those who find Meredith's verse unnecessarily obscure have here, perhaps, a point of inquiry.

William Morris wrote his first poems for a ready-made audience: the Exeter-Pembroke coterie at Oxford in the mid-fifties which was to produce the *Oxford and Cambridge Magazine.* The best-known members of this group were Edward Burne-Jones and Richard Watson Dixon. These and others had a new Morris poem read to them "almost every day" for some months, and the habit of giving such readings to such an audience became habitual with Morris. Jones was the resident member of a circle which included at different times the Rossettis, the Brownings, Jones's wife, Swinburne and some of the minor Rossetti courtiers. While *The Earthly Paradise* was being written, Morris called on the Joneses almost every evening for months to read and talk about the day's work. It is bound to seem preverse to assert at this point that Morris was utterly indifferent to others' reactions to his work, but there is much evidence that his readings were not meant as preliminaries to criticism from his auditors, but, like Swinburne's, as mere performances. Morris, according to even the friendliest observers, had no time for "ideas foreign to his own" and was always impatient of criticism. Wilfred Blunt has a detailed account of Morris's way of reading his own work: he read "as if he were throwing a bone to a dog, at the end of each piece breaking off with 'There, that's it,' as much as to say, 'You may take it or leave it, as you please' ".[5] On the whole, they seem to have taken it. Jones, the only regular consultant, was of a satisfactorily passive temperament, had uncertain taste (he wrote to Kipling especially to express fulsome admiration for the "Recessional"), and must have had passages like the following read to him without raising effective protest:

> The banners seemed quite full of ease,
> That over the turret-roofs hung down;
> The battlements could get no frown
> From the flower-moulded cornices . . .
>
> Bring up the men from the south gate
> To help me if I fall or win,
> For even if I beat, their hate
> Will grow to more than this mere grin.

Apart from the use of "beat" as a bottom-of-the-barrel synonym for "win," it is worth noting that "their" refers not to "the men from the south gate," but to a previous antecedent. The incapacity shown in both extracts is grounded in a concern not to communicate but merely to write. Morris was indifferent to the fate both of his manuscripts and of his published books; it was "work," the act of writing, that his nature demanded; he wrote (as he did everything else) with enormous speed and energy, and when a poem was finished was miserable until another was begun. The demand for "work" was too easily satisfied; Morris sacrificed the arduous and irritating task of communication to the unmixed pleasure of putting words down. No poet was more open to the temptations afforded by ownership of a private press, the temptations not to waste time correcting, or consulting the opinion of others, when the type was all waiting to be set up. He once said, and his practice bears it out, that for him poetry was "very easy to write," to which "easy writing's damned hard reading" is the correct answer.

Swinburne's readings of his own work approached even more closely than Morris's to the nature of turns. For twenty-five years these followed the same pattern: Swinburne's entry to his audience of the moment would be made in a state of high excitement, and he would be carrying in his hand or in his head a new poem or extract only a few hours old. The excitement would continue to be visible in nervous tremors of the shoulders and arms and, sometimes, in a repeated descent and ascent between a sofa or chair and the floor. The spectators included at different times John Nichol's "Old Mortality" group at Oxford, Morris, Jones and their Exeter-Pembroke coterie, and later their wives, the Rossettis and their circle, including Ruskin, and the guests at Monckton Milnes's *soirées*. Nothing suggests that comment was wanted, asked for, offered, or heeded at any of these widely varying auditions; everything suggests that it was not. The whole atmosphere of Victorian bardolatry, so important in this connection, was inimical to anything of that kind.

In 1879, when Swinburne set up house with Watts at Putney, the audience was reduced to one resident member, who after a time succeeded in substituting readings of Dickens for readings of new Swinburne. Finally, in the 80's, Swinburne is found reading his poems to the old miller who was putting him and Watts up during a summer holiday at Overstrand. Clara Watts-Dunton was amused enough to investigate:

> " . . . I think he liked reading to me," proudly remarked the old man with a *very* wise shake of the head. Such a confession inwardly entertained me, for it fully confirmed my opinion that Swinburne so fully appreciated an audience that he felt lost without one.

It seems that any conscious person would do.

The analogy with Morris becomes closer when it is remembered that Swinburne read his first poems to the evidently charming and talented Lady Trevelyan (wife of the naturalist Sir Walter Trevelyan), and obtained from her much the same reassurance and encouragement as Morris looked for from his Oxford set. Thereafter the pattern of furious work and determined readings of it is set, and remains similar for the next thirty years or so. Swinburne's speed of composition recalls Morris': 700 lines of *Jason* in a day, 17 pages of *Atalanta* in two afternoons. A more significant parallel, suggesting how little the readings of new work were tests of audience reaction, is that Swinburne habitually sent his original draft straight to the printer; Morris, as noted, actually became a printer. If the writing of poetry was, to Morris, a form of "work" conducted in isolation, for Swinburne it was the exercise of a power similarly unrelated to an audience. An anecdote of the later 70's may be of interest:

> Of "A Ballade of Dreamland" he told Miss Alice Bird that, going to his bedroom early one night, he sat down to write a poem with the refrain "Only the song of a secret bird," but that to his astonishment and disgust the words would not come. In the morning, when he awoke with rested brain, he wrote the ballade off without a halt.[6]

Twice in his life, however, Swinburne deviated from the pattern of work-plus-readings. The second divergence proved permanent as Watts, though declining to have the poems read out, became Swinburne's adviser and agent. There is no need to insist on the ineptitude of his advice, which was nearly always moral rather than poetical, and which Swinburne invariably took. Results of his more purely literary influence on Swinburne were the vapid childhood poems, the late "nature" poems, and the patriotic verse. Unless this or that poem was deemed "inadvisable," it was the best, "on every successive occasion," that Swinburne had ever written. Is the poetical decay at Putney to be wholly explained as the product of failing powers and personal loneliness?

To revert to Swinburne's earlier deviation from his usual practice: in 1870 he decided, for the only time, to pass a forthcoming book "through a crucible of revision, under the eyes of one of two friends," including especially the Rossettis. The book was *Songs before Sunrise*, and became its author's favorite. It was the only one of Swinburne's volumes written directly for an audience, however imperfectly visualized: Mazzini and the London Republican faction. If the poems in it have worn better than the bulk of Swinburne's work, its provenance may be an explanation.

Some earlier Victorian poets had implied by their practice an indifference to the problem of communication, but it was not until the English Decadence was under way that it was openly repudiated. A significant link is the veneration accorded Morris, Swinburne, and Meredith by the poets of the nineties. Officially sanctioned by Pater, defined and amplified by Wilde, the idea that the true artist can be detected first of all by his intention of working "solely for his own pleasure" would have been endorsed by the average Bodley Head poet, whose work can now be seen, in its dated posturing, to have followed out its author's intention in a more thorough sense than he would presumably have liked. Except in the short run, only those who write for an audience will reach one.

Though the findings of this article have obvious critical implications, these have been intentionally left, for the most part, as implications. Their application was felt to fall outside its scope, though it is hoped that they may be developed in a fuller study of the communication problem. The precision of a good deal of Rossetti's verse, even at its most orotund and marmoreal; the directness of Hopkins, together with his occasional "singular" quality and his later poetical sterility; the quietness of tone in Christina Rossetti's verse; the ineptitude in expression that was liable to afflict Thomson; the resolute obscurity of Meredith; Morris's lack of concern with finish; Swinburne's prolixity; the evaporation of appeal from the poetry of the 'nineties; all these things certainly seem to be traceable in part, sometimes in large part, to the attitudes to communication taken up by those concerned, and/or to their success, or lack of it, in finding a small inner audience suited to its function.

If even a slight general connection could be established between absence of concern to communicate and inability to produce work of lasting interest and value, perhaps the modern practitioners of a chap-fallen Romanticism may give up exhibiting themselves before their readers and at last set about telling them something.

Notes

[1] The suggestions can also be made that concern to communicate with a very large audience is bad for a poet's work. The later career of Tennyson is the example here. Gosse records how *Enoch Arden* was contemptuously received "by many hitherto dutiful worshippers" as "an intolerable concession to commonplace ideals." Meredith, FitzGerald, and others were indignant that Tennyson should have deliberately set out to please the general public in the 60's. Can the flabbiness of most political verse also be traced partly to this cause?

[2] IV, 111 *et seqq.*, 126; VIII, 172 *et seqq.*

[3] (London, 1918), 22 *et seqq.*

[4] *Letters,* ed. Abbott, CXXXVI (London, 1935).

[5] *My Diaries,* I, 70.

[6] Gosse, *Life* (New York, 1917), p. 241.

4.

Kristian Smidt

The Intellectual Quest of the Victorian Poets

Readers familiar with *The Oxford Book of English Verse* will know that one of Tennyson's poems included in the anthology is "The Lotos-Eaters," or at least its torso, the 'Choric Song.' They may not have noticed that 'Ulysses,' on the other hand, is omitted, although the latter poem really forms a companion piece to 'The Lotos-Eaters,' being related to it in subject and opposite in mood.

Both the choice and the omission are characteristic of the period when the anthology was compiled—around the turn of the century—and of the taste of the compiler, Sir Arthur Quiller-Couch. We are given the lotos-eating rather than the adventuresome aspect of Victorian poetry, the indolence rather than the energy. And far too many people right up to the present day have been apt to forget that the energy was there.

The truth of the matter becomes obvious as soon as we exchange our anthologies for the collected editions of any of the major poets. The dreamy emotionalism is still in evidence, but one is struck far more forcibly by the almost overwhelming quantity of poetry of ideas, good and bad. Some of it, in fact, is so tough to the intellect as to be positively ludicrous. It is hard enough to make sense of such lines as the following from Meredith's "The Empty Purse," even in their full context:

Reprinted by permission of the author and the editor from *English Studies*, Vol. 40, No. 2 (1959), pp. 90–102.

> Precedents icily written on high
> Challenge the Tentatives hot to rebel.
> Our Mother, who speeds her bloomful quick
> For the march, reads which the impediment well.

There is plenty of this sort of thing in Meredith, and passages almost as difficult could be culled from many of his contemporaries.

It is too late in the day now, of course, to pretend to originality in a general reassessment of the Victorians. Their rescue from the embraces of the sentimentalists and the condemnations of the cerebralists has long since taken place, and they have been recognized as not only capable of but actually given to daring and ambitious thought. The contents and directions of their thought have been analyzed in detail in such monumental works as Professor Fairchild's *Religious Trends in English Poetry, Vol. IV* (1957) and Professor Houghton's *The Victorian Frame of Mind* (1957), and there can hardly be much to add to the researches of these American scholars.

There does, however, still seem to be room for further adjustments of emphasis and for the drawing of more precise distinctions between different periods and individuals. In the following pages, therefore, I simply propose to emphasize a few important characteristics of Victorian poetry and to review some of the intellectual attitudes of the leading poets, to see if any further discrimination can be added to established insights.

There was probably just as much philosophy and metaphysics in the English poetry of the seventeenth and eighteenth centuries as in that of the nineteenth. But the thinking of the Victorian poets was different in kind from that of their predecessors, barring perhaps the Romanticists. When Milton set out to "justify the ways of God to men," the assumption was that he actually possessed sufficient knowledge to do so. And Pope in the eighteenth century echoed Milton's assurance as well as his words in wishing to 'vindicate the ways of God to Man,' The Victorian poets made no such claims, or if they did it was in a totally different spirit. Theirs not to expound and teach but to question why and how and what.

Characteristically the poetry of the Victorian period deals

with a search or quest—for knowledge or for something symbolizing knowledge and certainty. The ubiquity of the theme could be proved by examples from a great variety of works and writers. Tennyson's Ulysses is the representative figure,

> yearning in desire
> To follow knowledge like a sinking star
> Beyond the utmost bound of human thought.

Or another of Tennyson's figures, Sir Galahad, riding on and on in search of the Holy Grail. There is Browning's Paracelsus, seeking

> to comprehend the works of God
> And God himself, and all God's intercourse
> With the human mind; . . .

There is Matthew Arnold, recognizing

> an unspeakable desire
> After the knowledge of our buried life,
> A thirst to spend our fire and restless force
> In tracking out our true, original course;
> A longing to inquire
> Into the mystery of this heart that beats
> So wild, so deep in us, to know
> Whence our thoughts come and where they go.
> ("The Buried Life.")

Arnold's friend Arthur Hugh Clough was yet another seeker:

> Hints haunt me ever of a more beyond:
> I am rebuked by a sense of the incomplete,
> ("Dipsychus.")

And George Meredith found memorable phrases for his need of knowledge:

> Ah, what a dusty answer gets the soul
> When hot for certainties in this our life!
> ("Modern Love")

Or—a final example—to speak with Meredith's Martin in "Martin's Puzzle":

> But the worst of *me* is, that when I bow my head,
> I perceive a thought wriggling away in the dust,
> And I follow its tracks, quite forgetful, instead
> Of humble acceptance: for, question I must!

The search, as these quotations indicate, was definitely for knowledge, not primarily for passion, or for beauty or even for glory. And the knowledge which was sought was that of ultimate things, the matters that philosophy and religion usually make it their business to deal with: What is the nature of the universe? Is it guided towards some final purpose by a conscious will, or is it a meaningless dance of atoms? Is there a distinction between body and soul, and if so, what is it? What and who am I? Have I a moral nature, or is morality merely acquired?

Why, one may ask, having such problems to grapple with, did not these poets speculate in discursive prose and in philosophical language rather than in the surely recalcitrant medium of verse? Why did they not turn philosophers and do the thing systematically?

Only one answer is possible. They were dedicated men. They had a prophetic mission.

The Victorians were the direct heirs of the romantics, and knew it. Tennyson at fourteen heard the news of Byron's death and felt, says his grandson, "almost as though the world had come to an end." Browning at twenty idolized Shelley and in his first published poem, "Pauline," hailed him as the "Sun-treader." "The air seems bright with thy past presence yet," he wrote. Arnold, grieving for Byron, Shelley, and Obermann in his "Stanzas from the Grande Chartreuse," complained that

> The sufferers died, they left their pain;
> The pangs which tortured them remain.

The pangs, and, we may add, some of the fine enthusiasm.

Shelley, it will be remembered, concluded his *Defence of Poetry* by hymning the mystic powers of the poet:

> It is impossible to read the compositions of the most celebrated writers of the present day without being startled with the electric life which burns within their words. They measure the circumference and sound the depths of human nature with a comprehensive and all-penetrating spirit, and they are themselves perhaps the most sincerely astonished at its manifestations; for it is less their spirit than the spirit of the age. Poets are the hierophants of an unapprehended inspiration; the mirrors of the gigantic shadows which futurity casts upon the present; the words which express what they understand not; the trumpets which sing to battle, and feel not what they inspire; the influence which is moved not, but moves. Poets are the unacknowledged legislators of the world.

Anyone taking such views seriously and feeling that he had the gift of poetic inspiration must inevitably come to rely on poetry, including his own, to express true insight and understanding even if his thought was ordinarily bewildered. Shelley's *Defence* was not published till 1840, but his ideas were well known and there can be no doubt that the Victorian consciously accepted the prophet's mantle which he laid on their shoulders. They still felt that the poets were the philosophical leaders of mankind and its intellectual pioneers: ". . . but now / I shall be priest and prophet as of old," says the speaker of "Pauline." The philosophers proper might work out elaborate systems and publish them in learned volumes, but only the poets could bring out the central significance of their ideas and relate them to the times, turning them into beliefs and ideals for men of the nineteenth century and for their children.

But the Victorians inherited the enthusiasm of the romantic revolt without the possibility of repeating the grandiose negations and prophetic assertions of such as Shelley. For the intellectual climate was now more argumentative. It was no use now producing "words which express what they understand not"—when they did the words were in danger of expressing nothing at all, as Browning was to discover. Thoughts in this new age of science had to be precise and understandable, not "trumpets which sing to battle and feel not what they inspire." It was all very well for Shelley to speak of "electric life," but now "electric light" was on its way. The impact of the French Revolution, which had been felt so blissfully by the romantics, had died down, and instead there was the continuing but far more prosaic impulse of the Industrial Revolution. Jeremy Bentham's utilitarian pamphlets had succeeded Godwin's imaginative *Political Justice.* Poetic intuition was fighting against heavy odds.

The Victorian age was one of those which met a challenge to accepted beliefs only comparable to the intellectual upheaval which occurred in the late Renaissance. The challenge of Copernicus and Galileo revolutionized science and philosophy. But religion, after wavering rather dizzyingly for other reasons, finally accommodated itself to the new cosmology and remained relatively unshaken. So poets like Donne and Milton could go on describing the universe almost as if heliocentric astronomy had never been heard of, writing poetry based on unquestioning faith and taking care to make it poetry first and last.

Not so with the Victorians. Charles Darwin's challenge coincided with the direct challenge to religious beliefs represented by the Higher Criticism. In all fields at the same time science and scientific philosophy were clamorous for attention. Thus the first popular exposé of evolutionary theory, Robert Chambers's *Vestiges of the Natural History of Creation,* as well as George Eliot's translation of Strauss's rationalistic *Leben Jesu* and John Stuart Mill's positivistic *System of Logic* were all of them published in the eighteen-forties.

Belief in anything intangible and undemonstrable was made increasingly difficult, it was felt, by the advance of science. Fact was taking the place of faith. Even dreams were made impossible by the encroachment of fact, as Tennyson had complained as early as 1829, when he wrote his Cambridge prize poem "Timbuctoo." He first sees Timbuctoo in a Utopian dream as a city of mysterious loveliness. But then reality takes hold of his spirit and Discovery reveals the city for what it is:

> Black specks amid a waste of dreary sand,
> Low-built, mud-wall'd, Barbarian settlements,
> How chang'd from this fair City!

In some cases the poets clung strongly to the religious beliefs in which they had been brought up, and the resultant conflict caused an anguish of mind which was of a definitely intellectual kind. In 1830 Tennyson published a poem bearing the curious title "Supposed Confessions of a Second-Rate Sensitive Mind." Quite obviously the confessions of this poem are not merely "supposed" but perfectly genuine. The poem is tortured by guilt because he can no longer believe as his mother taught him to do:

> when with brows
> Propt on thy knees, my hands upheld
> In thine, I listen'd to thy vows,
> For me outpour'd in holiest prayer –
> For me unworthy!

Yet he cannot deny the discovery of his earliest youth that it is right to doubt and question

> and analyse
> Our double nature, and compare
> All creeds till we have found the one,
> If one there be?

He has entangled himself in an insoluble conflict of affirmation and doubt and ends the poem with a cry of despair: "O damned vacillating state!"

It is sometimes said that the death of Tennyson's friend Arthur Hallam, in 1833, was the event which mainly plunged the young poet into the metaphysical despair which is recorded in "In Memoriam." But his struggles had begun several years before Hallam died and were struggles of doctrinal faith against the onslaught of sceptical rationalism. Hallam's death naturally intensified the conflict and added great emotional force to it, but was hardly the cause. Nor was it responsible for its fundamentally intellectual character, which is also displayed in "The Two Voices," the poetic dialogue written just after the bereavement.

A similar struggle of the old-world faith to survive may be found in Browning. Though his childhood beliefs proved more resilient than Tennyson's, he felt throughout his life the restless "craving after knowledge" of his speaker in "Pauline."

No one, however, felt the conflict more agonizingly than Matthew Arnold, grown up under the influence of his remarkable father, Thomas Arnold of Rugby, whom he admired but could not follow. Thomas Arnold was a liberal Broad-Church man, but he knew his own mind in matters of belief and he was a stickler for discipline. Matthew Arnold, growing up somewhat later than Tennyson and Browning, neither knew his own mind nor had any relish for authority. His intellectual plight is poignantly expressed in "Stanzas from the Grande Chartreuse," where, thinking of his lost faith, he speaks of himself as

> Wandering between two worlds, one dead,
> The other powerless to be born,
> With nowhere yet to rest my head.

So the poets were left with the intellectual task, much more exacting perhaps than any that Shelley tackled, of writing poetry while trying to piece together a belief and a world view that should take adequate account of the assertions of scientists and positivists. They could no longer liberate their minds in revolutionary ardor, but were pressed to argue their beliefs and disbeliefs. There was a desperate need for certainty, to reconcile faith and knowledge in a higher enlightenment.

In particular, the poets could not remain indifferent to the theories of Evolution, and their various responses to these theories form one of the most interesting chapters of the intellectual and literary history of the age. The subject has been well explored recently by Dr. Georg Roppen in *Evolution and Poetic Belief* (Oslo, 1956), and I shall merely indicate certain distinctions which may still need to be clarified.

Tennyson was in search of the Age of Gold and at first sought a revelation of it in the past, and in myth. That stage is represented by "Timbuctoo" and also, perhaps, by his glimpses of Camelot and Bagdat and other cities of splendor. His early visions were destroyed by the advance of knowledge, or what he called "Discovery." But after a short while he came to accept, in a general way, the *pre-Darwinian* theories of evolution, and from then on pinned his faith in the future, finding in scientific thought, such as it was, at least a partial substitute for, or perhaps rather a supplement to, the dream of a religious paradise of perfection. "Locksley Hall" is a well-known example of his optimistic belief in evolution, as in the rapturous lines:

> For I dipt into the future, far as human eye could see,
> Saw the Vision of the world, and all the wonder that would be;

Or those other much-quoted lines:

> Yet I doubt not through the ages one increasing purpose runs,
> And the thoughts of men are widen'd with the process of the suns.

The "increasing purpose" is what Tennyson clung to. His evolutionary faith was teleological and connected with the undogmatic Christianity or "Higher Pantheism" in which he came to rest after his religious struggles. There are many indications in Tennyson's later poetry, however, that when he came to know Darwin's theory of natural selection with its emphasis on blind chance in the struggle for survival he lost much of his zest for evolution. And as time went on he felt more and more acutely how slow and haphazard a process it was bound to be. There was a new crisis of faith. And this, it seems probable, accounts for much of the despondency of his later verse, like "Lucretius" (1868), "Despair" (1881), "Vastness" (1889) and "The Dawn" (1892). The Voice of the Earth in "The Dreamer," though answered by a defiant optimism, still expresses an almost annihilating disappointment:

> I am losing the light of my Youth
> And the Vision that led me of old,
> And I clash with an iron Truth,
> When I make for an Age of gold . . .

The two poems to compare, of course, are "Locksley Hall," dating from 1842, and "Locksley Hall Sixty Years After," from 1886. Whatever optimism remains in the latter is much more hardly come by and much more guarded than that of the early poem. It is well represented by the couplet:

> Forward then, but still remember how the course of Time will swerve,
> Crook and turn upon itself in many a backward streaming curve.

The development from optimism to anxiety or even fear in relation to evolutionary ideas certainly seems an important strand in Tennyson's poetic woof.

If we turn to Browning, we shall find that he never accepted the idea that biological evolution would go on and on. The bodies of men and animals, he thought, had reached complete development with the appearance of man:

> And man appears at last. So far the seal
> Is put on life; one stage of being complete,
> ("Paracelsus.")

It only remains for man, and man alone, to continue developing his spiritual nature:

> the body sprang
> At once to the height, and stayed, but the soul, – no!
> ("A Death in the Desert.")

> progress, man's distinctive mark alone,
> Not God's, and not the beasts'
> (*Ibid.*)

This notion of completed evolution on the physical plane is not just an inconsistency in Browning's thought due to traditional conceptions of an ideal, static "chain of being." It is basic to his whole attitude.

After his initial Shelleyan revolt, Browning returned to a fairly central Christian position, agreeing with the mystics that evil and pain have a purpose in the larger scheme of things and thinking of our existence on earth as merely preliminary to a future spiritual state. Browning's vision of perfection, therefore, was eschatological. He believed in a heaven beyond this life on earth, which justified the deprivations and pains we suffer while in the body. Thus in "The Last Ride Together" the speaker of the monologue thinks he may have been deprived of complete happiness on earth in order to save him from forgetting that there is a heaven of happiness beyond; otherwise,

> Earth being so good, would heaven seem best?
> Now heaven and she are beyond this ride.

Browning characteristically sees the world as a place of trial and preparation. And after "Paracelsus" he quite consistently saw the Creator as transcendent, not immanent: "Externe / Not inmost, is the Cause, fool!" ("Francis Furini"). He even tried to assure himself that the questing intellect ought not to venture too far:

> where and when and how?
> Leave that to the First Cause! Enough that now,
> Here where I stand, this moment's me and mine,
> Shows me what is, permits me to divine
> What shall be.

Although these are the words of the dramatic character Francis Furini, the idea which they express can be found in numerous places in Browning's poetry.

There is little change in the larger philosophical implications of that poetry after "Paracelsus." In important respects it is determinedly and even refreshingly counter-evolutionary. This may seem surprising considering the age and Browning's usual optimism. But the only really surprising aspect of his philosophy as well as the only notable development of his thought, it seems to me, is in the idea which he gradually came to entertain of a continued spiritual and moral evolution in the hereafter. His Rabbi Ben Ezra enjoys a period of rest and understanding in old age before death sends him to a new sphere of evolutionary struggle:

> And I shall thereupon
> Take rest, ere I be gone
> Once more on my adventure brave and new:
> Fearless and unperplexed
> When I wage battle next,
> What weapons to select, what armour to indue.

This is indeed a rather startling picture of heaven, but it shows that Browning in at least one respect—that of spiritual growth—was more evolutionary than any other poet.

George Meredith, too, was interested in the development of man's mind and spirit. He dreamt of a time "when brain-rule splendidly towers." But unlike Browning, and to some extent unlike Tennyson, he wholly accepted the idea of a physical struggle for survival and of natural selection and was entirely content with the promise of perfection in this life involving man as a part of nature in general. As for Swinburne, he accepted the idea of evolution in a vague sort of way. But Swinburne really saw Man as the Creator, sharing the creative powers of nature rather than subject to a development over which he had no control. Man, if he only knew it, *is* fully developed. He only needs freedom. Not evolution, then, so much as revolution is Swinburne's gospel; and his thought is frequently political, especially in *Songs before Sunrise*. Thus 'Hertha' issues in a Utopian political vision, "Even love, the beloved Republic, that feeds upon freedom and lives."

Matthew Arnold for the most part held aloof from the evolutionary discussion, perhaps because of his belief that the poet should not engage himself too directly in practical and controversial issues. Aesthetes like Rossetti and Morris and Catholic poets like Christina Rossetti, Gerard Manley Hopkins and Coventry Patmore also kept evolution out of their poetry as a rule. They had found their answers. But most of the leading poets continually discussed it, and, as we have seen, it elicited widely divergent responses from them.

Even if the poets came to believe in some form of evolution, however, they had hardly solved their philosophical problems. For a belief in change and growth alone can hardly be a final philosophical standpoint. The truth of this is illustrated by the confused and confusing creed of Swinburne: from the point of view of thought Swinburne's 'Hertha' is surely one of the most incongruous poems in the English language. And the inadequacy of the evolutionary answer is abundantly proved again at the turn of the century by the pessimistic broodings of Thomas Hardy. Evolution possibly answers the question of how? but not those of why? and where to? Even Browning, who seems to have been reasonably happy in his solutions, was rather vague as to the nature of the transcendental life which he imagined after death.

Perhaps if the Victorians had been more clear-sighted, or if they had been more fortunate in their intellectual environment and stimuli, they might have found an answer to satisfy both philosophy and poetry. Some exciting new time concept might have worked the miracle—such as the idea that time, instead of flowing on and on with its burden of change and development without any apparent goal was only a dimension of our habitual experience and might itself be contained within a larger dimension which was timeless. Carlyle had some such intuition in *Sartor Resartus* and wrote poetically enough about it:

> Pierce through the Time-element, glance into the Eternal. Believe what thou findest written in the sanctuaries of Man's Soul, even as all Thinkers, in all ages, have devoutly read it there: that Time and Space are not God, but creations of God; that with God as it is a universal HERE, so is it an everlasting NOW.

An ancient idea, of course, as Carlyle himself points out, and one which, in its general mystical form, was quite familiar to the Victorians. But it had rather embarrassing associations with German idealism and could not be exploited a hundred years ago or even seventy years ago with any show of scientific support. The poets, at any rate, did not exploit or develop it to any significant extent. It was left to later generations of poets, those who caught the impact of a time-flouting depth psychology and who found support in a relativistically inclined science, to answer doubt and scepticism by a new vision of a timelessness beyond any process of evolution. The Victorians went on worrying.

It was a pity that the prophets were not better served by their inspiration. But perhaps they never really had sufficient faith in their oracular poetic medium, in the ability of poetry to turn their benighted thoughts into supernatural clarity. Arnold the critic might declare that "More and more mankind will discover that we have to turn to poetry to interpret life for us, to console us, to sustain us." To Arnold writing in prose, poetry was "an ever surer and surer stay." But what of Arnold the poet? And what of Tennyson and Browning?

Both Tennyson and Browning, especially the latter, somewhat distrusted poetry and the romantic-intellectual conception of poetry, never being entirely convinced of its adequacy to deal with the most important problems of life. Tennyson's "Palace of Art" and "The Lady of Shalott," in both of which art is more or less completely renounced for the sake of life, are good indications. In the former he describes the poet's soul enthroned in the Palace of Art:

Full oft the riddle of the painful earth
Flash'd through her as she sat alone,
Yet not the less held she her solemn mirth,
And intellectual throne.

And so she throve and prosper'd: so three years
She prosper'd: on the fourth she fell,
Like Herod, when the shout was in his ears,
Struck thro' with pangs of hell.

So when four years were wholly finished,
She threw her royal robes away,
"Make me a cottage in the vale," she said,
"Where I may mourn and pray.

Yet pull not down my palace towers, that are
So lightly, beautifully built:
Perchance I may return with others there
When I have purged my guilt."

This attitude of renunciation is most pronounced in Tennyson's early poetry. In Browning's case, however, it pervades almost all that he wrote. Naturally Browning recognized the value of poetry and art, witness all the artists of various kinds included in his portrait gallery. Fra Lippo Lippi is an eloquent defender of the high function of art:

we're made so that we love
First when we see them painted, things we have passed
Perhaps a hundred times nor cared to see;
And so they are better, painted—better to us.
Which is the same thing. Art was given for that;
God uses us to help each other so,
Lending our minds out.

But nevertheless, Browning always sees life as superior to poetry. He quotes himself in "Development" as habitually saying that "No dream's worth waking." Poetry, he admits in "The Last Ride Together," is "something, nay 'tis much"—"but them," he goes on to ask the poet,

> Have you yourself what's best for men?
> Are you—poor, sick, old ere your time—
> Nearer one whit your own sublime
> Than we who never have turned a rhyme?
> Sing, riding's a joy! For me, I ride.

The poet Cleon is admired even by King Protus. But his great achievements in poetry cannot make him happy, as he tries to explain to the King:

> Because in my great epos I display
> How divers men young, strong, fair, wise, can act—
> Is this as though I acted? If I paint,
> Carved the young Phoebus, am I therefore young?
> Methinks I'm older that I bowed myself
> The many years of pain that taught me art!
> ("Cleon.")

And in the prologue to "Fifine at the Fair" Browning finds poetry, like the sea, a glorious element to swim in, but he is glad he is in sight of "Land the solid and safe—."

So, of the two great prophets of Victorian poetry, one, Tennyson, doubted his message, and the other, Browning, had doubts of his medium. And they went on doubting too long. The Victorian age itself was too long. Once its initial challenge had been caught up, it settled down to a long process of uneasy adaptation, which lasted through the 1860's and seventies and eighties and nineties without any new intellectual upheavals of the first order to goad or stimulate the poets into rising on stepping-stones of their dead selves to higher things.

Great poets should die young if they cannot renew themselves or be renewed. But Tennyson and Browning both lived on into a ripe old age and certainly survived their own best efforts. Critics are right in detecting a certain hollowness at least in their later poetry. Not the poets' affirmations and beliefs were hollow, however—it was their doubts which had become mechanical gestures and for that reason perhaps insincere. Poetry let them down if they had ever believed with Shelley that it would do their thinking and prophecying for them. They spoke their doubts into its oracular orifice and it was still their doubts that came out, though sometimes in beautiful clouds of aromatic smoke, at the public end. But one cannot just go on doubting and remain a poet. And so the great age ended, not with a bang and not quite with a whimper, but with something indeterminately in between.

Having recognized this hollow sound towards the end of the period, we must still insist on the basic sincerity of the Victorian giants of poetry. They genuinely wrestled with intellectual problems and turned their struggles into art. They wrote verse because they were poets. Even Arnold was too much of a poet not to throw his speculations into verse. But they did not just happen to be poets *and* intellectual seekers, or poets who had lost their intellectual bearings. Poetry offered itself to them as a natural vehicle of thought because their intellectual dilemma was also an *emotional* one. I do not now mean emotional in the sense that the death of friends, or other events that touched them closely caused metaphysical distress. I mean that beliefs and ideas themselves necessarily have an emotional aspect. The attachment to an idea, like the attachment to a person, is itself an emotion, which will be colored by the kind of idea to which one is attached and which will sometimes be passionate. Further, it is emotionally reassuring simply to be able to believe in certain things at all; and the loss of once comforting beliefs may be very hard to endure. As Harold says in Tennyson's "Promise of May":

> Sometimes I wonder
> When man has surely learnt at last that all
> His old-world faith, the blossom of his youth,
> Has faded, falling fruitless—whether then
> All of us, all at once, may not be seized
> With some fierce passion, not so much for Death
> As against Life!

The poets, then, were concerned not only with speculating upon what they could or could not believe in, but with expressing, as T. S. Eliot would say, how it felt to be uncertain. The feeling of intellectual vacillation, as a matter of fact, is one that poetry can probably express far better than prose because it can present two alternative points of view as simultaneously attractive to the same mind: presenting them in the form of an argument perhaps, as in Tennyson's "The Two Voices" and Clough's "Dipsychus," but holding them in an emotional and rhythmical balance which may be more satisfying to the poetic imagination than the arrival at a definite conclusion.

There is an inner and natural connection between poetry and thinking. Sometimes, as in the seventeenth century, thought and feeling may be poetically fused by means of pregnant symbols and sublimated wit. But another perfectly valid method is to dramatize the thought, as the Victorians so often did, and so bring out its emotional intensity. Quite often, of course, ideas were simply worked out in the unwilling medium of verse. Mr. Eliot has said that Tennyson and Browning ruminated, and there is a fair amount of rumination in "In Memoriam" and, say, Browning's "Prince Hohenstiel-Schwangau." But at the best of times, as in other parts of "In Memoriam" or in "The Scholar Gipsy," the poets attained a unification of thought and feeling which is profoundly moving. They may not have added greatly to the world's store of knowledge, but they have added to our spiritual wealth. Which seems a sufficient justification for Clough's famous line:

Say not the struggle nought availeth.

5.

William O. Raymond

"The Jewelled Bow": A Study in Browning's Imagery and Humanism

In Browning's second letter to Elizabeth Barrett he uses the imagery of "white light" versus "prismatic hues" to represent the contrast between the full and direct reflection of her personality in lyric utterance, and the partial and oblique refraction of his own personality in the medium of the dramatic monologue. A little later, he reveals his consciousness of the limitations of his poetry through a kindred image: "these scenes and song-scraps *are* such mere and very escapes of my inner power, which lives in me like the light in those crazy Mediterranean phares I have watched at sea, wherein the light is ever revolving in a dark gallery, bright and alive, and only after a weary interval leaps out, for a moment, from the one narrow chink, and then goes on with the blind wall between it and you. . . ."[1] In response, Elizabeth Barrett, while deprecating the merit of her own poetry and paying tribute to the worth of Browning's, acknowledges the justice of his self-criticism: "and in fact, you have not written the R. B. poem yet—your rays fall obliquely rather than directly straight. I see you only in your moon" (1, 22). In one of her letters, though referring to "the glory of dramatic art," she urges: "Yet I am conscious of wishing you to take the other crown besides—and after having made your own creatures speak in clear human voices, to speak yourself out of that personality

Reprinted by permission of the author and the Modern Language Association of America from *PMLA,* Vol. 70, No. 1 (March, 1955), pp. 115–31.

which God made, and with the voice which he tuned into such power and sweetness of speech" (II, 182).

When contrasting lyric and dramatic poetry, it was inevitable that Browning should have in mind not only Elizabeth Barrett's verse, but also the art and personality of Shelley, whose influence upon him was so potent. It is probable that the imagery of "white light" versus "prismatic hues" was suggested by Shelley's lines in *Adonais*:

> Life, like a dome of many-coloured glass,
> Stains the white radiance of Eternity,

Previously, in *Pauline,* he had apostrophized Shelley as the "Sun-treader"; and the metaphor of "white light" is frequently introduced as representative of the aspiration, idealism, and spiritual quality of Shelley's life and poetry. In a more general sense, the imagery of "white light" is used by Browning in many connotations as a symbol of spiritual vertities which are absolute and ideal—the nature of God, Truth, Beauty, Goodness, Heaven, the Soul. In the initial reference from his correspondence I have cited, he identifies "the pure white light" with truth. Truth, in its absoluteness, is regarded by him as a divine endowment of the soul, enshrined in the depths of personality. As he wrote in *Paracelsus*:

> There is an inmost centre in us all,
> Where truth abides in fulness . . .
> (I.727–728)
> and to know
> Rather consists in opening out a way
> Whence the imprisoned splendour may escape,
> Than in effecting entry for a light
> Supposed to be without. (I.732–736)

The symbolism of "white light" and of "prismatic hues" is, in the main, confined in Browning's letters to an illustration of the limitation of his poetic medium of expression, the dramatic monologue. This, however, is a pendant to the comprehensive use of this metaphor in his poetry. Its occurrence is so frequent, and its application so varied, that it may be regarded as not merely illustrative, but of structural value. Before referring further to its employment in connection with Browning's art, I shall consider its wider significance. This involves basic aspects of the poet's life and thought which are both subjective and objective in their nature. They include two normative attitudes of mind or dispositions of spirit which, psychologically, have their sources in his individual personality. They also include two important environmental influences instrumental in moulding his philosophy of life. These are his artistic inheritance of the ideals of romanticism as represented by the poetry of Shelley, and his religious convictions as represented by evangelical Christianity. It is with these larger references in view that I have linked the imagery of the prism, the rainbow, the broken and deflected light, with the humanism of his poetry. While the "white light" of Browning's transcendentalism is of import, it is, as I shall strive to show, secondary to the "prismatic hues" of his humanism.

Although Browning for many years regarded himself as a disciple of Shelley, it is important to realize the basic differences between the two poets. Shelley's life and poetry are, in a sense, all of one piece. Browning's, on the other hand, are complex, motivated by his consciousness of the necessity of reconciling the absolute claims of the ideal with the concrete realities of man's existence on earth. "I . . . fear the pure white light, even if it is in me," Browning told Elizabeth Barrett. He was aware that one side of his nature was in kinship with Shelley. As a scion of the romantic era in English poetry he inherited its transcendental idealism. This dominant artistic influence was reinforced by phychical elements in his personality. In *Pauline,* as was noted by John Stuart Mill, the intense self-consciousness of the youthful poet is everywhere in evidence. Conscious of the prodigality of his intellectual and spiritual powers and of the boundless capacities of the soul, he, like Shelley, felt the urge to transcend the limitations of the external world, the barriers imposed by sense and time:

> How should this earth's life prove my only sphere?
> Can I so narrow sense but that in life
> Soul still exceeds it? (634–636)

The romantic aspiration to spurn the trammels of the finite in quest of the infinite, to seek "the pure white light," to give free expression to the fullness of personality, to press on towards the Absolute and its spiritual radiance of Truth, Beauty, and Goodness—these typical impulses and motifs of Shelley have their reflection in Browning.

There is, however, a strong counter-current in his life and poetry which flows like a gulf between him and Shelley. While the aspiration of the soul is infinite and its destiny immortal, Browning holds that it must stoop to conquer. The core of his ethics is that the limitations of this finite world are a school of discipline intended to serve the end of spiritual growth. Hence it is imperative for men to work within these, even though constantly striving to make reality conform more nearly to the standard of the ideal. Browning's philosophy of life, with its deep sense of human experience as poised between the absolute and the relative, is reinforced by his religious belief, the profound influence of the spirit and tenets of Christianity. His humanism is nowhere more in evidence than in the place given in his poetry to the Christian doctrine of the Incarnation. His interpretation of this is not a mere echo of the formal and traditional theology of English Puritanism. For him the Incarnation of Christ is not only a matter of historical record enshrined in a creed or a body of religious opinion. It is an eternal truth verified in his inner and personal experience, and made the subject of deep and individual reflection. In particular, it is inseparably linked with what has been called "the richest vein of pure ore" in his poetry, his view of the nature and function of love. The divine condescension to human weakness and imperfection is conceived of by Browning as flowing from the very essence of God as a being of infinite love:

> The very God! think, Abib; dost thou think?
> So, the All Great were the All-Loving too—
> So, through the thunder comes a human voice
> Saying, "O heart I made, a heart beats here!
> Face, my hand, fashioned, see it in myself!
> Thou hast no power nor mayst conceive of mine,
> But love I gave thee, with myself to love,
> And thou must love me who have died for thee!"
>
> (*Epistle of Karshish,* 304–311)

It is in *Pauline, Paracelsus,* and *Sordello,* elaborate studies of soul-development, that the interplay between the transcendental and humanistic elements of Browning's philosophy of life is most strikingly in evidence. In them we may trace the tension and conflict between what I have called the two basic attitudes or dispositions of his mind and spirit, and their reconciliation through the sovereign virtue of love. All poetry, Browning once wrote to Ruskin, is the problem of "putting the infinite within the finite."[2] It is this crux, in the sphere of life as well as art, that is the central theme of his three early monodramas; and it is also the poet's personal problem. The heroes of these poems are unmistakably of the romantic type. They are all characterized by a restless and eager self-consciousness, indomitable aspiration, illimitable desires, and a passion for the absolute which impel them to reject or scorn the bounds and imperfections of the finite. Images of white light or of the star are often introduced to symbolize their aims and qualities. The speaker in *Pauline* refers to his pride "in wandering o'er thought's world" to seek "the White Way for a star." Paracelsus, in his vain attempt "to contemplate undazzled some one star," confesses "what was a speck expands into a star . . . till I near craze." His mind, like Aprile's, became "dazzled by shapes that filled its length with light." Aprile is described as "the over-radiant star too mad to drink the life-springs." Sordello, "thrusting in time, eternity's concern," aspires to

> Compress the starriest into one star,
> And grasp the whole at once! (I.854–855)

Allusions to Shelley, the "Sun-treader," occur in all three poems, and it is clear that their principal characters reflect, in varying degrees, that side of Browning's nature which is in kinship with the transcendental idealism of Shelley. Aprile, in particular, embodies that conception of love as a spiritual principle, a thirst for the absolute, the pursuit of an eternal and perfect archetypal loveliness which is in harmony with the romantic Neo-Platonism of Shelley. Such a love, though "through the web of being blindly wove," can be but dimly foreshadowed in the perishable forms of earth. This concept of love strikes a responsive chord in Browning's being, and he has given it fine poetic expression in Part II of *Paracelsus*.[3] Yet the deeper significance of the poem is not fully revealed until Part v. In it Browning represents love not as an infinite aspiration in keeping with the romantic idealism of Shelley, but rather in the spirit of the Christian *Magnificat*. He visualizes it as a love that stoops to conquer, submits itself to the lowliness of human nature, and refuses to spurn the body or despise the world in the interests of an ascetic ideal of spirituality:

> love—not serenely pure,
> But strong from weakness, like a chance-sown plant—
> (v.698–699)
> Love which endures and doubts and is oppressed
> And cherished, suffering much and much sustained,
> And blind, oft-failing, yet believing love,
> A half-enlightened, often chequered trust . . .
> (v.702–705)

It is from the standpoint of the second disposition of his spirit that Browning is acutely conscious of the one-sidedness of the idealism of the romantic Titans he has portrayed in his monodramas. Blinded by a vision of the absolute, "the pure white light," they refuse to stoop to life on earth. They fail, as is pointed out in *Paracelsus,* because they have never grasped the deeper meaning of love. A comprehension of this would have taught them to sympathize with the weakness and imperfection of human nature, and not to disdain to work within the sphere of man's finite existence. This conception of love has its supreme prototype in the person of Christ, the Divine Love that for man's sake became poor and of low estate.

> 'T is the weakness in strength that I cry for! my flesh, that
> I seek
> In the Godhead! (*Saul* XVIII.22–23)

Browning parts company with Shelley in the interests of a noble humanism, and in accordance with the deepest convictions of his religious faith.

Browning's humanism has many facets. Its most obvious illustration is the variety and scope of his dramatic portrayal of individual character in flashes of crucial experience. "My Elixir of Life" was Rossetti's enthusiastic tribute to the delineation of human nature in *Men and Women,* a phrase revealing his delight in its vivacity and realism. The title of this collection of poems might aptly be regarded as summing up the central interest of the whole of Browning's poetry. While as a follower of the Romantic era he inherits its love of nature, he rarely describes nature for her own sake. Though there is much fine landscape painting in his poems, this is the background rather than the foreground of his canvas. Nature is subordinated to man. His portrayal of her is selective, designed to illustrate and enhance, either by likeness or contrast, those human moods or states which are the dominating motifs of his poetry.

The title *Men and Women* is also indicative of the particular quality of Browning's humanism. His primary concern is with the individual rather than with the group. The broad conception of humanity, so dear to the hearts of the poets of romanticism, is but faintly reflected in his verse. Nor is he greatly moved by the ideals of liberty, equality, and fraternity, associated with this humanitarian impulse in the epoch of the French Revolution. It is true that in *Sordello,* a work composed when Shelley's influence upon him was still potent, he represents his hero as finally dedicating himself to liberty and the service of humanity. But this generalized devotion to the principle of liberty and to man as man finds but little echo in the body of his verse. In his mature work he pays scarcely more than lip service to these concepts.

Nor is there evidence that the groupings of men in communal institutions, of which the nation is an outstanding example, kindled Browning's poetic imagination. In an early play, *Strafford,* he reveals his sympathy with the Puritans and the ideal of liberty they champion. Yet, even here, the drama is focused in the character of Strafford rather than in a national cause. As S. R. Gardiner comments: "from the beginning to the end of the play the personal relations between the actors are exaggerated at the expense of the political."[4]

Through his residence in Florence, Browning was in close touch with the Italian struggle for independence; and it is this which comes closest to being an inspiring patriotic motif in his poetry. There is, however, a contrast between the ardour of Mrs.

Browning's devotion to the national aspirations of Italy and her husband's more tempered sympathy. In particular, he never shared her enthusiasms for Louis Napoleon as the prospective deliverer of Italy from the yoke of Austria. Browning is far from indifferent. In occasional poems, such as *Pippa Passes, The Italian in England,* and *Old Pictures in Florence,* his support of Italy's cause is manifest. Yet in these his interest is incidental, subordinate in the first two instances to the dramatic representation of individual character, and in the third to the main theme of the paintings of the early Italian masters.

In the dedicatory letter to his friend Milsand, prefixed to *Sordello,* Browning wrote: "The historical decoration was purposely of no more importance than a background requires; and my stress lay on the incidents in the development of a soul little else is worth study." This statement would not be applicable to the whole of Browning's poetry without qualification. In *Pauline* and *Paracelsus* the poet is absorbed in the description and analysis of inner states of consciousness. There is no historical background in *Pauline* and only a minimum of it in *Paracelsus.* In *Sordello,* however, it assumes greater importance; and, beginning with the *Dramatic Lyrics* of 1842, the historical setting is a vital element in Browning's poetry. The men and women of his poems are representative of their eras and reflect the milieus—political, artistic, and religious—of the times in which they live. His interest in all the works of man is unflagging, and the fecundity of his humanism is finely illustrated by his panoramic vistas of the exhibition of these on the stage of history. His characters are not conceived in abstraction from their environments, but are motivated by the currents of active life and thought of their epochs, which range from ancient Israel and Athens to contemporary Italy and England.

Yet, despite this wealth of historical background, the primary and pivotal inspiration of Browning's poetry lies in the delineation of the individual rather than the group, and in inward consciousness rather than external circumstance. The historical settings of his poems are means to an end, their function being to influence or illumine cruxes in the lives of the men and women whose soul-development or soul-atrophy is his central theme. Unlike Tennyson, Browning shows little interest in social progress, the evolution of the race, laws and principles which have a general bearing on humanity as an entity. "Nor does he," as Edmund Dowden writes, "anywhere study political phenomena or events except as they throw light on an individual character."[5] It is significant that the favorite historical background of his poems is the Renaissance, an age of humanistic individualism, in contrast with the other-worldliness and social conformity of the Middle Ages.

The initial and most striking evidence of Browning's distinction as a humanist is the scope and variety of his portrait gallery of men and women, a wealth of character painting unsurpassed in modern poetry. In this connection he may be fairly compared with Chaucer, Shakespeare, and Scott. A master in the vivid, impressionistic medium of the dramatic monologue, he has given us a comprehensive vista of all manner and conditions of people, in climes and ages far asunder, in circumstances and situations of the most diverse sort.

My purpose, however, is not to enlarge upon Browning's dramatic portrayal of men and women, but rather to consider the intrinsic qualities of his humanism. In dealing with the relation between God and man, his convictions are those of a Christian humanist. However intimate their communion, the poet's sense of the pricelessness of individual personality prevents him from accepting any theory which would regard man as destined, here or hereafter, to be merged or absorbed in the being of God. Browning is not amongst the mystics of English poetry, and pantheism is abhorrent to him. In connection with man's life on earth, he constantly stresses its relative independence. There is a line of demarcation between God and man which God himself has ordained as a pledge and seal of the moral dignity of human freedom and responsibility.

> But also, God, whose pleasure brought
> Man into being, stands away
> As it were a hand-breadth off, to give
> Room for the newly made to live,
> And look at him from a place apart,
> And use his gifts of brain and heart,
> Given indeed, but to keep for ever.

> Man therefore stands on his own stock
> Of love and power as a pin-point rock!
> (*Christmas-Eve* V.27–33, 44–45)

This divorce of man's "rock" from God's "boundless continent" is restated, with variant imagery, in the parables of *Ferishtah's Fancies*[6] and elsewhere.

The humanism of Browning's ethics may justly be called the core of his philosophy of life. This pivots on the worth and paramount importance of the moral struggle in the life of the individual. For Browning, as for Keats, the world is the "vale of Soul-making." In the *Epilogue* to *Dramatis Personae* he pictures all the powers of nature flowing like the currents of ocean "towards some elected point of central rock," the personality of the individual:

> As though the pageant's end were to enhance
> His worth, and—once the life, his product gained—
> Roll away elsewhere, keep the strife sustained . . .
> (89–91)

In *By the Fireside* he exclaims:

> How the world is made for each of us!
> How all we perceive and know in it
> Tends to some moment's product thus,
> When a soul declares itself—to wit,
> By its fruit, the thing it does! (XLIX)

Browning's acute consciousness that the central purpose of life on earth is the fashioning of individual character led him to stress its hazards and hardships. The world is ordained to be a moral battle ground, a sphere of trial, testing, and probation. The limitations, obstacles, hostile forces with which man must grapple are the stern but indispensable conditions of soul-development. In order to accentuate the poignancy and arduousness of this process, the poet dwells with unflinching realism on the grim potency of evil and suffering. His distrust of human reason causes him to add to these the weakness of intellectual nescience:

Were knowledge all thy faculty, then God
Must be ignored . . .
(*A Pillar at Sebzevar,* 134–135)

Nevertheless in this moral warfare man does not fight unaided without the help of God. Browning's sceptical theory of knowledge never invalidates the evidence of his heart that God and man are in communion through the sovereign instrumentality of love. Yet it is characteristic of his humanism and his perception of the integrity of individuality that he never represents God as weakening man's moral fibre by impinging upon his freedom of choice in any moral crisis. God may even for a time seem to stand aloof in order that the will and resolution with which he has endowed his creature may be evoked and tested:

God, ever mindful in all strife and strait,
Who, for our own good, makes the need extreme,
Till at the last He puts forth might and saves.
(*Pompilia,* 1386–88)

This view of the relation between God and man is in keeping with Browning's emphasis on the distinction between the spheres of eternity and time. Were an unclouded vision of eternity vouchsafed to man it would thwart the moral purpose of his earthly life, the development of his soul in a finite world of travail and temptation. This is the central theme of *An Epistle of Karshish.* Lazarus, whom Christ raised from the dead, is an illustration of "Heaven opened to a soul while yet on earth, / Earth forced on a soul's use while seeing heaven" (141–142). Having beheld the white light of eternity he is incapacitated for the purposes of earth, blinded by remembrance of "a vast distracting orb of glory."[7]

A kindred aspect of Browning's humanism is his interpretation of the significance of the Incarnation as a historical event. Under human conditions man is incapable of comprehending the absolute fulness of God's being. But through the manifestation of God's nature in flesh and blood, in the person of Christ, the white light of His being is deflected in the prismatic hues of a revelation that can be grasped by man on earth in his weakness and finitude. In *The Ring and the Book* the Pope uses the imagery of the "spectrum" and the "convex glass" to illustrate the media through which the white light of eternal truth must pass to reach man's mind and heart, and in his meditation on the prismatic incarnation of God's nature in the historic life of Christ he reflects:

> Clouds obscure—
> But for which obscuration all were bright?
> Too hastily concluded! Sun-suffused,
> A cloud may soothe the eye made blind by blaze,—
> Better the very clarity of heaven:
> The soft streaks are the beautiful and dear.
> What but the weakness in a faith supplies
> The incentive to humanity . . .
> And that which men think weakness within strength,
> But angels know for strength and stronger yet . . .
> The divine instance of self-sacrifice
> That never ends and aye begins for man?
> (x.1643–50, 1653–54, 1657–58)

In *Parleyings with Certain People of Importance* Browning uses the imagery of the Sun as representative of God's absolute being, and the myth of Prometheus bringing fire from heaven in a hollow tube as a symbol of a revelation of the Divine nature which is adapted to the lowliness and imperfect faculties of man. It is true that the fire thus won is "glass-conglobed," and narrowed to "a pin-point circle." Nevertheless it is "the very Sun in little," sharing its elemental nature,

> Comprising the Sun's self, but Sun disrobed
> Of that else unconceived essential flame
> Borne by no naked sight.
> (*Bernard de Mandeville*, 307–309)[8]

While Browning's ethics are a pendant to his religious faith, it is in this sphere, as I have stated, that this humanism is most markedly in evidence. Though man's finite experiences, "this dance of plastic circumstance," are in their ultimate purpose "machinery just bent," like the potter's wheel, to shape the soul, it is clear that the poet attributes positive values to the material as well as the spiritual aspects of man's twofold nature. Nothing is more characteristic of his humanism than the importance he ascribes to the body and the senses. While his belief in the supremacy of the soul is unfaltering, he rejects any ascetic conception of man's nature. Although the body and the senses are from one point of view limitations of man's spiritual insight, they are the necessary conditions of his moral probation, the working tools through which the soul's development on earth is achieved. Throughout life the spiritual is bound up with the material; the body and the senses, so far from being spurned, are meant to serve as stepping stones to a realization of the spirit which uses these as vehicles of its temporal manifestation:

> Let us not always say,
> 'Spite of this flesh to-day
> I strove, made head, gained ground upon the whole!'
> As the bird wings and sings,
> Let us cry, 'All good things
> Are ours, nor soul helps flesh more, now, than flesh helps soul!'
>
> (*Rabbi Ben Ezra,* XII)

In *Fra Lippo Lippi* Browning reveals his sympathy with the humanism and realism of Renaissance art, its protest against the asceticism of the Middle Ages, its appreciation of "the value and significance of flesh," its conviction that "the world and life's too big to pass for a dream," its delight in earth's sensuous loveliness:

> —The beauty, and the wonder and the power,
> The shapes of things, their colours, lights, and shades,
> Changes, surprises,—and God made it all! (283–285)

In *Saul,* David exclaims:

> Oh, our manhood's prime vigour! No spirit feels waste,
> Not a muscle is stopped in its playing nor sinew unbraced.
> Oh, the wild joys of living! (IX.1–3)

Browning's ethical humanism has a further reach. Even the checks and obstacles, the evil and suffering that environ man on earth are the indispensable conditions of soul-development. Only through conflict with and victory over these can character be fashioned and God's purposes for man realized.

There is, consequently, a wide difference between the attitudes of Shelley and Browning to the whole range of human experience. For Shelley the limitations of man's life on earth, the finitude of his lot, are "stains"; they dim and obscure "the white radiance of Eternity." For Browning they are material for transmutation and transfiguration. So considered, the facets of man's chequered experiences in this finite world of space and time may be not stains but jewels, enriching the white light by mellowing and humanizing it into prismatic hues:

> Only the prism's obstruction shows aright
> The secret of a sunbeam, breaks its light
> Into the jewelled bow from blankest white,
> So may a glory from defect arise:
> (*Deaf and Dumb*, 1–4)

Browning makes frequent use of the imagery of the rainbow. In *Sordello* he writes:

> light, thwarted, breaks
> A limpid purity to rainbow flakes, (v.605–606)

In *Christmas-Eve* there is a superb description of a moon rainbow, and the poet reflects:

> Have I been sure, this Christmas-Eve,
> God's own hand did the rainbow weave,
> Whereby the truth from heaven slid
> Into my soul? (xx.46–49)

In *Numpholeptos* the symbolism of the rainbow pervades the entire poem.

Although this monologue of Browning's has been regarded by critics as strange and bizarre, it is of special interest as providing a link between the poet's ethical and artistic humanism and illustrating the likeness between them. The theme of this poem centers on a contrast between a nymph and her lover. The nymph is endowed with spiritual qualities of purity, goodness, and truth, absolute in their essence, but antecedent to and divorced from human experience. The imagery of the moon, of silver, of "quintessential whiteness" symbolizes the ideal but prenatal nature of her innocence. The lover who aspires to reach her feet must, as a mortal, pursue his aim under the conditions of life on earth. As he treads various paths to his goal, he is colored by the hues of his finite experiences in a world of trial, moral endeavor, and imperfection:

> Here I reek suffused
> With crocus, saffron, orange, as I used
> With scarlet, purple, every dye o' the bow
> Born of the storm-cloud. (82–85)

He describes himself to the nymph as, "Your pilgrim jewelled as with drops o' the urn/The rainbow paints from" (120–21). Browning emphasizes the disparity between the abstract idealism of the nymph and the humanism of her lover by making the color contrasts bold and vivid. The whiteness linked with the nymph is pallid, even cold. The imagery is that of pale moonbeams, delicate silver, rather than brilliant sunshine. On the other hand, the colors associated with the man are strong, positive, even crude, such as crimson and sulphurous yellow. Although these have origin in white light, the "blank pure soul" of the nymph is at once "the source and tomb of that prismatic glow." In the sequel the lover finds it impossible to satisfy the requirements of the nymph that he appear before her in a whiteness that corresponds with her abstract idealism, a state of being which is divorced from human struggle and achievement.

Betty Miller, in her recent work on Browning, has called *Numpholeptos* one of his autobiographical poems.[9] She compares its moon symbolism with that of *One Word More,* in which he apostrophizes his wife as "my moon of poets" and refers to himself as a "moonstruck mortal." There is, I believe, a slight autobiographical element in *Numpholeptos,* although of an indirect and glancing nature. In commenting on the moon imagery in *Pan and Luna,* William C. DeVane writes: "as we may see in *One Word More*, the *Epilogue to Ferishtah's Fancies,* the *Parley-*

ing With Daniel Bartoli and elsewhere, the moon in Browning was always, after 1855, a symbol for his wife."[10] This association of moon imagery with Mrs. Browning suggests the likelihood of its presence in *Numpholeptos*. Yet it seems evident that the primary contrast Browning has in mind in this poem is a difference between feminine and masculine natures. He refers to the nymph as endowed with

> that thrice-superfine
> Feminity of sense, with right divine
> To waive all process, take result stain-free
> From out the very muck. (144–147)

This abstract idealism, typically feminine, is set over against a masculine realism. The "quintessential whiteness" of the nymph is in keeping with Browning's conception of a woman as intuitively in touch with spiritual verities in their absolute essence. The "every dye o' the bow" in which the lover is garbed is symbolic of the fact that a man can only strive towards the white light of the ideal while following the paths of finite human experience and immersed in its variegated colors. Browning elsewhere, as has been noted, introduces the contrast between "white light" and "prismatic hues" to symbolize the difference between the undeflected spiritual idealism of his wife's lyric poetry and the trammelled humanism of his dramatic verse. This is an indication that in his comparison of feminine and masculine natures in *Numpholeptos* he has in the back of his mind a difference between Elizabeth Browning and himself. Yet this analogy is only secondary and indeterminate. It is absurd to regard *Numpholeptos* as in any sense literal autobiography, or representative of the psychological relations between Browning and his wife.

The allegorical significance of this poem, with its contrasts of color symbolism, is linked with the sphere of ethics. Since, however, in his letters to Elizabeth Barrett, Browning uses kindred imagery to describe the contrast between her poetry and his own, *Numpholeptos* is illustrative of a parallelism between his ethical and artistic humanism, and may serve as a point of transition to my discussion of the latter.

It is of interest to note that while Browning refers to the

prismatic hues of his dramatic monologues, he tells Elizabeth Barrett that there is white light in him, even though he fears it. This fear is indicative of an element of tension and conflict in his poetry. In his letter to Ruskin he reveals that the difficulty of "putting the infinite within the finite" was the central problem of his art as well as of his philosophy of life.

There is indeed "white light" in what may be called the Shelleyan side of Browning's complex nature. "I am made up of an intensest life," he wrote in *Pauline,* and he links with this "a principle of restlessness" in his inner consciousness "which would be all, have, see, know, taste, feel, all." A passion for the absolute, a desire to exhibit the fulness of personality, an urge to realize the boundless capacities of the soul, even in a finite world, is the noble ambition—yet the cardinal error—of the heroes of his early monodramas. They are all dazzled by the blinding vision of the white light of eternity while yet in the sphere of time.

The ethical problem of Browning's own life which is reflected in these monodramas has its aesthetic analogue. As a poet, the crux of the struggle was what seemed to him the almost insuperable task of subduing the wealth and prodigality of his spiritual powers—his imagination and intellect—to embodiment in the sensuous media of art. The infinite content of his thought continually out-paced and chafed against the confinement of it in finite form. He felt with peculiar poignancy the tension of

> Thoughts hardly to be packed
> Into a narrow act,
> Fancies that broke through language and escaped . . .
> (*Rabbi Ben Ezra* xxv.1–3)

This tension is at its height in Browning's early monodramas. In the attempt to chronicle not one but successive stages in the development of a soul, extending over a long period of time, the poet is lost in the mazes of his theme. "What was a speck expands into a star," as Paracelsus puts it. The myriad digressions, the tortuous convolutions, and complexity of *Sordello* are proverbial. Despite splendid lines and passages, the shower of sparks struck from "the quick forge and working-house of thought" are not fused to a steady flame. The poem lacks artistic restraint and discipline.

In contrast with his earlier poetry, Browning's fine series of dramatic monologues, published between 1843 and 1864, are a triumph of his individuality and his humanism. In them he solves, in a large measure, the problem of fitting to the finite his infinity. Through a wise economy he concentrates his psychological analysis on a single situation, a single moment of time, and often on a single character. Linked with these are the self imposed bounds of his thought and imagination by focusing them in dramatic representation.

Yet, while the white light of the undeflected radiation of Browning's personality is subordinated in the dramatic monologues of 1842–64 to the prismatic hues of his portrayal of men and women, it is too vital an element of his nature to be suppressed. Only occasionally does he attain the complete objective humanism of Shakespeare. His is seldom the art of the great playwright who stands aloof, as it were, letting character wait upon event and evolve with an independence and integrity not infringed by the personality of the dramatist. Browning, on the other hand, is prone to make his characters voice his own ideas, to grant them only semi-independence, or even to reduce them to mouthpieces of his personality. This complexity is in keeping with the constant interplay in his poetry and philosophy of the two basic dispositions of his mind and spirit. The tension of antinomies—Moral, spiritual, and aesthetic—is ever present in his consciousness. In Love alone he finds their resolution. Yet it seems evident that humanism rather than transcendence—the "prismatic hues" rather than the "white light"—is the dominating note and characteristic of Browning's life and poetry. His humanism is broadly rooted, and is nurtured by physical, psychical, and spiritual elements in his personality.

The intimate connection between Browning's humanism and his conviction of the worth and integrity of individuality may be illustrated in various ways. C. H. Herford has pointed out that this has a physical basis in the nature of the perceptions of his senses.[11] These fasten upon the differences and divergences between objects, which give them individual character, rather than likenesses blending them into a common unity. In his portrayal of Nature, Browning is more apt to dwell on the clear, definite outline of each separate feature in the scene he is describing than to subordinate these to the symmetry and harmony of the landscape as a whole. Often his demarcations are characterized by sharpness and abruptness. It is the line of cleavage between objects rather than the circle of inclusiveness, the edge, the angle, the salient, the roughness of texture—everything contributing to visual and tactile impressions of distinctness—which he stresses. It is the individuality of the multitudinous and intricate phenomena of Nature which Browning's acute and realistic sensibilities are quick to detect.

Physically and spiritually, the humanism of Browning's poetry is reflected in his life and personality. Despite the handicap of certain bodily ailments, such as frequent headaches and a nervous excitability of temperament, his constitution was, in the main, sound and vigorous. His son has stated that he can scarcely recall any time when his father spent a day in bed up till his last illness. Mrs. Sutherland Orr writes: "he was healthy, even strong, in many essential respects. Until past the age of seventy he could take long walks without fatigue, and endure an amount of social and physical strain which would have tried many younger men."[12]

Psychologically, Browning had a robustness and geniality of spirit which led him not only to accept but to rejoice in the natural pleasures and wealth of human association available to man on earth. As he tells us, he was one who "both lives and likes life's way." Since, in a recent biography of the poet, he has been pictured as inhibited by neurotic and pathological weaknesses, it is well to recall the testimony of his contemporaries to the sanity, balance, and humane qualities of his personality. Jowett described Browning as "entirely free from enmity, jealousy, or any other littleness, and thinking no more of himself than if he were an ordinary man."[13] Carlyle, in acknowledging his presentation copy of *Men and Women,* wrote to the poet: "My approval was hearty and spontaneous. . . . I shall look far, I believe, to find such a pair of eyes as I see there busy inspecting human life this long while—fresh, valiant, manful character, equipped with rugged humour, just love, just contempt, well carried and bestowed."[14] Such was the estimate of two noted men who cannot be accused of Victorian sentimentalism in their appraisal of character. The joy and tingle of Browning's contact with life in its sensuous as well as its spiritual aspects; his comprehensive and many-faceted vision of it as a theatre for the play of man's dual nature, both body and soul; the vitality and exuberance of his personality—overflowing in actuality the bounds of imaginative art—evince the generosity of his humanism.

"The soft streaks are the beautiful and dear." It is "the prismatic hues" of Browning's humanism which constitute his most important contribution to English poetry. To represent his fear of the "white light" as an apostasy from the ideals of Shelley, a tame submission to convention, a recreancy of mind and heart, is to travesty the independence and originality of his thought, and his depth of human insight. "So may a glory from defect arise." It is Browning's consciousness that the development of a soul on earth can be achieved only by the fashioning of it in the warp and woof of the colored strands of human experience which underlies his philosophy of life and imparts warmth and realism to his poetry.

Notes

[1] *Letters of R.B. and E.B.B.*, I, 17.

[2] *The Works of John Ruskin*, ed. E. T. Cook and Alexander Wedderburn (London, 1909), xxxvi, xxxiv.

[3] See in this connection Ch. 9 "Browning's Conception of Love as Represented in *Paracelsus*," in my book, The Infinite Moment and Other Essays in Robert Browning (Toronto, 1950).

[4] See his Introd. in Miss E. H. Hickey's edition of *Strafford* (London, 1840).

[5] *The Life of Browning*, Everyman's Library ed. (London, 1915), p. 111.

[6] Cf. 11. 31–39 in "Plot-Culture":

> "Thou wouldst not stand
> Distinctly Man,"—Ferishtah made reply,
> "Not the mere creature, did no limit-line
> Round thee about, apportion thee thy place
> Clean-cut from out and off the illimitable,—
> Minuteness severed from immensity.
> All of thee for the Maker,—for thyself.
> Workings inside the circle that evolve
> Thine all,—the product of thy cultured plot."

[7] A similar idea is expressed in 11. 625–55 of *Bishop Blougram's Apology:*

> Naked belief in God the Ominiptent,
> Omniscient, Omnipresent, sears too much
> The sense of conscious creatures to be borne.
> It were the seeing him, no flesh shall dare.

[8] Cf. the imagery of the use of "an optic glass" in *A Death in the Desert*. This is symbolic of the way in which, through the Incarnation of Christ, the truth of God's nature is adapted to man's apprehension by being "reduced to plain historic fact" and "diminished into clearness."

[9] *Robert Browning: A Portrait* (London, 1952), pp. 259–61. I agree that Browning's statement to Furnivall, "I had no particular woman in mind," does not preclude an autobiographical element in *Numpholeptos*. The poet was frequently evasive in answering questions of members of the Browning Society, especially when they semed to pry into the privacy of his personal life. Moreover, the autobiographical reference is, as I have said, indirect and glancing, confined to the point of contrast between the nymph's idealism and her lover's humanism.

[10] *A Browning Handbook* (New York, 1935) p. 410.

[11] *Robert Browning* (Edinburgh and London, 1905).

[12] *Life and Letters of Robert Browning* (London, 1891), p. 20.

[13] Evelyn Abbott and Lewis Campbell, *Life of Jowett, I*, 400–401.

[14] Letter of 25 April, 1856.

6.

Shiv K. Kumar

The Moment in the Dramatic Monologues of Robert Browning

In one of her earliest letters to Robert Browning, Elizabeth Barrett attempts to categorize his "vision" in terms of the traditional dualism: "You have in your vision two worlds, or to use the language of the schools of the day, you are both subjective and objective in the habits of your mind. You can deal with abstract thought and with human passion in the most passionate sense."[1] Indeed, Browning often does indulge in explicit statements, or what Fairchild calls his "giveaways,"[2] and he sometimes seems to oscillate between the rational and the intuitive, the empirical and the transcendental. In spite of this seeming paradox, however, it is not difficult to see that his genius is essentially concerned with the immediacy of human experience: he is constantly attempting to penetrate the vital core of *Existenz,* not intellectually, but intuitively "in the most passionate sense," shorn of all metaphysical trappings. This kernel of experience, Browning feels, manifests itself not in the grey "dailiness"[3] of life, but in certain dramatic moments of heightened perception when a seemingly trivial experience becomes charged with fresh significance.

It seems that Browning's *modus operandi* is to capture such moments of illumination. In a letter to Elizabeth Barrett, he remarks: " . . . that is a way of mine which you must have observed; that foolish concentrating of thought and feeling, *for a moment,* on some one little spot of a character or anything else

Written especially for this book.

indeed, and in the attempt to do justice and develop whatever may seem ordinarily to be overlooked in it,—that over-vehement *insisting* on, and giving an undue prominence to, the same—which has the effect of taking away from the importance of the rest of the related objects which, in truth, are not considered at all . . ."[4] But it is in another letter to Elizabeth Barrett that he uses the metaphor of *phare* to emphasize momentariness as the prime basis of his poetic experience. Here he describes his poems as "very escapes of my inner power, which lives in me like the light in those crazy Mediterranean phares I have watched at sea, wherein the light is ever revolving in a dark gallery, bright and alive, and only after a weary interval leaps out, *for a moment,* from the narrow chink, and then goes on with the blind wall between it and you."[5] And again, in a letter to Julia Wedgwood, he refers to his poetic concept of instantaneous illuminations, those "rare flashes of momentary conviction that come and go in the habitual dusk and doubt of life."[6]

It is through such moments of sudden revelation that Browning achieves his true poetic identity. Whereas such longer poems as *The Ring and the Book* and *Sordello,* in spite of their dramatic framework, meander expansively into intellectual casuistries, and his shorter poems like *Rabbi Ben Ezra* and *Bishop Blougram's Apology* offer merely a series of generalities abstracted from experience, it is only in his shorter dramatic monologues that he establishes direct contact with actuality. The moment in such dramatic monologues carries within itself its *raison d'être,* its very genesis and meaning.

Before we undertake to assess the multifaceted significance of the moment, appearing in the dramatic monologues of Robert Browning under such protean guises as the moment *naked, terrible, fateful, burning, warm, mighty, rapturous, blessed, eternal* (indeed, he seems to have run through the entire gamut of adjectives suggesting the intense quality of such moments), it is imperative to define its most distinctive characteristic. The moment in Browning's poetry is akin, in many respects, to the existential "atoms of eternity." It is not merely *chronos,* it is *kairos,* or "the infinite reflection of eternity in time."[7] The protagonist in each of his dramatic monologues is not a mere entity in an abstract Hegelian process, but an individual caught existentially in a state of tension which, according to Kierkgaard, is "the frontier between time and eternity."[8] At the point where the present moment encounters eternity, and is transformed into the eternal "now,"[9] the individual perceives a fresh meaning in life; he is transformed into a new existence; he realizes thereafter his peculiar relation to his environment. It is the function of a poet to symbolize this intersection between time and eternity; as Browning observes in a letter to Ruskin, all poetry is fundamentally concerned with the problem of "putting the infinite within the finite."[10] To isolate time from eternity would be to reduce it to mere *chronos* and divest it of all meaning and purpose. This is what John implies in *A Death in the Desert* when he warns his ignorant disciples against the folly of living merely in time, which must inevitably lead to anguish and frustration:

> . . . Ye would withdraw your sense
> From out eternity, strain it upon time . . .

Meaningful existence, therefore, is not merely quantitative, but qualitative in essence; it recognizes the paradox of infinity in the finite, and eternal Being in temporal Becoming.

Let us now examine how the moment in Browning's dramatic monologues manifests itself on the emotional, aesthetic and religious planes, respectively.

On the emotional plane, Browning holds up for closer scrutiny the moment of greatest intensity between man and woman, when nothing distracts the heart from participating fully in the experience of love. He selects from the stream of diurnal routine certain luminous moments in which the lover realizes his true identity in relationship to his beloved. Eternity congeals itself in that instant, and conversely the moment acquires cumulatively the vitality of eternity. This nature of "the moment eternal" Browning describes in a lyric of exquisite beauty entitled "Now." Here the lover is so deeply absorbed in the ecstatic moment that, unconcerned as to "how long such suspension may linger," he tries to achieve complete identification, however transient, with his beloved. All that he asks is a moment of complete affirmation, so that they both may "condense,/ In a rapture of rage, for perfection's endowment,/ Thought and feeling and soul and sense—/ Merged in a moment . . . " It is significant to note here that Browning considers it essential for the lover to bring his entire being to bear on such a consummation, for in "ecstasy's utmost we clutch at the core . . . "

The lover in *The Last Ride Together* passes through a moment of suspense, "a breathing-while or two/With life or death in the balance," before his beloved grants him his last request. And then as the ride begins, so also starts the process of ever-deepening intensification towards *le moment consommé*. First as "lay she a moment on my breast," the lover feels his passion drawing "cloud, sunset, moonrise, star-shine too," "till flesh must fade for heaven was here!" Browning here aptly uses the metaphor of the soul smoothing "itself out," like "a long-cramped scroll/Freshening and fluttering in the wind." With each thrust of ironic pity at other roles of existence—a statesman's, a soldier's, a poet's, a sculptor's, a musician's—he penetrates deeper into himself, until he is suddenly enraptured by "the moment eternal." "The instant made eternity," may well be conversely taken to imply "eternity made this instant," as the lover in wishing his moment of supreme felicity to run on for ever, is actually charging the instant with the vitality of a whole eternity. However, in his attempt to arrest the moment "We, fixed so, ever should so abide?"/the lover still perceives it as a fragment of eternity. Deep down in his soul he knows that, the ride over, his beloved will again dissolve into eternity, which flows relentlessly on and on.

But Porphyria's lover, in an outburst of frenzied passion, freezes this movement by strangling his beloved, so that she, as a living and growing organism, may not ever move away from him. "That moment she was mine, mine, fair,— / Perfectly pure and good." In a sense, though perverted, he has attempted, like his counterpart in *The Last Ride Together* to make her love for him eternal. " . . . all night long we have not stirred," and yet as the day will break, and another night descend, he must realize the futility of it all, the insanity of attempting to freeze the moment mechanistically by detaching it permanently from eternity, which alone lends it identity and meaning. In saying, "give herself to me for ever," and by strangling her, he is left only with the corpse of a living and vibrant reality.

On the aesthetic plane, Browning's theory of art—of music, painting and poetic creation—also recognizes the ecstatic moment as a point in perception when the object reveals itself in its entirety from the inside; it is seen and felt rather than remembered and categorized. In the process of creative incubation, when the secondary imagination is at work, the artist is suddenly caught up in the "naked moment," like an excalibur thrust out of water, and all the disparate strands of thought and feeling merge esemplastically into a harmonious pattern. His vision, hitherto partial, casual and fragmentary, achieves its totality and all "the broken arcs" melt into "a perfect round"; all multiplicity is unified.

Abt Vogler, one of Browning's most dynamic monologues, is a typical example of his treatment of the moment. Abt Vogler has been "extemporizing upon the musical instrument of his invention," symbolizing the free play of the mind. Uninhibited by any written score, he is conjuring up notes "fresh from the Protoplast," his "manifold music" resisting the imposition of any "structure," when suddenly "a flash of the will that can," makes him exclaim, "But here is the finger of God!" "What never had been, was now; what was, as it shall be anon;/ And what is,—shall I say, matched both? for I was made perfect too." The "earth had attained to heaven, there was no more near nor far." This vision of cosmic reality, transcending all limitations of time and space, descends upon him epiphanically, as "when a great illumination surprises a festal night." Again, the moment becomes a dynamic *kairos*; "eternity affirms the conception of an hour." But once the moment of revelation fades away ("Well, it is gone at last . . . Gone! and the good tears start"), Abt Vogler descends to the lower plane of conceptual reasoning, till, "sliding by semitones," he sinks to "the common chord again," "The C Major of this life." He who had earlier realized that "God has a few of us whom he whispers in the ear;/ the rest may reason and welcome," now himself takes recourse to rational analysis, only to be thrown back on his ordinary perspective.

The painters in Browning's dramatic monologues are equally

concerned with capturing such moments when, to quote Pictor Ignotus, the artist is "straight like thunder, sunk to the center, of an instant." From the continuum of the life-flow, the painter, in a moment of heightened perception, apprehends the potential of a seemingly trivial gesture, motion or glance. Fra Lippo Lippi, for instance, describes how he waits for a momentary vision of "the breathless fellow at the altar-foot, fresh from the murder," "the proper twinkle in your eye," or "your cullion's hanging face." Likewise, in the course of his rambling monologue, Andrea Del Sarto's eye is arrested for a moment by Lucrezia's hand ("Your soft hand is a woman of itself"), and her smile ("You smile? why, there's my picture ready made,/ There's what we painters call harmony!") In fact, it is obvious that Del Sarto's monologue somewhat like Abt Vogler's musical improvisation, runs on a *flux ininterrompu,* externalizing his repressed urges and impulses, with Lucrezia's laconic smiles forcing him momentarily into confrontation with the painful reality. She is clearly amused at her husband's humiliating self-debasement, his pathetic outpourings of protestations, till he announces, in a moment of dramatic affirmation, his unconditioned commitment to her.

> Four great walls in the New Jerusalem,
> Meted on each side by the angle's reed,
> For Leonard, Raphael, Agnolo and me
> To cover—the three first without a wife,
> While I have mine!—still they overcome
> Because there's still Lucrezia,—as I choose.

The note on which this poem ends acquires an intense poignancy as it brings into sharp focus two diametrically conflicting commitments: that of Del Sarto's to his wife and Lucrezia's to the cousin. His affirmation clashes with her denial, and as he hears "Again the Cousin's whistle!" and says "Go, my love," the reader imagines him achieving a new sense of self-realization before he lapses into the "common chord" of life again.

Though the Duke of Ferrara is not a painter, his susceptibilities are markedly aesthetic; in fact, he prefers to be amply compensated by Fra Pandolf's portrait of his wife rather than live with a young woman whose "looks went everywhere." His appreciation of "that piece a wonder," "the depth and passion of its earnest glance," "the faint/Half-flush that dies along her throat,"—shows the sensitive perception of a seasoned connoisseur of art. So in murdering his wife and zealously preserving her portrait, he has salvaged what he considers to be the kernel and thrown the husk away. The image of the duke himself, as it emerges from *My Last Duchess,* is subtly complex, wrapped in subterfuges and innuendoes. What, then, is his basic motivation? He reveals his innermost soul, not in analyzing overtly his motive, but in making a casual observation about his bronze statue. As he invites the Count's envoy to "meet the company below," he pauses for a moment on the steps in front of the statue:

> Notice Neptune, though,
> Taming a sea-horse, thought a rarity,
> Which Claus of Innsbruck cast in bronze for me!

Here in a casual aside is crystallized for the reader the duke in his full amplitude—a man charged with overwhelming possessiveness, uncompromising egotism and self-complacency, who must bend everything to his inviolate will.

On the plane of religious experience, the moment, in some of Browning's dramatic monologues, symbolizes the incarnation, God's revelation as the Christ, through His infinite love and compassion for man. Cosmic experience, otherwise a remote concept of man's relation to the infinite, now concretizes itself in the shape of the Christ. But it will not be sufficient to say that in Christ "eternity became time,"[11] (as propounded by Karl Barth, for instance), "unless we also concede that eternity is dynamic and redemptive, capable of dealing with the successive and durational time of man as man knows and engenders it. Such is the true accommodation of a divine God-manhood."[12] This may offer a clue to the understanding of Browning's presentation of both the incarnate and epiphanic revelations.

It is unnecessary to trace any direct theological or philosophical influences on Browning's mind. Was he, for instance, influenced by the epiphany feast?[13] Or did he get the idea from the pagan festivals associated with the Dionysiac cult,[14] at which the god appeared momentarily (the "epiphany" of Dionysus) as his frenzied worshippers burst into *ekstasis*,[15] only to disappear soon into another world? If some of his poems are epiphanic in overtones, it is probably because Browning was guided more by his poetic sensitivity than by any formal ritual or dogma.

Browning's so-called religious poems, which center around the themes of revelation and the incarnation, fall into two distinct categories; firstly, those poems in which the main character's mental processes persistently follow a predetermined course until he achieves the final illumination, and, secondly, those poems in which the epiphanic revelation explodes upon the mind, "as if in a thunder peal." Although both kinds of religious experience ultimately culminate in sudden spiritual enlightenment, it is obvious that the involuntary or unpremeditated mode of dramatic perception comes closer to Browning's innate sensibilities. In Bergsonian terminology, these two varieties of religious experience are like two distinct planes of mental tension: one on which the mind deliberately summons up images from the past and is thus involved in a process of *mémoire volontaire*, and the other plane on which remembrances flow into the mind intuitively and involuntarily signifying *mémoire par excellence*.

Let us first consider those poems in which revelation comes as a sequel to premeditation. Take, for instance, *Christmas Eve* in which the soliloquist depicts himself in a Florentine church, on a particular Christmas eve, reflecting on the utter inadequacy of the purely formal and soulless modes of worship ("the pig-of-lead like pressure/ of the preaching man's immense stupidity/ As he poured his doctrine forth"). As he walks away from the congregation, and finds himself alone on the hillside, "suddenly/ The rain and the wind ceased." He senses the presence of Christ.

> All at once I looked up with terror.
> He was there.
> He himself with his human air,
> On the narrow pathway, just before.
> I saw the back of him, no more . . .

In that "rapturous moment," he sees the Heavenly vision; he reaches for "the flying robe;" he then realizes

> We are made in his image, to witness him . . .
> No mere exposition of morality
> Made or in part or in totality
> Should win you to give it worship . . .

Again, in *Easter Day* the phenomenon of revelation emerges as a result of contemplation. "How very hard it is to be/ A Christian!" is the note on which this poem opens. Browning sets out, against his native genius, on a discursive exposition of the nature of belief, faith, doubt and empirical reasoning. His analysis weaves its labyrinthine cobweb ("And as I said/ This nonsense throwing back my head/ With light complacent laugh"), he sees a vision of the Last Judgment.

> Suddenly all the midnight round
> One fire. The dome of heaven had stood
> As made up of a multitude
> Of handbreath cloudlets, one vast rack
> Of ripples infinite and black
> From sky to sky.

But Christ, through his infinite compassion, offers love and light to the true seeker:

> Then did the form expand, expand–
> I knew Him through the dread disguise
> As the whole God within His eyes
> Embraced me.

In *Saul* Browning works out a more skillful blending of these two varieties of religious experience: the premeditated and the truly epiphanic. As Saul lies in his tent, immersed in deep despair, agonized, "drear and stark, blind and dumb," David walks in with his harp to sing him back to faith and deed. At first he sings traditional psalms in praise of the Lord, only to feel the irrepressible urge to forge "a new harmony." "I shall dare to discover some province, some gift of my own." And then in a desperate effort to quicken Saul back into new life, he breaks into his own, unpremeditated song: "Oh, speak through me now!" At this ecstatic moment, when David ascends from a purely formal to an intensely personal love of God, the vision of the Saviour takes shape before his eyes:

> 'T is the weakness in strength, that I cry for! my flesh, that I seek
> In the Godhead! I seek and I find it. O Saul, it shall be
> A face like my face that receives thee; a Man like to me,
> Thou shalt love and be loved by, for ever: A Hand like this hand
> Shall throw open the gates of new life to thee!
> *See the Christ Stand!*

New vistas open before him as he feels himself reborn into the eternal now:

> The whole earth was awakened, hell loosed with her crews;
> And the stars of the night beat with emotion, and tingled and shot
> Out in fire the strong pain of pent knowledge . . .
> . . . he felt the new law.

In *An Epistle*, the Arab Physician's twenty-second letter to his master Abib, the former experiences the dramatic moment of affirmation without the least possible premeditation. Written in a fluid and colloquial style, following the lines and curves of his thoughts, the poem depicts him suddenly confronted by a unique phenomenon, which his scientific mind cannot comprehend. Both Lazarus's resurrection, and his transformation into new dimensions of perception, are beyond the limited compass of "this picker of learning's crumbs." Not equipped to understand the depth and complexity of an experience transcending both life and death, Karshish refers to it as a mere triviality "to avoid the stuffing of my travelscript." But "The Man had something in the look of him—/ His case has struck me far more than 't is worth." He rambles on in his perplexity, when suddenly in an ecstatic moment of dramatic affirmation, he senses the authenticity of the miracle. His analytical perspective can no longer ignore the power and the glory of the Christ, the self-giving Love:

> The very God! think, Abib; dost thou think?
> So, the All-Great, were the All-Loving too—
> So, through the thunder comes a human voice
> Saying, "O heart I made, a heart beats here!
> "Face, my hands fashioned, see it myself!
> "Thou hast no power nor mayst conceive of mine,
> "But love I gave thee, with myself to love,
> "And thou must love me who have died for thee!

Although *Cristina* is essentially a love lyric, in it Browning also plumbs the depths of true religious experience. Here he suggests that a life completely devoid of any moments of illumination would be dark, mute, almost evil. It is Satan's prime objective to keep man wrapped up in routine responses, his mind chained in rational self-complacency. But

> Oh, we're sunk enough here, God knows!
> But not quite so sunk that moments,
> Sure tho' seldom, are denied us . . .

Indeed, these "flashes struck from midnights," these "fire-flames that noondays kindle," are God's mysterious signs by which the eternal breaks into the temporal that man may "catch God's secret," and earth may commune with heaven.

Notes

[1] *The Letters of Robert Browning & Elizabeth Barrett 1845–46,* I, (New York, 1899), 8 (letter dated January 15, 1845).

[2] Hoxie N. Fairchild, "Browning the Simple-Hearted Casuist," *University of Toronto Quarterly,* XIVIII (April 1949), 234–40.

[3] Virginia Woolf, *A Writer's Diary* (London, 1953), p. 63.

[4] *The Letters of Robert Browning & Elizabeth Barrett,* I, 354–55.

[5] *Ibid.,* p. 17.

[6] *Robert Browning & Julia Wedgwood: A Broken Friendship as Revealed by Their Letters,* ed. Richard Curle (New York, 1937), p. 7 (letter dated June 25, 1864).

[7] Soren Kierkegaard, *Concept of Dread* (Princeton, 1944), p. 79.

[8] Berdjaev uses the expression "on the frontier of two worlds."

[9] See H. A. Slaatte, *Time and Its End* (New York, 1962), pp. 33 ff.

[10] *The Works of John Ruskin,* eds. E. T. Cook and Alexander Wedderburn (London, 1909), p. xxxiv.

[11] *Die Kirchliche Dogmatik,* Band II, halbband I, pp. 694 ff.

[12] H. A. Slaatte, *Time and Its End,* p. 140.

[13] "Epiphany," *Encyclopaedia of Religion and Ethics,* ed. James Hastings, V (New York, 1951), 331–32.

[14] Edwin Rohde, *Psyche: the Cult of Souls and Belief in Immortality Among the Greeks* (New York, 1925), pp. 258–61. (Chapter: "The Thracian Worship of Dionysos.")

[15] *Ibid.,* p. 259.

[16] In spite of Katherine H. Porter's attempt to associate Browning with a particular spiritual group (see *Through a Glass Darkly—Spiritualism in the Browning Circle,* Lawrence, Kansas, 1958), it remains doubtful if Browning subscribed to a formal creed or dogma. Nor would it be correct to define his religion as "a vague subjective theism in which Christian belief counted for little or nothing," H. N. Fairchild in "*Le Saisiaz* and *The Nineteenth Century,*" *Modern Philogy,* XLVIII (1950), 105.

[17] Henri Bergson, *Matter and Memory,* trans. N. S. Paul and W. S. Palmer (London, 1913), pp. 95 ff.

7.

Milton Millhauser

Tennyson: Artifice and Image

The first half of Tennyson's career, through *In Memoriam* or perhaps *Maud,* was one long striving toward poetic growth, and was marked not only by intellectual development—although that catches the eye more readily—but by increasingly varied and ever more exacting demands upon technique. Again and again he adapted language and imagery to some new conception or attitude or form; again and again he refined, experimented, pruned away excess and dross, until he had rendered his style the completely flexible and exquisitely sensitive instrument of his poetic will. His power to find the right, the fully expressive word or rhythm is evident in any handful of his verses; looking back from the mid-'fifties over the patient succession of those labored volumes, we are struck also by an expanding range of interests, an insistent deepening of theme and of emotional penetration, which by the problems they must have posed further underline the quality of his purely technical achievement.

It is emblematic of the fickleness of taste that this achievement could have been so widely satisfying to his own generation and so generally disappointing to ours. We tend to think of him as a craftsman without substance. Yet whatever other faults may be charged against Tennyson—sentimentality, conventionality, superficiality—none of these can be entirely divorced from technique; it is his treatment of his subject-matter, rather

Reprinted by permission of the author and the editor from *Journal of Aesthetics and Art Criticism,* Vol 14, No. 3 (March, 1956), pp. 333–38.

than the subject-matter in itself, the naked argument, that determines our response to his poems. The complaint is that we are not emotionally or imaginatively convinced, and what is to convince us if not the poet's very words? Why do we accept Malory's Galahad and not Tennyson's, except that Tennyson's is the rather self-conscious and hollow being his own speech makes him? Art works through artistry, whose function is to realize for us the artist's intuition of his theme; we know its depth and weight and texture only as he has embodied them for us in the materials of his craft. Broaden the term to include some elements of management and presentation, and the failure of Tennyson to endow his conceptions with vitality was in some degree a failure of technique—of style. And if Tennyson failed in this, despite his arduous dedication to it as the central labor of his life, some consideration of his whole work from that point of view, some effort to fix the cause and character of his failure, will surely be in order.

Now, the error of a virtuoso will lie not in the quality but in the direction of his effort; he will have done superlatively some ill-advised thing. Whether we like his vein or not, Tennyson thought deeply and felt deeply, and wrote out of his heart and head. If he could develop a style remarkable even in a remarkable century for beauty, variety, and modulation, and could then still fail to communicate more than once or twice anything like the reach and urgency of his own experience, he must have applied his unique talent somewhat less than wisely; if he could adapt his marvelous technique to pose and compromise and sham heroics, this must have been accompanied by some modification in the direction of sham and pose and compromise in the technique itself. A fine style will not smirk or simper, but speak out. Tennyson's words do what he asks of them, and yet ring false, or thin; we are justified in suspecting that at some point, purely as a craftsman, he must have followed false lights. He did; he followed late Romantic and Victorian ones. (It might be fairer to say that he followed Romantic models with Victorian eyes.) And I believe that, among the many possibilities of error that his time left open to him, we can distinguish at least two that operated directly to the detriment of his technique: a misconception as to the elements of poetic style, and a misconception as to the use and value of his essentially lyric endowment.

These, if my supposition is correct, will manifest themselves in particular devices and mannerisms and patterns of approach, which we should be able to recognize both as characteristic and as limitations: factors which admit both the peculiar beauty and the peculiar externality of Tennyson's effects. Specifically, I think we will find two things: a shallow and apologetic use of imagery, and a disposition to make use of forms and figures uncongenial to his own imagination.

Let us consider first the problem of style. His own text is all the evidence we need that Tennyson thought of poetry in terms of line and image: the line being the unit of statement and melody, the image functioning principally as decoration; the overall effect intended being one of loftiness, luxuriance, and congruity among the several parts. Now, this is a fine style, but there are resources that it does not tap. The modern taste, having tired of it or exhausted its possibilities, has discovered a diametrically opposite system of devices, aiming at a beauty familiar, spare, and centered about irony or tension; the line today is exploited as a unit of rhythm—a wiry, incisive rhythm—rather than of "tone color"; the image is an instrument of expression rather than of embellishment or enforcement of mood; incongruities stand deliberately unresolved. There is, of course, no absolute reason for preferring one of these over the other; but the fertility of the terse and nervous modern style, its command over our imaginations, the partial anticipations of it by such contemporaries as Browning and Meredith, will suggest the actual limitations amid which Tennyson worked, and the restrictions of tone and manner to which, however powerful his individual genius, his understanding of his models committed him.

One such limitation is indicated by the characteristic modern preference for a poetic subject that is felt and thought at the same time, whereas Tennyson's was one in which feeling follows thought, and is presented to the reader as a logically separable part of his experience. "The Wasteland" is a *locus classicus* of the first sort of poetry, "Locksley Hall" (which admittedly suffers by the comparison) of the other, and the effect of each is conditioned by its style; in one the images are the poem itself, and sustain the theme, in the other they are consciously added to it. We can interpret "a cycle of Cathay" or "the ringing grooves of change" into a logically adequate prose equivalent, whose sense underlies them in the poem; "the drowned Phoenician sailor," whatever we may make of him afterward, operates *in the reading* directly on the reader's mind. This is merely to say that Tennyson tends even in his lyric inspiration toward the reflective mode, which raises its matter deliberately to poetic pitch, and to which a decorative or illustrative style is congenial; the modern is a metaphysical, for whom the poetic experience is immediate and indivisible, and whose imagery must convey simultaneously the concept and its accompanying tone.

We tend today to overestimate our own devices, as though the long line of reflective poets from Lucretius on could be brushed aside by the little magazines as a minor aberration of cultural history. A more catholic taste might admit Spenser to some minor eminence, perhaps not quite alongside Andrew Marvell. Still, it is true that the immediate image is a compellingly powerful psychic instrument, and the poet who does not avail himself of it is denying himself a whole range of subtle and penetrating effects. "The Wasteland" is not only a more honest poem than "Locksley Hall"; it is more intense, aesthetically more coherent, and is accepted on a deeper level of the mind. And this, I suggest, is largely for stylistic reasons; with a wealth of feeling to convey, Tennyson did not have available some of Eliot's most valuable resources. Tennyson followed Keats, but seems to have learned from him opulence rather than immediacy; the Keats of the great Odes phrased his most poignant experiences directly, so that their meanings are implicit in them, and touch us as experiences rather than as propositions; but Tennyson is forever commenting on his most pointed images. He loses thereby not only spontaneity but the fusion and reciprocal heightening of all the elements of the poetic moment which the metaphysical technique makes possible. He separates the reader from the poem, our current favorite among the "ancients," Donne, says "Go and catch a falling star" and lets the image stand alone; Tennyson says "Thy voice is on the rolling air;/ I hear thee where the waters run," and hastens to explain: "I seem in star and flower/ To feel thee some diffusive power"—a kind of pseudo-chemical proposition which does not add perceptibly to the beauty or even the meaning of the first, but merely divides the image from the sense. (The whole lyric—the next to the last of *In Memoriam*—wavers in this way between poetry and opinion; "I prosper, circled with thy voice" is impassioned mysticism, but "Mix'd with God and Nature thou" is sentimental eschatology.) Compare this, a very favorable example of his style, with the old song that begins:

> O western wind, when wilt thou blow,
> That the small rain down may rain?
> Christ! that my love were in my arms . . .

of which half the beauty is that, although the first part is intended to reflect on the second, the lines of connection are *not* drawn, save in the subconscious of the reader. But Tennyson will have everything explicit, even at the price of a descent in tone. We start with "Break, break, break/ On thy cold grey stones, O sea," and end with "the tender grace of a day that is dead," which is merely pretty; we start with "such a tide as moving seems asleep," and end with "I hope to see my Pilot face to face," which, with its reduction of the Godhead to a sort of super-Peggotty, is positively ludicrous. It is not merely that the thing is said twice, but that it is said in two different ways that pull against each other; the image remains the keynote, but it might have been the vehicle of the idea.

These are extreme examples, chosen to define a tendency that is not usually so clearly marked; and it is only fair to add that each of the poems thus drawn upon is a very great and very beautiful one. Only they might have been greater and more beautiful if the craftsman had stood aside and allowed the poet's imagination to speak unimpeded to his audience. Indeed, for the modern taste the one remaining objection is that the images would still be too pretty, too transparent, to trouble us very deeply; they would still be understood before they were intimately felt. Perhaps this was a fault of taste—the age's fault: agreeing in this instance with a rather bookish, rather sentimental turn of mind. At any rate, this sort of lucid loveliness was precisely Tennyson's conception of poetry; it is what we should expect of an art that was reflective, not intuitive. For a lyric temperament, his approach to his themes was singularly detached and workmanlike; it was no part of his plan to cut beneath the psychic surface.

This understanding of his art, and the decorative technique that is its embodiment, actually contribute more or less directly to the overall pallor and stiltedness with which modern criticism charges Tennyson when it troubles to consider him at all. It is not only that the image loses immediacy and the poem force. The reflective manner also makes it easier to impose an arbitrary, an externally determined tone on the poetic experience; once separated from statement, the image can gloss over a theme instead of realizing it. And Tennyson really wanted his experience to have a tone that was not native to it. He wanted the clarion certainty of "thy foot/ Is on the skull which thou has made," not the faint hope of "Thou seemest human and divine." He wanted to be Ulysses, not a Second-rate Sensitive Mind. Living in a world as complex, false, and contradictory as our own, sensitive to its every jar and shadow, he felt himself obliged to present these under the form of a harmony and dignity appropriate to a golden age; he was faithful to the matter of his experience, but he tried to infuse into it the quality of the stateliest kind of classical verse. That way lay compromise and surface rhetoric: the facile Epilogue to *In Memoriam* succeeding to the tortured central stanzas; the Victorian equation of Galahad with Grundy and commercial progress with utopia. And that way lay a language chosen for what it could bring to the subject rather than what it could reveal in it—the opaquely brilliant lapidary style. Tennyson's poet "in a golden clime was born." He did not need to be immediate, because he wanted to be golden rather than sharp or real.

In this connection, the influence of classical studies as a possible reinforcement of Tennyson's own temperamental disposition, although a minor point, is worth considering. The Latin poetry to which he was most attracted was smooth and lofty and ornate, and it was studied (in the nineteenth century) by way of the analysis of particular devices. It may well have fixed his attention upon the most readily analyzed elements of poetic technique, such as tonal harmony, expressive rhythm, and precision of epithet: elements peculiarly subject to intellectual control, and elements which, almost from his first publication, he made the basis of his art. Such studies would tend to identify creativity with craftsmanship. But a more general effect might be to suggest (as they did to Arnold) a certain vigor and loftiness of attitude as the most appropriate poetic mode. These, the time made impossible for Tennyson, whose direct speech would be of bitterness, confusion, and despair: impossible, unless he refused to speak directly. How inviting, then, was the dramatic and heroic mode! I suspect, from the whole tenor of his work, that he had little heart to begin with for direct and painful speech. I suspect that he was willing enough to shift and compromise for his heart's ease, trusting faintly amid the terrible Victorian toppling of ideals; I suspect, too, that innate shyness made him turn away from faith in his first gift, which may have been his best, of compact lyric expression. Now here were doctrine and illustrious example telling him to prefer finish to depth, serenity to immediacy and anguish: and by means over which he had superb control. Was not Virgil cool, objective, and remote? It does not matter that this was a superficial reading of the classics; what matters is that it was most probably his reading, as it was his century's, and that it fell in with the natural reticence of a divided soul.

At any rate, the personal note is rare in his poetry, and very rare after 1842; where it is heard at all, it is heard most often not in pure lyrics (like the songs from *The Princess*) but in half-dramatic pieces like "Love and Duty" or "Supposed Confessions," where the character can mask the poet. From the first it must contend against an objective-idyllic strain, the strain of "The Lotus-Eaters" and "Morte d'Arthur": a strain less intimately his than the other, but beautifully executed, and a much readier means of presenting an escape or an ideal. Among the happiest of the characteristic effects are those, like "Ulysses," in which the ideal posture and the inner longing blend—standing, as it were, a little way outside the poet. Like Arnold, Tennyson wanted poetry to be "bracing"; unlike him, he could not wait elegiacally between two worlds. He must have some comforting message, some image of noble endurance or patient love or "faith that comes of self-control"; he must bring strength or beauty, not awareness, to his world. He longed for dignity and purpose, not catharsis. One name for that temptation is the Victorian Compromise: another is "The May Queen" or "Lady Clare." The wonder is not that he yielded, but that he yielded so slowly and grudgingly; it was twenty-five years before the laureate-pieces and vatic exercises, the half-epics and the tedious dramas, had crowded out the stubborn sincerities of "The Two Voices" and *In Memoriam* and *Maud.* In the latter two, however, the disposition toward compromise and rationalization is already strong; in *Maud* we can sense, standing between the poet and ourselves, not only the melancholy "happy ending" but the whole arbitrary and conventional management of what might have been a moving lyric poem.

At bottom, of course, this was a spiritual choice: an acceptance of respectable commonplace, a comfortable determination to deny denial, to which any strictly literary considerations were irrelevant. But the fact remains that this choice invited, or a least accommodated, a particular literary attitude, into which his technical dexterity made it easy for him to fall. It was the choice that suited his career. Since 1830 he had been inclined, in the intervals of inspiration, to act out his conception of a poet, selecting themes on which he could ring the considered decorous changes for the world's plaudits and behoof. The trait persisted: even the fine 1842 volume is the work of a man determined to add to his poetic stature by taking thought, and there is much of jeweler's work and gallant bathos in *Maud*; at length it clouded over his more personal genius, and became a habit and a public function.

This, on one side of him, was what he had always wanted, it was a kind of shy self-realization, not of the artist but of his art. Certainly it was the direction of his most conscious ambition and his steadiest growth. And it permitted him the mastery he coveted; no style could be better adapted than Tennyson's to this rather formal vision of poetry, no vision could propose fitter subjects for his style. Only his accomplishment was incomplete. This was his power, but not all his power; it answered to his spirit, but not to his spirit's depths. He had command over his themes, but the moment came early when his themes no longer took command over him. The style runs smooth and thin, like a light wine; the symbols—Merlin, Galahad—are canonical: vestmented and pale. How many Geraints and Enids would we not sacrifice for another St. Simeon Stylites, original and real as a Browning character is real. We have "Tiresias" and "The Revenge" and a long roll of stately harmonies; but we miss the edge that could touch the raw nerve.

> Be near me when my light is low,
> When the blood creeps, and the nerves prick
> And tingle; and the heart is sick,
> And all the wheels of being slow.
> Be near me when the sensuous frame
> Is rack'd with pangs that conquer trust;
> And Time, a maniac scattering dust,
> And Life, a Fury slinging flame.
> Prophet, curse me the blabbing lip,
> And curse me the British vermin, the rat. . . .
> Arsenic, arsenic, sure, would do it,
> Except that now we poison our babes, poor souls!
> It is all used up for that.

We do not hear that voice—that almost modern voice—again. In its place we have a cool and sane and very lovely art, whose one weakness is that it conceives of its medium as rooted in device rather than imagination: a poet who stands off from his poem and applies "beauties" to it methodically, like brush-strokes to a canvas, until the planned effect has been built up. We have the art that lay implicit in that clear, unruffled style. This was the art of artifice, beneath which, finally, Tennyson's original gift lay all but buried: the greater part of him, but not the greatest: not an error, not a false trail, but a drastic limitation of his magnificent and many-sided genius.

8.

Allan Danzig

The Contraries: A Central Concept in Tennyson's Poetry

Nearly every book or article on Tennyson alludes to the poet's characteristic ambiguity, one neither of syntax nor of meaning but inherent in his very choice of subject and thus an essential aspect of his imagination. Few cirtics, however, have even tried to build a unified thesis from their isolated perceptions of, for instance, Tennyson's simultaneous concern with macrocosm and microcosm, the similarity and mutual attraction of opposites in his poetry, and, over all, his assumption of the dualistic nature of things. Most references to these phenomena are as brief, but rarely so significant, as Eliot's evaluation of the success and failure of *In Memoriam,* which calls attention to the poem's expression at once of the most obvious and the most sensitive: "Tennyson's surface, his technical accomplishment, is intimate with his depths: what we most quickly see about Tennyson is that which moves between the surface and the depths, that which is of slight importance."[1]

The first section of E. D. H. Johnson's *Alien Vision of the Victorian Poets* (Princeton, 1952) is based on the opposition of Tennyson's public and private selves, but even this most thorough-going of all attempts to deal with the problem stresses only one of its manifestations and, I believe, a secondary one. It is by a careful examination of the poetry itself that we may

Reprinted by permission of the author and the Modern Language Association of America from *PMLA,* Vol. 77, No. 5 (December, 1962), pp. 577–85.

discover the existence and finally the meaning of Tennyson's dualistic universe.

From his earliest poetry Tennyson deals in antithetical relationships. They appear in the juvenile *Poems by Two Brothers,* that pastiche of Byronic sentiments and Biblical sententiousness, made up principally of laments for lost innocence, laments for vanished civilizations, and laments for friends and family supposedly deceased.[2] Most of the poems now ascribed to Alfred present the traditional Christian paradox of life attained through death, or turn on the dualistic nature of man.

> Why should we weep for those who die?
> They fall—their dust returns to dust;
> Their souls shall live eternally
> Within the mansions of the just.
> They die to live—they sink to rise. . . .
> I was cursed from my birth,
> A reptile made to creep on earth,
> An hopeless outcast, born to die
> A living death eternally!
> With too much conscience to have rest,
> Too little to be ever blest . . .
> Yet I cling
> To life, whose every hour to me
> Hath been increase of misery.

The heavy oxymoron of these passages, the opposition in lines five and six of the second, and the inexplicable fact presented in the last three lines, may forecast Tennyson's later interest in the apparent contradictions of sensate life, just as they obviously if crudely suggest his rhetorical development. Or they may simply be memories of Pope and the declamatory gesture of Byron and Moore.

Timbuctoo,[3] Tennyson's prize poem of 1829, is somewhat better poetry and a much clearer example. The ostensible subject, set by the prize committee, is merely the vehicle for a consideration of the opposing claims of fact and imagination. A bright seraph shows the poet a vision of the city, "a wilderness of spires, and chrystal pile/ Of rampart upon rampart, dome on dome," but mourns,

> The time is well-nigh come
> When I must render up this glorious home
> To keen Discovery: soon yon brilliant towers
> Shall darken with the waving of her wand;
> Darken, and shrink and shiver into huts,
> Black specks amid a waste of dreary sand,
> Low-built, mud-wall'd barbarian settlements.

Yet this retreat cannot really endanger the seraph's empery, for he remains the living spirit of

> All th' intricate and labyrinthine veins
> Of the great vine of Fable, which, outspread,
> With growth of shadowing leaf and clusters rare,
> Reacheth to every corner under heaven,
> Deep-rooted in the living soil of truth.

Neither the poet nor the seeker of fact may alone claim to serve truth, which emerges from their interaction. This dialectic was to become characteristic of Tennyson's later poetry. The Emperor of "Akbar's Dream," published in 1892, declares,

> If every single star
> Should shriek its claim "I only am in heaven"
> Why that were such sphere-music as the Greek
> Had hardly dream'd of.

Akbar goes on to affirm the validity of every partial manifestation of truth. The underlying concept is the same as that of *Timbuctoo,* though in 1829 Tennyson had not yet formulated his position so clearly.

In the volume published in 1830 appear several poems which simply present contrary affirmations. Of these the most obvious are the companion pieces "Nothing Will Die" and "All Things Must Die," inconsequential poems despite their clear technical advance over the earlier "Why Should We Weep For Those Who Die?" based on the same paradox. Tennyson does not develop his conceit; indeed, once stated it can be taken no farther. The world, promises one poem, is constantly evolving in cyclic recreation; "It will change, but it will not fade." Yet, answers the second, it had a beginning and so must have an end: "Ye will come never more,/For all things will die."

In other poems there is some attempt at a conclusion. "The Mystic" presents a sage who lives in constant presence of "the still serene abstraction," beholding the unity behind multiplicity and affirming them both. Contradiction is only apparent, too, in "*οι ρέοντες*," which claims, "All thoughts, all creeds, all dreams are true," though with a note that "this very opinion is only true relatively to the flowing philosophers." Later in his life Tennyson was to hold less timidly to this declaration, as the passage from "Akbar's Dream" just quoted makes clear. And in "The Two Voices" opposing and equally valid arguments are superseded by a third term which is above all argument, an effort of the will to believe. Though the final assertion of the troubled narrator is weak and may even seem fortuitous in this poem, it foreshadows the similar and more satisfactory resolution of *In Memoriam.*

The ultimate explanation of these resolutions, essential to an understanding of Tennyson's poetry, lies beyond logic. It is based on an intuition seen at its simplest in the slight poem "Dualisms." Here, in a paradigm of contrary relationships, opposites are immediately understood by their mere juxtaposition to be expressions of a common unity. Two bees gather pollen from the same flower, two birds "woo each other, carolling together."

> Two children lovelier than Love adown the lea are
> singing . . . :
> Like, unlike, they roam together
> Under a summervault of golden weather;
> Like, unlike, they sing together
> Side by side,
> MidMay's darling goldenlockèd,
> Summer's tanling diamondeyed.

The contrast of the blond and the brunette "tanling" does not argue that either is to be preferred, still less that either is less validly a child. The two partake of a single reality more full for their specific contrasts. Each is the *contrary* of the other, but neither is the other's *negation.*

The Blakean distinction between contrary and negation is basic to Tennyson's perception of the world and thus to his poetry. Every quality, every manifestation of the sensual world, inevitably implies its contrary. It follows that, so long as human life continues, this pair may not finally be resolved to a third term of synthesis. Rather, they exist in constant dialectic tension; they do not destroy each other, as do negations. Life and death, reality and appearance, the unity and multiplicity of "The Mystic": man must recognize and accept their mutual existence. not seeking to simplify them by denying one or the other. He must give each its due until, balanced, "like, unlike, they sing together / Side by side." Thus he achieves a necessary harmony, an apparent stability, in a world he yet knows as a bewildering flux of multiplicity.

The two children of "Dualisms" develop into all the balanced contrary pairs of characters in later poems, such as old James and the poet Leonard of "The Golden Year," and the heroines of *The True and the False,* Elaine and Guinevere, Enid and Nimuë (afterwards Vivien). The twin brothers Balin and Balan are the best known and the most successful of a series of close relatives who embody contraries while demonstrating their fundamental unity. More complex versions of the same situation appear as well as in three melodramatic poems, spanning Tennyson's poetic career, which turn on the relation between a pair of sisters or, in one case, cousins. Closeness of blood and opposition of interests establish the sense of likeness in unlikeness.

The first, "The Sisters" (published in 1832), is a tale of revenge; the speaker tells how she murdered her sister's seducer. Both sisters love the Earl, and each successively wins his love; for the first this means to die, for the second to kill. Within this neatly symmetrical pattern the speaker herself weighs the opposed claims of her love and hate. These contraries can have no resolution, and they outlive their common object.

The second of these poems, published in 1880 and also called "The Sisters," is bewilderingly full of contraries. The male speaker of the poem had loved first Edith, then Evelyn, twin sisters. Edith had stepped aside to permit Evelyn's marriage, but died of a broken heart. Evelyn, learning of the sacrifice, declined and died, leaving two children, also called Edith and Evelyn. Now a suitor wavers for a moment in his choice of one or another of the girls, thus furnishing a reason for the recounting of the story. Their father advises him, "The graver is perhaps the one for you / Who jest and laugh so easily and so well. / For love will go by contrasts, as by likes." Each pair of sisters embodies a contrary relationship. The mistake of confusion in the first generation is balanced by its rectification in the second; this in turn is made possible by yet another contrary, the gay young man and his grave bride.

Sentimental as this poem, and even more "gothick" than the first, is "The Ring," published in 1889. The story is too complicated to summarize briefly, and the poem does not merit extended treatment. It is enough to say that here too there is a confusion in the wooing of two girls, cousins named Miriam and Muriel. The lover marries first one and, at her death, the other. Jealous Muriel is eventually punished and the worthy Miriam watches contentedly from beyond the grave as her daughter, also named Miriam, inherits her ring on her wedding day. The passing of names from one generation to the next, which in the second "Sisters" implies the continuation of the original problem, here sets up a contrary: the mother's doubt and the daughter's certainty of the security of love. None of these poems is worth consideration for its own sake. But they show Tennyson's interest continuing for sixty years in a device first handled in "Dualisms," and demonstrate the process of his non-finalist dialectic: the two terms of a contrary, in precarious balance, are equally valid and equally necessary to human life, which exists in the tension of their irresolvable polarity.

That this tension may produce at least a moment of harmony is attested by "Roses on the Terrace." The contraries are essentially as simple as those in "Dualisms" despite the sixty years between their writing; to be sure, in the later poem their expression is more sophisticated. *What has been* is reconciled with *what is,* cancelling time for an instant; the real work of the poem, a compliment to an old friend, is borne by the suggested metaphor equating girl and blush and flower. Tennyson's familiar love of distance both of time and space is combined with his equally familiar precision of detail. Thus there operate in the poem contraries making up the poet's familiar stance, and, on another level, those of time past and time present.

Despair and hope are the contraries seen as harmony in the uncomplaining endurance of "The Dreamer." Less explicit but perhaps more clear is the same synthesis presented in "A Voice Spake Out of the Skies"; so similar in concept to the earliest poems, these appeared in the posthumous volume of 1892. From his earliest to his latest work Tennyson considers the coexistence of contraries in such complementary relationships, in a harmony which yet conserves their opposition. Probably the best-known example is "Flower in the Crannied Wall" (published in 1869, mid-way in his career, with its Blakean unity of microcosm and macrocosm. Clearly isolated in poems of such simple—or at any rate single—subjects is the view underlying his most complex work.

If the idea of the contrary itself remained virtually static throughout the poet's life, his ability to make something dramatically satisfying of it grew with time. The force and successful pathos of "Lucretius" arises from the philosopher's incapacity to come to terms with the contraries, or even to recognize their existence. Throughout his monologue Lucretius exposes seeming antitheses. On the most simple level of natural description he observes that yesterday's dusty hollows have overnight become riotous watercourses. He knows that Nature of "the all-generating powers and genial heat" is one with the fierce-forked lightning; creation large in light is no more real than the darkness of the illimitable inane. Helen's breasts, capable of nourishing, may destroy as well. Similarly the nature of the gods is two-fold; Venus the human-amorous trifler is yet Venus Genetrix, and all-seeing prophet Apolo is blind to men and their destinies.

While Tennyson would accept these apparent contradictions as equal truths in a larger system of reality, Lucretius, a logician, seeks to reduce multiplicity to a single principle internally consistent at every point. As his philtre-confused mind conjures a satyr from a quivering bush and a melting cloud, he cries, "Him I proved impossible; / Twy-natured is no nature." But the satyr goes on about his brutish business. Unlike his would-be exorcist he is single-minded and sure of his goal, for it is central to this poem as to so much of Tennyson's poetry that from its deepest springs creation is "twy-natured." The demand for single-term logic unlooses chaos, while the recognition of contraries alone can produce a coherent and satisfying world view.

With pitying and tender irony Tennyson requires Lucretius to state and restate this principle but never to recognize it. The syntax of the philosopher's argument exposes paired contraries for both of which, as he comes on them in turn, he claims equal validity. But, because he enunciates these contraries at widely separated points in his discussion, he can generally avoid admitting they exist. Thus he affirms the pathetic transience of life, yet asserts the possibility of eternal calm. So too, as we have glimpsed, he admits in nature the principle of destruction, certain as that of creation. His gods are by definition eternal, but they are, similarly by definition, atomic and therefore subject to dissolution. This last is the only contrary he actually formulates, and his logic requires him to see in it only an intolerable negation. Because of his inability to transcend logic, for Lucretius the contraries do anything but "sing together, side by side"; monstrous, they menace him.

Lucretius is unable to profit from his own perfectly correct observations. He declares that nature emerges "balmier and nobler from her bath of storm," but can make of this perception only a useless precept for his own behavior: he merely seeks to compose himself as the storm has been allayed. He fails to go one step further, to realize that, as the storm is as integral a part of nature as her calm, so the brute turbulence of his blood is as essential to him as mental tranquillity. He does indeed admit that the one is as much a part of him as the other, but this knowledge is productive only of self-contempt. Because he has previously affixed values to these contrary moods he can see them only as negations. Their inseparability is the cause of his despair; since "twy-natured is no nature," one of them must be abnormal. Through a logic he regards as more perfect than himself he is drawn irresistibly to suicide as the only resolution of an unbearable confusion. But not even Lucretius' passion for logic is without its internal ambivalence; we can recognize in the decision to kill himself less the influence of reason than that of simple terror at his own helplessness.

The poem begins with twenty-five lines of introductory narrative. Two contrary and inescapable claims are immediately stated, and Lucretius, we understand, more or less ignores the one of them represented by his wife.

> For when the morning flush
> Of passion and the first embrace had died
> Between them, tho' he loved her none the less,
> . . . the master took
> Small notice, or austerely, for . . .
> he past
> To turn and ponder those three hundred scrolls
> Left by the Teacher, whom he held divine.

His wife Lucilla can only believe she has a rival. It is important to remember that the aphrodisiac she administers does not change Lucretius' fundamental nature, or introduce an alien power. "Tickling the brute brain within the man's," it merely loosens mechanically the indigenous passions he would restrain. The main portion of the poem presents his effort to reestablish self-control; as he moves between the poles of calm and fury Lucretius cannot appreciate the dialectic he defines.

He begins by trying to order his three dreams. With a complete faith in logic he believes that if he can work out a reasonable explanation for them their power will be broken. The first, though a nightmare vision of chaos, has nevertheless been an apocalypse in Lucretian terms; he acknowledges it his and, thus attaching it to a recognizable system, subdues it. Like many other Tennysonian dreamers, such as the heroine of "Mariana in the South" who, "dreaming . . . knew it was a dream," Lucretius stands outside his dream looking on. The simile of the dog, which Tennyson took from the historical Lucretius' own illustration of his theory that we continue in dreams our waking life,[4] intimates as well that the dreamer can anticipate and even direct his dream in a relation like that between hunter and hound. The second dream has shaken this belief. He had expected dragon warriors to spring from the ground under its rain of blood, parallel to the civil war which, waking, he had expected to answer Sylla's tyranny. Instead there had arisen "girls, Hetairai, curious in their art,/Hired animalisms."

These phrases progress from recognition to disgust, reflecting Lucretius' growing loss of control as the women had pressed closer to him, half-suffocating him until, he says, "I yell'd aloud." The undignified "yell'd" is a measure of his terror at the as yet unexampled mutiny of his mind. Worse was to follow.

> Then, then, from utter gloom stood out the breasts,
> The breasts of Helen, and hoveringly a sword
> Now over and now under, now direct,
> Pointed itself to pierce . . . ;
> and as I stared, a fire,
> The fire that left a roofless Ilion,
> Shot out of them, and scorch'd me that I woke.

The symbolism of this little tableau is rich, but it is enough here to say that the passage forecasts the end of the poem; a terrible beauty renders impotent the force which opposes it and, irreducible itself to logic or pity, imposes its own revenge.

Tennyson has a clear understanding of the effect of external stimuli on the sleeping mind. Three thunderstorms gave rise to Lucretius' dreams and provided their background of turbulence; a great lightning-bolt had perhaps suggested the scorching fire of Helen's breasts. But now the storms are over. Nature is the clearer for her purgative rage. Lucretius seeks similarly to recompose himself, and the reduction of his dreams to logical exposition seems to help him.[5] Thereafter he largely succeeds in keeping his uncertainty on an abstract plane. As he turns to consider the nature of the gods there pulses beneath his unanswerable question the more immediate problem of his own nature, but thus intellectualized it is manageable. Even when he first considers suicide (ll. 145–155) his discussion is a model of control—however uncontrollable the need which drives him to such a consideration.

It is only when memories of his recent humiliating visitations return to him (ll. 155–163) that the soothing habit of rationality is disturbed. But not for long; even this disquiet is transmuted from an emotional to an intellectual question: Why is the mind subject to such disorders? asks Lucretius. Does it secretly love erotic titillation? Or is it temporarily overborne by the sheer multitude of unworthy images? We may recognize in both these suggestions threats to that primacy of the mind on which Lucretius insists; a helpless mind, for the purposes of his system, is little better than one actively corrupt. But for the moment Lucretius is satisfied. He has seemingly eliminated one of the contraries.

Working beneath this appearance of logic, it is the incursion of a system not dreamt of in his philosophy which precipitates his suicide. A satyr and an oread, creatures of his dream, now break in upon him fully awake. There follows a rapid succession of violent emotions. At first, once more the detached observer, he hopes the nymph will escape her pursuer. But when she lasciviously rushes upon Lucretius he is swept under by his former panic: "Catch her, goatfoot," he cries. Immediately regretting this humiliating destruction of his new-found calm, he amends his words: "Nay, / Hide, hide them, million-myrtled wilderness." Revolted, he wants nothing to do with this further evidence of his mind's faithlessness.

Does he recognize the creatures as his own imaginings, or does he think them real? We cannot know, for he characteristically turns to analysis less productive of emotion. It is at this point significant to state that Lucretius is not by nature removed from the joy of life. Rather, as Jebb approvingly declares in his article on the poem, in Tennyson's work "as in the *De Rerum Natura,* one feels instinctively that Lucretius is *lonely* . . . [He] stands apart from the life of his day . . . [But] a certain sustained intensity [makes us] feel that the agony described is not of a cold mind stung, but of an eager mind baffled." His is a "confusing torment of the senses, mingled with . . . clear-minded despair";[6] in short, immersion in a world of contraries. Examining his own suspect desires, he seeks to make of them objects separable from himself, and thus to exempt himself from "twy-nature."

> Do I wish—
> What?—that the bush were leafless? or to whelm
> All of them in one massacre?

This questioning, a pitiful attempt to return to disengagement, cannot save him, for neither voyeurism nor rage will accord with "the sober majesties / Of settled, sweet, Epicurean life."

Sure now that he can rely on nothing, least of all his own mind, Lucretius falls into a weary pathos. For him uncertainty is an end, while Tennyson would take it for a beginning. Logic is replaced by word-play. "I often grew / Tired of so much within our little life, / Or of so little in our little life." One of Tennyson's favorite devices is this rhetorical opposition; in this poem he uses it altogether functionally to show Lucretius' habit of mind which maintains at all times the appearance of logic. At the same time it suggests here the persistence of the contraries he seeks by logic to resolve.

Earlier in the poem antithesis had provided a harmless flourish to Lucretius' question: "Was it the first beam of my latest day?" (l. 59). Now, all substance of argument gone, rhetorical opposition plays with straws and flowers. Soon it will grow sinister, seeming to lend logical sanction to a decision emotionally arrived at. Despite the formally logical appearance of his "since" and "therefore" in the final portion of his monologue (ll. 230–273), his apparently careful building from cause to effect, Lucretius, we find, argues from metaphor (l. 234) and from merely rhetorical syllogism (ll. 231–232; 271–272): "Why should I, beastlike as I find myself, / Not manlike end myself?" Unable to accept "twy-nature" he can only negate all nature in his suicide. He makes human life impossible, at least for himself, by demanding the forcible elimination of contraries in the name of the logical unity of a system.

Tennyson, as much as Lucretius, appreciates calm of mind. However, the poem insists, it is not calm but despair which is reached by reducing all explanations to single causes or perfect systems. Other poems counsel success by accepting and thus (for a moment) reconciling the dualistic or pluralistic nature of the sensual universe. It is of course fruitless to label Tennyson a considered dualist, either philosophical or psychological, and downright false to call him a theological or ethical one.[7] Yet it is clear in what direction his feelings lie. Hallam Tennyson reports, in his notes to "Akbar's Dream," "During one of the Bishop of Ripon's last visits my father said to him: 'Looked at from one point of view, I can understand the Persian dualism; there is much which looks like the conflict of powers of light and darkness'."[8] In the note there follows a prose sketch of a proposed poem on the Zoroastrian creation. The Almighty creates Ormuzd and Ahriman, the spirits of light and of darkness, who together create the world. Each holds to his own incontrovertible principle, and it is only the Almighty who can know the system which includes them both.

This idea, expressed in more human and in more conventionally Christian terms, had previously struck the keynote in the introduction to *In Memoriam:*

> Our little systems have their day;
> They have their day and cease to be;
> They are but broken lights of thee,
> And thou, O Lord, are more than they.

God's is, by definition, a perfect system, but we cannot fathom it, must accept its very existence on faith. Man is worse than mistaken to magnify one beam in darkness and think it universal illumination. In "Vastness" we meet "Craft with a bunch of heal-all in her hand, follow'd up by her vassal legion of fools." For there can be no all-healing solution to the world's ills, nor even to a single one, and those who claim to have a universal panacea are either guileful or gullible. Lucretius must remember, with the speaker of *In Memoriam* (section LIII), that pushed beyond her proper limits "divine Philosophy" becomes "Procuress to the Lords of Hell." No matter how perfect the will of the systematizer, by the very act of systemization a necessarily fragmented appreciation of the good is perverted. Tennyson succinctly states this in the much-quoted but little examined lines in "Morte D'Arthur":

> God fulfils himself in many ways,
> Lest one good custom should corrupt the world.

"E.g., chivalry, by formalism of habit or by any other means," he adds in his note, but the warning is obviously capable of extension to include all human perceptions of the good.

Denial of contraries, reliance on system, becomes pathetic tragedy in "Lucretius" and contributes to the grander tragedy of the *Idylls of the King*. Not by a process of negation, but in the movement of a dialectic towards a final resolution it can never reach, may man best balance the contraries in an approximate answer to his needs.

We may see this movement in "Locksley Hall." The disappointed lover first mourns the faithlessness of his still-beloved Amy; then his love is countered by his despite of her. He merges these emotions as he envisions her life with a brutal husband. This synthesis becomes the first term in a new opposition, as he turns from personal emotion to celebration of his "wondrous Mother-Age." These in turn merge to a vision of progress, a personal redemption as well as that of the world. The dialectic very generally sketched here is successful; that is, the speaker has attained a self-confidence, though not a calm, which Tennyson's Lucretius could have admired.

Of course this is true only if we stick to the limits of the poem and do not unfairly bring in "Locksley Hall Sixty Years After" as evidence against the speaker. Yet it is very much to the point that the second "Locksley Hall" exists. The earlier confidence has here vanished, and it is not yet calm which has succeeded. For the balance of contraries cannot last. It may be more viable than such a monistic system as Lucretius seeks to impose upon the universe; it may provide a moment's satisfaction, as in "Locksley Hall," or even a permanent solution to some minor aspect of the situation, as in "Dualisms." But the contraries change their ground.

This we have seen them do in *Timbuctoo* and "Lucretius," slipping back into flux and demanding endless redefinition. Since they cannot finally be resolved, the stability implied and established by their harmony is only temporary. It is Arthur's recognition of this fact which brings the *Idylls of the King* so close to full-scale tragedy. Knowing from the first that any system outlives its usefulness as the postulates on which it is based dissolve and re-form,[9] Arthur can achieve *cette tristesse majestueuse* which Racine, in the introduction to *Bérénice,* claims as the essence of tragedy; Tennyson himself declared, "Tragedy is all balance throughout."[10] It is only as an octogenarian that the speaker of the two "Locksley Halls" foreswears system, and, with nothing to replace it, falls into a despair which mocks his earlier easy solution.

Tennyson's world is ever in constant contrary process. As

many critics have commented, in nearly every poem reality lies beyond its sensual manifestation. "This double seeming of the single world" is the theme of more than "The Ancient Sage," in which this formula appears. We find it in poem after poem, though rarely is it so overt as in "The Two Greetings." These are a pair of contraries; as Wilfred Ward sums up, "The second greeting considers the reality of the child's life and its meaning, the first only its appearance."[11] The speaker of "Supposed Confessions" cries out against man's "damned vacillating state," in an agony like the later Lucretius', but he is at least willing to endure the world of contraries.

> Shall we not look into the laws
> Of life and death, and things that seem,
> And things that be, and analyse
> Our double nature, and compare
> All creeds till we have found the one,
> If one there be?

"Our double nature" here refers specifically to the Christian dualism, but understood in the larger context of Tennyson's mature poems it implies, like Lucretius' "twy-nature," so many reservations on the possibility of human perfectibility that we may wonder how serious critics could ever have confused Tennyson with the hero of "Locksley Hall."[12] The poet is never certain that he is "heir to all the ages, in the foremost files of time"; in "Supposed Confessions" he asks, "Oh! wherefore do we grow awry / From roots which strike so deep?" He laughed pityingly at the story of a Brahman who had smashed a microscope which showed him animalcules fighting in a drop of water. "As if we could destroy facts by refusing to see them," he commented.[13] "Nature, red in tooth and claw" is always behind his hope, almost a plea, that man may realize the highest within himself. Without this hope, he felt, man would find life impossible, "reel back into the beast."

Accordingly, in *In Memoriam,* he built his hope into a faith. But it is clear that even in that poem the reconciliation of contraries is not a final answer. Section CVI ("Ring Out, Wild Bells") is, in its context, as desperate as it is triumphant, an incantation designed to create hope as much as a prophecy of its realization. Its mixture of faith and a larger fear was set forth long before the old man of the second "Locksley Hall" was to speak of "Evolution ever climbing after some ideal good, / And Reversion ever dragging Evolution in the mud."

Maud is very similar to "Locksley Hall," both in its general outline and in its treatment of contraries. In each a hero, tainted with hyper-Tennysonian black bile aggravated by an orphaned and troubled childhood, inveighs in similar terms against the age's moral corruption and love of gold. In each a love affair, unhappily terminated at least in part by the selfish intervention of the girl's relatives, leads to a frantic despair, which is in turn soothed by the hero's dedication to a cause, one, furthermore, with which we cannot wholly sympathize.

However this similarity of plot is not nearly so marked as the difference in poetic treatment. "Locksley Hall" is written in a florid, gesticulating style which makes it easy, at least for the modern critic, to regard its hero as a dramatic creation. The steady gallop through almost all the stronger emotions warns us we cannot accept them at face value. *Maud,* an altogether more finished work despite the influence of the lurid Spasmodic school, is so much finer in its emotional modulation as to seem to claim complete moral validity, and thus to demand an acceptance we are unwilling to extend.

Tennyson is still censured for puffing a tawdry war into a gimcrack scheme of universal salvation. In fact he probably agreed with the defender of *Maud* who wrote, "The Omniscient has accorded to warfare an appointed function in human affairs."[14] But W. C. Bennett's fierce satire *Anti-Maud* and Gladstone's objection to the poem are unfair. The latter writes, "A vision of the beloved image . . . 'spoke of a hope for the world in the coming wars,' righteous wars of course, and the madman begins to receive light and comfort; but, strangely enough, it seems to be the wars, and not the image, in which the source of consolation lies."[15] Only to a flat and literal mind is this true. Tennyson, it is safe to say, is rarely, and certainly not here, concerned with war at all.

Certain of the Laureate's patriotic songs are jingoistic, but it must not be argued, drawing on a line from "Rizpah"[16] and such poems as "The Sailor Boy," that in *Maud* he is advocating a militaristic social program. These are all poems about the race between an individual and his personal devil to find work for idle hands; they are not discussions on unemployment, nor even cautionary tales on what happens if the devil gets there first. We may sense in Tennyson's bewildered reaction to public outcries at his supposed bloodthirstiness that the poet was not really (perhaps not adequately) concerned with the specific story he was telling. The sailor boy is just as likely to be setting out to join a grain ship as a gun-boat; the circumstances of the poem are accidental to its meaning. And "Rizpah" is spoken by a mad old woman. It was to dissociate the poet from his *personae* that Hallam Tennyson quotes his father, in his note to "Locksley Hall," with special reference to *Maud* as well: "In a certain way, no doubt, poets and novelists, however dramatic they are, give themselves in their works. The mistake that people make is that they think the poet's poems are a kind of 'catalogue raisonné' of his very own self, and of all the facts in his life, not seeing that they often express a poetic instinct, or judgment of characters real or imagined, and on the facts of lives real or imagined."[17]

The final sentence of Wells's *Tono-Bungay* may be read as a prose statement of "The Lady of Shalott" and "Crossing the Bar"; "London passes, England passes. . . . We are all things that make and pass, striving upon a hidden mission, out to the open sea." The same idea is everywhere in Tennyson's poetry, and rarely is it more cogent than in *Maud*. Indeed the poem closes with a situation almost identical with that of *Tono-Bungay:* the hero on a warship, hailing the open sea and the fearsome but intoxicating future he will help shape. Wells has never been attacked as a warmonger for this symbolic conclusion. The grim certainty of his hero is critically accepted as the indictment of a society. We are reluctant to see the same indictment in the salvation the hero of *Maud* finds in war when peace fails to offer an object worthy his dedication. But this is clearly how the poem is to be read.

To put it another way, we may understand the poem as a further Tennysonian tentative in the endless reconciliation of contraries, moving in the now-familiar dialectic. Melancholy is opposed by love of Maud the girl, and the hero has a momentary vision of personal happiness. This is wiped out by the duel, the separation, and Maud's death, and he is driven through despair to madness. Maud, now seen as universal love, slowly lifts him to selflessness, and he can declare, "I am one with my kind."[18] It should not worry us, as it worried Gladstone, that this statement of human solidarity is called forth by a war; the fact only underlines the persistence of the contraries. Both Maud and the cause in which her lover engages his energies are to be seen as complementary metaphors describing a merely apparent opposition; thus the poem deals with a typically Tennysonian problem. Its hero, like the speaker of "Locksley Hall," at last believes that he has won through to dynamic equilibrium, and in his own terms he has. It does not compromise his victory that into the warrior's vision of eternally balanced contraries intrudes our further knowledge: this is not the furthest demand we would make, this is no final answer; not even our demand can mark a limit. We have only to look at *In Memoriam,* a poem which attempts and ultimately rejects a final reconciliation of the contraries, to know that the process can have no end.

Notes

[1] T. S. Eliot, "In Memoriam," *Essays Ancient and Modern* (London, 1936), p. 189.

[2] It is well known that in fact three brothers contributed to the volume; Frederick, Charles, and Alfred were nineteen, eighteen, and seventeen respectively at the time of its publication in 1826 (the book is postdated 1827 on the title page). It is Charles who in successive poems kills off father, grandmother, brother, sister, various lovers, and Lord Byron, while Alfred is repeatedly horrified as he contemplates the destruction of Peru, Jerusalem, Druidical Britain, Babylon, Persia, Egypt, and Hindostan. All three confess to depths of depravity hardly to be expected in youths of such retired upbringing in a quite Lincolnshire rectory.

[3] All references to the poems are to the *Works of Tennyson,* ed. Hallam Tennyson, Eversley Edition, 9 vols. (London, 1908), hereafter referred to as *Works.*

[4] Tennyson had previously used this idea in "Locksley Hall," where, however, it serves mainly as an insult to Amy's future husband: "Like a dog he hunts in dreams, and thou art staring at the wall."

[5] In this they resemble the "sad mechanic exercise" of writing poems with which the speaker of *In Memoriam* controls his grief. But for Lucretius it is the reduction of the inexplicable to logic which is important, while in *In Memoriam* it is precisely the leap into intuition which eventually will provide reassurance.

[6] R. C. Jebb, "On Mr. Tennyson's 'Lucretius'," *Macmillan's Magazine,* XVIII (1868), 98–99, 103.

[7] It is often a serious falsification, or at best a mistake of emphasis, to attach a poet to a philosophical system unless, like Pope, he deliberately sets himself up as its spokesman. In Tennyson's case we may with certainty identify his position as one opposed to philosophical materialism. This may be seen in his interest in the Metaphysical Society, which he helped found and for whose first meeting he wrote "The Higher Pantheism." The idea is strongly confirmed by numerous poems, most notably *Lucretius.* As E. D. H. Johnson points out in *The Alien Vision of the Victorian Poets,* it is from the conflict between Tennyson's idealism and what he felt was his duty to pronounce on social questions that most of his more notable failures proceed. Conversely, it is through the understanding that the conflict exists that we may arrive at a sympathetic reading of these poems. Many of the objections to *Maud,* for example, disappear or in any case are minimized if we consider the poem as a dramatic presentation ("A Monodrama"), one specific solution to the problem of appearance and reality dealt with variously in "Locksley Hall," *The Princess,* and *In Memoriam.*

[8] *Works,* VII, 383.

[9] It is well to remember that the line, "The old order changeth, yielding place to new," appears in "The Coming of Arthur" as well as in the "Passing."

[10] Hallam Tennyson, *Alfred, Lord Tennyson: A Memoir,* 2 vols. (London, 1897), II, 226, hereafter referred to as *Memoir.*

[11] Wilfred Ward, "The Comments of Tennyson on One of his Later Ethical Poems," *Tennyson and his Friends,* ed. Hallam Tennyson (London, 1911), p. 478.

[12] The supposed belief in progress for which Tennyson is too often ridiculed may properly be understood as one among other metaphors for the endless balancing of contraries.

[13] *Memoir,* I, 278.

[14] Robert Mann, *Tennyson's 'Maud' Vindicated: An Explanatory Essay* (London, 188–), p. 76.

[15] William Gladstone, "Tennyson's Poems," *Quart.,* CVI (1859), 461.

[16] "The King should have made him a soldier, he would have been one of his best."

[17] *Works,* II, 341.

[18] In this he echoes the speaker of *In Memoriam:* "The shade by which my life was crost, / Which makes a desert in the mind, / Has made me kindly with my kind" (LXVI), and "I will not shut me from my kind" (CVIII). But *In Memoriam* arriving at a conclusion so similar to that of *Maud,* traces an altogether different path. This fact serves to reinforce the claim that the Crimean War has no essential meaning for the latter poem.

9.

Allan Brick

Equilibrium in the Poetry of Matthew Arnold

The usual effect of Victorian poetry is to prove that a truth exists, that the search for it must be unrelenting, and that its very attainment promotes a further search for a more ultimate truth—*ad infinitum.* This search is the penetration of self, an interior journey on which the individual draws away from the world of appearance, from the encrustations of social personality and ever closer to innermost reality. Like Shelley and Coleridge, the major Victorians express themselves in terms of idealist philosophy; their poetic form schematizes the self into subject-object relationships. If, as compared with their predecessors, they seem to be more distant from the individual consciousness, more interested in the neat recounting of "stories," on closer examination one finds the "stories" are dramatizations for philosophical inculcation.

In *Prometheus Unbound* and *The Rime of the Ancient Mariner,* all individuals and objects may be readily understood as dramatic correlatives for the forces and attitudes at work within the mind. The freeing of Prometheus symbolizes the freeing, through the painful process of consciousness, of the innermost Understanding. The relationship between the Wedding Guest and the importunate Mariner who has journeyed into spiritual reality and is now returned to make his report is essentially the relationship between normal perception and Kantian Appercep-

Reprinted with the permission of the author and the editor *University of Toronto Quarterly,* Vol. 30, No. 1 (October, 1960), 45–56.

tion; for in hearing the story retold the ego is jolted out of its adventitious social pose and, in uniting with the Mariner on the continually recurring voyage, is moved ever deeper into the spirit power in which all ego is grounded.

Tennyson's *Maud* seems closely analogous to the *Rime* in its recounting of the various stages of madness through which the consciousness must pass before it can exchange malaise in the world of phenomena for spiritual health through idealist vision. *In Memoriam* and Browning's *Saul* examine this process in the perspective of *Prometheus Unbound* by dramatizing the resurrection of the Understanding; the raising of the Christ in both *In Memoriam* and *Saul* is achieved by the same self-revelatory suffering that frees Prometheus. Tennyson moves between hope and despair, each cycle more and more intense, until he envisions the dead Hallam resurrected with the living Christ and feels that all "the truths that never can be proved" are proved as "we close with all we loved / And all we flow from, soul in soul";[1] in Kantian terms, phenomenal appearance has fallen away to reveal a glimpse of noumenal reality. In *Saul,* after an upward spiralling between reason and faith, the individual ego attains its "unity of Apperception" and thence for an instant recognizes its fusion with the noumenal reality essential to all things.

Browning is actually a more complete idealist than Tennyson, for he admits of no objectivity at all in that one eternal moment of conversion, even though he shows that objectivity and the world of appearance more or less return as the ego slips back into the limitations of normal everyday consciousness. Whereas for Browning the ego can fuse with reality in the moment of conversion, for Tennyson ultimate reality may be glimpsed now only as a vision, and not fully attained until some future time. For Tennyson there is even at the deepest point of penetration into the self an inescapable tension between the transcending subject and the existential personality, and thus a necessary separation between the striver and the goal. For both Browning and Tennyson the journey of penetration, which has culminated in either complete transcendence or at least a glimpse of impending reality, entails heightened consciousness for the ego on its return to normal life. The reward is an increased ability to sense the transcendent reality behind all individual perceptions, to synthesize the fragmentary objects of everyday consciousness. Thus the resultant condition of Browning's David, emerging fresh from his union with the essential Saul, is sustained conversion:

> Anon at the dawn, all that trouble had withered from earth—
> Not so much, but I saw it die out in the day's tender birth;
> In the gathered intensity brought to the grey of the hills;
> In the shuddering forests' new awe; in the sudden wind-thrills;
> In the startled wild beasts that bore off, each with eye sidling still
> Though averted with wonder and dread; in the birds stiff and chill
> That rose heavily, as I approached them, made stupid with awe!
> E'en the serpent that slid away silent—he felt the new Law.
> The same stared in the white humid faces upturned by the flowers;
> The same worked in the heart of the cedar, and moved the vine-bowers;
> And the little brooks witnessing murmured, persistent and low,
> With their obstinate, all but hushed voices—"E'en so, it is so!"
>
> (*Saul,* XIX)

Matthew Arnold rejects the assertion that the "outer world" (both as physical and as conceptual phenomena) exists only in relation to a transcendental power which focuses through a perceiving ego. Thus he does not, like Shelley, Coleridge, Tennyson, and Browning, write poetry in which all setting, characters, and events serve to dramatize the structure and function of the ego. He does not imagine, for example, that the appearance of the woods, hills, and animals in his poem depends upon the perceiving consciousness of the hero, whose movement through them is correlative to the subject ego's penetration into itself as objective envelopment. For Arnold, rather than the ego transforming —even determining—the appearance of the "outer world," quite the reverse is true: the ego is impinged upon by that outer reality which it foolishly, tragically, pretends to dominate. Arnold insists that there is an objective reality over which man's will has no control—an amoral Nature which is not man's friend nor his foe nor in any way cognizant of him, and which subjects him to the rules of change and death. While recognizing that it is natural for man to persist in the illusion that he can understand or even contain "reality," Arnold reveals a world thoroughly independent of the "dreams" which constitute human consciousness. He berates Clough for his unavailing struggle to contain all reality within some recognizable structure of his own ego:

> You ask me in what I think or have thought you going wrong: in this: that you would never take your assiette as something determined final and unchangeable for you and proceed to work away on the basis of that: but were always poking and patching and cobbling at the assiette itself—could never finally, as it seemed—"resolve to be thyself"—but were looking for this and that experience, and doubting whether you ought not to adopt this or that mode of being of persons qui ne vous valaient pas because it might possibly be nearer the truth than your own: you had no reason for thinking it *was,* but it *might* be—and so you would try to adapt yourself to it.[2]

Arnold tries to show this idealist *par excellence* that there is a definite stance to be assumed, a position to be held: "You are too content to *fluctuate*—to be ever learning, never coming to the knowledge of the truth. This is why, with you, I feel it necessary to stiffen myself—and hold fast my rudder."[3] Arnold seeks a point of balance between activity and repose.

Most of his poems deal with an individual whose stance is already determined; they merely define that stance and its implications. Arnold's lonely individual is denied the idealist potentiality of joining "soul in soul," of joining (in the manner of Browning and Tennyson) with a noumenal reality essential to all men. In "A Republican Friend" the idealist who subordinates outer reality to the human will is portrayed as a man of social action who believes he can make a better world; but the narrator in the poem reduces this social idealist to a political activist: one who pretends foolishly that he can strive for a utopian goal untainted by the "lust, avarice, envy" of worldly existence. Thus Arnold's individual, with the perspective of this narrator, makes his first step in the process of self-consciousness, or rather of "reality"-consciousness: withdrawal from society. This step is more or less complete before the time of the poem. Arnold's individual sympathizes with the purposes of "A Republican Friend," saying, "I am yours, and what you feel I share,"[4] but at the same time admits that activism, even if admirable, is delusive. He steps away from his friend (p. 7)—as from the activist self of his own past—

> Seeing this vale, this earth, whereon we dream,
> Is on all sides o'ershadow'd by the high
> Uno'erleap'd Mountains of Necessity,
> Sparing us narrower margin than we deem.

Recognizing the idealist arrogance of that other self, he admits that human beliefs are illusory and human efforts fruitless. Yet it is only as double-self that he is human; man's life must circle paradoxically between resolute withdrawal and credulous activism, for even in making the effort to cut away he increases the tension with his existence as foolish hero. Seduced into a desire to rejoin, to receive the bodily investment of, the worldly self, he must increase the puritanical vigour of his rejection.

Thus Arnold's individual is profoundly bohemian (p. 7), intensely antibourgeois, sharing thoroughly the despite republicans hold for

> The barren optimistic sophistries
> Of comfortable moles, whom what they do
> Teaches the limit of the just and true.

But he insists that the republicans, in freeing themselves from the somnolent blindness of ordinary men, pretend far too much vision. How can they be so foolish as to believe they can acquire sure knowledge about and then impose changes upon complex world realities? "To an ambitious friend" he says (p. 47),

> Omit, omit my simple friend,
> Still to enquire how parties tend,

> Or what we fix with foreign powers.
> If France and we are really friends,
> And what the Russian Czar intends,
> Is no concern of ours;

and he warns that such social buzzing falls far below life's better task, the crowning of Eugenia's hair with rose garlands. Yet Arnold does not make this point final—as does the idealist Browning of "Love among the Ruins"; for fair Eugenia might very well be scornful, and then it would be best to consider what time and change will do to her beauty and your desire. Thus idealist absolutes are as impossible in the romantic sphere as in the political.

For Arnold the discovery of reality is the discovery of self *vis à vis* the outer world; it comes at a point of equilibrium between, on the one hand, engagement in society, in love, in ideals and, on the other, isolation from action, from passion, from principle, indeed, from life itself. Neither the self nor the outer world are noumena which can be seen into or, except in the most limited and exterior manner, understood; and this fact can force man either to accept oversimplified forms (illusions) in place of reality, or to despair of imposing upon complex existence any forms whatsoever. At a point of equilibrium man must develop the humility and the strength to "hold his rudder fast" against winds that would blow him to either side.

King Mycerinus, with only six years to live, decides his notions of religion and justice are illusory forms, "mere phantoms of man's self-tormenting heart," and abandons them, along with the entire context of social existence, to find what meagre reality he can in "the silence of the groves and woods" (p. 10). His withdrawal is to be neither a retirement nor an escape, but a modest affirmation. In the woods, however, he enters upon an endless cycle of satiation and desire, thus replacing the illusions of social activism and religious belief with those of hedonist indulgence. There, as before, he discovers that every perceived phenomenon, every presumed reality, disappears precisely at the instant of possession—that every "feast" insofar as it occurs is gone, leaving no sustaining after taste. It is at this point that Mycerinus, having learned the full lesson about idealist participation, might be imagined to feel the need for a more ultimate withdrawal (p. 11).

> It may be that sometimes his wondering soul
> From the loud joyful laughter of his lips
> Might shrink half startled, like a guilty man
> Who wrestles with a dream; as some pale shape
> Gliding half hidden through the dusky stems,
> Would thrust a hand before the lifted bowl,
> Whispering: *A little space, and thou art mine!*

Thus "it may be" that there is no ultimate withdrawal save death, and that the King does well to continue in sensual indulgence, struggling to confine beneath smooth brow and clear laugh his fear of that sole reality. Or "it may be" that for the brief interval before death, even as the feasting continues, Mycerinus pauses inwardly to "take measure of his soul," and is thereby "calm'd, ennobled, comforted, sustain'd." In the darkness, peering at the noumenon of self, the poet cannot assert anything definite. All he can do is chronicle from a distance Mycerinus' problem, and speculate on the existence of a solution. The poem ends in mystery, as Arnold represents the impossibility of narrator and audience ever discovering anything about noumenal Mycerinus—the impossibility of the ego ever discovering anything essential about itself and what surrounds it (p. 12):

> And when the mirth wax'd loudest, with dull sound
> Sometimes from the grove's centre echoes came,
> To tell his wondering people of their king;
> In the still night, across the steaming flats,
> Mix'd with the murmur of the moving Nile.

Mycerinus' inward projection of withdrawal itself provides the point of view in "A Modern Sappho." The narrator, Sappho, personifies that subject ego which struggles to hold fast the rudder, now against the force of participation and later against the force of death. At the moment the force of participation, her lover, dominates the entire ego; Sappho (helpless at the helm, as it were) must sit resolutely longing for the proper balance. The lover, like "a republican friend," and Mycerinus engaged in fleeting pleasures, is now impassioned over the world of illusion: the young and sensuous other woman. Sappho, in torture, awaits the day when time will conquer this love, allowing her hero to be drawn to her. Then, dominating, she may effect for the entire ego an interval of essential equilibrium between the passion of life and the dissolution of death. The torturing mystery lies in the question whether or not such an interval can exist; can there be before death *any* life other than that of a sensual, passionate, self-deluded lover? For it is possible that her very longing is in its violence an uncontrollable impulsion toward death, and that the supposed point of balance, once reached, cannot be held (p. 20):

> —Let my turn, if it *will* come, be swift in arriving!
> Ah! hope cannot long lighten torments like these.
> Hast thou yet dealt him, O life, thy full measure?
> World, have they children yet bow'd at his knee?
> Hast thou with myrtle-leaf crown'd him, O pleasure?
> —Crown, crown him quickly, and leave him for me!

This theme is treated more profoundly in "Tristram and Iseult," for which "A Modern Sappho" may have been a preliminary sketch. Here Tristram symbolizes the participative ego. He is involved with two Iseults, neither of whom can fully receive his love—Iseult of Ireland can't because of her separation from him as wife of King Marc, and Iseult of Brittany can't because Tristram is blinded to her by his love for Iseult of Ireland. The first two parts of the poem tell of Tristram's sickness from his love for the unattainable Iseult of Ireland; he dies blinded by the "flooding moonlight" of her beauty. In this portion of the poem Iseult of Brittany is mentioned repeatedly in Tristram's love ravings, but only as the Iseult he does *not* want, despite her admitted purity and goodness. Part Three is devoted to Iseult of Brittany, who, having loved the living Tristram in vain, now survives him. Before, her presence in the poem was covert, but now it is clear that she has been the implicit centre for the poet's sympathy. She is revealed as precisely that inward projection of withdrawal personified by Sappho. Thus the story Iseult tells the children at the end of the poem is the wish fulfillment of Sappho's plea that "life" and the "world" "Crown, crown him quickly, and leave him for me!" Iseult envisions herself as Vivian contriving to cast a spell on the old, but still passionate, magician Merlin, and trapping him fast within her "daisied circle."

The longings of Sappho and Iseult of Brittany represent an inward pull toward stoical control without which the "lover," drawing away into "life" and the "world," would dash himself to pieces—as, indeed, Tristram does. But this pull toward control may result not simply in the inhibition but also in the destruction of the participating self, may effect a virtual suicide. The question is how much force the withdrawing self must exercise in order to restrain the idealist who would be ruthless destroyer of the total ego. Undercurrent, therefore, to the controlled equilibrium envisioned by Sappho and Iseult-Vivian, is the threat of the loved hero's imprisonment or even murder by the *femme fatale*.

The suicide in its most basic form is evident in "The Sick King in Bokhara." Identifying a part of himself with a man who seeks the punishment of death for such sins as are common to all humanity, the King rules: "if he seek to fly, give way,/Hinder him not, but let him go"; then the King "softly" casts the first stone, as the sinner, looking up at him with joy, stays to embrace his execution. The King makes the extraordinary command that the corpse be brought to him; but his Vizier, at a loss to understand such sympathy for strangers, reminds him of the dignity of kingship, and of the law commanding that such a man be stoned "even were he thine own mother's son." In thus counselling the King, the Vizier perceives that the executed sinner is in a sense the King himself, that the King is similarly human. The King's sickness is his inability to escape from exactly that awareness; if he could harken to the Vizier and thus stoically ignore his disease of humanity, he could have health, release from tension. The King struggles to hold a balance between the sinner who succumbed to his thirsts and the Vizier who, being old, need not contend with any desire. If all three represent divisions of the human spirit, the final stanzas epitomize the proper action of the will in holding a firm balance between the cold indifference of reason and the consuming life of passion. The King concludes (pp. 94–5), "What I would, I cannot do," but "what I can do, that I will":

> I have a fretted brick-work tomb
> Upon a hill on the right hand,
> Hard by a close of apricots,
> Upon the road of Samarcand;
>
> Thither, O Vizier, will I bear
> This man my pity could not save,
> And, plucking up the marble flags,
> There lay his body in my grave.
>
> Bring water, nard, and linen rolls!
> Wash off all blood, set smooth each limb!
> Then say: 'He was not wholly vile,
> Because a king shall bury him.'

A similar "suicide"—the killing, or at least abandonment, of the social self by the withdrawing self—is effected by the wine of "The World and the Quietist," by "The Strayed Reveller," and by the self-imposed estrangement, the bohemianism, of "The Forsaken Merman" and "The Neckan." "The Scholar Gypsy" seems to achieve an equilibrium by abandoning his participating self; and yet, insofar as he retreats from society, the question arises does he, did he ever, exist at all? Arnold's most profound treatment of this theme is "Empedocles on Etna." It is a mistake to read this poem simply as a direct comment on Arnold's age. "Empedocles" is no Victorian "Wasteland"—no bitter lament over the death of idealism, the impossibility of holding absolute values in this withering modern age—rather it is Arnold's interpretation of the tragedy implicit in human existence in every age. Society will always banish, or at least estrange, its just ruler, and, more important, the just ruler will always find it necessary to withdraw from society; insofar as he is honest and courageous he will destroy his activist self, obliterating the pretension and arrogance of idealism. As Arnold said to Clough, Empedocles says, "Know thyself," but in that very assertion inveighs against the Emersonian idealism which defines the inner self as part and parcel of all things (p. 419):

No eye could be too sound
To observe a world so vast,
No patience too profound
To sort what's here amass'd;
How man may here best live no care too great to explore.

But we—as some rude guest
Would change, where'er he roam,
The manners there profess'd
To those he brings from home—
We mark not the world's course, but would have *it* take *ours*.

And all human knowledge is pretentious, so is human "pleasure" (p. 424):

Pleasure, to our hot grasp,
Gives flowers after flowers;
With passionate warmth we clasp
Hand after hand in ours;
Now do we soon perceive how fast our youth is spent.
At once our eyes grow clear!
We see, in blank dismay,
Year posting after year,
Sense after sense decay;
Our shivering heart is mined by secret discontent.

Thus Arnold spurns all idealism—hedonism as well as religion. He seems to end Act One of "Empedocles" with a direct attack upon Tennysonian idealism, asking (p. 425), must we

. . . feign a bliss
Of doubtful future date,
And, while we dream on this,
Lose all our present state,
And relegate to worlds yet distant our repose?

In Act Two of "Empedocles" Arnold deals with the paradox that life in its most essential form may be death, that indeed there may be no equilibrium possible between participation and utter dissolution. As in "A Modern Sappho," he suggests that release from tension comes only with the annihilation of the participant self, and results in nothing less than the eternal loss of personality. On the volcano's summit Empedocles is poised between the longing for participation and the longing for death. Down the mountainside is his life of participation in the world of men, who will "help him unbend his too tense thought" "till the absence from himself/. . . grow unbearable" and he must again come up here to solitude. But (pp. 435–6),

> . . . he will find its air too keen for him,
> And so change back; and many thousand times
> Be miserably bandied to and fro
> Like a sea-wave, betwixt the world and thee,
> Thou young, implacable God! and only death
> Can cut his oscillations short, and so
> Bring him to poise. There is no other way.

Looking back on such an existence, Empedocles can no longer see any reason to struggle for balance; indeed, to do so may also be an arrogant assertion of idealism. How can he, a prisoner of consciousness, who sees only through its "forms, and modes, and stifling veils," know he is not deluding himself in assuming the possibility of balance. And yet, we might ask, how can he know he is any *less* deluded in believing he can eternalize his "dwindling faculty of joy," can achieve some ultimate equilibrium by precipitate reunion with the elements? Actually we are left in complete doubt, as is Empedocles; for even as he plunges he feels that his belief in finding a life of eternal repose among the elements was but "for a moment." What seems a puzzling blank—a failure in the conception of "Empedocles"—is, rather, its necessary conclusion. We are left with an absolute question: whether Empedocles' joining with the elements is a transcendentalist assertion (and thus itself a valid idealism), as Empedocles hopes it is, or is instead an act of nihilistic futility. The answer cannot be determined, man cannot know that much about himself *vis à vis* outer reality.

The same theme is essential to "Sohrab and Rustum," where Arnold portrays the impact between the two impulses in its most violent form. The world-weary Rustum, now aware that it is his own son—his activist self—whom he has slain, repeats the pity of the "Sick King" for the dead sinner (p. 85):

> . . . rather would that I, even I myself
> Might now be lying on this bloody sand,
> Near death, and by an ignorant stroke of thine,
> Not thou of mine! and I might die, not thou;
> And I, not thou, be borne to Seistan;
> And Zal might weep above my grave, not thine;
> And say: *O son, I weep thee not too sore,*
> *For willingly, I know, thou met'st thine end!*

Rustum has complained about never achieving repose:

> But now in blood and battles was my youth,
> And full of blood and battles is my age,
> And I shall never end this life of blood.

However, Rustum has killed his activist self and repose is apparently near. The poem ends (p. 86):

> So, on the bloody sand, Sohrab lay dead;
> And the great Rustum drew his horseman's cloak
> Down o'er his face, and sate by his dead son.
> As those black granite pillars, once high-rear'd
> By Jemshid in Persepolis, to bear
> His house, now 'mid their broken flights of steps
> Lie prone, enormous, down the mountain side—
> So in the sand lay Rustum by his son.
> And night came down over the solemn waste,
> And the two gazing hosts, and that sole pair,
> And darkne'd all; and a cold fog, with night,
> Crept from the Oxus. Soon a hum arose,
> As of a great assembly loosed, and fires
> Began to twinkle through the fog; for now
> Both armies moved to camp, and took their meal;
> The Persians took it on the open sands
> Southward, the Tartars by the river marge;
> And Rustum and his son were left alone.
> But the majestic river floated on . . . .

After the violent impact of activity with necessity, comes equilibrium. The withdrawing self has made the murderous sacrifice, and now, at the shoreline of existence, has its eternal moment of union with the still warm body. Or so—gazing into the expanding scene, into the mythological depths of the past—do we strive to imagine. For in the fast-dimming picture it seems impossible to measure what a small, insignificant portion of all "reality," if *any* portion, is comprised by the dual human figure. And the tragedy here portrayed may be not so much the universal self's suicidal struggle and resulting ennoblement as it is our own struggle to feel sure that such a story, with some sort of meaningful conclusion, could occur. The repose—or is it anxiety?—communicated at the end of this poem is the result of our own contemplation of the mysteries of existence—one of the greatest of which is whether we may presume so to contemplate.

For Arnold, the end of poetry is communication not of the idealist power that fuses Saul and Hallam with the resurrected Christ, but of the necessary futility of activism braving an alien reality. Although he emphasizes a search for self-knowledge, a withdrawal from social unreality, this is not the continuing process which for Tennyson, Browning, and their romantic predecessors becomes itself the ultimate truth. In the end Arnold permits nothing but the question: what is man, even to believe he can make such a search?

Notes

[1] *In Memoriam,* CXXIX.

[2] *The Letters of Matthew Arnold to Arthur Hugh Clough,* ed. Howard Foster Lowry (London, 1932), p. 130.

[3] *Ibid.,* p. 146.

[4] *The Poetical Works of Matthew Arnold,* eds. C. B. Tinker and H. F. Lowry (London, 1950), p. 7. Subsequent page references are to this edition.

10.

Lionel Trilling

Kipling

Kipling belongs irrevocably to our past, and although the renewed critical attention he has lately been given by Edmund Wilson and T. S. Eliot is friendlier and more interesting than any he has received for a long time, it is less likely to make us revise our opinions than to revive our memories of him. But these memories, when revived, will be strong, for if Kipling belongs to our past, he belongs there very firmly, fixed deep in childhood feeling. And especially for liberals of a certain age he must always be an interesting figure, for he had an effect upon us in that obscure and important part of our minds where literary feeling and political attitude meet, an effect so much the greater because it was so early experienced; and then for many of us our rejection of him was our first literary-political decision.

My own relation with Kipling was intense and I believe typical. It began, properly enough, with *The Jungle Book.* This was my first independently chosen and avidly read book, my first literary discovery, all the more wonderful because I had come upon it in an adult "set," one of the ten green volumes of the Century Edition that used to be found in many homes. (The "set" has become unfashionable and that is a blow to the literary education of the young, who, once they had been lured to an author, used to remain loyal to him until they had read him by the yard.) The satisfactions of *The Jungle Book* were large and numerous. I suppose a boy's vestigial animal totemism was pleased; there were the marvelous but credible abilities of Mowgli; there were the deadly enmities and grandiose revenges, strangely and tragically real. And it was a world peopled by wonderful parents, not only Mother Wolf and Father Wolf, but also—the fathers were far more numerous than the mothers—Bagheera the panther, Baloo the bear, Hathi the elephant, and the dreadful but decent Kaa the python, a whole council of strength and wisdom which was as benign as it was dangerous, and no doubt much of the delight came from discovering the benignity of this feral world. And then there was the fascination of the Pack and its Law. It is not too much to say that a boy had thus his first introduction to generalized notion of society. It was a notion charged with feeling—the Law was mysterious, firm, certain, noble, in every way admirable beyond any rule of home or school.

Mixed up with this feeling about the Pack and the Law, and perfectly expressing it, was the effect of Kipling's gnomic language, both in prose and in verse, for you could not entirely skip the verse that turned up in the prose, and so you were led to trust yourself to the *Barrack Room Ballads* at a time when you would trust no other poetry. That gnomic quality of Kipling's, that knowing allusiveness which later came to seem merely vulgar, was, when first experienced, a delightful thing. By understanding Kipling's ellipses and allusions, you partook of what was Kipling's own special delight, the joy of being "in." Max Beerbohm has satirized Kipling's yearning to be admitted to any professional arcanum, his fawning admiration of the man in uniform, the man with the knowhow and the technical slang. It is the emotion of a boy—he lusts for the exclusive circle, for the sect with the password, and he profoundly admires the technical, secret-laden adults who run the world, the overalled people, majestic in their occupation, superb in their preoccupation, the dour engineer and the thoughtful plumber. To this emotion, developed not much beyond a boy's, Kipling was addicted all his life, and eventually it made him silly and a bore. But a boy reading Kipling was bound to find all this sense of arcanum very pertinent; as, for example, it expressed itself in *Plain Tales from the Hills,* it seemed the very essence of adult life. Kipling himself was not much more than a boy when he wrote these remarkable stories—remarkable because, no matter how one judges them, one never forgets the least of them—and he saw the adult world as full of rites of initiation, of closed doors and listeners behind them, councils, boudoir conferences, conspiracies, innuendoes, and special knowledge. It was very baffling, and certainly as an introduction to literature it went counter to all our present educational theory, according to which a child should not be baffled at all but should read only about what he knows of from experience; but one worked it out by a sort of algebra, one discovered the meaning of the unknowns through the knowns, and just as one got without definition an adequate knowledge of what a *sais* was, or a *dâk*-bungalow, and what the significance of *pukka* was, so one penetrated to what went on between the Gadsbys and to why Mrs. Hauksbee was supposed to be charming and Mrs. Reiver not. Kipling's superior cryptic tone was in effect an invitation to understand all this—it suggested first that the secret was being kept not only from oneself but from everyone else and then it suggested that the secret was not so much being kept as revealed, if one but guessed hard enough. And this elaborate manner was an invitation to be "in" not only on life but on literature; to follow its hints with a sense of success was to become an initiate of literature, a Past Master, a snob of the esoteric Mystery of the Word.

"Craft" and "craftily" were words that Kipling loved (no doubt they were connected with his deep Masonic attachment), and when he used them he intended all their several meanings at once—shrewdness, a special technique, a special *secret* technique communicated by some master of it, and the bond that one user of the technique would naturally have with another. This feeling about the Craft, the Mystery, grew on Kipling and colored his politics and even his cosmological ideas quite for the worse, but to a boy it suggested the virtue of disinterested professional commitment. If one ever fell in love with the cult of art, it was not because one had been proselytized by some intelligent Frenchman, but because one had absorbed Kipling's creedal utterances about the virtues of craft and had read *The Light that Failed* literally to pieces.

These things we must be sure to put into the balance when we make up our account with Kipling—these and a few more. To a middle-class boy he gave a literary sanction for the admiration of the illiterate and shiftless parts of humanity. He was the first to suggest what may be called the anthropological view, the perception that another man's idea of virtue and honor may be different from one's own but quite to be respected. We must remember this when we condemn his mindless imperialism. Indians naturally have no patience whatever with Kipling and they condemn even his best book, *Kim,* saying that even here, where his devotion to the Indian life is most fully expressed, he falsely represents the Indians. Perhaps this is so, yet the dominant emotions of *Kim* are love and respect for the aspects of Indian life that the ethos of the West does not usually regard even with leniency. *Kim* established the value of things a boy was not likely to find approved anywhere else—the rank, greasy, over-rich things, the life that was valuable outside the notions of orderliness, success, and gentility. It suggested not only a multitude of different ways of life, but even different modes of thought. Thus, whatever one might come to feel personally about religion, a reading of *Kim* could not fail to establish religion's factual reality, not as a piety, which was the apparent extent of its existence in the West, but as something at the very root of life; in *Kim* one saw the myth in the making before one's very eyes and understood how and why it was made, and this, when later one had the intellectual good luck to remember it, had more to say about history and culture than anything in one's mere experience. *Kim,* like *The Jungle Book,* is full of wonderful fathers, all dedicated men in their different ways, each representing a different possibility of existence; and the charm of each is the greater because the boy need not commit himself to one alone but, like Kim himself, may follow Ali into the shrewdness and sensuality of the bazaars, and be initiated by Colonel Strickland into the cold glamour of the Reason of State, and yet also make himself the son of the Lama, the very priest of contemplation and peace.

And then a boy in a large New York high school could find a blessed release from the school's offensive pieties about "service" and "character" in the scornful individualism of *Stalky*

& Co. But it was with *Stalky & Co.* that the spell was broken, and significantly enough by H. G. Wells. In his *Outline of History* Wells connected the doings of Stalky, McTurk, and Beetle with British imperialism, and he characterized both in a way that made one see how much callousness, arrogance, and brutality one had been willing to accept. From then on the disenchantment grew. Exactly because Kipling was so involved with one's boyhood, one was quick to give him up in one's adolescence. The Wellsian liberalism took hold, and Shaw offered a new romance of wit and intellect. The new movements in literature came in to make Kipling seem inconsequential and puerile, to require that he be dismissed as official and, as one used to say, intending something aesthetic and emotional rather than political, "bourgeois." He ceased to be the hero of life and literature and became the villain, although even then a natural gratitude kept green the memory of the pleasure he had given.

But the world has changed a great deal since the days when that antagonism between Kipling and enlightenment was at its early intensity, and many intellectual and political things have shifted from their old assigned places. The liberalism of Wells and Shaw long ago lost its ascendency, and indeed in its later developments it showed what could never in the early days have been foreseen, an actual affinity with certain elements of Kipling's own constellation of ideas. And now when, in the essay which serves as the introduction to his selection of Kipling's verse, Mr. Eliot speaks of "the fascination of exploring a mind so different from my own," we surprise ourselves—as perhaps Mr. Eliot intended that we should—by seeing that the similarities between the two minds are no less striking than the differences. Time surely has done its usual but always dramatic work of eroding our clear notions of cultural antagonisms when Kipling can be thought of as in any way akin to Eliot. Yet as Mr. Eliot speaks of the public intention and the music-hall tradition of Kipling's verse, anyone who has heard a record of Mr. Eliot reading *The Waste Land* will be struck by how much that poem is publicly intended, shaped less for the study than for the platform or the pulpit, by how much the full dialect rendition of the cockney passages suggests that it was even shaped for the music hall, by how explicit the poet's use of his voice makes the music we are so likely to think of as internal and secretive. Then it is significant that among the dominant themes of both Kipling and Eliot are those of despair and the fear of nameless psychological horror. Politically they share an excessive reliance on administration and authority. They have the same sense of being beset and betrayed by the ignoble mob; Kipling invented and elaborated the image of the Pict, the dark little hating man, "too little to love or to hate," who, if left alone, "can drag down the state"; and this figure plays its well-known part in Mr. Eliot's poetry, being for both poets the stimulus to the pathos of xenophobia.

Mr. Eliot's literary apologia for Kipling consists of asking us to judge him not as a deficient writer of poetry but as an admirable writer of verse. Upon this there follow definitions of a certain ingenuity, but the distinction between poetry and verse does not really advance beyond the old inadequate one—I believe that Mr. Eliot himself has specifically rejected it—which Matthew Arnold put forward in writing about Dryden and Pope. I cannot see the usefulness of the distinction; I can even see critical danger in it; and when Mr. Eliot says that Kipling's verse sometimes becomes poetry, it seems to me that verse, in Mr. Eliot's present sense, is merely a word used to denote poetry of a particular kind, in which certain intensities are rather low. Nowadays, it is true, we are not enough aware of the pleasures of poetry of low intensity, by which, in our modern way, we are likely to mean poetry in which the processes of thought are not, by means of elliptical or tangential metaphor and an indirect syntax, advertised as being under high pressure; Crabbe, Cowper, and Scott are rejected because they are not Donne or Hopkins or Mr. Eliot himself, or even poets of far less consequence than these; and no doubt Chaucer would be depreciated on the same grounds, if we were at all aware of him these days. I should have welcomed Mr. Eliot's speaking out in a general way in support of the admirable, and, as I think, necessary, tradition of poetry of low intensity. But by making it different in kind from poetry of high intensity and by giving it a particular name which can only be of invidious import, he has cut us off still more sharply from its virtues.

Kipling, then, must be taken as a poet. Taken so, he will

scarcely rank very high, although much must be said in his praise. In two evenings, or even in a single very long one, you can read through the bulky Inclusive Edition of his verse, on which Mr. Eliot's selection is based, and be neither wearied, in part because you will not have been involved, nor uninterested, because Kipling was a man of great gifts. You will have moments of admiration, sometimes of unwilling admiration, and even wish that Mr. Eliot had included certain poems in his selection that he has left out. You will be frequently irritated by the truculence and sometimes amused by its unconsciousness—who but Kipling would write a brag about English understatement? Carlyle roaring the virtues of Silence is nothing to it—but when you have done you will be less inclined to condemn than to pity: the constant iteration of the bravado will have been illuminated by a few poems that touch on the fear and horror which Mr. Wilson speaks of at length and which Mr. Eliot refers to; you feel that the walls of wrath and the ramparts of empire are being erected against the mind's threat to itself. This is a real thing, whether we call it good or bad, and its force of reality seems to grow rather than diminish in memory, seems to be greater after one's actual reading is behind one; the quality of this reality is that which we assign to primitive and elemental things, and, judge it as we will, we dare not be indifferent or superior to it.

In speaking of Kipling's politics, Mr. Eliot contents himself with denying that Kipling was a fascist; a tory he says, is a very different thing, a tory considers fascism the last debasement of democracy. But this, I think, is not quite ingenuous of Mr. Eliot. A tory, to be sure, is not a fascist, and Kipling is not properly to be called a fascist, but neither is his political temperament to be adequately described merely by reference to a tradition which is honored by Dr. Johnson, Burke, and Walter Scott. Kipling is not like these men; he is not generous, and, although he makes much to-do about manliness, he is not manly; and he has none of the *mind* of the few great tories. His toryism often had in it a lower-middle-class snarl of defeated gentility, and it is this, rather than his love of authority and force, that might suggest an affinity with fascism. His imperialism is reprehensible not because it *is* imperialism but because it is a puny and mindless imperialism. In short, Kipling is unloved and unlovable not by reason of his beliefs but by reason of the temperament that gave them literary expression.

I have said that the old antagonism between liberalism and Kipling is now abated by time and events, yet it is still worth saying, and it is not extravagant to say, that Kipling was one of liberalism's major intellectual misfortunes. John Stuart Mill, when he urged all liberals to study the conservative Coleridge, said that we should pray to have enemies who make us worthy of ourselves. Kipling was an enemy who had the opposite effect. He tempted liberals to be content with easy victories of right feeling and with moral self-congratulation. For example, the strength of toryism at its best lies in its descent from a solid administrative tradition, while the weakness of liberalism, arising from its history of reliance upon legislation, is likely to be a fogginess about administration (or, when the fog clears away a little, a fancy and absolute notion of administration such as Wells and Shaw gave way to). Kipling's sympathy was always with the administrator and he is always suspicious of the legislator. This is foolish, but it is not the most reprehensible error in the world, and it is a prejudice which, in the hands of an intelligent man, say a man like Walter Bagehot or like Fitzjames Stephen, might make clear to the man of principled theory, to the liberal, what the difficulties not merely of government but of *governing* really are. And that is what Kipling set out to do, but he so charged his demonstration with hatred and contempt, with rancor and caste feeling, he so emptied the honorable tory tradition of its intellectual content, that he simply could not be listened to or believed, he could only be reacted against. His extravagance sprang from his hatred of the liberal intellectual—he was, we must remember, the aggressor in the quarrel—and the liberal intellectual responded by hating everything that Kipling loved, even when it had its element of virtue and enlightenment.

We must make no mistake about it—Kipling was an honest man and he loved the national virtues. But I suppose no man ever did more harm to the national virtues than Kipling did. He mixed them up with a swagger and swank, with bullying, ruthlessness, and self-righteousness, and he set them up as necessarily antagonistic to intellect. He made them stink in the nostrils of youth. I remember that in my own undergraduate days we used specifically to exclude physical courage from among the virtues; we were exaggerating the point of a joke of Shaw's and reacting from Kipling. And up to the war I had a yearly struggle with undergraduates over Wordsworth's poem, "The Character of the Happy Warrior," which is, I suppose, the respectable father of the profligate "If."[1] It seemed too moral and "manly," the students said, and once when I remarked that John Wordsworth had apparently been just such a man as his brother had described, and told them about his dutiful and courageous death at sea, they said flatly that they were not impressed. This was not what most of them really thought, but the idea of courage and duty had been steeped for them in the Kipling vat and they rejected the idea with the color. In England this response seems to have gone even further.[2] And when the war came, the interesting and touching phenomenon of the cult of Richard Hillary, which Arthur Koestler has described, was the effort of the English young men to find the national virtues without the Kipling color, to know and resist their enemies without self-glorification.

In our day the idea of the nation has become doubtful and debilitated all over the world, or at least wherever it is not being enforced by ruthless governments or wherever it is not being nourished by immediate danger or the tyranny of other nations. Men more and more think it best to postulate their loyalty either to their class, or to the idea of a social organization more comprehensive than that of the nation, or to a cultural ideal or a spiritual fatherland. Yet in the attack which has been made on the national idea, there are, one suspects, certain motives that are not expressed, motives that have less to do with reason and order than with the modern impulse to say that politics is not really a proper human activity at all; the reluctance to give loyalty to any social organization which falls short of some ideal organization of the future may imply a disgust not so much with the merely national life as with civic life itself. And on the positive side too something is still to be said for nations, the case against them is not yet closed. Of course in literature nothing ever is said; every avowal of national pride or love or faith rings false and serves but to reinforce the tendency of rejection, as the example of the response to Kipling shows. Yet Kipling himself, on one occasion, dealt successfully with the national theme and in doing so implied the reason for the general failure—the "Recessional" hymn is a remarkable and perhaps a great national poem; its import of humility and fear at the moment of national success suggests that the idea of the nation, although no doubt a limited one, is still profound enough to require that it be treated with a certain measure of seriousness and truth-telling. But the occasion is exceptional with Kipling, who by the utterances that are characteristic of him did more than any writer of our time to bring the national idea into discredit.

Notes

[1] The war over, the struggle is on again.

[2] George Orwell's essay on Kipling in *Dickens, Dali and Others* deals bluntly and fairly with the implications of easy "liberal" and "aesthetic" contempt for everything Kipling stood for.

11.

T. S. Eliot

Swinburne As Poet

It is a question of some nicety to decide how much must be read of any particular poet. And it is not a question merely of the size of the poet. There are some poets whose every line has unique value. There are others who can be taken by a few poems universally agreed upon. There are others who need be read only in selections, but what selections are read will not very much matter. Of Swinburne, we should like to have the *Atalanta* entire, and a volume of selections which should certainly contain *The Leper, Laus Veneris,* and *The Triumph of Time*. It ought to contain many more, but there is perhaps no other single poem which it would be an error to omit. A student of Swinburne will want to read one of the Stuart plays and dip into *Tristram of Lyonesse*. But almost no one, today, will wish to read the whole of Swinburne. It is not because Swinburne is voluminous; certain poets, equally voluminous, must be read entire. The necessity and the difficulty of a selection are due to the peculiar nature of Swinburne's contribution, which, it is hardly too much to say, is of a very different kind from that of any other poet of equal reputation.

We may take it as undisputed that Swinburne did make a contribution; that he did something that had not been done before, and that what he did will not turn out to be a fraud. And from that we may proceed to inquire what Swinburne's

From *Selected Essays of T. S. Eliot;* reprinted by permission of Harcourt, Brace & World, Inc., New York, Faber and Faber Ltd., London.

contribution was, and why, whatever critical solvents we employ to break down the structure of his verse, this contribution remains. The test is this: agreed that we do not (and I think that the present generation does not) greatly enjoy Swinburne, and agreed that (a more serious condemnation) at one period of our lives we did enjoy him and now no longer enjoy him; nevertheless, the words which we use to state our grounds of dislike or indifference cannot be applied to Swinburne as they can to bad poetry. The words of condemnation are words which express his qualities. You may say "diffuse." But the diffuseness is essential; had Swinburne practiced greater concentration his verse would be, not better in the same kind, but a different thing. His diffuseness is one of his glories. That so little material as appears to be employed in *The Triumph of Time* should release such an amazing number of words, requires what there is no reason to call anything but genius. You could not condense *The Triumph of Time*. You could only leave out. And this would destroy the poem; though no one stanza seems essential. Similarly, a considerable quantity—a volume of selections—is necessary to give the quality of Swinburne although there is perhaps no one poem essential in this selection.

If, then, we must be very careful in applying terms of censure, like "diffuse," we must be equally careful of praise. "The beauty of Swinburne's verse is the sound," people say, explaining, "he had little visual imagination." I am inclined to think that the word "beauty" is hardly to be used in connection with Swinburne's verse at all; but in any case the beauty or effect of sound is neither that of music nor that of poetry which can be set to music. There is no reason why verse intended to be sung should not present a sharp visual image or convey an important intellectual meaning, for it supplements the music by another means of affecting the feelings. What we get in Swinburne is an expression by sound, which could not possibly associate itself with music. For what he gives is not images and ideas and music, it is one thing with a curious mixture of suggestions of all three.

> Shall I come, if I swim? wide are the waves, you see;
> Shall I come, if I fly, my dear Love, to thee?

This is Campion, and an example of the kind of music that is not to be found in Swinburne. It is an arrangement and choice of words which has a sound-value and at the same time a coherent comprehensible meaning, and the two things—the musical value and meaning—are two things, not one. But in Swinburne there is no *pure* beauty—no pure beauty of sound, or of image, or of idea.

> Music, when soft voices die,
> Vibrates in the memory;
> Odours, when sweet violets sicken,
> Live within the sense they quicken.
> Rose leaves, when the rose is dead,
> Are heaped for the beloved's bed;
> And so thy thoughts, when thou art gone,
> Love itself shall slumber on.

I quote from Shelley, because Shelley is supposed to be the master of Swinburne; and because his song, like that of Campion, has what Swinburne has not—a beauty of music and a beauty of content; and because it is clearly and simply expressed, with only two adjectives. Now, in Swinburne the meaning and the sound are one thing. He is concerned with the meaning of the word in a peculiar way: he employs, or rather "works," the word's meaning. And this is connected with an interesting fact about his vocabulary: he uses the most general word, because his emotion is never particular, never in direct line of vision, never focused; it is emotion reinforced, not by intensification, but by expansion.

> There lived a singer in France of old
>   By the tideless dolorous midland sea.
> In a land of sand and ruin and gold
>   There shone one woman, and none but she.

You see that Provence is the merest point of diffusion here. Swinburne defines the place by the most general word, which has for him its own value. "Gold," "ruin," "dolorous": it is not merely the sound that he wants, but the vague associations of idea that the words give him. He has not his eye on a particular place, as:

> Li ruscelletti che dei verdi colli
> Del Casentin discendon giuso in Arno . . .

It is, in fact, the word that gives him the thrill, not the object. When you take to pieces any verse of Swinburne, you find always that the object was not there—only the word. Compare

> Snowdrops that plead for pardon
> And pine for fright

with the daffodils that come before the swallow dares. The snowdrop of Swinburne disappears, the daffodil of Shakespeare remains. The swallow of Shakespeare remains in the verse in *Macbeth;* the bird of Wordsworth

> Breaking the silence of the seas

remains; the swallow of "Itylus" disappears. Compare, again, a chorus of *Atalanta* with a chorus from Athenian tragedy. The chorus of Swinburne is almost a parody of the Athenian: it is sententious, but it has not even the significance of commonplace.

> At least we witness of thee ere we die
> That these things are not otherwise, but thus. . . .
> Before the beginning of years
> There came to the making of man
> Time with a gift of tears;
> Grief with a glass that ran. . . .

This is not merely "music"; it is effective because it appears to be a tremendous statement, like statements made in our dreams; when we wake up we find that the "glass that ran" would do better for time than for grief, and that the gift of tears would be as appropriately bestowed by grief as by time.

It might seem to be intimated, by what has been said, that the work of Swinburne can be shown to be a sham, just as bad verse is a sham. It would only be so if you could produce or suggest something that it pretends to be and is not. The world of Swinburne does not depend upon some other world which it simulates; it has the necessary completeness and self-sufficiency for justification and permanence. It is impersonal, and no one else could have made it. The deductions are true to the postulates. It is indestructible. None of the obvious complaints that were or might have been brought to bear upon the first *Poems and Ballads* holds good. The poetry is not morbid, it is not erotic, it is not destructive. These are adjectives which can be applied to the material, the human feelings, which in Swinburne's case do not exist. The morbidity is not of human feeling but of language. Language in a healthy state presents the object, is so close to the object that the two are identified.

They are identified in the verse of Swinburne solely because the object has ceased to exist, because the meaning is merely the hallucination of meaning, because language, uprooted, has adapted itself to an independent life of atmospheric nourishment. In Swinburne, for example, we see the word "weary" flourishing in this way independent of the particular and actual weariness of flesh or spirit. The bad poet dwells partly in a world of objects and partly in a world of words, and he never can get them to fit. Only a man of genius could dwell so exclusively and consistently among words as Swinburne. His language is not, like the language of bad poetry, dead. It is very much alive, with this singular life of its own. But the language which is more important to us is that which is struggling to digest and express new objects, new groups of objects, new feelings, new aspects, as, for instance, the prose of Mr. James Joyce or the earlier Conrad.

12.

Austin Warren

Instress of Inscape: Gerard Manley Hopkins

The early Hopkins follows Keats and the "medieval school" (as he called the Pre-Raphaelites). The latest Hopkins, who wrote the sonnets of desolation, was a poet of tense, economic austerity. Their nearest parallel I can summon would be Donne's "holy sonnets": "Batter my heart" and "If poisonous minerals." For the mode of "Andromeda" and the later sonnets (1885–1889), Hopkins himself projected "a more Miltonic plainness and severity": He was thinking of Milton's sonnets and the choruses of *Samson.* In 1887 he invoked another name: "My style tends always more towards Dryden."

The middle period, which opens with the "Wreck of the Deutschland" (1885) and closes with "Tom's Garland" and "Harry Ploughman," both written in 1885, is the period of experiment. But it is also the most Hopkinsian—the most specially his own.

Middle Hopkins startles us by its dense rich world, its crowded Ark, its plenitude and its tangibility, its particularity of thing and word. There is detailed precision of image ("rose moles all in stipple upon trout that swim"). The poet is enamored of the unique, the "abrupt self."

The exploration of Middle Hopkins—its style, the view of life and art implicit in its style—may well start from the institutions and movements from which the poet learned, in which he participated. The motifs are the Ritualist Movement, Pre-Raphaelitism, Aestheticism, linguistic renovation, England, the Catholic church. In Hopkins' celebration of the sensuous, the concrete, the particular—his "instress of the inscapes"—all of these converge.

As a Catholic, Hopkins was an incarnationist and a sacramentalist: the sacraments are the extensions of the Incarnation. As a Catholic he believed that man is a compound of matter and form and that his body, resurrected, will express and implement his soul through all eternity. "Man's spirit will be flesh-bound when found at best. But unencumbered. . . ." Like all Catholic philosophers, he believed in an outer world independent of man's knowing mind—he was, in the present sense of the word, a "realist."

Hopkins was an Englishman, of a proud and patriotic sort. This is not always remembered, partly because he became the priest of a church viewed by other Englishmen as Continental, or Italian, or international. But there is an English way of being Catholic. Hopkins was not an "old Catholic" of the sturdy, unemotional variety nourished on Challoner's *Garden of the Soul;* no convert could be that. But, like his admired Newman, and unlike Manning and Faber (also converts), he was "Gallican," not ultramontane; British, not Italian, in his devotional life and rhetoric. He remembers when England was Catholic, when the pilgrims frequented the shrine of Our Lady of Walsingham.

> Deeply surely I need to deplore it,
> Wondering why my master bore it,
> The riving off that race
> So at home, time was, to his truth and grace
> That a starlight-wender of ours would say
> The marvelous Milk was Walsingham Way
> And one—but let be, let be:
> More, more than was will yet be.

The four real shapers of Hopkins' mind were all Britons; we might go farther and say that all were British empiricists

—all concerned with defending the ordinary man's belief in the reality and knowability of things and persons.

Two of them were encountered at Oxford. Pater, who remained his friend, was one of his tutors. Against the abstractions of the academic world, Pater boldly defended the concrete—in the visual arts and music, in perception. "Every moment some form grows perfect in hand or face, some tone on the hills or the sea is choicer than the rest. . . ." Though Hopkins could not conceivably have written so representatively, abstractly ("hills. . . . sea. . . . choicer") the famous Conclusion to *The Renaissance* pleads for a stressing of the inscapes. Hopkins followed some lectures by Pater on Greek philosophy; perhaps he heard, in an earlier version, Pater's lectures on Plato and Platonism, in which, with monstrous effrontery, the Doctrine of Ideas was praised as giving contextual interest to the concrete.

With Ruskin, whose *Modern Painters* he read early and admiringly, Hopkins revolted against the neoclassical grandeur of generality praised by Johnson and expounded by Reynolds. The influence of Ruskin—art medievalist, devout student of clouds, mountains, trees—is pervasive in Hopkins' sketches (five of which are reproduced in the *Note-Books*) and in his journalizing, his meticulously technical descriptions of church architecture (often neo-Gothic) and scenery.

Hopkins follows the general line of Ruskin in more than art. He does not find the humanly satisfactory and well-furnished world such an effect of its Creator as the watch of the watchmaker. Nor does he, after the fashion of some mystics and Alexandrians, dissolve Nature into a system of symbols translating the real world of the Spirit. Like Ruskin, he was able to recover the medieval and Franciscan joy in God's creation. And, like Ruskin, he protested against an England which is "seared with trade. . . . and wears man's smudge." His political economy, as well as it can be construed, was Ruskinian—what may be called tory socialist or distributist.

It was to Newman, his great predecessor, that Hopkins wrote upon deciding to become a Roman Catholic. And Newman's closest approach to a philosophical work, his *Grammar of Assent* (1870), interested Hopkins enough so that in 1883 he planned to publish (had Newman agreed) a commentary on it. There were marked temperamental and intellectual differences between the men. Newman, much the more complex and psychologically subtle, could feel his way into other men's minds as Hopkins could not. Hopkins was the closer dialectician and scholar. He did not share Newman's distrust of metaphysics (including the scholastic), his tendency to fideism; but he was, like Newman—in words the latter used of Hurrell Froude—"an Englishman to the backbone in his severe adherence to the real and the concrete."

The great medieval thinker who most swayed Hopkins' spirit to peace, Duns Scotus, was also a Briton, had been an Oxford professor. He was "of reality the rarest-veinéd unraveler": he was able to analyze, disengage from the complex in which they appear, the thinnest, most delicate strands ('vein' may be either anatomical or geological). Perhaps "rarest-veinéd unraveler" is a kind of kenning for the philosopher's epithet, the Subtle Doctor. Scotus, the Franciscan critic of the Dominican Aquinas, was centrally dear to Hopkins as undertaking the philosophical validation of the individual. In the individual's relation to his species, Aquinas taught that the "matter" individuates, while the "form" is generic: that is, that the individuals of a species reproductively multiply their common originative pattern. Scotus insisted that each individual has a distinctive "form" as well: a *haecceitas*, or thisness, as well as a generic *quidditas*, or whatness.

After having discovered this medieval Franciscan, Hopkins, upon "any inscape of sky or sea," thought of Scotus. The word, of Hopkins' coinage, occurs already in his Oxford notebooks. Modeled presumably on "landscape," "inscape" stands for any kind of formed or focused view, any pattern discerned in the natural world. A central word in his vocabulary and central motif in his mental life, it traverses some range of meaning: from sense-perceived pattern to inner form. The prefix seems to imply a contrary, an outerscape: that is, an "inscape" is not mechanically or inertly present but requires personal action, attention, a seeing and a seeing into.

The earliest "Notes for Poetry" cite: "Feathery rows of young corn. Ruddy, furred and branchy tops of the elms backed by rolling clouds." "A beautiful instance of inscape *sided* on the *slide,* that is successive sidings on one inscape, is seen in the behavior of the flag flower." In 1873, two years before the "Deutschland," he "saw a shoal of salmon in the river and many hares on the open hills. Under a stone hedge was a dying ram: there ran slowly from his nostrils a thick flesh-coloured ooze, scarlet in places, coiling and roping its way down so thick that it looked like fat."

He made notes on ancient musical instruments and on gems and their colors: "beryl—watery green; carnelian—strong flesh red, Indian red. . . ." His love of precise visual observation never lapsed, nor did his taste for research. Like Gray, he had a meticulous antiquarianism, suited to botany or archeology, to notes and queries, details, studies in place names, amateur etymologies.

Perhaps his most brilliant prose celebrates the Self and its wonders: "That taste of myself, of I and me above and in all things, which is more distinctive than the taste of ale or alum." Other selves were mysterious. As a shy man, he found it easier to reach natural "inscapes." He wrote no psychological portraits matching for sharpness and delicacy his notations of ash trees. The men in his poems are seen as from a distance—sympathetically but generically.

But he gloried in the range and repertory of mankind. Chesterton was concerned that, lying down with the lamb, the lion should "still retain his royal ferocity"; and Hopkins, also, wanted monks to be mild and soldiers to be pugnacious. He imagined Christ incarnate again as a soldier. He didn't want other men to be like himself; he was drawn to his anti-types—to soldiers; miners; Felix Randall, the blacksmith, and Harry, the ploughman; to manual laborers. Moreover, each of these men he wished to be functioning not only characteristically but intensely, violently, dangerously—on their mettle, like the Windhover, like Harry Ploughman, like the sailor of the "Eurydice" who, "strung by duty, is strained to beauty."

In poetry he desired both to record inscapes and to use words as objects. His was a double particularity.

Poetry, he wrote shortly before composing the "Deutschland," is "speech framed to be heard for its own sake and interest even over and above its interest of meaning. Some (subject) matter and meaning is essential to it but only as an element necessary to support and employ the shape which is contemplated for its own sake. Poetry is in fact speech for the inscape's sake—and therefore the inscape must be dwelt on."

In 1862 he was already collecting words. The earliest entries in the *Note-Books* are gritty, harshly tangy words, "running the letter,": "grind, gride, grid, grit, groat, grate" and "crock, crank, kranke, crick, cranky." He collected dialectal equivalents: "whisket" for "basket," "grindlestone" for "grindstone." He notes linguistic habits: that an observed laborer, when he began to speak "quickly and descriptively—dropped or slurred the article." He attends to, and tries to define, the sundry modes of Latin pronunciation. He inquires concerning the character of the Maltese language; wants to learn Welsh—not primarily in order to convert the local Wesleyans back to their ancestral faith.

In his early poetry Hopkins followed Keats and the "medieval school." Even in his middle style there remain vestiges of the earlier decorative diction, frequent use of "beauty," "lovely," "dear," "sweet" ("that sweet's sweeter ending"). But as early as 1866, "The Habit of Perfection," though dominantly "medieval," anticipates the later mode:

> This ruck and reel which you remark
> Coils, keeps, and teases simple sight.

"The Wreck of the Deutschland" (1875) inaugurates Hopkins' middle period (his first proper mastery). The diction is quite as extraordinary as the rhythm. Characteristic are homely dialectal words, sounding like survivors from Old English, and compound epithets suggestive of the same archetype. From the concluding stanzas of the "Deutschland" come these lines:

> Mid-numbered He in three of the thunder-throne!
> Not a dooms-day dazzle in his coming nor dark as he came....

and

> Dame, at our door
> Drowned, and among our shoals,
> Remember us in the roads, the heaven-haven of the Reward.....

From "The Bugler's First Communion":

> Forth Christ from cupboard fetched, how fain I of feet
> To his youngster take his treat!
> Low-latched in leaf-light housel his too huge godhead.

That Hopkins was influenced by Old English poetry is an easy assumption. In his excellent *New Poets from Old: A Study in Literary Genetics,* Henry Wells observes that all the technical features representative of that poetry appear conspicuously in Hopkins; judge him far nearer to Cynewulf than to Chaucer; and finds a plausible parallel to a passage in *Beowulf.* But, by his own statement, Hopkins did not learn Anglo-Saxon until 1882 and seems never to have read either *Beowulf* or Cynewulf. In any case, he was already a student of Welsh poetry and an attentive reader of linguistic monographs. Like Pound and Eliot, he belongs among the poets who can be incited to poetry by scholars' prose.

In 1873–1874, while teaching a course in rhetoric at Manresa House, Hopkins wrote the observations collected in the *Note-Books.* In his notes he used the 1859 *Lectures on the English Language* by the American scholar, George P. Marsh, a book calculated to incite a poet. Marsh has a real interest in the future (as well as the past) of the language and a real interest in the literary (as well as the pragmatic) use of words. The whole direction of his book suggests that literary experiment can find much to its purpose in literary history and that new poetry can be engendered by old. Ending his lecture on "Accentuation and Double Rhymes," he urges: "We must enlarge our stock [of rhyming words] by the revival of obsolete words and inflections from native sources," or introduce substitutes for rhyme; in the following chapter he excitingly discusses alliteration (with illustrations from *Piers Plowman*), consonance, e.g., "bad, led"; "find, band" (with illustrations from Icelandic poetry and invented English examples), and assonance (with illustrations from the Spanish). Hopkins' quotations from *Piers* are Marsh's; only in 1882 did he study *Piers,* and then without admiration, regarding its verse as a "degraded and doggerel" form of Anglo-Saxon sprung rhythm.

To both Bridges and Dixon, curious concerning the new poetic method of the "Deutschland," Hopkins says nothing of Old English or of *Piers Plowman* but speaks of nursery rhymes, the choruses of Milton's *Samson,* and his readings in Welsh poetry (which he began studying in 1875). "The chiming of the consonants I get in part from the Welsh, which is very rich in sound and imagery." Traits common to Old English and Middle Hopkins (scant use of articles, prepositions, and pronouns; constant use of compound words) are shared by both with Welsh poetry.

There is a third lineage for the diction of Hopkins. Through Barnes and Furnivall, at least, he derives from an imprecisely defined group of Victorian historians and philologists, who challenged the dominance of the Latin and Romance—the "civilized," learned, abstract—elements in our language. One of these linguistic protestants was the Oxford historian, E. A. Freeman, who chronicled the Norman Conquest and himself resisted it. As early as 1846 he was praising the Teutonic part of our language as affording "expressions mostly of greater strength than their Romance synonyms for all purposes of general literature"; and he used the phrase "pure English" for a diction purged of these synonyms. Another Anglicizer was F. J. Furnivall, a founder, in 1864, of the Early English Text Society, and a constant editor of texts, who began his intellectual career under the influence of Ruskin and Maurice and declared that his interest in early literature was not linguistic but social. Another founder of the E.E.T.S., R. C. Trench, gave a chapter of his *English, Past and Present* (1855) to a consideration of "English as it might have been" without a Norman Conquest. Though our present cerebral and technical words derive from the classical languages, he argues that the Anglo-Saxon might have developed—chiefly by compounding, as German has done—such a vocabulary. Even "impenetrability" could have been matched, accurately, by "unthoroughfaresomeness." And theological language would be understood by farm hand as well as by scholar if we said "again-buying" for "redemption."

In the tradition of Trench, but much more violent, William Barnes lamented the linguistic conquest of English and declared the old stock still capable of extension by compounding. Instead of "photograph," we should say "sunprint" or "flameprint." Indeed, all our current Latinisms we should replace out of the "wordstores of the landfolk." Barnes's nominations are all flavorsome; samples are "overyearn" (commiserate), "gleecraft" (music), "outclear" (elucidate), "faithheart" (enthusiasm). He regretted the loss of "inwit" in place of "conscience"; and to serve instead of "subjective" and "objective" (those psychological-philosophical terms which Coleridge introduced from Germany) he suggested "inwoning" and "outwoning."

Barnes had something of a following among literary people; was publicly praised by Patmore, Gosse, Bridges, Hardy. His poetry, early read, Hopkins preferred to that of Burns, liking its "West Country instress." But he leaned most from the prose. Barnes's *Speechcraft* [i.e., Grammar], says Hopkins, is "written in an unknown tongue, a soul of modern Anglo-Saxon, beyond all that Furnival in his wildest Forewords ever dreamed. . . . It makes one weep to think what English might have been, for in spite of all that Shakespeare and Milton have done with the compound ["impure" English] I cannot doubt that no beauty in a language can make up for want of purity. In fact, I am learning Anglo-Saxon and it is a vastly superior thing to what we have." He cites Barnes's wonderous "pitches of suchness" (for "degrees of comparison"): "We *ought* to call them so, but alas!"

Hopkins' characteristic critical and philosophical terminology follows closely the counsel of Trench and Barnes: that is, it is a compounding of Old English roots and suffixes to suit new needs and to replace Latinic terms. "Inwit" (for "conscience") and Barnes's "inwoning" (subjective) may have suggested "instress" and "inscape." Hopkins explains his special use of "sake" (the being a thing has outside itself) by analytic parallel of the compounds "forsake," "namesake," "keepsake." The terminology of the *Comments on the Spiritual Exercises* (1880) is particularly Hopkinsian (e.g., "pitch," "stress," "burl"). To Bridges, Hopkins wrote of his manuscript book on rhythm, "It is full of new words, without which there can be no new science."

His doctrine of the language for poetry, nowhere exposited, we can infer to have been quite different. Archaism—the use of obsolete words for literary effect—he repudiated. His oddities (like "pashed," "fashed," "tucked," "degged") are generally dialectal; and it is safe to assume that his words of Old English lineage were collected and used by him as dialectal, still-spoken English: not 'inkhorn' terms but folk speech. Even when he thought he was improvising, he was—at least in one instance—remembering: his alleged coinage, "louched" (slouched, slouching) was, as Bridges observed, to be found in Wright's Dialect Dictionary.

Whenever Hopkins explained his words (as he always stood ready to do), their particularity, their compactness and detail, were manifest. "Stickles—Devonshire for the foamy tongues of water below falls." "Bole" is not only used by poets but seems technical and proper and in the mouth of timber merchants and so forth. Of "flit," questioned by a correspondent, he writes: "I myself always use it and commonly hear it used among our people. I think it is at least a North Country word, used in Lancashire, for instance."

His compoundings are another matter. Though analogues can be offered from Browning, Hopkins came to them, it is probable, by way of medieval poetry, English and Welsh, and by way of Marsh, Trench, and Barnes. His defense would doubtless be that to compound freely was to restore to the English language a power it once had possessed. But the words thus compounded, or the root and suffix or prefix, were separately familiar and oral. He writes "spend-savour salt" (the salt which is spending its savor and on its way to being the biblical salt which has lost its savor); "bloomfall"; "trambeam"; "backwheels"; "though worlds of *wanwood leafmeal lie*" ("leafmeal" is on the model of "piecemeal"; suffix means "by bits," "by portions").

Judged by its effect and its internal intent, Hopkins' poetry finds partial parallels in Holst, Delius, and Vaughan Williams. Avoiding the archaism of Warlock and Dolmetsch, they sought to resume the line of English music where its genuine succession was interrupted—at the Restoration, and to go creatively back to the English glory of folksong and madrigal and the modal scales, to Dowland, Bull, and Byrd. Similarly, Hopkins seems to be reaching back, while he is reaching forward, to an "English" poetry. Probably, we may add, to an "English Catholic" poetry; and suppose that his pushing back of the Elizabethans had some incentive in his desire to get back of the Reformation to an England at once Catholic and English.

Like the poetry of the bards and the scops, Hopkins' poetry is oral, yet not conversational but formal and rhetorical. It uses dialectal words without intending, like Barnes's *Poems of Rural Life,* to be local and homely; it uses folk words in "serious" poetry. Hopkins' poems were written for an ideal audience, never existent in his day or ours, composed of literarily perceptive countrymen and of linguistically adept and folk-minded scholars. What his poetry assumed as convention, he had, by artifice, to create. "The Wreck" and "Tom's Garland" suggest or predict a greater poetry than they achieve. Hopkins' experiments are yet more important than his achievement; his comparative failures more interesting than his good "whole poems."

The ideal of poetry must be to instress the inscapes without splintering the architecture of the universe and, expressionally, to make every word rich in a way compatible with a more than additively rich total poetic structure. But in Hopkins' poems, the word, the phrase, the "local excitement," often pulls us away from the poem. And in the more ambitious pieces, the odes as we may call them ("The Wreck," "Spelt form Sibyl's Leaves," "Nature Is A Heraclitean Fire"), there is felt a discrepancy between texture and structure: the copious, violent detail is matched by no corresponding intellectual or mythic vigor. Indeed, "The Wreck of the Deutschland" is an "occasional," commissioned piece at which Hopkins works devotedly and craftfully, like Dryden at his *Annus mirabilis,* but which, like Dryden's poem, falls apart. Hopkins was not a story-teller, and he was not able to turn his wrecks into myths of wreck; they remain historical events accompanied by commentary. "The Bugler-Boy" and other poems suffer from the gap between the psychological naïveté and the purely literary richness. To try prose paraphrases of the middle poems is invariably to show how thin the "thinking" is. Hopkins' mind was first aesthetic and then technical: he reasoned closely upon metaphysical and prosodic matters. But his reflections upon beauty, man, and nature—his humanistic thoughts—are not distinguished.

The meaning of Hopkins' poems hovers closely over the

text, the linguistic surface. The rewarding experience of concern with them is to be let more and more into words and their ways, to contemplate the protopoetry of derivation and metaphorical expansion, to stress the inscapes of the English tongue.

13.

W. W. Robson

Pre-Raphaelite Poetry

The poets of the Victorian age were numerous, and they included some people of talent and even of genius. But the greatest imaginative writers of the period are novelists, not poets. The reasons for this decline of poetry are disputable, but the fact of the decline itself can hardly be questioned. For Victorian poetry, though it often reaches a high degree of sophistication and shows a conscious care for style and form, does not satisfactorily embody the life of the age; it is not at its best when it tries to put to poetic use a wide range of the emotional, intellectual, and moral interests of an intelligent adult. It is usually more successful when it either ignores these or transposes them, by more or less subtle means, into some mode of evasion. And this is true even of the poets who dutifully attempt to grapple with the world they lived in; who offer thought, or a moral burden for the times; since their success as poets, when they are truly poets, is significantly *like* the achievement of their avowedly undidactic successors: in creating a dream world; in withdrawing to memories of childhood over which a glamour of ideality is thrown; or in making incantation, decoration, emotional overtones, and other incidental beauties of style, serve as beguiling substitutes for the centrality of themes, and completeness of command of them, characteristic of great poetry. This comes out clearly when we consider the nature of the contrast between the good and the bad things in Tennyson's work. But it can also be said of Matthew Arnold's: which is a striking tribute to the strength of "tradition" in limiting "the original talent" not robust enough to oppose it. Browning's case is rather different; but even he cannot be considered a triumphant exception.

Perhaps Arnold had this contemporary situation in mind when he made his celebrated formulation: "Poetry is at bottom a *criticism of life*." Certainly he was the opponent, in his critical propaganda, of a trend which he discerned in the work of the great Romantic poets: a separation between "poetry" and "life." It is these poets whose joint influence constitutes the Victorian poetic tradition. And the influence of none of them—not even Wordsworth's—was such as to counteract the trends which Arnold saw. One of them, indeed, was a chief inspiration and sanction to poets in the phase of Victorian Romanticism succeeding that of Tennyson and Ruskin; the original high priest of their Religion of Beauty was John Keats.

The Religion of Beauty is today somewhat *en baisse*. The work of the Pre-Raphaelites (like that of their successors in the Aesthetic Movement) is now generally judged to be not only inferior to, but in some ways deeply unlike, that of Keats. Pre-Raphaelite poetry is seen to bear a derivative and subordinate relation to that of the great Romantics, and even to the contemporary poetry of Tennyson and Browning. Its relation to Tennyson I shall discuss presently; I shall merely note here that the influence of Browning on Rossetti (as in *Jenny*) has not often been emphasized; and, correlatively, there is a "Pre-Raphaelite" element in Browning:

> Only, they see not God, I know,
> Nor all that chivalry of his,
> The soldier-saints who, row on row,
> Burn upward each to his point of bliss.
> *(The Flight of the Duchess)*

And so it is relevant to mention here a related symptom of this change of taste: the enlistment of Gerard Manley Hopkins as a "modern" poet, alongside T. S. Eliot and the later Yeats; and the consequent exalting of him above Tennyson and Browning, the official great poets of the Victorian period. Hopkins himself remains unmistakably a Victorian—as those who read him as a living poet are the first to acknowledge; but his art, the way in which he uses the resources of the English language, has been aptly characterized (by F. R. Leavis) as "un-Tennysonian." Pre-Raphaelite poetry, on the other hand, though not exactly like Tennyson's, contains far less that is likely, either by its matter or its manner, to disturb the admirer of Tennyson. And so it has suffered the neglect which has befallen other Victorian poetry of which the same could be said. My purpose here is not to suggest reasons for reversing this implicit verdict; nor to discuss whether other poets—notably Hopkins, but perhaps also Beddoes, Darley, or John Davidson—have better claims to be regarded as the true heirs of the great Romantics. I wish rather to consider what kind of interest Pre-Raphaelite poetry can be made to yield to the reader who shares, substantially, Arnold's view of the right relation between "poetry" and "life."

By "Pre-Raphaelite poetry" I mean the poetry of Dante Gabriel Rossetti (1828–1882), of his sister Christina (1830–1894), and of William Morris (1834–1896)—though other poets, from Swinburne to Yeats, have Pre-Raphaelite connections. D. G. Rossetti, the strongest personality and effective organizer of the group, deserves the chief critical attention. But he has hardly received it: His picturesque life and habit of confession have proved a biographical lure too strong for most critics. What is now known as the "cult of personality" existed among the Pre-Raphaelites themselves and their followers; and the flood of autobiography, memoirs, and letters has not yet subsided. I am not of course saying that Rossetti's private life is irrelevant to the study of his poetry; any more, or any less, than the relation between devoutness and morbidity in Christina Rossetti, or the activity of Morris as designer, printer, or propagandist of Socialism, is irrelevant to the study of theirs. These things have their importance even for the literary critic: But they must be recalled in their due place, as ancillaries, not as substitutes, for the study of poetry, which is the study of what poets do with words.

But at this point an obvious objection must be met. Is it proper, or useful, to discuss Pre-Raphaelite poetry without discussing Pre-Raphaelite theory and practice in painting? The term "Pre-Raphaelite" itself, as is well known, came to be used when the young Holman Hunt and the young J. E. Millais adversely criticized Raphael's *Transfiguration*, challenged the "classical" doctrines expounded by Sir Joshua Reynolds, and extolled the superior purity and simplicity of the Italian primitives. And the movement began, at the close of the 1840s, as an attempt to introduce into visual art, not only the qualities of medieval Italian painting, but the naturalistic accuracy of detail thought appropriate to the dawning age of science. But by the 1850s what is now associated with Pre-Raphaelite painting—the merely decorative neomedievalism, the subjectivity, the dreaminess—had become its dominant style. Painters were turning their eyes away from a contemporary industrial and urban world which was *ipso facto* hideous and hence, on Ruskinian principles, intractable to treatment in art. In any case, Rossetti himself—who is the literary critic's first concern—seems to have had no very intense interest in the philosophical basis of the early naturalism of Hunt and Millais. (The general lack of wide intellectual interests in the circle of Rossetti and Morris comes out clearly in contemporary accounts.) And that dogmatic concern with precision of detail, which excited the admiration of Ruskin and the scorn of Dickens, appears in Rossetti—the Rossetti of *Ecce Ancilla Domini*—only as a transient phase of style. He was always essentially a "literary" painter, and the Pre-Raphaelite Brotherhood was fundamentally literary and preoccupied with literature. A literary approach, therefore, seems to be quite in order.

The adjective "Pre-Raphaelite" in *literary* criticism suggests certain idiosyncrasies of style—sometimes they are hardly more than tricks—associated with the Rossettis and the early Morris. Yet many of them are to be seen in earlier poetry: in Tennyson's *Mariana* poems; in Coleridge's *Christabel* (which might be called the first Pre-Raphaelite poem); or in Keat's *The Eve of St. Mark*. There is the deliberate simplicity (or *simplesse*) of manner, often found in conjunction with that curious trick of particularizing, e.g. numbers:

> She had three lilies in her hand,
> And the stars in her hair were seven.
>
> (Rosetti, *The Blessed Damozel*)

There were five swams that ne'er did eat
The water-weeds, for ladies came
Each day, and young knights did the same,
And gave them cakes and bread for meat.
(Morris, *Golden Wings*)

There is the particularity of sensory detail, of which again the thematic relevance is not obvious; visual detail, as here:

Without, there was a cold moon up,
Of winter radiance sheer and thin;
The hollow halo it was in
Was like an icy crystal cup.
(Rosetti, *My Sister's Sleep*)

Or auditory detail:

Twelve struck. That sound, by dwindling years
Heard in each hour, crept off, and then
The ruffled silence spread again,
Like water that a pebble stirs.
Our mother rose from where she sat;
Her needles, as she laid them down,
Met lightly, and her silken gown
Settled: no other noise than that.
(*My Sister's Sleep*)

There is the archaizing and medievalizing, the cultivation of the ballad-mode and similar archaic forms, accompanied (especially in Morris) by a liking for archaic technical vocabulary:

"They hammer'd out my basnet point
Into a round salade," he said.
"The basnet being quite out of joint
Natheless the salade rasps my head."
(Morris, *Old Love*)

There is a characteristic Pre-Raphaelite taste in decoration, as in:

Raise me a dais of silk and down;
Hang it with vair and purple dyes;

Carve it in doves and pomegranates,
And peacocks with a hundred eyes;
Work it in gold and silver grapes,
In leaves and silver fleur-de-lys;
(Christina Rossetti, *A Birthday*)

But these are superficial traits of style. More important for the critic is the recurrence of certain habits of feeling; especially a mood associated with autumn, regarded as the season of listlessness, decay, desolation, death; never, in Pre-Raphaelite poetry, the "close bosom-friend of the maturing sun," but Tennyson's "spirit" that "haunts the year's last hours, Dwelling amid these yellowing bowers"; as in

. . . the sere
Autumnal springs, from many a dying year
Born dead;
(Rossetti, *The Stream's Secret*)

. . . the year grown old
A-dying mid the autumn-scented haze,
That hangeth o'er the hollow in the wold,
Where the wind-bitten ancient elms enfold
Grey church, long barn, orchard, and red-roofed stead,
Wrought in dead days for men a long while dead.
(Morris, *The Earthly Paradise: October*)

[Life's] very bud hangs cankered on the stalk,
Its very song-bird trails a broken wing,
Its very Spring is not indeed like Spring,
But sighs like Autumn round an aimless walk.
(Christina Rossetti, *Later Life*)

Finally, there is the habit suggested by such passages as these:

O thou who at Love's hour ecstatically
Unto my lips dost evermore present
The body and blood of Love in sacrament;
Whom I have neared and felt thy breath to be
The inmost incense of his sanctuary;
(Rossetti, *Love's Redemption*)

> This feast-day of the sun, his altar there
> In the broad west has blazed for vesper-song;
> And I have loitered in the vale too long
> And gaze now a belated worshipper.
>
> (Rossetti, *The Hill Summit*)

This is religiosity: the use of religious language for evocative purposes, by a man to whom real religion means nothing. But with this example we have left the Pre-Raphaelite group as a whole and become aware of the need to make distinctions; religiosity is not a characteristic of Morris's poetry: formal religion meant little to him, and he was not tempted to exploit its language in this way; neither was Christina Rossetti—though for an opposite reason. But it is significant that the last two passages quoted from Rossetti could be endlessly parallel in other Victorian poetry.

One feature all these examples have in common with each other, and with mid-Victorian poetry in general: their obvious literariness. In Rossetti especially, whether in his simple or his elaborate manner, one is conscious all the time of the artifice, the sophistication, of a poet using a diction and movement which he well knows to have been used before by other poets. There is little that is fresh, spontaneous, unliterary, immediate. The contrast with another poet-painter, William Blake, is illuminating. In reading Blake's successful poems (*O Rose, thou art sick,* for example) we do not merely hear words, we "see" things, and our "seeing" is not confined to mere visualization ("In my mind's eye, Horatio") ; since Blake's own "seeing" is an activity of the intelligence, manifesting itself in an almost clairvoyant power of notation of mental and spiritual realities. In a Rossetti sonnet—to show the contrast with Blake at its most extreme—our response is predominantly a response to *words,* words heavily charged with literary association and reminiscence; there is nothing that is strong in imagery or concrete in evocation:

> So it happeneth
> When Work or Will awake too late, to gaze
> After their life sailed by, and hold their breath.
> Ah! who shall dare to search through what sad maze
> Thenceforth their incommunicable ways
> Follow the desultory feet of Death?
>
> (*Known in Vain*)

We have only to ponder the metaphorical value of "sailed" or "maze" here, or the literal meaning of "incommunicable," to see how small a part they play in the total effect. The words seem to be "saying" a great deal, but to be "doing" very little; and when we look up the passage in its context, the impressiveness of this "saying" seems to be the *raison d'être* of the whole poem.

A care for finish of style and polish of phrasing takes the place of a scrupulous effort at definition of meaning. And when we admire the phrasing and music of

> Thenceforth their incommunicable ways
> Follow the desultory feet of Death?

and try to characterize more exactly the spirit of Rossetti's manipulation of the language, it is tempting to recall his Italian origin. But this use of English is an important part of English poetic history from Spenser and Milton to Keats and Tennyson. And the reservation we have about this use of language is not only that it leaves out, or does not employ creatively, so much that is centrally characteristic of English, the language of Shakespeare: its concrete expressiveness and mimetic vigor, its colloquial force, and the much richer music that arises from the playing-off of its speaking rhythm against the patterns of formal meter. It is not merely that the "Italianate" use of English deprives it of the typically English energy of the verbs. The great limitation of the "music" cultivated by Tennyson and Rossetti is that it is a medium unsuited to precise expression *of any kind*. This, no doubt, could be said to some extent of its earlier phases of development, in Spenser or in Milton. But it would be easy to find passages from those earlier poets in which there is plenty of general mental activity going on; whereas the Victorian development of this use of English, even in a "sage-poet" like Tennyson, tends towards confusion, vagueness, and a progressive emaciation of the *content* of poetry. Thus, while Swinburne has his own music, which is not Tennyson's or Rossetti's, his well-known sacrifices of sense to sound, his rhythmic self-intoxication, his hypnotic cadences, his hallucinations of meaning dissolving inextricably into one another, may be considered as an exotic variant of the same tradition.

What is most important, for critical purposes, in this verbal music, appears not so much in frankly incantatory peotry like much in the early Morris (*The Blue Closet,* for example), but in passages where the poet is making a sustained offer of thought and "message." It will be noted that the passage quoted above from Rossetti is sententious. And though Rossetti does not come before us, as Tennyson sometimes does, in the role of the Sage, but rather as a fellow-sufferer, his mature poetry is quite as sententious as Tennyson's, and ostensibly stakes quite as much on the reader's thoughtful acceptance of a message solemnly delivered. (Rossetti is never humorous or ironic in his successful poetry—at any rate, not in the *House of Life* sequence, where the moral-philosophical ambition is as apparent as the stylistic virtuosity.) And the admirer of Rossetti discovers "fundamental brainwork" even in the more lush and mannered specimens of his later style (*The Stream's Secret,* for example). But it seems fairest to verify the attribution of "fundamental brainwork" by considering a poem in which Rossetti appears to be offering a deliberated and credal affirmation of his religion of beauty. This is the famous sonnet *Sibylla Palmifera,* from which I quote the sestet:

> This is that Lady Beauty, in whose praise
> Thy voice and hand shake still,—long known to thee
> By flying hair and fluttering hem—the beat
> Following her daily of thy heart and feet,
> How passionately and irretrievably,
> In what fond flight, how many ways and days!

Those who do not dislike this poem are not likely to be persuaded to do so by detailed fault-finding. But such is not my intention: I wish merely to show, by a particular inspection of the way Rossetti uses words, that the poem does not owe what impressiveness it has to "fundamental brainwork," to the communication of anything precisely definied or clearly imagined; it is, rather, a gesture in a *general* direction, depending for its effect on the reader's anterior readiness for vague sympathy with the attitude suggested. Poetic skill is certainly there, in the means by which the despairing yet unchecked pursuit of "Beauty" is communicated by the delayed caesura of the fourth line, the assimilation through alliterativeness of the *"flying* hair" and *"fluttering* hem" to the poet's "Following"; and, more subtly, by the breathlessness conveyed in the associated aspirates in "hair" and "hem" and "heart and feet." But it is a skill which does little but display itself; we are merely *told* what this ardent though desperate pursuit, of which we are given a general sense, is a pursuit *of*; "Beauty" remains something only vaguely gestured at, as in the poem's opening:

> Under the arch of life, where love and death,
> Terror and mystery, guard her shrine, I saw
> Beauty enthroned . . .

If we dislike the poem, we will be inclined to say that "Beauty" from beginning to end remains as much a mere word as "life," "love," "death," "terror," and "mystery" in this poem. And if we find ourselves resisting the hierophantic manner of the opening lines, we may be provoked in reaction to a closer examination of the seeming impressiveness of phrasing, the appearance of lapidary conciseness, exemplified in the sestet—" . . . in whose praise/Thy voice and hand shake still." If we reflect for a moment—which the lines do not encourage us to do—on the meaning of "shake" here, it will appear that whatever propriety the verb has in regard to the "voice" of the poet trembling in praise of "Beauty," it cannot have in regard to the "hand" (of the painter); the word "shake," in fact, represents the articulation of one vague meaning with another even vaguer. There is no real gnomic or graphic precision, only an appearance of it. Similarly with " . . . the beat/Following her daily of thy heart and feet": the appearance of compression, or effective zeugma, dissolves immediately we bring the meaning of the word "beat" here into focus. But bringing into focus is not, of course, what we are supposed to do. It is only the general effect that matters to the admirer of this poem; the predisposition to accept an attitude which is never more than suggested by the poet. But in compensation, the tone in which the suggestion is made combines grandiloquent expansiveness with unction. And it is on this tone of voice that objections will primarily centre; even the most sympathetic reader-aloud of the sonnet will find it hard to play down its unctuous rectitude:

> The alloted bondman of her palm and wreath.

It is significant that those who dislike this poem are usually told that they have an initial prejudice against its subject ("aestheticism"). But this retort in a way itself confirms the observations made above about the character of this sonnet; what is approved, or disapproved, by one reader or another, remains something *general,* something ouside the poem which the poem itself merely gestures at; what is found impressive, or unimpressive, as the case may be, is nothing more specific than a manner and a tone of voice.

Rossetti, of course, wrote much better poems than *Sibylla Palmifera.* Nor is the range of his powers best seen in things like *The Blessed Damozel,* charming as that is. His most interesting work, in my opinion, is his turbid, mannered love-poetry, with its characteristic alteration of the hectic and the languid, of over-ripe voluptuousness and the chill of desolation.

> Stand still, fond fettered wretch! while Memory's art
> Parades the Past before thy face, and lures
> Thy spirit to her passionate portraitures:
> Till the tempestuous tide-gates flung apart
> Flood with wild will the hollows of thy heart,
> And thy heart rends thee, and thy body endures.
>
> (*Parted Love*)

Over-sophisticated as this is, it has a certain power, though perhaps not of a very pleasing kind: the power of

> "O ye, all ye that walk in Willowwood,
> That walk with hollow faces burning white"; . . .
> Alas! the bitter banks in Willowwood,
> With tear-spurge wan, with blood-wort burning red.
>
> (*Willowwood*)

Willowwood is everywhere in this poetry: romantic idealization, and half-glimpsed behind it, its corollary of selfishness, and incapacity for a mutually respecting relation with another; ahead of it, the nemesis of inevitable disappointment, weariness with oneself, sense of irretrievable waste and loss. The Rossetti of *Barren Spring,* of *Lost Days,* of *"Retro Me Sathana!,"* could have echoed Baudelaire's:

> Mais mon coeur, que jamais ne visite l'extase,
> Est un théâtre où l'on attend
> Toujours, toujours en vain, l'être aux ailes de gaze!

But the comparison with Baudelaire reminds us that the Rossetti of such poems is still the Rosetti of *Sibylla Palmifera.* They reveal subtler ways in which the poetry insinuates an over-valuation of the experience it presents, but their limitation is essentially the same; the temptation, yielded to by the poet, to find in spiritual sickness the occasion for suggesting a spiritual superiority. That temptation is insidious, and I do not say that Baudelaire always overcame it; but his greatness is surely that he succeeded, in his finest poems, in diagnosing his own malady, and thereby making us see his own very special case in relation to more universal feelings, principles of health, and moral judgments. If Baudelaire's weaknesses as a poet are due to his Romanticism, his strength is that he was able at times to turn it into a creative force. Rossetti's guilt, remorse, and sensation of spiritual bankruptcy remain egocentric. The result is that doom of the emotionalist: monotony; the monotony which so soon afflicts the reader of his poetry, small in bulk though it is. Worse still is the pretentiousness which commonly accompanies the over-valuing of one's experience:

> Because our talk was of the cloud-control
> And moon-track of the journeying face of Fate,
> Her tremulous kisses faltered at love's gate
> And her eyes dreamed against a distant goal:
> But soon, remembering her how brief the whole
> Of joy, which its own hours annihilate,
> Her set gaze gathered thirstier than of late,
> And as she kissed, her mouth became her soul.
>
> (*Secret Parting*)

The relation of the highfalutin of the opening to what follows is very obvious and very distasteful; the last line of the quotation is curiously vulgar. It is clear that the Meredith of *Modern Love* had forerunners.

But that is Rossetti at his worst. And there is at least one poem in which we glimpse a remarkable freshness and directness of perception, which suggest that Rossetti's potentialities as a poet were greater than his achievement. I am thinking of *Song IV* in the *House of Life,* the poem called *Sudden Light,* which begins:

> I have been here before,
> But when or how I cannot tell:
> I know the grass beyond the door,
> The sweet keen smell,
> The sighing sound, the lights around the shore.

From the first line onwards we have an unusually direct presentment of an individual's experience in a sensitively particularized situation. This particularity is very different from anything in *The Blessed Damozel*: It contributes functionally to the recreation of that peculiar state, at once one of bewilderment and of clarity ("sudden light"). We notice how it brings in a lightness, a fresh air, "the sweet keen smell"—so un-Rossettian, un-Pre-Raphaelite, un-Tennysonian. The "sighing" is no mere poeticality; it is precise in evocation, and the stanza as a whole, with all its rich suggestiveness, has no incantation, but rather the effect of statement.

But for critical purposes, the stanza in its context can only confirm the general judgment on Rossetti's poetry. For the poem modulates back into a familiar Pre-Raphaelite key: the static, dreamy atmosphere, which has not the transitory vividness of real dreams, but rather the insubstantiality of a waking dream or reverie:

> Shall we not lie as we have lain,
> Thus for Love's sake,
> And sleep, and wake, yet never break the chain?

In view of Rossetti's love-poetry in general, with its ardors, hungers, opiates, and derelictions, it is interesting to note the plausibility here lent to Freud's theory that the *déjà vu* sensation is associated with the wish to return to the mother. But here we reach the frontier between criticism and psychiatry. And we may leave Rossetti to pass the final judgment on his own work in those characteristic lines:

Look in my face: my name is Might-have-been;
I am also called No-more, Too-late, Farewell.
(*A Superscription*)

Christina Rossetti's poetry has the Rossetti skill and the careful concern with form and design, and it has a Pre-Raphaelite vocabulary and coloring. But it has none of the over-sophistication and artificiality of her brother's poetry; it is never lush or mannered; nor does it succumb to the temptations, gross or subtle, which beset the poet who must seek, as becomes a devotional poet, to express an attitute of humility and self-forgetfulness. It is significant that one finds oneself appraising her work in these negative terms. For negation, denial, deprivation are the characteristic notes of Christina's religious poetry: and it must be admitted that an extensive reading of it is depressing. The sadness, often morbidity, which is felt even in her delightful poetry for children, even in *Goblin Market,* certainly in *The Prince's Progress;* the felt absence of any outlet for aggressive impulses, deepening into depression or resignation; the compensating yearning for death imagined as an anodyne, an eternal anesthetic—these are familiar to every reader of her poetry. And it is difficult to find many poems in which she either transcends them or turns them into the conditions for major creation.

One of the rare occasions on which her religion appears in her poetry as a source of revival and refreshment is the (significantly titled) sonnet *A Pause:*

They made the chamber sweet with flowers and leaves,
And the bed sweet with flowers on which I lay;
While my soul, love-bound, loitered on its way.
I did not hear the birds about the eaves,
Nor hear the reapers talk among the sheaves:
Only my soul kept watch from day to day,
My thirsty soul kept watch for one away: —
Perhaps he loves, I thought, remembers, grieves.
At length there came the step upon the stair,
Upon the lock the old familiar hand:
Then first my spirit seemed to scent the air
Of Paradise; then first the tardy sand

Of time ran golden; and I felt my hair
Put on a glory, and my soul expand.

The simplicity and naturalness of this writing, the trace of the speaking (not intoning) voice:

Perhaps he loves, I thought, remembers, grieves

The exquisite good taste and spiritual good manners (if the expression be permitted) of the way in which the two worlds are related—the religious and the everyday—are characteristic distinctions of Christina's poetry. And a comparison of her better-known *Sping Quiet* ("Gone were but the Winter") with Hopkins's early *Heaven-Haven* ("I have desired to go") brings out a certain community of temperament (though even the latter, slight as it is, has Hopkins's idiosyncrasy—"sharp *and sided* hail"). But it reminds us also that *Heaven-Haven,* unlike *Spring Quiet,* by no means represents a high point of its author's achievement.

The distinctiveness and the limitation of Christina Rossetti's talent are alike illuminated by the parallel her sonnet "Remember" offers to Shakespeare's 71st sonnet ("No longer mourn . . . "). Perhaps, indeed, she was remembering Shakespeare's poem when she wrote it.

Remember me when I am gone away,
Gone far away into the silent land;
When you can no more hold me by the hand,
Nor I half turn to go yet turning stay.
Remember me when no more day by day
You tell me of our future that you plann'd:
Only remember me; you understand
It will be too late to counsel then or pray.
Yet if you should forget me for a while
And afterwards remember, do not grieve:
For if the darkness and corruption leave
A vestige of the thoughts that once I had,
Better by far you should forget and smile
Than that you should remember and be sad.

The superficial similarity of theme does not disguise the deep difference between the two poems. Shakespeare's sonnet, though not one of his greatest, is characteristic of his best work in the Sonnets, in the effect it produces of a mind intent upon its argument, charged with the determination to deliver its meaning, and taking the emotional effect of that meaning so much for granted, that the poet can afford to deploy his statement in a highly formal, "logical" progression. For all the element of poignancy, the total effect is therefore akin to wit; the satisfactory following-through of an exaggeration, a hyperbole, to its completion. The result is that a poem which, on the face of it, expresses as much loving self-abnegation and tender humility as Christina's, conveys at the same time a graceful compliment and a hint of rebuke. And thus the *precise* value we are to give to Shakespeare's overt humiliation of himself and his poetry has been beautifully defined, and the beauty of this defining is the beauty of the poem. Christina's poem calls for no such subtle adjustment; the shy reserve, tenderness, and wistfulness of the speaker are presented simply and truthfully, and our acceptance of her truthfulness is bound up with our recognition of her authentic speaking voice:

> Yet if you should forget me for a while,
> And afterwards remember, do not grieve . . .

But by the time we reach the closing lines, with their (hardly successful) epigrammatic turn of phrasing which sends us back to the Shakespeare sonnet, we feel a slight discomfort with the poem; its modest acceptance of very limited pretension which makes it seem, if not mawkish, a little *mièvre:*

> Better by far you should forget and smile
> Than that you should remember and be sad.

The comparison with Shakespeare's sonnet leads us to call the other sonnet, with a limiting intention, "feminine": in the absence of the verve and chargedness there is felt to be a thinness, a lack of substance.

But what is also evident in this poem is the very welcome absence of anything like the sonorous and vatic manner, at one and the same time declamatory and embarrassingly intimate, which we associate with Mrs. Browning—and, perhaps, with one or two later women poets. If we pay Christina Rossetti the archaic compliment of calling her a lady, this will be understood to have no implication of snobbery.

The deprived, depressed, monotonous quality of her poetry is to be accounted for, as we know, very largely by the circumstances of her life and her renunciation. But in one form or another this is a common feature of Victorian Romantic poetry. And if we ignore the personal accent of Christina Rossetti, and the devotional vocabulary and setting of her poems, their moods and tones are immediately recognizable as moods and tones of the period. This is certainly not because of any affectation of fashionable melancholy on Christina's part: no poet could be more touchingly sincere and disinterested. Yet we may wonder if, had she been in contact with a tradition allowing the exercise, in serious verse, of her sharp wits and her astringency, the substance of her work might not have been more considerable and its styles more various. Certainly, after reading her poetry, we are keenly reminded of the advantages enjoyed by some seventeenth-century religious poets.

William Morris is, in my opinion, much the least interesting of the three poets considered here. What he can do best is illustrated in the early (1858) *Defense of Guinevere* volume, especially the title poem; yet we may find even that poem plaintive and picturesque, rather than rising to the tragic possibilities of its subject; and for the other poems in the volume only a limited compliment seems appropriate, such as that implied when we say they are "charming." Arnold, regretting Burn's background, remarked that it is a great advantage to the poet to live in a beautiful world; and so it must have seemed to the Morris of *Golden Wings:*

> Midways of a walled garden,
> In the happy poplar land,
> Did an ancient castle stand,
> With an old knight for a warden.
>
> Many scarlet bricks there were
> In its walls and old grey stone;
> Over which red apples shone
> At the right time of the year.

On the bricks the green moss grew,
    Yellow lichen on the stone,
    Over which red apples shone;
Little war that castle knew.

Deep green water fill'd the moat,
    Each side had a red-brick lip,
    Green and mossy with the drip
Of dew and rain. . . .

This is certainly charming. But the "beautiful world," from which everything harsh or disagreeable is excluded, turns out to be a daydream world and, in no very long run, an uninteresting one. Morris, of course, has his characteristic emotional tone, his pathos, in these shorter poems, and it might well be said that even the happier ones imply the sadness from which they withdraw. But in his poetry Morris's protest against the actual world is confined to the protest of ignoring it.

The Life and Death of Jason makes pleasant reading, but again one cannot feel that Morris has glimpsed the tragic power of the story he is telling; the sin of Jason seems to have little moral significance; the poet's activity as poet is directed, again, to charming incidentals of visual observation, of costume, color, and landscape. In *The Earthly Paradise,* however much Morris may have felt himself the successor of Chaucer, there is none of Chaucer's vigorous interest in and command of life in so many of its forms, the sense of *nihil humanum a me alienum puto*. Morris's interest is always in the picturesque, the decorative, in the romantic "feel" of the legends, as in the "northernness" of *Sigurd the Volsung*. When human beings are at the ostensible center of interest, there is a queer externality, difficult to illustrate convincingly just because it is so pervasive. Hence it would be futile to enter the controversy about *The Earthly Paradise*—if it not really poetry of escape, but a sociological sermon in the form of an allegory? Whatever Morris's deeper intention, no effective message of the kind he is credited with could be delivered in such verse.

We almost always have the sense in reading Morris's poetry —and indeed his prose romances, too—that what he is doing is quite marginal, quite apart from the main activities of his life.

Outside his poetry we know Morris as an energetic, strenuous figure and strong character, the last of the great Victorian "prophets," and more than a "prophet" in being a man of action and a maker. But in his poetry—even after his "Pre-Raphaelite" phase—we observe in an extreme, and a naïve form, the Pre-Raphaelite separation of "art" from "life." "Art" for Morris was essentially a relaxation, an amusement, something to do; writing poetry came easily to him, and he was not the poet to resist the temptations (of profusion and careless workmanship) inherent in being one's own publisher and printer:

> The fascination of what's difficult
> Has dried the sap out of my veins, and rent
> Spontaneous joy and natural content
> Out of my heart.

Morris the poet could not have applied to himself these words of Yeats. And it is significant that there is no parallel between *his* development and that of Yeats—who also began as a Pre-Raphaelite, born out of due time.[1] Indeed, 'development' is not a word with any obvious application to Morris's poetry. His work as translator of epic and saga—and the greater part of his verse is translation—shows him as responding to certain "romantic" qualities which may well be in his originals but which are not necessarily the most important there. The socialist songs have their merits, but they hardly concern the student of poetry.

It is difficult, then, to give Morris a high place purely as a writer. Even in the prose work, *News from Nowhere,* in which his dreamworld is realized more interestingly than in his poetry, it is still the impulse to "Forget six counties overhung with smoke" that predominates. His lack of human centrality, the lack of concentration and pressure in all his imaginative writing, the daydream habit of his verse, may be mainly attributed to his having other things to do. The expression of the robuster side of his nature was to be reserved for the Anti-Scrape Society, the settlement-house, and the socialist meeting; above all, for the noble effort to fulfill (in the world of Victorian industrialism, Karl Marx, and Mr. Podsnap) the prophecy of John Ruskin. But the poetic tradition which he accepted was not, anyway, calculated to encourage the expression of anything robust, and one of the most telling criticisms of it may be that it confined William Morris to minor poetry.

Note

[1] 'The dream-world of Morris was as much the antithesis of daily life as with other men of genius, but he was never conscious of the antithesis and so knew nothing of intellectual suffering:' W. B. Yeats, *Autobiographies*. (London, 1955), p. 175.

PART III Fiction

14. The Modern Values of Victorian Fiction

Lionel Stevenson

During the past twenty years, critical and scholarly opinion has undergone a radical transformation in its attitude toward the works of the mid-nineteenth-century novelists. Prior to the last war, the whole literature of the Victorian period languished in the depths of critical disfavor, and the novels were considered if possible even more contemptible than any of the other literary genres. When I was a graduate student I would scarcely have ventured to confess that I had read the works of Dickens, Thackeray, and the Bontës, let alone that I enjoyed them.

The principal reason for this neglect, of course, was the normal cycle of literary taste which inevitably revolts against the immediately preceding era, and only the more violently when that preceding era has been especially eminent and revered. As long as the Victorian age was reviled for smugness, sentimentality, and vulgar taste, the fiction that reproduced it so faithfully was bound to incur those strictures to the extremist degree.

A particular reason for the antipathy toward the novel was the rigid code of critical dogmas that began to come into effect after 1880. Henry James confidently proclaimed that the art of the novel depended essentially upon exact realism, with the corollary that the author's personal views and feelings ought to remain invisible. George Moore reinforced James's influence

Reprinted by permission of the author and the editor, *College Language Association Journal,* Vol. 4, No. 1 (September, 1960), 1–7.

by propagating the French naturalistic school's doctrine that fiction must depict human behavior—mainly its violent and bestial manifestations—with the ruthless impartiality of an anatomist's dissection.

Not only by practical example in their own novels but also by persuasion in their prefaces and critical essays, James and Moore established the primacy of realism so effectively that the English fiction of the preceding generation appeared hopelessly naïve and archaic. The authoritative treatises that were published in the 1900's, notably *The Craft of the Novel,* by Percy Lubbock, and *Aspects of the Novel,* by E. M. Forster, were written by devout Jamesians who could not conceive that his axioms could ever be challenged.

Being blissfully unaware of these austere axioms, the Victorian novelists had given emotional coloring to everything they wrote about; they had expressed their own attitudes and sympathies without constraint; they had written in individual styles that sometimes burst into the extravagance of oratory or the luxuriance of poetry; their complicated plots had often included melodramatic suspense or farcical absurdity; many of them were committed to overt social purpose, and yet paradoxically their earnest crusades were so mingled with genial laughter that literal-minded students could accuse them of irresponsibility.

The critics and scholars in the early twentieth century could not be oblivious to the fact that a great many people still enjoyed reading the fiction of the earlier era; but this became merely another count in the indictment. Anything that existed primarily to give pleasure to a wide indiscriminate audience was automatically debarred from the sacred canon of good literature.

A general revival of appreciation for Victorian literature was certain to occur as soon as the era faded far enough into the past to make possible a normal perspective. The artistic and intellectual stature of the Victorian authors, and their astonishing variety of achievement, began to be tentatively and grudgingly acknowledged by pontiffs of modern criticism such as T. S. Eliot and Edmund Wilson. As the tensions of this present age of anxiety increased, readers turned nostalgically to the literary landscape of an epoch that seemed to enjoy security and confidence. As soon as intelligent people started to read Victorian literature without preconceived notions, they discovered with amazement that the major authors, far from being the complacent optimists depicted in the accepted stereotype, were vitally concerned with the basic issues of social change and were distressed by most of the current trends of their century. A new explanation for the temporary eclipse of the great Victorians became apparent: the reading public of the early twentieth century had ignored them in an instinctive evasion of the disquieting warnings that the average person was unwilling to accept or even to perceive. The Victorians had been all too prescient in their anxiety about such a materialistic and competitive society as the modern world proceeded to adopt.

The Victorian novel naturally shared in the restored prestige of its period. The mid-nineteenth century was the first epoch when prose fiction had reached full parity with the other types of literature in critical esteem, and had surpassed them in popular appeal. Hence the combined opportunities of fame, profit, and influence attracted a wide assortment of ambitious and able authors, who might otherwise have expressed themselves in the older literary media. The energy and richness of Victorian fiction more than compensates for occasional deficiencies in technical skill. In fact, one of the most compelling reasons for studying Victorian fiction is that it offers a unique opportunity for observing a new literary genre in the very process of maturing. Each author was supplying his individual component, all were experimenting freely and borrowing from one another, while no rigid system of critical theory had yet come into existence to dictate practice and to prohibit innovation. By analysis of Victorian fiction we can learn a great deal about the processes of literary evolution.

To account for the abrupt accession of interest in the Victorian novelists, cynics may suggest that the pressure upon professors to find new material for publishable books and articles, and upon graduate students to select topics for dissertations, obliged them to venture beyond the approved areas of scholarly research, and that Victorian fiction by its very bulk proved to be a virtually inexhaustible territory for exploration. It is true that adequate interpretation and explication had been impossible without certain indispensable tools of a sort that can never be satisfactorily provided until a couple of generations have elapsed. The most noteworthy of these tools are Gordon Ray's massive edition of Thackeray's letters, Gordon Haight's of George Eliot's, Bradford Booth's of Trollope's, Edgar Johnson's exhaustive biography of Dickens and Ray's of Thackeray, all of which have appeared within the past fifteen years. Indeed, the solid three-volume Nonesuch collection of Dickens's letters, which was hailed as a scholarly landmark when it was published in 1938, is already so obsolete and undependable that a vast new edition, three or four times as extensive, is now in preparation.

Once provided with the essential sources of factual information, the analysers were able to work more confidently upon the novels. When Bradford Booth in 1945 cautiously started a journal to facilitate communication among the scattered scholars who shared his interest in Anthony Trollope, he was amazed by an inundation of articles on other Victorian novelists also; he changed the name of his periodical to *Nineteenth-Century Fiction*, and it is now firmly established among the important academic quarterlies.

The resurgence of Victorian fiction, however, cannot be attributed primarily to the quest for a new area of research, or to the provision of documents and biographical data and the establishment of new media of publication, or even to the general rehabilitation of all Victorian writers. A more definite reason can be found in the influence exerted upon critical theory by the psychological study of the unconscious.

The dominance of realism in the novels of the late nineteenth century was postulated upon the rationalistic assumptions of the physical scientists. Henry James concerned himself exclusively with the conscious processes in the minds of his characters; and in his determination to avoid overt discussion of them he was obliged to show the characters engaged in interminable analytical discussion of their own and one another's motives and attitudes. Even the naturalists, who claimed to be displaying the primitive instincts of their characters rather than the intelligent decisions, nevertheless accepted the scientific method of tracing a logical train of cause and effect in human conduct. The novelists of the early twentieth century, such as Wells and Galsworthy, who enlarged their focus to include the study of social groups and movements, were just as fully committed to scientific principles.

All this cool reasonableness was invalidated when the theories of Freud and Adler and Jung gained currency. The psychoanalysts concentrated upon the irrational element in behavior; and since prose fiction is the literary form best suited to detailed recording of what goes on within individuals, the novelists promptly undertook to find ways of revealing the inner processes that are not susceptible to coherent exposition.

To communicate the impression of dreams and reveries and all the divagations of each individual's reactions to experience, it became apparent that the novelist must use distortions, metaphors, rhythm, incongruity, and any other possible stimuli to emotional and imaginative response that they could devise. Moreover, the psychoanalysts soon joined hands with the cultural anthropologists to emphasize the primitive and traditional elements in our mental equipment. Myths, folklore, and fairy tales gained new significance. The theories of Miss Maude Bodkin and Miss Jessie Weston about archetypes and symbolic ritual exerted immense influence upon critics and creative writers alike. In the second decade of the twentieth century the most enterprising writers of fiction were seeking for methods of combining these age-old intuitions and legends with the sophisticated externals of modern civilization.

The experimental fiction of half a century ago seemed to be radically new because it broke away from the tedious uniformity of external realism. Ironically, however, scholars are now realizing that Lawrence and Joyce were at the same time paving the way for a restored appreciation of the Victorian novelists. Foreshadowings of the "stream of consciousness" have been recognized in early novels of Dickens, particularly in his studies of fear and guilt in such criminals as Bill Sikes and Jonas Chuzzlewit. Another recent critic has pointed out an affinity between Molly Bloom's drowsy reverie at the end of *Ulysses* and Flora Finching's scatterbrained conversation in *Little Dorrit*.

Once the shibboleths of external realism were abandoned, Dickens could no longer be dismissed as a mere caricaturist because he exaggerated and distorted the appearance and behavior of his characters, or as a mere sensationalist because he portrayed emotional agonies. Emily Brontë ceased to be regarded as a neurotic girl who spun an implausible horror-story out of her reading of Byron. George Meredith was relieved of the stigma of wilful obscurity and gratuitously oblique implications.

One result of the changed critical attitude has been a weakening of the artificial barrier between prose fiction and poetry. Simile and metaphor, rhythm and echo, fantasy and symbol are now accepted as serving valid functions in a novel as well as in a poem. And this in turn has led to a more exact study of the art of fiction. The old assumption used to be that the Victorian novelists were "natural story-tellers" who simply rambled on through interminable sequence of confused episodes. Now students are discovering structural design, verbal patterns, recurrent images, symbolic correspondences, and all manner of other technical subtleties that were previously invisible mainly because a novel is so much larger and more complex than a poem that its minute aesthetic details are less conspicuous.

In the long run, the chief value of the revulsion in critical and scholarly opinion is that intelligent people can now undertake the reading of Victorian fiction without a guilty conscience. Exempted from the tyranny of categorical condemnation, we can approach each novel with an open mind, ready to appreciate its particular merits and leniently to observe its incidental defects. One must remember, of course, that the relationship between author and reader was vastly different a hundred years ago. It would be unwise to pick up *Vanity Fair* or *Bleak House* or *Framley Parsonage* or *Middlemarch* like a paperback murder-mystery at an airport newsstand, to while away the three hours of a jet flight. Most of the Victorian novels came out serially in weekly or monthly installments, often running for as long as two years; and ordinarily they were read aloud in the family circle, a few pages every evening, to prolong the enjoyment to the utmost. One of the most pleasurable features of Victorian fiction is the refuge that it provides from the precipitate tempo of the modern age. The ideal procedure in reading a novel by

Thackeray or Dickens, Kingsley or Mrs. Gaskell, Borrow or Bulwer-Lytton is to forget about technical analysis and stylistic devices, to spread the reading over several weeks as an intermittent relief from more strenuous tasks and to enter with imaginative sympathy the author's fully realized world, which is just as vivid as the actual world around us, just as unreasonable in its mixture of triviality and crisis, of absurdity and profundity, just as frustrating in its unreconciled tensions, and which nevertheless in some elusive way is an individual work of art, surviving apart from temporal vicissitudes. After one has finished reading such a novel for the sheer pleasure of the vicarious experience that it provides, one can then look back over its voluminous bulk and recognize the artistic dexterity and the creative insight with which it was constructed.

15. U. C. Knoepflmacher

Religious Humanism and the Victorian Novel: A Postscript

The one charge that cannot be levelled at the Victorians is that they belittled their tasks: "The thing is," wrote Matthew Arnold in *Literature and Dogma* (1873), "to recast religion."[1] By the latter third of the nineteenth century, the empirical spirit which Carlyle had challenged decades before had been consolidated by evolutionary science. The prophets of the 'seventies and 'eighties thus redoubled their efforts to find a compromise between the orthodoxies of science and religion. Through the process of a dialectical balancing of the "sweet" and the "reasonable," the potential and the factual, the "Hebraic" and the "Hellenic," Victorian critics of culture and religion hoped to amass truths untainted by error and to weld them into new and eclectic creeds. Their reconciliations were shadowed by fear. The new "development hypothesis," according to Walter Pater, had threatened to invade all products of the mind: "Races, laws, arts, have their origins and end, are themselves ripples only on the great river of organic life; and language is changing on our very lips."[2] Rooted in time, man found himself on a level with the animals whose paragon he once had been supposed to be. Yet despair also quickened the eagerness to devise new ways of countering the "Everlasting No." If man was an evolutionary creature subjected to the motions of the flux, might he not also be lifted unto a higher plane of experience? An imaginative interpretation of the mechanics of history seemed

Written especially for this book.

imperative to resolve even the most personal and private dilemmas. The prophet in search of assurance invariably glanced backwards: Only the past could yield the prescriptions for the future.

Such prophetic reconciliations called for ingenuity as well as integrity. In a famous passage in *Culture and Anarchy* (1869), more noted perhaps for its rhetorical power than for its historical accuracy, Matthew Arnold predicted the imminent resurgence of his ideals by going back in time to the era of the 1832 Reform Bill. Resorting to his favorite metaphor of the stream (equally precious to so many other Victorians), Arnold asserted that the "currents of feeling" generated by the Oxford movement, though severely broken in the 1830's by its material-minded foes, had for three decades "swelled the tide of secret dissatisfaction" with both the "vulgarity of middle-class Liberalism" and "the grotesque illusions of middle-class Protestantism." This underground stream, he assured his readers had kept up its communications with the future and was now ready to resurface under new auspices—his own. For, though emphatically rejecting the theological foundations of "Dr. Newman's movement," Arnold did not at all hesitate to appropriate its "keen desire for beauty and sweetness" for his own polemical purposes. Climaxing his free arrangement of history with a dubious prophecy, he confidently predicted that the same stream "which has mined the ground under the self-confident Liberalism of the last thirty years" would now contribute to the triumph of his own secular faith in "culture."[3]

Arnold soon turned his attention to dogma itself in the theological essays where he would even more directly try to fit the "sweetness" of the Bible into a "reasonable" cult for his own times. But the celebrated passage from *Culture and Anarchy* is important, not only because it anticipates the direction that Arnold was to take in *Literature and Dogma* or *God and the Bible,* but also because it bears comparison to a work of fiction, George Eliot's *Middlemarch.* In her greatest novel, begun but two years after *Culture and Anarchy,* George Eliot produced the most complex expression of her fictional attempts to validate "that religious and moral sympathy with the historical life of man which is the larger half of culture."[4] Resorting to the same method of retrospection and prophecy employed by Arnold, she too examines the England of the Reform Bill era in order to assess the "origins" of her own present. Mixing wishfulness with irony, she likewise contrast an ardent "desire for beauty and sweetness" to the stultifying impact of a prosaic reality. While Arnold's "Dr. Newman," the apostle defeated by history, is incidental to the essayist's definition of "culture," the pyrrhic victory of a young idealist who had wanted to live "in the time of the Apostles" becomes the novelist's prime parable about that forward struggle against determining conditions "in which great feelings will often take the aspect of error, and great faith the aspect of illusion."[5] Arnold's ambivalent attitude towards the semi-fictional "Dr. Newman" is not unlike George Eliot's own attitude towards the fully fictitious Dorothea Brooke. In the opening "Prelude," Dorothea's imminent journey is ironically likened to the child-pilgrimage undertaken by the infant Saint Theresa; in the novel's "Finale," Dorothea's mellowed idealism is explicitly endorsed by her creator. Though partially defeated, she is now praised for having contributed to the forward flow of higher aspirations. In a novel which studies the rippling effects of human actions, the former Miss Brooke is likened to a deflected river which, like Arnold's underground "currents," has nonetheless generated impulses destined to burst out anew:

> Her full nature, like that river of which Cyrus broke the strength, spent itself in channels which had no great name on the earth. But the effect of her being on those around her was incalculably diffusive: for the growing good of the world is partly dependent on unhistoric acts." ("Finale," p. 495)[6]

In *Literature and Dogma* Arnold specified that the advocate of "culture" must possess "a very wide experience from comparative observation in many directions, and a very slowly acquired habit of mind."[7] The narrator of *Middlemarch* is an observer whose command of both scientific as well as moral and aesthetic cultures has led him to care "much to know the history of man, and how the mysterious mixture behaves under the varying experiment of Time" ("Prelude," p. 1). Like the *persona* adopted by Arnold in his essays, this narrator offers the products of a collective human experience through the gradual unfolding of a self-inclusive irony. Both authors rely on juxtaposition and analogy, allusion and archetype. If the Arnold of *Culture and Anarchy* compresses the verities of religion and rationalism by pairing off Hebraist and Hellenist, the mottoes of Bishop Wilson and Montesquieu, the George Eliot of *Middlemarch* plays Dorothea's quest against that of another would-be reformer, the young doctor Tertius Lydgate. Dorothea's archetype is Saint Theresa (the saint who, according to Arnold, best emulated the "sweetness" of Jesus); Lydgate's model is the anatomist Andreas Visalius, a fighter for the "light" of empirical truth. Their opposition to each other, as well as their interaction with the remaining Middlemarchers, helps to define George Eliot's own priorities. At the end of the novel, a reversal of roles has taken place. In an Aristotelian *peripateia,* Dorothea, the once inactive idealist, has become an active healer, while Lydgate, the onetime believer in the self-sufficiency of his material science, has become her passive and grateful patient. The physician who had earlier disparaged Dorothea's moral enthusiasm now enthusiastically celebrates her "sweetness": " 'This young creature has a heart large enough for the Virgin Mary' " (ch. 76, p. 361). Devoid of Dorothea' inbred "consciousness of Christian centuries," Lydgate's own heart has been wasted on the sentimentalism which caused him to convert his wife into an "accomplished mermaid." Lacking the "righteousness" defined by Arnold in *Literature and Dogma,* Lydgate must learn that for George Eliot, as for Arnold, "conduct, plain matter as it is," remains the prime ingredient of culture.[8] George Eliot's choice of a medical man to assert the primacy of "conduct" coincides with Arnold's own remarks on moral illness: "Medical science has never gauged,—never, perhaps, enough set itself to gauge,—the intimate connexion between moral fault and disease."[9]

These parallels have been drawn for an obvious reason: Clearly George Eliot's novel, all too frequently misread as but a photographic "slice" of English provincial life, is a meticulous intellectual construct which addresses itself to questions quite similar to those which inform Arnold's imaginative prose. If Arnold was thrown upon the form of the essay because he felt that his age denied him the substance for poetry, it was the prosaic *"architectonicè"* of the novel which yielded that "allegory" which he had rejected as an aim for his poems. The dynamic framework of *Middlemarch* makes full use of that dual process of looking backward and forward which Arnold employed in his prose and which George Eliot described as the "divine gift of memory which inspires the moments with a past, present, and a future, and gives a sense of corporate existence."[10] In *Culture and Anarchy,* Arnold must strip the great Oxford Apostle of his other-worldly religion in order to convert him into an acceptable ally for the author's own secular "culture." In *Middlemarch,* George Eliot also strips the apostolic Dorothea of all those elements of belief which do not correspond to her own agnostic standards. But whereas Arnold's handling of Newman remains a rhetorical sleight-of-hand, George Eliot, by adopting the form of the novel, can rely on a more substantial mode of persuasion. The "sweetness" of her Dorothea is not juxtaposed to Arnoldian abstractions such as "the grotesque illusions of middle-class Protestantism" or the "vulgarity of middle-class Liberalism," but rather to the credible illusions of a banker who frantically regards himself as the executor of God's "will" and to the equally credible vulgarity of a Liberal candidate whose unimaginativeness manifests itself at the hustings. Thus, while Arnold must wishfully impose his predilections on contemporary history, George Eliot can transplant her "sympathy with the historical life of man" into the purely fictitious realm of "unhistoric acts." The intrusiveness of Arnold's creative imagination alienates those who misread *Culture and Anarchy* as factual history and even distresses those who are fully aware of the significance of his ideas. It is seldom recognized that in a novel like *Middlemarch,* these very same ideas have acquired the security and permanence of great art.

In *Religious Humanism and the Victorian Novels: George Eliot, Walter Pater, and Samuel Butler* (Princeton, 1965), I tried to examine the efforts of three writers who, unlike Arnold, did turn to the novel in order to assert the possibility of a secular belief in a world ruled by the capriciousness of the temporal flux. In my study I gave equal attention to each writer's particular ideas and to their artistic incarnation. Yet I chose George Eliot, Walter Pater, and Samuel Butler, not only because of their representativeness as thinkers or their accomplishments as novelists, but also because their work illuminates that transforming process (so notable in the nineteenth century) which, by converting private doubts into public assertions, can give tentative ideas the finality of art. Modern scholars of the nineteenth century still fall into two distinct camps. The one regards a work of creative literature as but a repository of intellectual, sociological, or biographical insights; the other denies the validity of an historical approach. The dangers of either extreme are evident. A study which would treat a lesser novel like Mrs. Humphry Ward's *Robert Elsmere* as the culmination of the history of an "idea" conveniently sets aside the book's artistic faults; even worse, to treat a masterpiece like *Middlemarch* solely in terms of its ideas or ethical "values," without attending to its chosen mode of persuasion, its shape or texture, is to reduce the criticism of fiction into the elucidation of the barest of expository prose.[11] On the other hand, it has become increasingly fashionable in recent years to ignore the definite ideological basis underlying so much of Victorian literature. To treat a novel like *Middlemarch* as if it had been written by Flaubert or Henry James is to neglect the special qualities of George Eliot's art which James himself was the first to recognize.[12]

James found *Middlemarch* inferior to the craftsmanlike *Silas Marner* because it was, according to him, too overt an "echo of Messrs. Darwin and Huxley." Although his value judgment seems questionable today, it did stem from a correct appreciation of the nature and intentions of George Eliot's later novel: "Fielding was didactic—the author of *Middlemarch* is really philosophic."[13] At first glance, this distinction seems cryptic: Fielding, like George Eliot, had resorted to the novel for "philosophic" ends. Through the deliberate artifice of his plots and the calculated effect of his digressions, Fielding could imply the existence of a reasonable order, even though this order was only dimly perceived by the characters peopling his teeming "histories." Yet George Eliot could no longer avail herself of her predecessor's atemporal frame of reference. In Chapter Fifteen of *Middlemarch,* she therefore makes sure to dissociate herself from his example. Though a "great historian" and colossus, Fielding lived in a simpler age, unburdened by the preoccupations inherent in her own time-bound philosophy. As a "belated historian" who tells the story of a late-born Theresa, the narrator of *Middlemarch* protests that his task is more limited. He must content himself with examining the texture of life on this earth and not disperse his light over "that tempting range of relevancies called the universe." This protestation is telling. Far from belittling her own role as a novelist, the narrator's faint irony calls attention to George Eliot's own very definite preoccupations with the universe. For it is the altered nature of that universe which is the true object of her comparison. Fielding, confident of a divinely ordered world, can well afford to spend his days on earth by chatting slowly in all "the lusty ease of his fine English." But time is far more precious to the belated historian. As a novelist, George Eliot cannot "linger" after Fielding's example. Her predecessor, she claims, has had the happiness to have lived over a hundred and twenty years before, in a secure and static eighteenth century. The narrator of *Middlemarch,* however, lives in an era in doubt of its future. Unlike Fielding, this narrator must become a genuine historian and find in history those laws which previous novelists could take for granted. To do so, he must extricate these laws from the casual network of actuality: "I at least have so much to do in unravelling certain human lots, and seeing how they are woven and interwoven . . ." George Eliot's distinction is clear. Despite her affinity to Fielding, despite her affection for the didactic lectures so resonantly delivered from his armchair, she cannot mount the same proscenium. The traditional forms of the English novel can no longer satisfy the "philosophic" needs of a writer steeped in the evolutionary lore of the mid-nineteenth century.

George Eliot's movement from the essay to the novel in the late 1850's anticipated by almost two decades the similar paths which both Walter Pater and Samuel Butler were to take in the 1870's; some of her earlier efforts to test out her assumptions, in novels like *The Mill on the Floss* (1860) or *Romola* (1862–1863), bear distinct resemblances to the "philosophic" fiction written by her two successors.[14] Yet although *Middle-*

march (1871–1872) resolves the difficulties which George Eliot met in her previous experimentations with form, it is itself sharply separated from her last two productions, *Daniel Deronda* (1876) and the sketches of *Impressions of Theophrastus Such* (1879). For George Eliot was as much affected as Pater and Butler by the wave of re-assessment and reconsideration which took place in the 'seventies. Her *Daniel Deronda,* Pater's *Marius the Epicurean* (begun around 1879 and published in 1885), and Butler's *The Way of All Flesh* (begun in 1873 and finished in 1884) spring from the same climate of re-evaluation and controversy–from a period also marked by Arnold's theological "palinodes," by Morley's *On Compromise,* by Huxley's and Tyndall's lectures on the self-sufficiency of science, by Mill's posthumous *Essays in Religion,* as well as by the multiple debates conducted in journals, pamphlets, lecture halls, and on the premises of the "Metaphysical Society."

Almost simultaneously, George Eliot, Pater, and Butler underwent a turnabout which led them to reconsider some of their earlier tenets of unbelief. The George Eliot who had succeeded, in *Middlemarch,* in balancing the divisions that had marred some of her previous productions, now abandoned the ironic equipoise of her greatest novel in favor of the synthesis which takes place in the apocalyptic *Daniel Deronda.* In her last novel, she abandoned the empirical standards maintained in her earlier fiction and refused to disguise her blatant use of the coincidental, the improbable, and even the supernatural. Walter Pater was also led to redefine a philosophical position which he had expressed through historical distortions far more arbitrary than Arnold's manipulations in *Culture and Anarchy.*[15] Made painfully conscious of his questionable use of historical fact, Pater cautiously moved from the "real" sketches of *The Renaissance* (1873) to the "imaginary portraits" of his fiction. In each of these philosophical parables he depicted the plight of a lonely seeker who yearns for the "influence" of a meaningful "atmosphere," "background," "perspective," or "environment" (these five terms recur with an amazing frequency throughout his stories and essays) among the physical or intellectual milieus of the past. Butler, whose *Erewhon* (1872) had appeared in the same year as *Middlemarch,* had tenuously blended religion and evolutionism through the form of the Utopian novel. Yet increasingly dissatisfied with the Darwinian explanation to which he had given his ready assent, Butler slowly began to test out alternate theories of his own in essays even more fanciful and personal than Pater's had been. Eventually, *The Way of All Flesh,* he too lighted upon the form of an apocalyptic novel as a way of mastering his self-division.

The stories of Daniel Deronda, Marius the Epicurean, and Ernest Pontifex reveal the earnestness with which their creators sought to order an impersonal world of flux. In the concluding portions of *Middlemarch,* still set in a past of a "hopefulness" much "checked in our days," George Eliot had allowed Dorothea to escape: Her "heart" can thrive only outside the confines of the community which had defeated her aspirations. In *Daniel Deronda,* however, which is set in a contemporary scene, the mediocrity of the Middlemarchers has spread to an entire nation characterized by its purposelessness. The irreligious society headed by the Mallingers needs a far more transcendent model: Brought up as an English aristocrat, Daniel Deronda finds himself converted into an exotic Jewish patrician who can sail into a new realm of purpose and dedication. As a member of "the heart of mankind," Israel, this over-idealized figure acts out a purely exemplary role; the England he leaves behind must be reminded of its own "Hebraic" heritage. In *Marius the Epicurean,* the longest and most elaborate of his "imaginary portraits," Pater transports another young idealist to the "atmospheres" provided by an age of transition and decadence much like his own.[16] Hovering indecisively between two opposing historical cycles, Pater's melancholy pilgrim discovers in death the unity granted to Deronda. If George Eliot's Hebraist is freed from his temporal enslavement to a material order, Pater's Hellenist, though a victim of time, resolves the antagonisms which had lamed him by detecting at least the continuity which links the noblest of Roman philosophies to the worship of the early Christian church. In *The Way of All Flesh,* Butler fused the extremes which had thwarted Marius by altering the identity of still another truth-seeker, Ernest Pontifex. By reverting to the ancestral vitality of his pagan forefather, the carpenter John Pontifex, Ernest obeys instinctively the mandates of a temporal deity—"God the Known"—which Butler had cast in the image of his fondest wishes. Through the fantasy of Ernest the bridge-builder, his creator transmuted autobiography into fiction, satire into earnestness, and an Erewhonian daydream into a Utopian faith.

Ideologically, George Eliot, Samuel Butler, and Walter Pater may be linked to three important currents within the mainstream of nineteenth-century thought: a humanism inspired by Continental philosophers, critics, and historians; a scientism based on the discoveries of native geologists and biologists; and an aesthetic movement related both to its counterpart across the Channel and to the Catholic revival and Pre-Raphaelite "renaissance" in England. Although these currents are not strictly separable, it is possible, for the sake of simplification, to identify each novelist with the predominant concerns of only one of these movements. George Eliot, as Henry James remarked, wished to "recommend herself to a scientific audience."[17] Yet she enlisted the very tools she had received from evolutionism for what amounted to a reaction against its materialist assumption. Although her "recommendations" were addressed to the scientific-minded, they were largely inspired by the second wave of a Continental humanism which, in a previous generation, had already prompted Coleridge and Carlyle to challenge the tenets of science. Like Matthew Arnold, whose belief in "culture" had similar origins, she tried to present her age with a Christian "essence" that would conserve the ethics of the old religion while rejecting its metaphysics. Unlike George Eliot, Samuel Butler belonged more squarely in a native tradition. Initially a Darwinian, Butler moved from science to pseudo-science in order to regain the teleology of his lost belief. Although he went far beyond George Eliot in his efforts to impose design on the evolutionary universe of Wallace, Darwin, and Huxley, the rational order he built as a substitute was, as he well knew, the outgrowth of an irrational "dream." For all its Lamarckian trappings, the vitalist faith of Ernest Pontifex (which was to be refined by D. H. Lawrence and by Shaw) was primarily the product of his creator's ingenuity. The curious aestheticism of Walter Pater falls between the humanism of George Eliot or Matthew Arnold and the scientism of Samuel Butler. Like

Butler, Pater was a Hellenist who believed in the sole validity of the sensational impression. But Pater also believed with Arnold and George Eliot in the urgency of retaining a morality based on a Judaeo-Christian "essence." As a result, he turned to ritual and religious art in order to find in their "atmospheres" a source for moral impressions.

Artistically, the experimentations of these three writers opened the way for later novelists who likewise chose to replace the revelations of the Bible with the prophecies of their fiction. The search of Marius the Epicurean, the young and "constitutionally impressible" Roman whose austere religious temperament is so much at odds with his keen desire for beauty leads logically to that of Stephen Daedalus, the ascetic Dubliner who becomes the acolyte of his own religion of art. Similarly, the abrupt loss of faith which chastens the ardor of Dorothea Brooke stuns, even more violently, the benevolent Mrs. Moore: Stripped of their provincial outlook, each woman finds that the words of "poor little talkative Christianity"[18] have become supplanted by the mocking rhythm of a wider, yet impersonal and alien order. Lastly, the "crossing" undertaken by the matured Ernest Pontifex and by the children whom he reschools in the ways of the flesh anticipates the "deliverance" of many a Lawrencian hero.

The desire to transcend time led these three Victorian novelists to go beyond the purely sequential or episodic form of the traditional novel. The intricate causal web which, in *Middlemarch,* so inextricably connects the notions of all characters, is enriched by a network of allusions to history, literature, and myth which endows each of the unhistoric events examined in the foreground with wider and universal implications. Likewise, in *Marius* and in the "imaginary portraits," Pater's skillful use of Greek mythology makes the actions of his time-burdened protagonists seem universally recurrent, part of an unending cyclical pattern. If Marius' passive absorption of one "atmosphere" after another makes his spiritual pilgrimage seem a protracted Victorian version of Johnson's *Rasselas,* it is the novel's symbolic framework, its mythic dimensions, which also reveal its distinct kinship to a modern work like Mann's *Magic Mountain.* The book's complex system of antithesis and analogy, like that of *Middlemarch,* is designed to obviate the exclusiveness of any one view of life. Though a lesser work than George Eliot's novel, *Marius* expresses through its very structure the same desire to master the perpetual flux which renders all things relative. *Daniel Deronda* and *The Way of All Flesh,* concerned with vindicating a new faith, are less balanced and more exhortatory. In them, actuality mixes with escapism and the destructiveness of satire blends uneasily with the exaltation of Utopian ideals; the submission of the witty Gwendolen Harleth to the priestly Daniel Deronda is as unsatisfying as the submergence of Ernest the priest into the witty disciple of Overton. Yet both works take the Victorian novel to its outermost boundaries. The temporal disruptions which George Eliot uses in *Daniel Deronda* to create unexpected links between the various plot lines were to be carried further by Joseph Conrad; the curious compression of levity and earnestness of *The Way of All Flesh* was to find a more balanced expression in the experimental comedy of James Joyce.

Thus it was that Victorian humanism brought a new dimension to the English novel. As actual creeds, George Eliot's and Pater's reductions of religion into tradition or Butler's diminution of heritage into heredity were hardly destined to endure. Their confident amalgam of all idealism and materialism has in our own times turned into a most brittle compound. Yet their search for new modes of belief led these three writers to reproduce in the *"architectonicè"* of their fiction the very same divisions that Matthew Arnold had declared to be inimical to the creation of enduring art. The intensity with which Joyce, Lawrence, and Forster utilized the novel in their own search for a principle of perpetuity would probably have been impossible without the efforts of these nineteenth-century prophets. *Ulysses,* that modern compendium of the best that has been thought and said, can be understood in terms of the same dialectic which informs *Middlemarch.* United, the Hellenic Daedalus and the Hebraic Bloom could, like Lydgate and Dorothea, provide an ideal synthesis; kept apart, they represent, as do the two exiles from Middlemarch, the fragmentation of modern existence. *Middlemarch*—like *Daniel Deronda, Marius,* and *The Way of All Flesh*—did not only set a limit to the development of the old-fashioned novel. They mapped out the direction in which modern fiction would grow.

Notes

[1] *Literature and Dogma: An Essay Towards a Better Apprehension of the Bible* (London, 1873), p. xi.

[2] *Plato and Platonism: A Series of Lectures* (London, 1910), p. 21.

[3] *Culture and Anarchy: An Essay in Political and Social Criticism* (London, 1869), pp. 35–39.

[4] *The George Eliot Letters,* ed. Gordon S. Haight (New Haven, 1954–1955), IV, 97.

[5] *Middlemarch,* 3 vols., Cabinet Edition (Edinburgh, n. d.), "Finale," p. 464. Future references to this edition are given in the text.

[6] Cf. *The Mill on the Floss* (1860), where the "destiny" of Maggie Tulliver, another idealist thwarted by ordinary life, is also likended to an underground river. In the earlier novel, however, this destiny is tragic: Life by the Ripple gives way to death on the destructive Floss.

[7] *Literature and Dogma,* p. 283.

[8] *Ibid.,* p. 354.

[9] *Ibid.,* p. 143.

[10] "The Modern Hep! Hep! Hep!" in *Impression of Theophrastus Such,* Cabinet Edition (Edinburgh, n. d.), p. 261.

[11] This method unfortunately underlies a work as valuable as Mr. Bernard J. Paris' *Experiments in Life: George Eliot's Quest for Values* (Detroit, 1965).

[12] In his excellent study, *The Art of George Eliot,* W. J. Harvey tries to counter the strictures invoked by Jamesian critics against George Eliot's art, but he does so, not by defending the validity of her philosophical "form," but rather by making her out to be as much (or more) a formalist than James.

[13] James' 1873 review, "George Eliot's *Middlemarch,*" is reprinted in *Nineteenth-Century Fiction,* VIII (December, 1953), 161–70. The quotation occurs on p. 170.

[14] *The Mill on the Floss* contains interesting analogues both to Pater's use of the historical flux in his "imaginary portraits" as well as to Butler's application of ideas about heredity in *The Way of All Flesh.* For a connection between *Romola* and Pater's work, see David J. DeLaura, "*Romola* and the Origin of the Paterian View of Life," *Nineteenth-Century Fiction,* XXI (December, 1966), 225–34.

[15] Speaking about the "great movement which goes by the name of the Renascence," Arnold had noted: "I have ventured to give the foreign word *Renaissance,* destined to become of more common use amongst us as the movement which it denotes comes, as it will come, increasingly to interest us, an English form" (*Culture and Anarchy,* p. 159).

[16] In 1852 Arnold wrote Clough what amounts to a thumbnail sketch of a figure like Marius the Epicurean: "We deteriorate in spite of our struggles—like a gifted Roman falling on the uninvigorating atmosphere of the decline of the Empire" (*The Letters of Matthew Arnold to Arthur Hugh Clough,* ed. H. F. Lowry [London and New York, 1932], p. 123).

[17] "George Eliot's *Middlemarch,*" p. 169.

[18] E. M. Forster, *A Passage to India* (New York, 1924), p. 150.

16.

George Levine

Determinatism and Responsibility in the Works of George Eliot

The nature and degree of George Eliot's commitment to a deterministic world view have been the source of considerable difficulty in the criticism of her work. Critics who concern themselves with the subject take, for the most part, the view either that her belief in determinism seriously marred her art or, on the other hand, that despite appearances she was not a consistent determinist.[1] In both cases, however, determinism evokes extraordinary intensity of feeling, almost everyone agreeing that a commitment to it tends to be detrimental to the artist because it forces a distortion of the facts of existence (or at least a depressing interpretation of them) and leads to an underestimation of man's capacity for action and of his potential dignity.

I shall argue, however, that in one important and widely acceptable use of the term, George Eliot was a consistent determinist, and that this sense is in no way incongruous with her continuous emphasis on moral responsibility and duty. Her novels, letters, and essays suggest that her position—never, so far as I know, fully articulated in print—was very close to John Stuart Mill's, and that if she was inconsistent she was no more so than Mill. Mill's views on determinism, moreover, though they have never pleased absolutists, have considerable philosophical support, belonging as they do to a tradition which stems back at least as far as Hume's *Inquiry* and extending

Reprinted by permission of the author and the Modern Language Association of America from *PMLA,* Vol. 77, No. 3 (June, 1962), 268–79.

forward to one of the most powerful contemporary schools of academic philosophy—that of linguistic analysis. With the philosophical tools at their disposal neither Mill nor George Eliot could have carried analysis as far as contemporary analysts do; but the position is not an easily discredited one, either philosophically or, as it is embodied in George Eliot's works, artistically: it does at least as much justice to the facts of existence as any indeterminist position or any less flexible determinist one.

The danger in a detailed discussion of this position, of course, is to treat George Eliot as a philosopher rather than an artist. For although she was widely read in philosophy and translated Spinoza's *Ethics,* Feuerbach's *Essence of Christianity,* and Strauss's *Life of Jesus,* the fact that she never felt impelled to set down her own thoroughly worked out system or to state finally her views on the problem of determinism should suggest that at best she was an amateur philosopher using her wide reading for purposes essentially unphilosophical. Her novels and essays are full of protests against the rigidity of systems,[2] but refusal to work out an all-embracing philosophical system is not necessarily incompatible with consistency. And her determinism was flexible enough, she thought, to be applicable without distortion to the life she tried to represent with scrupulous fidelity. Determinism informed her artistic vision; she not only believed in it as an abstract truth but saw it working even in the routine actions of ordinary life. To be sure, in her novels she does not use it as an abstract argument, but it is persistently there; and for this reason it is important that it be understood by her critics and, where necessary (though abstractions are regarded by critics with a kind of horror), even discussed in the abstract.

There are three basic stances taken by philosophers on the matter of determinism: (1) that the world is rigidly determined and that, in fact, there is no such thing as human responsibility,[3] (2) that though almost everything is determined, the relation of cause and effect is broken in matters of human choice: thus man is free and therefore responsible;[4] (3) that the world is rigidly determined, even in cases of human choice, but that man remains responsible for his actions. The last position of course causes most of the logical difficulties, and it is this position which, I believe, George Eliot shared with Mill.

If one can accept it (as most contemporary analytic philosophers do), one not only avoids the underestimation of man's capacity to learn and to act with dignity and responsibility which many writers feel is an inevitable conjunct of determinism; one sees it also as it was for George Eliot, an indispensable means of rationally defending the possibility of just those qualities. She found, one might infer from available materials, that the only valid interpretation of her vision was deterministic, for it was the only one that could adequately account, among other things, for her sense of man's dependence on man, his ability to learn and grow, and his obligation always to follow the promptings of duty. The key to her determinism lies in her refusal to discount the human will. Thus, an investigation of what her deterministic position was and of why she made so full a commitment to it, may make it possible to move a little closer to understanding how determinism actually works in her novels and in what important ways it affected, whether to distort and darken or to enrich, her particular artistic perception of the world.

For George Eliot determinism was an entirely secular position—the belief that every event has its causal antecedents. Although in her early years she was a pious Calvinist, her mature belief in determinism was entirely divorced from the Calvinistic concept of predeterminism, which suggests some supernatural power figuring beforehand the necessary course of things. Her novels, for example, are not fatalistic, whatever the appearances, since they always make it abundantly, sometimes terrifyingly, clear that her characters' fate is in large measure of their own making. Lydgate's "spots of commonness" are as much responsible for his failure as Rosamond's callous egoism. We may, it is true, be asked to feel sympathetic to Dolly Winthrop when she says, "We may strive and scrat and fend, but it's little we can do arter all—the big things come and go wi' no striving o' our'n—they do that they do."[5] But Mrs. Poyser is much more clearly George Eliot's spokesman when, perplexed by the conflicting theories of conflicting sects, she argues, "I see plain enough we shall never do it without a resolution, and that's enough for me."[6] In the end, this common sense position adequately summarizes George Eliot's most important views on freedom and responsibility (and the views of Mill and many other modern analysts as well).

But having turned from religion she still felt the pull of Calvinist determinism, and she looked to science and philosophy for an explanation. She saw that determinism was clearly implicit in Newton's physics and in the theory of the association of ideas, and that utilitarians and positivists were committed to the view that there were fixed laws of nature and that man, a part of nature, was subject to those laws. Thus Comte argued: "all events what ever, the events of our own personal and social life included, are always subject to natural relations of sequence and similitude, which in all essential respects lie beyond the reach of our interference."[7] George Eliot had committed herself to such a view fairly early. To Charles Bray, author of *The Philosophy of Necessity* and the man who was probably the first to expose her to a systematic and scientific-seeming determinism, she wrote in 1857,

> in the fundamental doctrine of your book—that mind presents itself under the same condition of invariableness of antecedent and consequent as all other phenomena (the only difference being that the true antecedent and consequent are proportionately difficult to discover as the phenomena are more complex)—I think you know I agree.[8]

This is Comtean, even to the parenthetical qualification.[9]

The scientific bias of this view would seem to push in the direction of amorality (as, for instance, it did much more clearly though not yet finally with Pater as early as 1866 in his essay on "Coleridge"),[10] but as is obvious in most of the philosophical writings of this "age of ideology," almost every theory had a strong moral bias. As the universe tended to become for certain thinkers more materialistic and amoral, they struggled fearfully and vigorously to control the forces of irrationality and violence which would be unleashed with the destruction of traditional sanctions. Thus we find Comte, Mill, and Spencer outlining possible sciences of society (with various degrees of belief in the possibility of finally achieving such sciences) according to which men might live together in utopian harmony, and we find George Eliot, with what amounts at times almost to desperation, taking up a moral stance at every point.

I

Despite her emphasis on the claims of duty and the power of the will, the world which George Eliot describes in her novels is meant to be consistently deterministic. And I should like here to look briefly at some of the most important philosophical and moral implications for her of the deterministic idea—simple at bottom but leading to enormous complications—that every event has its causal antecedents.

(1) George Eliot saw a deterministic universe as a marvelously complex unit in which all parts are intricately related to each other, where nothing is really isolable, and where past and future are both implicit in the present. Nothing in such a universe is explicable without reference to the time and place in which it occurs or exists. This suggested that one can never make a clear-cut break with the society in which one has been brought up, with one's friends and relations, with one's past. Any such break diminishes a man's wholeness and is the result of his failure to recognize his ultimate dependence on others, their claims on him, and the consequent need for human solidarity. For George Eliot, every man's life is at the center of a vast and complex web of causes,[11] a good many of which exert pressure on him from the outside and come into direct conflict with his own desires and motives.

It is obvious that George Eliot's extraordinary insight into the workings of society is closely related to this view, probably both as cause and effect. The full scale portrayals of small town society which we get in *The Mill on the Floss* and pre-eminently in *Middlemarch* depend on a rich and vital sense of the way in which every man's life impinges on many others. A refusal to accept responsibility for the claims that society puts upon one leads to destruction or dehumanization. So old Peter Featherstone dies a defeated, willful animal cut off from all normal human relationships. So Maggie, having cut herself off from society by her one yielding to impulse, has to die (however melodramatically) in her effort to reestablish normal human relationships. And any character who, like Tito or Bulstrode, attempts to blot out the past or cut himself off from old friends or relatives, fails inevitably; the result of his attempts is moral disintegration. The persistent theme of egoism which isolates man from his natural ties is also related to the notion of a complex deterministic universe. This theme is worked out almost in paradigm in the story of Hetty Sorrel in *Adam Bede,* but we see it again in the brief but brilliant portrait of Mrs. Transome in *Felix Holt* and in the story of Gwendolen Harleth in *Daniel Deronda.*

In her review of Riehl's *Natural History of German Life* George Eliot emphasizes the importance of continuity. Riehl, she notes approvingly, sees "in European society *incarnate history,* and any attempt to disengage it from its historical element must, he believes, be simply destructive of social vitality. What has grown up historically can only die out historically, by the gradual operation of necessary laws." But what applies to society as a whole applies equally well to the individual. This view accounts in part for her insistence on the importance of early life in the formation of character in, for instance, the portraits of Maggie and Gwendolen. It accounts, moreover, for what seems her almost melodramatic concern with people cut off from their real parents (Hetty, Esther Lyon, Arthur Transome, Tito, Gwendolen, Deronda, and even the Spanish Gypsy). The view, moreover, confirmed George Eliot in what she regarded as a conservatism which, as a child, she breathed in with the Midland atmosphere.[12] Thus, we find her "radical" novel, *Felix Holt,* to be firmly antirevolutionary, and her radical hero actually forced to battle with the proletariat whose interests he in theory protects. Since real change can only come about through the slow increment of myriad causes working through history, revolution is doomed to failure.

The insistence on unity, harmony, duty, and slow growth, which we see in George Eliot's broad social analyses and in her minute psychological investigations of egoism and division within a single human soul, obviously has its roots in a moral bias. But the bias, for George Eliot, has its rational justification in determinism.

(2) A deterministic universe, as George Eliot understood it, is a democratic one. The emphasis rests not on the Byronic and extraordinary but on the ordinary; the occurrence of large heroic action is unlikely though not by any means impossible. Since, as John Holloway says, George Eliot believed that "Man is a part of Nature, and Nature is a vast and complex system of which the parts are subordinate to impersonal forces governing the whole," she felt as well that "the individuals that belong to such a system cannot be heroes."[13] Determinism, of course, need not necessarily be anti-heroic: the Hegelian version, for instance, raises to almost godlike stature the world-historical figure who, acting from a vision which is far ahead of his time's, prepares the way for the future changes which further reveal the working out of the mind of God in history. Marxism too, as an antimetaphysical outgrowth of Hegelianism, has its world-historical heroes. But even in these systems, the hero is a rare figure behind whom the great masses of people struggle helplessly in the grip of historical processes.

The heroic, as we shall see, is not entirely excluded from George Eliot's novels, but even the strongest figures in the novels—with the possible exception of Savonarola, Deronda, and Mordecai—could be better described as ordinary than heroic. For the most part, George Eliot was concerned with ordinary life and felt it dangeorus to emphasize the heroic. Her contempt for the Byronic hero echoes throughout her letters, *Felix Holt,* and *Daniel Deronda* precisely because she felt that a concentration on the heroic, out of reach of all but a handful of great men, tended to make one dissatisfied with life as it has to be lived. Moreover, the heroic—even the nobly heroic—is inevitably combined with egoism and a consequent tendency to disregard the necessary but ordinary ties which bind man to his friends, relatives, and society. No man is entitled to expect much personal gratification from so complex a universe running according to invariable laws which apply indifferently to all men. The external pressure of these laws (or, as they manifest themselves in the novels, the external pressure of society) is too great for any single man completely to overcome. "There is no creature," she warns, "whose inward being is so strong that it is not greatly determined by what lies outside it."[14] Thus, in all the novels but *Daniel Deronda,* heroism takes the shape of resignation exclusively, a willingness to renounce not only personal satisfactions but the possibility of great achievement for good causes. The brilliant hovering irony of the portrait of Dorothea in the early part of *Middlemarch* suggests how, even for the characters with whom she tended to sympathize excessively, George Eliot was aware of the important and debilitating role egoism plays in the shaping of heroic objectives.

The one significant exception to this tendency deserves more extended treatment than it can be given here. But in Daniel Deronda and Mordecai George Eliot creates characters who are meant to have heroic stature. Their activities are to help create a new nation. It is not surprising that they are two of the weakest (if still the most interesting) characters George Eliot ever created. Their kind of heroism was what she aspired to, but it was also incompatible with her particular vision; it suggested the possibility of great and rapid changes, of significant and conscious tampering with the course of history, where, as a determinist, she instinctively felt that such tampering had become almost impossible. To create such characters she had to go outside the limits of the ordinary life of England, which her novels (except *Romola,* of course) had hitherto described, into a world which, however wide her reading, she did not really understand.

It is important to note, on the other hand, that George Eliot did not believe, as Holloway argues, that individuals, if they can't be heroic, must then be obscure and petty. Certainly they must remain obscure, but, she insisted, "there is nothing petty to the mind that has a large vision of relations, and to which every single object suggests a vast sum of conditions."[15] Since, that is, every act is related in some way to every other, the most apparently unimportant act may have important ramifications, and the most apparently unimportant person must be accorded considerable respect. "We insignificant people," she says in the famous "Finale" of *Middlemarch,*

> with our daily words and acts are preparing the lives of many Dorotheas, some of which may present a far sadder sacrifice than that of the Dorothea whose story we know. . . . The growing good of the world is partly dependent on unhistoric acts.

(3) Deterministic theory translated into the practice of her fiction became grounds according to which one might abjure coincidence and condemn chance. Nothing, she argued, happens accidentally, and a belief in the possibility of some kind of occurrence not usually produced by the normal workings of the laws of nature became to her one of the positive signs of moral weakness. Since similar events have similar effects (unless other causes are secretly at work), George Eliot believed it morally reprehensible to rely on the unlikely or unusual, even if there is a remote chance that it might happen. For example, Gwendolen expects triumph from her marriage with Grandcourt, Arthur expects nothing to come of his liaison with Hetty, Lydgate imagines he can break his vow of temporary celibacy without hurting his scientific work: in each case the more likely upshot helps destroy the character who would rather hope for the unlikely. When "chance" does occur, to be sure, George Eliot is not suggesting that it is outside the normal laws of nature, but only that the elaborate and complex system of causes has been working beyond the knowledge of her characters.

In *Daniel Deronda* and *Middlemarch* "chance" becomes a dominant motif: the vivid opening scene in *Deronda* in which Gwendolen plays passionately at the luridly lit gaming table introduces the theme and sets its moral tone; and this tone is close to that of *Middlemarch* when Lydgate succumbs to the vice he had previously despised in Mr. Farebrother and becomes feverishly absorbed in gambling at billiards. In less obvious ways it appears in all her novels and is always associated with evil. "Favourable Chance," she says in *Silas Marner,*

> is the god of all men who follow their own devices instead of obeying a law they believe in. Let even a polished man of these days get into a position he is ashamed to avow, and his mind will be bent on all the possible issues that

may deliver him from the calculable results of that position (Ch. ix).

(4) Finally, and most important for George Eliot, a deterministic world such as she envisioned is one in which duty becomes primary (as it does, of course, in Comte's positivistic system). Since, as we have already remarked, every act, no matter how trivial, has a vast number of consequences, not all of them traceable, she felt that it behooves every human being to exercise the greatest care in his actions to avoid causing misery to others. To F. W. H. Myers she made a remark which has since become notorious: that although God was "inconceivable," and immortality "unbelievable," Duty was "peremptory and absolute."[16] In a letter written to Mrs. H. F. Ponsonby in 1874 she explained this severe and tough-minded view:

> I suppose that there is not a single man, or woman, who has not more or less need of that stoical resignation which is often a hidden heroism, or who, in considering his or her past history, is not aware that it has been cruelly affected by the ignorant or selfish action of some fellow-being in a more or less close relation of life. And to my mind there can be no stronger motive, than this perception, to energetic effort that the lives nearest to us shall not suffer in like manner from us.[17]

This idea is so fundamental to the novels that examples here would be superfluous.

It would seem that at least a fifth implication should follow from the belief that every event has its causal antecedents, and this, perhaps, the most important of all: that what man is, what he wills, what he becomes, is necessarily determined in such a way that he is incapable of anything but acquiescence in the pull of his unconscious desires and the push of external forces. But this is precisely the view that George Eliot despised as morally enervating and vicious, and which she tended to call necessitarianism.[18] Along with John Stuart Mill, she insisted that this position did not follow.[19] Both began their attack on it from a position of common sense. Mill, as we shall see more fully later, began with a perception that the word "Necessity" was misleading, that it

> carried with it a misleading association; and that this association was the operative force in the depressing and paralyzing influence which I had experienced: I saw that though our character is formed by circumstances; and that what is really inspiriting and ennobling in the doctrine of free-will, is the conviction that we have real power over the formation of our character; that our will, by influencing some of our circumstances, can modify our future habits or capacities of willing."[20]

Just as Mill began his analysis of the term "Necessity" out of a deep personal need to throw off the weight of depression that determinism had laid upon him, so George Eliot worked her way out of the dilemma of determinism because of her deep moral bias. Aware of the philosophical commonplace that no one can be obliged to do something unless he is capable of doing it, yet feeling with equal strength the call of duty, she, like Mrs. Poyser, asserted the common sense point that nothing will get done unless we make the effort and that experience tells us we can make it:

> Every fresh morning is an opportunity that one can look forward to for exerting one's will. I shall not be satisfied with your philosophy till you have conciliated necessitarianism . . . with the practice of willing strongly, of willing to will strongly, and so on, that being what you certainly can do and have done about a great many things in life."[21]

This is clearly not yet a sufficient justification of the position, but it is an important first step toward what might very well be the solution of the modern school of linguistic analysis (an immediate descendant of positivism). What it amounts to, however, is that in matters of choice determinism is "ethically irrelevant."[22]

It is important to see, however, on what grounds Mill and, one might safely infer, George Eliot were able satisfactorily for themselves to reconcile determinism with responsibility. The attempt has been made by philosophers over many centuries, but no one not a partisan of a particular contemporary view can look back over the history of the problem and be wholly satisfied that the reconciliation has been accomplished. W. D. Ross, one of the most eminent of twentieth-century moral philosophers, after a long discussion of the problem, says:

> This attempt to reconcile responsibility with Determinism can, then, hardly be deemed successful. . . . A philosophical genius may some day arise who will succeed in reconciling our natural thought about freedom and responsibility with acceptance of the law of causality; but I must admit that no existing discussion seems to be very successful in doing so.[23]

And although there have been a good many brilliant assaults on the problem since Ross wrote these words,[24] it is apparent that neither side is going to make any important concessions. In the face of the confusion of professional philosophers I do not pretend here to offer a solution. What I wish to do is outline the way Mill and George Eliot made the reconciliation and to suggest that if their answer is not *the* answer, it is *an* answer which must be accorded respect; if this is the vision embodied in George Eliot's works, one cannot dismiss her determinism out of hand.

II

The problem really begins with what Ross calls "our natural thought about freedom," that is, our instinctive feeling that somehow we are free to will whatever we wish within the limits of physical possibility, and that we are responsible for what we do. It is the point from which George Eliot seems to begin. To Mrs. Ponsonby she wrote:

> As to the necessary combinations through which life is manifested, and which seem to present themselves to you as a hideous fatalism which ought logically to petrify your volition—have they, *in fact,* any such influence on your

> ordinary course of action in the primary affairs of your existence as a human, stoical, domestic creature? And if they don't hinder you from taking a bath, without which you know you cannot secure the delicate cleanliness which is your second nature, why should they hinder you from a line of resolve in a higher strain of duty to your ideal, both for yourself and others?[25]

This certainly is typical of the way in which, for George Eliot, determinism reinforced a moral bias. She didn't allow philosophy to alter her instinctive and most strongly felt impressions (rather, with some analysts today, she used it to fortify them); what is essential is that she *felt* she was free to will and responsible for her acts at the same time that she believed in universal causality.

Before indicating in more theoretical terms how George Eliot justified her sense of responsibility, it is important to repeat that she was committed to universal causality. Certainly, there are occasions when she appears to be taking a fuzzy, religio-metaphysical libertarian position, but on these occasions she is usually talking metaphorically or attacking some of the cruder positions which determinism might produce.[26] In a letter to Bray, who ruled out the possibility of free will altogether, and who was so infatuated with his deterministic system that he minimized the importance of the individual, she wrote of "our total inability to find in our natures a key to the Divine Mystery."[27] And in her outraged rejection of the view that "the relations of men to their neighbours may be settled by algebraic equations,"[28] she seemed to be rejecting the possibility of a science of society based on the fixed laws of moral causation. But in fact, in these and many other similar arguments she is not rejecting the laws of causality. Rather, she is indicating that there are severe limitations to man's knowledge and that the phenomena of mind and of moral behavior are, as Comte argued before her, far too complicated to be reducible to formulas. All of her objections to ordering the phenomena of consciousness into precise formulas seem to be little more than an outgrowth of her insistence on the importance of the individual. It is on this point that she differed from Bray, Comte, and the other philosophers whose systems tended to overvalue Man at the expense of man.[29]

The three major aspects of George Eliot's reconciliation of determinism with responsibility seem to correspond to those of Mill: (1) her sense of the great and bewildering complexity of the causes which form human behavior; (2) her recognition of the difference between cause and compulsion; (3) her belief that each man's character plays an important role in determining what he becomes.

(1) *Complexity*. Her view of this point is similar to that of Comte and John Stuart Mill, although again, as in most cases, it is probably only the details which she borrowed from them. Here is Mill's statement:

> The agencies which determine human character are so numerous and diversified (nothing which has happened to the person throughout life being without its portion of influence), that in the aggregate they are never in any two cases exactly similar. Hence, even if our science of human nature were theoretically perfect, that is, if we could calculate any character as we can calculate the orbit of any planet, *from given data;* still as the data are never all given, nor ever precisely alike in different cases, we could neither make positive predictions, nor lay down universal propositions.[30]

As a philosopher George Eliot recognized this complexity,[31] but as an artist she emphasized it. She tried to show, as Bourl'honne remarks, that

> l'homme n'est pas un, qu'il est un composé de tendances multiples et diverses, le plus souvent opposées entre elles, et que, par consequent, suivant les rapports et l'équilibre qui s'établissent entre ces tendances, l'homme devient ceci ou cela. Il y a donc une certaine indetermination dans la destinée de l'individu; le caractère n'est pas continué des l'origine d'une manière absolue et définitive.[32]

But this proves that each individual is likely to be different and, perhaps, that his fate is not determinable by man, not that there is a certain indetermination in his development; it implies, on the contrary, that were it possible to know every causal factor in a character's life, one could, as Mill himself argues, accurately work out what he would become.[33] Accordingly, the argument from complexity merely suggests that man is too ignorant to know *how* he is determined, and that whatever laws apply to character, they are more complex than physical laws. Complexity may account for the "mystery" in human behavior and even for man's natural feeling that he is a morally free agent, but it cannot logically justify that feeling.

(2) *Cause and Compulsion.* On this point, George Eliot has very little explicitly to say, but in her treatment of character the idea is often implicit. Again, Mill's statement seems to me close enough to her view to be useful:

> human actions . . . are never (except in some cases of mania) ruled by any one motive with such absolute sway, that there is no room for the influence of any other. The causes, therefore, on which action depends, are never uncontrollable; and any given effect is only necessary provided that the causes tending to produce it are not controlled.[34] That a person holding what is called the Necessitarian doctrine should on that account *feel* that it would be unjust to punish him for his wrong actions, seems to me the veriest of chimeras. Yes, if he really "could not help" acting as he did, that is, if his *will* could not have helped it; if he was under the action of such a violent motive that no fear of punishment could have any effect; which, if capable of being ascertained, is a just ground of exemption, and is the reason why, by the laws of most countries, people are not punished for what they are compelled to do by the immediate danger of death.[35]

The point is that although every action is caused, few causes are uncontrollable in the sense that no effort to alter them can succeed.[36] As long as the cause is not a compulsion, that is, as long as it is not physically impossible or excessively dangerous to will differently and as long as one is not so mentally ill that one cannot will differently even if one wants to, one is responsible for his actions. To take an example: in *Adam Bede,* Arthur Donnithorne was free to avoid the circumstances which drew him into sexual relations with Hetty Sorrel. He was aware that he should have told Mr. Irwine about his feelings, but he chose not to. And even though he was helped in avoiding confession by Irwine's overly decorous refusal to make him talk, Arthur was under no compulsion to be silent. At one point in the conversation between Arthur and Irwine, Irwine figuratively and implicitly makes the distinction between cause and compulsion. Arthur says to him:

> "Well, but one may be betrayed into doing things by a combination of circumstances, which one might never have done otherwise."
>
> "Why, yes [Irwine replies], a man can't very well steal a bank-note unless the bank-note lies within convenient reach; but he won't make us think him an honest man because he begins to howl at the bank-note for falling in his way." (Ch. XVI)

The banknote's presence, that is to say, is one of the causes of the theft, but there is nothing in its presence serving as a compulsion to make a man steal it. The thief could have avoided stealing it had he wanted to strongly enough, and he was therefore responsible for his action. Significantly, a bit earlier in the same chapter in which Arthur and Irwine have the preceding conversation, Arthur says to Adam,

> I fancy you would master a wish that you had made up your mind it was not quite right to indulge, as easily as you would knock down a drunken fellow who was quarrelsome with you.

And a bit later:

> You've got an iron will, as well as an iron arm. But however strong a man's resolution may be, it costs him something to carry it out, now and then. We may determine not to gather any cherries, and keep our hands in our pockets, but we can't prevent our mouths from watering (Ch. xvi).

Of course, the point about Arthur is that once his mouth started watering, an action truly compelled because he has no control over his salivary glands, he would take his hands out of his pockets and start picking cherries. The second action, however, is not compelled by the loveliness of the cherries or the actions of his salivary glands; it is merely caused by them and several other things—primarily by a weakness of will. The mark of strong will, according to George Eliot, is the ability to avoid being influenced by merely selfish causes. Thus Adam Bede, watering mouth or not, would keep his hands in his pockets. And in the novels there are no occasions I can think of in which a character is *compelled* to make an important choice. Many of the moments of choice do, however, give the impression that the main character is coerced into the action by some internal compulsion. One thinks of Tito, suddenly confronted by the escaped Baldassare at the Duomo in Florence. His rejection of his foster father escapes from him almost instinctively. But what George Eliot is suggesting in this incident and in many others in her novels is that we frequently make our decisions long before we are required to make them public. Thus Tito, through his elaborate course of deceit about Baldassare before the encounter at the Duomo, had in fact already chosen to reject him. In less obvious ways, this is true of Gwendolen's decision, in the brilliant proposal scene in *Daniel Deronda,* to marry Grandcourt, and of Maggie's avoidance of a decision, as she is rowed down river by Stephen Guest. These characters are responsible for their decisions as fully as if they had, at the moment when the choice was necessary, balanced the alternatives carefully in their minds and hearts.

For the most part, it is true, George Eliot concerns herself in her novels with external pressures or internal desires which give the appearance at least at some point of being remediable. She does not press back to ask what were the causes which shaped the susceptibility or what were the causes which shaped the causes which shaped the susceptibility. Her concern is with the immediate and the practical (but this we see is true of Mill as well). The typical George Eliot story shows how a character (Lydgate, for example), under the influence of strong social pressures, reveals certain flaws in his character which, in combination with the social pressures, cause his moral failure. But it is important to see that George Eliot holds him responsible for his own character and his own motives.

Moreover, she doesn't suggest that Adam Bede, for example, because he is strong, is less fully determined in his actions by external and internal causes than Arthur, who is weak. For George Eliot strong will is a sign rather of a man who, aware of the power of causes to shape him (as Tito, for example, was not aware), is educated by this awareness. Felix Holt's self-justifying speech to Esther Lyon states the case plainly:

> It all depends on what a man gets into his consciousness—what life thrusts into his mind, so that [the desire to give up "worldly good"] becomes present to him as remorse is present to the guilty, or a mechanical problem to an inventive genius. There are two things I've got present in that way: one of them is the picture of what I should hate to be. I'm determined never to go about making my face simpering or solemn, and telling professional lies for profit; or to get tangled in affairs where I must wink at dishonesty and pocket the proceeds, and justify that knavery as part of a system that I can't alter. If I once went into that sort of struggle for success, I should want to win—I should defend the wrong that I had once identified myself with. I should become everything that I see now beforehand to be detestable. (Ch. xxvii)

(3) *Character.* This brings us to what Mill regarded as the strongest argument against necessitarianism: a man is himself one of the causes of what he becomes. As we have already seen, in his *Autobiography* Mill indicates that this idea is what saved him from the overpowering depression belief in determinism had forced upon him. Here is his most systematic statement of the view:

> [Man] has, to a certain extent, a power to alter his character. Its being, in the ultimate resort, formed for him, is not inconsistent with its being, in part, formed *by* him as one of the intermediate agents. His character is formed by his circumstances (including among these his particular organization); but his own desire to mould it in a particular way, is one of those circumstances, and by no means one of the least influential. . . . We are exactly as capable of making

> our own character, *if we will,* as others are of making it for us.[37]

Man is on this account no longer a merely passive figure compelled by the power of innumerable causes, but an active force with some power to choose among a number of possible alternatives. According to this argument, it is true, a man's action can never be uncaused. If, however, we put the idea in different terminology—"He can never act without a motive, conscious or otherwise"—it loses its depressing effect.[38] And his character, shaped in the past by experience of right and wrong, pain and pleasure, can act on what the experience taught, if it will. George Eliot never puts the argument in such thoroughly Benthamite terms (although she does specifically recognize the usefulness of legal punishment), but the view, slightly modified, runs through all her works. When her characters come to a point at which they must make a crucial decision, she does not mean the decision to be a mere formality. Arthur really has an opportunity to confess to Mr. Irwine, just as Romola has the opportunity *not* to return to Tito at Savonarola's prompting, and Gwendolen not to marry Grandcourt. The difference lies in the characters' consciousness of their own motives. Arthur yields to the habits of his nature without fully understanding them. Romola, on the other hand, behaves in a way counter to her usual proud nature, and humbles herself before Tito. A character, for George Eliot, becomes what he makes himself: he can, in some limited degree, move counter to the push of external circumstance, and, by allowing himself to become aware of his own motives, can even at times overcome them by changing them. In "Janet's Repentance," for example, Janet Dempster, an alcoholic and therefore almost compelled, not merely caused, to drink, is saved from moral destruction by her own powerful desire to overcome her habit (and by Mr. Tryan).

There is nevertheless no indication in George Eliot's writings that, as Ernest Baker wishfully remarks, for her "Ultimately, the will is free."[39] She did not believe that the will had to be "free" in the sense of "uncaused" (the sense to which, unless specifically stated otherwise, I am attempting to restrict it in this paper) in order that every man be responsible for his actions.

It is likely, rather, that she accepted Mill's arguments, when, in combating the necessitarian position, he wrote,

> to think that we have no power of altering our characters, and to think that we shall not use our power unless we have a motive, are very different things, and have a very different effect upon the mind. A person who does not wish to alter his character, cannot be the person who is supposed to feel discouraged or paralyzed by thinking himself unable to do it. The depressing effect of the fatalist doctrine can only be felt where there *is* a wish to do what that doctrine represents as impossible. It is of no consequence what we think forms our character when we have no desire of our own about forming it; but it is of great consequence that we should not be prevented from forming such a desire by thinking the attainment impracticable, and that if we have the desire, we should know that the work is not so irrevocably done as to be incapable of being altered.[40]

This is very similar to the argument which George Eliot used in the letter to Mrs. Ponsonby I have already quoted. Her insistence that every man should exercise his will did not commit her to the view that every man is capable of any choice. As Irwine says to Donnithorne, "A man can never do anything at variance with his own nature" (Ch. xvi). But within the limits of his nature, man is capable of altering his character by willing to alter it. Only people who surrender hopelessly to their impulses or to the pressures of external circumstances—people like the young Arthur Donnithorne—appear wholly determined in their actions by forces external to themselves. And even they, since they almost deliberately refuse to be more than passive and unaware of the forces that are driving them, are contributing to the external causes of their moral decline.

III

It might seem that for a moralist, belief in a universe wholly governed by the laws of cause and effect is the starting point for little more than a series of subtle wranglings about the possibility of any moral act whatever. On the contrary, however, according to George Eliot and to most determinist moral philosophers, a deterministic universe is the *only* kind of universe in which moral acts are possible. In a wholly or even partially undetermined universe, every act would be capricious because it need not be the result of one's own past thinking and experience or of one's consciousness of its possible effects. It would, as W. D. Ross says, "have no moral value. . . . because it would not be the result of any thought about the nature of the act, and of any consequent impulsion to do it. It would be an unintelligent and unmotived leap in the dark."[41] Since in such a world there would be no necessary or consistent connection between the past and the present, between one's thinking and one's actions, between *any* two things, morality, as we presently conceive it, would be impossible. As I have already suggested determinism was for George Eliot a theory which she used to support her moral biases; without determinism she could have found no rational justification for them.

It is therefore, George Eliot says, the presence of "undeviating law" which "alone can give value to experience and render education in the true sense possible."[42] Experience is valuable only in so far as it can teach, and it can teach only in so far as it is consistent. If, for instance, a certain act produces an undesirable effect, one will avoid doing it again unless one wants to produce that effect. But if the effect does not consistently follow from the action, one can have learned nothing (and may therefore, for example, put his hand on hot stoves frequently, only occasionally, if at all, to be burned). One will not know whether any act is worth doing, and whatever one chooses to do in the future cannot be rationally dependent on what one did in the past. The great moral teacher in the world, as George Eliot saw it, was experience, and at its best dogma—unquestioned rule inherited from the past—could only serve as a frequently misleading shortcut:

> The divine yea and nay, the seal of prohibition and of sanction, are effectually impressed on human deeds and aspirations, not by means of Greek and Hebrew, but by that inexorable law of consequences, whose evidence is confirmed instead of weakened as the ages advance; and human duty

> is comprised in the earnest study of this law and patient obedience to its teaching . . . every past phase of human development is part of that education of the race in which we are sharing; every mistake, every absurdity into which poor human nature has fallen, may be looked on as an experiment of which we may reap the benefit. A correct generalization gives significance to the smallest detail.[43]

But where no generalization is possible, she implies, nothing has significance.

Thus, for George Eliot morality and responsibility are wholly bound up in determinism, and they are not achievable, as libertarians would have it, by denying the universality of cause and effect. A man is only good in so far as he has trained himself to exercise his will for what past experience has taught him is the good. George Eliot believed that the only way one can transcend circumstance is by recognizing clearly that the "law of consequence" is irrevocable and invariable—"human duty is comprised in the earnest study of this law and patient obedience to its teaching"—that the past is a permanent part of one's character, and one's society is, and should be, a very powerful influence on one's actions. In other words, one overcomes the depressing effects of determinism by understanding it. This can be viewed, of course, as just another version of the vicious Hegelian-Marxist paradox that freedom is the recognition of necessity. But a theory has it value, in good part, in the context which it fills. For Hegel and Marx the paradox was intended to shift responsibility from the individual to the state and to make the individual a passive creature of the state. And it is to the credit of George Eliot that she indulges this paradox in its most acceptable form—not to diminish man's responsibility or to submit him to some higher power, but to increase it and to give meaning and direction to his activity for good.

Moreover, the determinist-freedom paradox, as George Eliot resolves it, is not paradoxical at all. The difficulty, according to her implicit analysis, is essentially linguistic. If we mean by free "uncaused," then our actions are never free and the paradox is meaningless. But if we are willing to shift the meaning of "free" to "capable of reasonable choice in accordance with our motives" (which all the novels or letters allow), then there is no conflict between determinism and "freedom." This kind of semantic shift is unlikely to satisfy those who argue that man is wholly the master of his fate, and who mean something quite different by the word. But such "freedom" has its attractions: it is the condition of a man who knows why he does what he does, who knows the probable effects of his actions, who understands the forces of habit, emotion, and circumstance working upon him, and who is therefore able to avoid succumbing irrationally to their influence.

And this is the condition of George Eliot's heroes when they arrive at their moral maturity. They all share a sense of their littleness in the universe and a consequent willingness to renounce their own desires for "wider and nobler" ends. All of them come to understand that their lives are irrevocably dependent on the lives of others. On the other hand, the unhappy characters, the ones who strive blindly for romantically inaccessible ends, are unhappy precisely because they are not conscious of the invariable "law of consequence" and allow their egoistic desires to push them toward ruin by forcing them to demand too much of the world. In *Daniel Deronda,* the clearest sign of Gwendolen Harleth's regeneration is her recognition for the first time that "her horizon was but a dipping onward of an existence with which her own was revolving" (Ch. lxix). And in *The Mill on the Floss* even Maggie's wretchedness after her father's bankruptcy is blamed on her lack of "knowledge of the irreversible laws within and without her, which, governing the habits, becomes morality, and developing the feelings of submission and dependence, becomes religion" (Bk IV, Ch. iii).

Determinism, then, manifests itself in George Eliot's works, not only in her analysis of how her weak characters degenerate, but equally in her description of the growth to maturity of her heroes and heroines. Determinism, for her, is at the root of education, and it therefore pervades her novels: in the constant interplay between the individual and society and the consequent elaborate portraits of, for example, the towns of St. Oggs, Florence, and Middlemarch; in the instinctive and traditional shrewdness of Mrs. Poyser in *Adam Bede,* the Dodsons in *The Mill on the Floss,* and the Garths in *Middlemarch;* in the ineluctable reactions of their deeds upon the virtuous and villainous alike, in the traditionalism and fundamental conservatism of the strong-willed, powerful Adam Bede and Felix Holt, in her analysis of the debilitating effects of egoism and of the moral power of external goodness (as exemplified by Maggie's edition of *The Imitation of Christ* or the homiletic and tedious Daniel Deronda). And the insights and limitations of these specifically deterministic aspects of her work are linked—whether as cause or effect is not clear—to her vivid sense of introspective psychology, and of social relations in a universe undirected by any supernatural being and therefore indifferent (as any later naturalist would have seen it) to the problems of humanity.[44]

Whatever her philosophical conclusions might have been, George Eliot's handling of the problem was artistic rather than theoretical. Determinism was for her not a rigid and depressing system but an aspect of the world which she saw and dramatized. She was concerned with the practical rather than the philosophical consequences of her views. She knew that somehow evil was to be avoided and her interest was not in finding someone to blame for it—in discovering whether or not she had a philosophical right to blame anyone—but in averting it. For her, the man who excuses himself from responsibility because he was caused to do wrong is arguing beside the point. In *Adam Bede,* when Arthur Donnithorne suggests that a man is excusable if he succumbs to a severe temptation, Mr. Irwine replies with what must be George Eliot's own answer: "Our deeds carry their terrible consequences, quite apart from any fluctuation that went before—consequences that are hardly ever confined to ourselves. And it is best to fix our mind on that certainty, instead of considering what may be the elements of excuse for us" (Ch. xvi). And Mrs. Poyser takes a similar common sense position: "I see plain enough we shall never do it without a resolution, and that's enough for me" (Ch. xvii).

Notes

[1] Most of the critics who discuss her determinism do so in order to criticize. See, especially, Gerald Bullett, *George Eliot: Her Life and Books* (London, 1947): "Determinism is a form of death because it makes everything, including our own thinking, a mindless mechanism." More recently, William J. Hyde in "George

Eliot and the Climate of Realism," *PMLA,* LXXII (March, 1957), has written: "What matters is that George Eliot based her sequence of action not so much on direct observation and recording of life, as she did her characters, but on a preconceived moral theory of consequences that served to direct it toward an end" (p. 163). This is an argument similar to David Cecil's in his *The Early Victorian Novelists* (London, 1934). See especially p. 319. Again, Robert Preyer in a valuable article, "Beyond the Liberal Imagination: Vision and Unreality in 'Daniel Deronda,'" *Victorian Studies,* IV (September, 1960), argues that the Deronda half of the novel is important because in it for the first time George Eliot breaks through the restricting dogma of determinism. Implicity Mr. Preyer assumes that determinism for George Eliot is equivalent to necessitarianism.

[2] See especially her essay on the German philospher Gruppe (*Leader,* 28 July 1855, pp. 723–24) in which she makes plain her distaste for German system-making and praises Gruppe for his refusal to indulge in it. One of her most famous comments on the dangers of dogma and general systems comes in *The Mill on the Floss:*

> All people of broad, strong sense have an instinctive repugnance to the men of maxims; because such people early discern that the mysterious complexity of our life is not to be embraced by maxims, and that to lace ourselves up in formulas of that sort is to repress all the divine promptings and inspirations that spring from growing insight and sympathy. And the man of maxims is the popular representative of the minds that are guided in their moral judgment solely by general rules, thinking that these will lead them to justice by a ready-made patent method, without the trouble of exerting patience, discrimination, impartiality—without any care to assure themselves whether they have the insight that comes from a hardly-earned estimate of temptation, or from a life vivid and intense enough to have created a wide fellow-feeling with all that is human. (Bk. VII, ch. ii)

All quotations from George Eliot's works, unless otherwise noted, are from the Cabinet Edition, 24 vols. (London and Edinburgh, n. d.).

[3] See, for example, C. D. Broad, *Determinism, Indeterminism and Libertarianism* (Cambridge, England, 1934).

[4] George Eliot's contemporary, J. A. Froude, though not a philospher himself, took this position. He wrote, a conviction assures us that there is somewhere a point of freedom. What that point is, where other influences terminate and responsibility begins, will always be of intricate and often impossible solution. But if there is such a point at all, it is fatal to necessitarianism, and man is what he has been hitherto supposed to be—an exception in the order of nature, with a power not differing in degree but differing in kind from those of other creatures. ("Spinoza," *Westminster Review,* LXIV [July, 1885], 20). To Sara Hennell George Eliot wrote about this article, "I don't at all agree with Froude's own views" (*The George Eliot Letters,* ed. Gordon S. Haight, 7 vols. [New Haven, 1954–56], II, 211; henceforward *GEL*),

[5] *Silas Marner,* Ch. XIV.

[6] *Adam Bede,* Ch. XVII.

[7] Auguste Comte, *A General View of Positivism,* tr. J. H. Bridges, Academic Reprints (Stanford, n. d.), pp. 28–29.

[8] *GEL,* V, 403.

[9] It is important, however, to see that though George Eliot's thought seeems pervaded by the details of positivistic and contemporary scientific philosophy,

her position was probably not so much caused by them as refined by them. Her temperament and her own broad intellect shaped most of her major beliefs before she was exposed to the systematic philosophies of Mill, Spencer, and Comte. She wrote,

> I never had any personal acquaintance with J. S. Mill . . . . and though I have studied his books, especially his Logic and Political Economy, with much benefit, I have no consciousness of their having made any marked epoch in my life.
>
> Of Mr. Herbert Spencer's friendship I have had the honour and advantage for twenty years, but I believe that every main bias of my mind had been taken before I knew him. Like the rest of his readers, I am of course indebted to him for much enlargement and clarifying of thought. (*GEL*, VI, 163)

For more on this point, see Paul Bourl'honne, *George Eliot: essaie de biographie intellectuelle et morale, 1819–1854* (Paris, 1933), p. 112, and Michael Wolff, "Marian Evans to George Eliot: The Moral and Intellectual Foundation of her Career," a microfilmed doctoral dissertation (Princeton, 1958), pp. 145–46. The latter is the most useful and thorough intellectual biography of George Eliot I have seen.

[10] Pater's ideas met with George Eliot's fairly strong disapproval, despite the similarity of their views on history and systems. See *GEL*, V, 455.

[11] Several critics have called attention to the persistent web imagery in *Middlemarch*. Quentin Anderson, for instance, suggests that "the master image of the book . . . is the image of human relationships as a web" ("George Eliot in Middlemarch," *From Dickens to Hardy*, The Pelican Guide to English Literature, ed. Boris Ford, [London, 1959], VI, 276–77).

[12] *Impressions of Theophrastus Such*, Ch. ii, "Looking Backward." This chapter in particular is useful to anyone interested in establishing the "non-intellectual" influences on the development of her mature views.

[13] *The Victorian Sage: Studies in Argument* (London, 1958), p. 127.

[14] *Middlemarch*, "Finale."

[15] *Mill on the Floss*, Bk. IV, Ch. i.

[16] F. W. H. Myers, *Essays Modern* (London, 1885), p. 269.

[17] *GEL*, VI, 99.

[18] She said she hated "the ugly word" (*GEL*, VI, 66).

[19] As I have already suggested, George Eliot's views on determinism and necessitarianism, as far as I can find them expressed explicitly in her writings, are strikingly similar to (though not necessarily dependent on) those of Mill and, less completely, of Comte. All three writers emphasize the moral implications of the views, and Mill, with George Eliot, stresses the importance of the individual in a deterministic scheme and the possibility of his altering in some measure the course of things. Anyone wishing to find a more systematic and full exposition of the position would do well to read the Sixth Book of Mill's *System of Logic*, "On the Logic of the Moral Sciences," especially Chapters ii, x, and xi. In the following discussion I shall be relying heavily on Mill's exposition. All references are to the first edition, *A System of Logic; Ratiocinative and Inductive* (London, 1843), 2 vols.

[20] *Autobiography of John Stuart Mill* (New York, 1924), p. 119. Both Mill and George Eliot regard the problem of freewill in terms which would be unac-

ceptable to contemporary philosophical analysts, although their manner of solution is similar. The central distinction lies in what the analysts might call their failure to perceive that the "will" is not a faculty, acting, as it were, divorced from the whole person. Gilbert Ryle has been the most outspoken of contemporary philosophers on this point. He rejects, as Mill and George Eliot did not, the extension of the mechanical model of the universe from physical nature to moral and voluntary acts, and has therefore changed all the major terms of the discussion of "freewill." See especially his *The Concept of Mind* (London, 1949), Ch. iii. Ryle's essay on the subject, "It Was to Be," in *Dilemmas* (Cambridge, England, 1953), is a good example of his method.

[21] *GEL,* VI, 66.

[22] Stephen Pepper, *Ethics* (New York, 1960), p. 46.

[23] *Foundation of Ethics* (Oxford, 1939), p. 230.

[24] See especially A. J. Ayer, *Philosophical Essays* (London, 1954), Ch. xii; P. H. Nowell-Smith, *Ethics,* Penguin Books (London, 1954), Chs. xix–xx, and, by the same author "Freewill and Moral Responsibility," *Mind,* LVII (1948), 45–61; also Stuart Hampshire, *Thought and Action* (London, 1959), *passim.*

[25] *GEL,* VI, 98.

[26] See, for example, her argument against "men of maxims" in note 2, above.

[27] *GEL,* II, 403.

[28] *Essays,* "The Natural History of German Life: Riehl."

[29] Indeed, it is astonishing that there are so few records of her criticism of Comte. His assertion, that "the only real life is the collective life of the race; that individual life has no existence except as an abstraction" (*A General View,* p. 404), must certainly have infuriated her as did Young's poetry or Dr. Cumming's evangelical preaching.

[30] *System of Logic,* II, 494. Here is Comte's view on the subject:

> invariability in all primary aspects is found compatible with modifications in points of secondary importance. These modifications become more numerous and extensive as the phenomena are more complex. The reason of this is that the causes from a combination of which the effects proceed being more varied and more accessible, offer greater facilities to our feeble power to interfere with advantage . . . the extensive modifications of which society admits, go far to keep up the common mistake that social phenomena are not subject to any constant law. (*A General View,* pp. 31–32)

[31] See, for example, her essay on Riehl.

[32] *George Eliot,* p. 155.

[33] This, however, is to say little more than that if you know everything about a man you know everything about him. Gilbert Ryle makes an important distinction between being able to predict what will happen and determining it, and he suggests that there is nothing binding on a person whose actions have been predicted. In other words, ability to predict does not imply necessitarianism (*Dilemmas,* Ch. ii).

[34] *System of Logic,* II, 484.

[35] John Stuart Mill, *An Examination of Sir William Hamilton's Philosophy,* 2 vols. (New York, 1874), II, 296–97.

[36] I recognize the circularity of this reasoning. To say that a cause is controllable by other causes is simply to push the question back, not to resolve it. The act of controlling a cause is itself caused, and one might go on infinitely asking what causes the cause which causes the cause, etc. This is precisely the kind of difficulty the analytic philosophers would object to. One must recognize, for example, the difference between robbing a bank because one wants the money and robbing it because one is forced at gunpoint to do so. Nowell-Smith makes explicit, it seems to me, the point of view that Mill is taking up here when he attacks the libertarians who, making the objection of circularity to an argument like Mill's ask, "Can we justly blame a man if vicious actions are due to hereditary epilepsy or to the influence of a corrupt and vicious court?" Nowell-Smith replies,

> To this the answer is that we can and do. So long as we persist in supposing that, to be moral, an action must be uncaused, we could only push the moral responsibility back in time; and this, so far from solving the problem, merely shows the impossibility of any solution on these lines" ("Freewill and Moral Responsibility," p. 50).

[37] *System of Logic,* II, 485.

[38] Hume in the eighteenth century and Nowell-Smith in the twentieth make the same point. Hume says, "By liberty, then, we can only mean a *power of acting or not acting according to the determinations of the will*" (*An Inquiry Concerning the Human Understanding,* sec. 8); Nowell-Smith puts it a little differently, "To be 'free' in this sense is to be free to do what one wants to do, not to be able to act in spite of one's desires" (*Ethics,* p. 279).

[39] *History of the English Novel,* 10 vols. (London, 1930), VIII, 235.

[40] *System of Logic,* II, 486.

[41] *Foundation of Ethics,* p. 231.

[42] "Mackay's Progress of the Intellect," *The Writings of George Eliot,* Warwickshire Edition, 25 vols. (Boston, 1907), XXII, 279.

[43] Ibid.

[44] "For if it be true that Nature at certain moments seems charged with a presentiment of one individual lot, must it not also be true that she seemes unmindful, unconscious of another?" (*Adam Bede,* Ch. XXVII).

17.

Angus Wilson

The Heroes and Heroines of Dickens

To examine the heroes and heroines of Dickens is to dwell on his weaknesses and failures. Only a strong conviction of Dickens's extraordinary greatness can make such an examination either worth while or decorous; since the literary critic, unlike the reviewer, can always choose his fields and should seek surely to appreciate rather than to disparage. Even in the weak field of his heroes and heroines, Dickens made remarkable advances, for though he matured—or, to use a less evaluating word, changed—late both as a man and as an artist, his immense energy drove him on through the vast field of his natural genius to attempt the conquest of the territory that lay beyond. The development of the heroes and heroines of his novels is indeed a reflection of this change or maturing, and a measure of his success in going beyond the great domain he had so easily mastered. Some of the dilemmas that lay at the root of his difficulties were personal to him; but others were historical, and some perhaps will never be solved by any novelist.

In general, the subject of Dickens's heroes has not received much attention from serious critics. Admirers have preferred to dwell on his excellencies; detractors have found more positive qualities to excite their antipathy. The child heroes and heroines brought tears to the eyes of contemporary readers, and have

Reprinted by permission of the author, the editor, and Curtis Brown Ltd. from *Review of English Literature,* Vol. 2, No. 3 (July, 1961), 268–79.

found equal portions of admiration and dislike in later times. There has been some general recognition that the now highly acclaimed late novels owe something of their declared superior merit to a greater depth in the portrayal of the heroes and the heroines.

I shall not here discuss the child heroes and heroines, except to suggest that as Dickens matured he found them inadequate centers for the complex social and moral structures he was trying to compose. The children too gained in realism by being removed from the center. The peripheral Jo has a deeply moving realism that is not there in the necessarily falsely genteel Little Nell or Oliver. It is also perhaps worth noticing as a mark of Dickens's rich genius that he could be prodigal with his gifts, making masterly child portraits of Paul, David, and Pip serve merely as fractions of a large structure. Most post-Jamesian novelists would have exhausted their total energies in such portrayals of the childhood vision.

It is, however, the adult heroes and heroines with whom I am concerned. Let me first suggest the limitations which I believe hampered Dickens in successfully creating central figures in his works, and then, by analysis of the development of the heroes and heroines through his novels, throw some light perhaps upon how far he overcame or could overcome these limitations.

The historical limitations of the Victorian novelists are too well known to be worth more than a mention. The happy ending is an unfortunate distortion in Dickens's work as it is in that of the other great Victorians, but, despite the change made to *Great Expectations,* it goes deeper than a mere capitulation to the whims of readers. With Dickens as with Thackeray, though for different reasons, the contemporary idea of domestic happiness as the resolution of, or perhaps more fairly one should say, the counterpoise to social evil, was a strongly held personal conviction. Even more vital to Dickens was the idea of pure love as the means of redemption of flawed, weak, or sinful men. Neither of these beliefs can properly take the weight that he imposed upon them; though the latter, at any rate, is not such a psychological falsity perhaps as many twentieth-century critics have thought. The main destructive effort of this exaggerated view of love as a moral solvent falls upon those characters in the novels who, under any view, could be regarded as heroes and heroines. Closely allied to the popular prejudice in favor of wedding bells and the patter of tiny feet is the contemporary absolute demand for sexual purity. There has been a recent tendency to play down the effects of this on the Victorian novel. True, these effects have so often been discussed as now to be trite, but that does not unfortunately diminish them. This censorship did, in fact, reduce the great Victorian novelists in the sexual sphere to a childish status beside their continental contemporaries. It is surprising how often they can get past the ban by suggestion; it is surprising how often the ban does not matter to an imaginative reader; again, our freedom is only relative and has its own danger of absurdity; all this is true—yet the fact remains that our great Victorian novelists were forced at times to devices that are false, ridiculous, or blurred. And these faults occur too often at the moral heart of their work. In English fashion, and with reason, we may take pride in the degree to which our Victorian novelists achieved greatness in spite of this—but we can't efface it. No characters, of course, suffer so greatly as the heroes and heroines. Once again, however, I would suggest that Dickens had a special personal relationship to this sexual censorship—and that, while it sometimes led him into exceptionally absurd devices, it also produced a characteristically powerful effect. The sexual life of Charles Dickens, like that of most Victorians, has become a shop-soiled subject, but one may briefly say four things of it—he was a strongly sensual man, he had a deep social and emotional need for family life and love, he had a compensating claustrophobic dislike of the domestic scene, and he woke up to these contradictions in his sexual makeup very late. Surely the distressing feature about the famous letter to the press upon the breakup of his marriage is not so much the tasteless publicity, but the tasteless publicity sought by a man of Dickens's years and standing. He acted at best like a young man blinded by new fame. His emotional life, in fact, for all his many children, was by most standards immature. Thackeray, very percipient where his dislike of Dickens was concerned, hit the right note, when he said of Kate, "the poor matron." Dickens behaved not as a middle-aged man but as a young fool or as an old fool.

The contemporary censorship, in fact, went along with, rather than against, Dickens's natural inclinations. His submerged, but fierce, sensuality was to run some strange courses from the days of John Chester until it came to light in the diverging streams of Wrayburn and Headstone. Seduction withheld, deferred, foiled—at any rate never accomplished—produced many interesting and complex characters, who would not have been born in a fiction that reflected the real world where men are more resolute and women are weaker.

Perhaps even more important in its effect on his heroes and heroines than the imperfect view of love and the impossible view of sex that Dickens shared with his readers, was the ambiguous view of Victorian society that he shared with so many of the artists and intellectuals of his age. Broadly speaking, one could say that the young Dickens aspired to a respectable middle-class radicalism attacking particular social evils, and ended as a middle-aged revolutionary with a peculiar hostility to the middle classes. Such an evolution in a man not given to intellectual self-analysis inevitably produced ambiguities in his portrayal of every social class at one time or another. And in no group of characters is this unconscious evolution with its accompanying contradictions more clearly displayed than in the young men who stand at the heroic center of his books. This uneven course in his social opinions, now veering, now tacking, yet, for all its changes, moving in one final direction, affected his attitude to the future and to the past, to all classes, to education, to money, to ambition, to work, to play, to conformity, and to rebellion. This strange and complex pattern of life may be observed working out in various ways among his heroes and heroines.

Any account of Dickens must start with *Pickwick Papers,* the novel which announces an age of innocence before the course has begun. Perhaps Dickens never produced so satisfactorily a hero as Mr. Pickwick again—a man, who like his author, imperceptibly changes; but not from hope to despair, rather from nullity to positive goodness. None of the problems of Dickens are met in this book: Mr. Pickwick developed in the garden of Eden before the fall, the next step from him was to Oliver and Nell—children, at least, have their measure of original sin. Yet no article on Dickens's heroes should fail to salute the perfection of Mr. Pickwick before it goes on to the real story.

Apart from the children, the first group of heroes may be seen leading up to the self-portrait of David Copperfield. Like Mr. Pickwick, this "walking gentleman," genteel hero group begins in near nullity: one cannot discuss Harry Mayley or Edward Chester, for they are not there. Nicholas and Martin advance us a few steps: they are haters of hypocrisy, cant, and cruelty; sharp tongued and humorous; hot-tempered; inclined to selfishness; a bit weak and spoilt; pale reflections, with their eye for the absurd, of the uninstrospective young Dickens as he saw himself. Martin, with Jonas and Chevy Slyme for his relations, can hardly claim gentility; but Nicholas is a born gentleman of a somewhat ill-defined kind, although his uncle is a money-lender. The young socially unsure Dickens had need not only of false gentility and of hatred of the aristocracy, he needed also a suffused and vague love of the past—a mark of the genteel. So Nicholas's first act, when he became a rich and prosperous merchant, was to buy his father's "old house . . . none of the old rooms were ever pulled down, no old tree was ever rooted up, nothing with which there was any association of bygone times was ever removed or changed."

It is something of the same undefined traditional gentility which so endears to David Copperfield Dr. Strong's vaguely traditional old school and the aroma of scholarship given off by his improbable dictionary. David is the culmination, in fact, of these purely genteel heroes for whom Pip was later to atone. Of course, being a self-portrait, he has more life, but, after childhood, it's a feeble ray. To begin with, who can believe that he is a novelist? Indeed, although he is said to be a model of hard work, we never have any sense of it except in his learning shorthand. Dickens was far too extrovert in those days to analyze the qualities in himself that made for his genius. It is notable that David is no more than "advanced in fame and fortune," where Dickens was advanced in literary skill and imaginative power. It is also notable that after childhood, nothing happened to David himself except the passion of his love for Dora and the shock of her death—and these, which should be poignant, are somehow made less by being smiled back upon through the tears as part of youth's folly and life's pageant. *David Copperfield* is technically a very fine novel of the sentimental education genre, but the mood of mellow, wise reflection is surely too easily held; and, when we think of Dickens's age at the time of its writing, held all too prematurely. "Advanced in fortune and fame," as a result, has inevitably a smug sound, and "my domestic joy was perfect" seems to demand the Nemesis that was to come in real life.

Nor is this smug, genteel, conformist quality of David helped by Agnes. A successful novelist guided by her "deep wisdom" would surely become a smug, insensitive, comfortable old best seller of the worst kind. Agnes, indeed, is the first of the group of heroines who mark the least pleasing, most frumpy and smug vision of ideal womanhood that he produced. Agnes, in fact, is betrayed by Esther Summerson, when Dickens in his next book so unwisely decided to speak through his heroine's voice. It is not surprising that this wise, womanly, housekeeping, moralizing, self-congratulating, busy little creature should have needed a good dose of childlikeness, a dose of Little Nell to keep her going when she reappears as Little Dorrit. If we cannot believe in the child-woman Little Dorrit, at least we are not worried as we are by Agnes or Esther Summerson about her complete lack of a physical body—a deficiency so great that Esther's smallpox-spoilt face jars us because she has no body upon which a head could rest.

But if nothing happens to David himself after Mr. Murdstone goes off the scene, something does happen in the novel, about which David (Dickens uses language that suggests that there lies the real drama—as well he may, for with Steerforth's seduction of Em'ly, and indeed with Steerforth himself, we are at the beginning of all those twists and turns by which Dickens eventually transforms a somewhat stagey villain into a new sort of full-sized hero. From Steerforth to Eugene Wrayburn is the road of self-discovery. Of all the would-be seducers in Dickens's novels, James Steerforth alone gets his prey; yet he is the only one, until Wrayburn, whom Dickens seems to have wished to redeem. If we look at the facts of Steerforth's character, it may be difficult to see why. From the moment that he so revoltingly gets Mr. Mell dismissed at Creakle's school until his carefully planned seduction of Em'ly he does nothing to commend himself. Yet David (and surely Dickens) uses language that would save if it could—"But he slept—let me think of him so again—as I had often seen him sleep at school; and thus, in this silent hour I left him. Never more, oh God forgive you, Steerforth, to touch that passive hand in love and friendship.

Never, never more!" . . . "Yes, Steerforth, long removed from the scenes of this poor history! My sorrow may bear involuntary witness against you at the Judgement Throne; but my angry thoughts or reproaches never will, I know." And at the last—"among the ruins of the home he had wronged, I saw him lying with his hand upon his arm, as I had often seen him lie at school." If Dickens could have redeemed Steerforth he surely would have done so. And, indeed, he did; for Eugene Wrayburn is as much a redemption of Steerforth as Pip is a scapegoat for the falsities in David. On the whole, as I suggest, redemption through Wrayburn is a somewhat arbitrary business; but before that redemption came about, the figure of Steerforth had suffered under many guises and, in the course of his translation to hero, had borne witness to many changes in Dickens's social and moral outlook, had even assisted in the birth of a heroine more adequate to Dickens's mature outlook than either Little Nell or Agnes, or indeed the strange hybrid figure of Little Dorrit.

To trace these changes we should perhaps go back before Steerforth to earlier seductions in the novels. At the start the seducer is a cynical rake or libertine—John Chester or Sir Mulberry Hawk. He stands full square for the aristocratic dandy whom the middle-class radical Dickens detests as the source of outdated arbitrary power. Yet we have only to look at Boz in his early pictures to see the beringed and ringleted dandy—or is it the "gent"? Dick Swiveller is kindly treated. In his adolescence surely it was among the would-be swells of Dick Swiveller's world that Dickens moved—the direct butt, no doubt, of any real dandy's contempt and laughter. The seducer, then, up to *Dombey,* is a crude class symbol.

Dombey and Son brings us further forward. Carker has some genuine sensuality, of the cold, calculating, rather epicene imitaton-Byron kind that the early nineteenth century must often have bred. True, he is vulgar, hypocritical, and apparently subservient—but then, unlike Steerforth, he has to scheme and work for his living. Like Steerforth, his Byronic professional seducing spills over into other sorts of pleasure loving—a somewhat ornately comfortable villa. There are four things in which Steerforth differs from him, apart from age: Steerforth despises the world, he puts other values above work, he sometimes wishes that he was not wasting his life, he has the vestige of a power to love or at any rate to want to be loved. It is not very much luggage, yet it proves enough to make the long journey to Eugene Wrayburn. Carker fails in his seduction, but then in Edith Dombey he has a much more difficult job than little Em'ly presents to Steerforth. There were two roads open for the Dickensian seducer—glamour (it was presumably this that Steerforth used, though little Em'ly's last note to Peggotty shows small evidence that she has felt it) or boredom. Boredom and self-distaste, these were the marks of the woman who had already sold herself into loveless marriage—Edith, Louisa Bounderby, Honoria Dedlock, if she had not already been seduced before the novel began. Pride saves Edith Dombey; pride would have saved Lady Dedlock; pride and an instinct of self-preservation save Louisa. Yet it is hardly a fair contest—Mr. Carker emits his faint ray of vulgar sensuality, James Harthouse his rather superior brand of Steerforth's worldly charm. But, if it only takes one to make a rape, it takes two to make a seduction; and there is nothing in Edith or Louisa to respond. They are looking for flight from a desperate situation and indeed they take it; but they are not looking for any species of sexual love. The female equivalent to the sort of professional minor Byronism that Steerforth and Harthouse and Gowan, no doubt, in his relations with Miss Wade, offer, is the minor, rather half-hearted coquetry that is touched on in Dolly Varden, punished in Fanny Dorrit and Estella, and finally redeemed in Bella Wilfer. But Estella and Bella are more than coquettes, they are proud, frozen, unhappy women anxious to be free of desperate homes, they combine in fact the nearest approach that Dickens gets to a sensually alive woman with the proud cold beauties—Edith, Louisa, and Honoria. *Our Mutual Friend,* in fact, contains the most developed hero and the most developed heroine in Dickens's fiction. The one has come a long journey from the seducer-villain; and the other, almost as long a journey from the coquette and the runaway wife. Even so they remain separate, each is reclaimed by a nullity, John Harmon and Lizzie Hexam. Yet in them Dickens has admitted to the saved a degree of sexual reality that argues well for the future.

We may leave Bella on one side; she has brought some frailty, some liveliness, and some sexual warmth to Dickens's heroines;

but she plays little part in the evolution of Dickens's social or moral outlook—it was not a woman's role to do so.

Eugene Wrayburn is a far more interesting case. His salvation is really immensely arbitrary. Even after he has left Lizzie for the last time before Headstone's murderous attack, he has not given up his ideas of seduction entirely—his father's voice tells him, "You wouldn't marry for some money and some station, because you were frightfully likely to become bored. Are you less frightfully likely to become bored marrying for no money and no station?" It is indeed his rival's blows that save him. Yet we have seen that Steerforth had certain pleas to offer; Wrayburn offers all the same pleas and by this time they have become more urgent to Dickens. First, contempt for the world and for success—this, once a hidden admiration, is now the center of Dickens's moral values. Private income, public school and university education, all these may be forgiven if they produce a despiser of bourgeois society. Dandy insolence, once the mark of an arbitrary, outdated order is now the badge of rejection of Podsnap. Other values above work and duty? This has been amply confirmed by a rather separate but very successful hero, the sad, Calvinist-destroyed Clennam. Then the vestige of regret for a wasted life has gone through many fires since Steerforth's day; it has been purified by Richard Carstone and above all by Sidney Carton, whom Shrewsbury, gentlemanly bohemianism, and the Bar could not entirely destroy. Above all the need for love has also been through Carton's fire so that Lucie can say to Darnay, "remember how strong we are in our happiness, and how weak he is in his misery." Loneliness, failure, pride, bitter rejection of all that made up Victorian progress and Victorian morality, a considered rejection of duty and hard work as moral ends, Dickens comes through to acceptance of these in the person of Eugene Wrayburn. And sensuality? Does he also redeem his own strong sensuality? This, I think, is less certain. The thin, calculated sensuality that runs from the Byronic Steerforth to the Yellow Book Wrayburn is not surely of the obsessive, tortured kind that we suspect in Dickens. Does not this real sensuality peep through in more sinister places? In Pecksniff's scene with Mary Graham, in Jonas's wooing of Mercy, in Uriah's glances at Agnes—there is more real lust there than in all the wiles of Steerforth and Harthouse, in all the brutalities of Gowan. And now the lust comes up again on the wrong side, in slavery to the Victorian doctrines of hard work, of fact, of ambition and of self-betterment—all things that had played a large part in Dickens's own life and which he had now rejected. The obsessive lust of Bradley Headstone finds no redemption. Yet as he rolls on the ground, after Charlie Hexam has left him, I believe that Dickens feels as strong a pity for him as David had felt for Steerforth. Would Dickens perhaps have left from here on another long pilgrimage deep into the holy places of his own soul? Can Jasper be the next strange step in that new pilgrimage?

18.

Geoffrey Tillotson

Truth About the Whole Range of Society: Thackeray

About society . . . [Thackeray] has much to say. It is indeed his broadest theme:

> The social human heart, man in relation to his kind—that is his subject. His actors are distinct and individual,—truthfully, vigorously, felicitously drawn; master-pieces in their way; but the personal character of each is not the supreme object of interest with the author. It is only a contribution to a larger and more abstract subject of contemplation. Man is his study; but man the social animal, man considered with reference to the experiences, the aims, the affections, that find their field in his intercourse with his fellow-men: never man the individual soul.[1]

Some of his social commentary is direct; more is implicit in the picture he draws.

He accepts the social structure as it stands, even though there is much in it that pains him. His position seems to be that of Pen in his notable debate with Warrington. On coming into his property, Pen is obliged by his friend to take stock of the philosophy by which his life is being conducted. Politics are broached first, and then the structure of society:

"... I see men who begin with ideas of universal reform, and who, before their beards are grown, propound their loud plans for the regeneration of mankind, give up their schemes after a few years of bootless talking and vain-glorious attempts to lead their fellows; and after they have found that men will no longer hear them, as indeed they never were in the least worthy to be heard, sink quietly into the rank and file,—acknowledging their aims impracticable, or thankful that they were never put into practice. The fiercest reformers grow calm, and are fain to put up with things as they are: the loudest Radical orators become dumb, quiescent placemen: the most fervent Liberals, when out of power, become humdrum Conservatives, or downright tyrants or despots in office. Look at Thiers, look at Guizot, in opposition and in place! Look at the Whigs appealing to the country, and the Whigs in power! Would you say that the conduct of these men is an act of treason, as the Radicals bawl,—who would give way in their turn, were their turn ever to come? No, only that they submit to circumstances which are stronger than they,—march as the world marches towards reform, but at the world's pace, (and the movements of the vast body of mankind must needs be slow,)—forego this scheme as impracticable, on account of opposition,—that as immature, because against the sense of the majority,—are forced to calculate drawbacks and difficulties, as well as to think of reforms and advances,—and compelled finally to submit, and to wait, and to compromise."

"The Right Honourable Arthur Pendennis could not speak better, or be more satisfied with himself, if he was First Lord of the Treasury and Chancellor of the Exchequer", Warrington said.

"Self-satisfied? Why self-satisfied?" continued Pen. "It seems to me that my scepticism is more respectful and more modest than the revolutionary ardour of other folks. Many a patriot of eighteen, many a Spouting-Club orator, would turn the Bishops out of the House of Lords to-morrow, and throw the Lords out after the Bishops, and throw the throne into the Thames after the Peers and the Bench. Is that man more modest than I, who take these institutions as I find them, and wait for time and truth to develop, or fortify, or (if you like) destroy them? A college tutor, or a nobleman's toady, who appears one fine day as my right reverend lord, in a silk apron and a shovel-hat, and assumes benedictory airs over me, is still the same man we remember at Oxbridge, when he was truckling to the tufts, and bullying the poor under-graduates in the lecture-room. An hereditary legislator, who passes his time with jockeys and black-legs and ballet-girls, and who is called to rule over me and his other betters because his grandfather made a lucky speculation in the funds, or found a coal or tin-mine on his property, or because his stupid ancestor happened to be in command of ten thousand men as brave as himself, who overcame twelve thousand Frenchmen, or fifty thousand Indians—such a man, I say, inspires me with no more respect than the bitterest democrat can feel towards him. But, such as he is, he is a part of the old society to which we belong: and I submit to his lordship with acquiescence; and he takes his place above the best of us at all dinner parties, and there bides his time. I don't want to chop his head off with a guillotine, or to fling mud at him in the streets. When they call such a man a disgrace to his order; and such another, who is good and gentle, refined and generous, who employs his great means in promoting every kindness and charity, and art and grace of life, in the kindest and most gracious manner, an ornament to his rank —the question as to the use and propriety of the order is not in the least affected one way or other. There it is, extant among us, a part of our habits, the creed of many of us, the growth of centuries, the symbol of a most complicated tradition—there stand my lord the bishop and my lord the hereditary legislator—what the French call *transactions*[2] both of them,—representing in their present shape mail-clad barons and double-sworded chiefs, (from whom their lordships the hereditaries, for the most part, *don't* descend,) and priests, professing to hold an absolute truth and a divinely inherited power, the which truth absolute our ancestors burned at the stake, and denied there; the which divine transmissible power still exists in print—to be believed, or not, pretty much at choice; and of these, I say, I acquiesce that they exist, and no more. If you say that these schemes, devised before printing was known, or steam was born; when thought was an infant, scared and whipped; and truth under its guardians was gagged, and swathed, and blindfolded, and not allowed to lift its voice, or to

> look out or to walk under the sun; before men were permitted to meet, or to trade, or to speak with each other—if any one says (as some faithful souls do) that these schemes are for ever, and having been changed and modified constantly are to be subject to no farther development or decay, I laugh, and let the man speak. But I would have toleration for these, as I would ask it for my own opinions; and if they are to die, I would rather they had a decent and natural than an abrupt and violent death."[3]

Like Pen, Thackeray accepts things as they are and as, left to themselves, they are becoming.

His main concern in the long novels is with the higher grades of society. There are several reasons for this choice. One of them is that riches and the social glories that go with them are things of interest to the ordinary man. If a single principle is at work in the social scene it seems to him to be snobbishness, by which he means social climbing. To his sense of the widespread operation of snobbishness there is *The Book of Snobs* as ready witness, a series of some fifty papers on snobs royal, aristocratic, clerical, professional, mercantile, provincial, not to mention "dinner-giving," Irish and club snobs— the whole representing an effort of sustained criticism as remarkable as the poetical effort that gave the book brilliance and life. It is towards the glory of rank, as he sees it, that society as a whole aspires. In choosing to write much of that glory he knows he will interest readers, who enjoy the sight of the life that most would take the chance of living if they could. On the other hand, he writes much about the poor, especially in his minor writings, because he enjoys their ways with something of a Dickensian relish; and sometimes even out of bravado—the very point of *Catherine* is that she is a rogue who does not exchange drabness for splendor, and her end is so crudely bloody that when the novel was reprinted in the collected edition of 1875 much of it was suppressed. In *Our Street,* which Thackeray may have planned as a companion piece for Miss Mitford's *Our Village,* all the inhabitants are given due attention, even the cheerful "spawn of the alleys about Our Street."[4] And there is the squalid household of Dennis Haggarty, and the squalid testimony of James Yellowplush. Then again, Thackeray is the author of a poem of the kind we associate with Ebenezer Elliott, called, as if it were a picture, "Daddy, I'm Hungry. A Scene in an Irish Coachworker's Family, Designed by Lord Lowther, July 1843", which has verses like the following:

> He turns from their prattle as angry as may be,
> 'O, daddy, I'm hungry', says each little brat;
> And yonder sits mammy, and nurses the baby,
> Thinking how long there'll be dinner for that.[5]

Though Thackeray cannot forget his own social position, as Mrs. Gaskell and George Eliot could, his examination of members of the lower orders, both in the earlier and later writings, is often thorough. And often tender—in a late piece, a "Roundabout" paper, "Autour de mon Chapeau," we hear that

> The milkman becomes a study to him; the baker a being he curiously and tenderly examines.

A good instance of tenderness from the earlier writings occurs in *A Shabby Genteel Story* where one of the personages is a servant girl beautifully drawn.

In the later novels there is more of the lower orders than is sometimes credited to Thackeray. They are particularly evident in *Pendennis,* the hero of which has "sympathy with all conditions of men."[6]

Having much about the rich and also about the poor, he has much about them as master and servant, especially in the big novels, where the picture is on all scales from grand to shabby. The relationship fascinated him, and one of the Roundabout papers, "On a Chalkmark on the Door," analyzes its moral and human basis with a searchingness fresh and fearless as Johnson's. The standpoint adopted is somewhere in what Roscoe described as his favorite territory, "the debateable land between the artistocracy and the middle classes."[7] Taking that standpoint, he cannot but look down at the servants. The perspective is arranged in the first chapter of *Esmond,* which advances a theory of the proper way to write history. Speaking for Thackeray—witness statements in his prose of thinking[8]—Esmond suggests that we widen the range of histories to take in Louis XIV's barber as well as Louis XIV. Hogarth and Fielding, he judges, "will give our children a much better idea of the manners of the present age in England, than the *Court Gazette* and the newspapers which we get thence"—the instancing of the newspapers as well as the *Court Gazette* shows how wide a meaning Thackeray is here giving to manners. Sometimes the rank of his personages is that of Louis XIV, but his favorite ground, especially in the long novels, is the debatable one discriminated by Roscoe. On this ground the rich and the shabby genteel spring up in their hundreds, complete with domestics, spongers, and blackmailers. The poor come into the novels, therefore, mainly as they barber their patrons, and if Thackeray "knows the secrets of a thousands footmen,"[9] the secrets are mainly about their masters. In *Vanity Fair* a chapter is headed "How to live well on nothing a-year": We note the word "well," and know that it means "very well." The downward range of the long novels is not unfairly suggested by the principle advanced in the commentary of *Pendennis,* that there is no

> more effectual plan . . . to get a knowledge of London society, than to begin at the foundation—that is, at the kitchen-floor.[10]

This principle determines the structure of *Lovel the Widower,* in which "the parlour and kitchen . . . are on the same level."[11] That is not so in any of the other later works, unless it be *Denis Duval,* but in the middle sections of *Pendennis* and in the relevant sections of *Vanity Fair* the reader is given a sense of London society complete. In any of these novels we come on remarks such as

> A pauper child in London at seven years old knows how to go to market, to fetch the beer, to pawn father's coat, to choose the largest fried fish or the nicest ham-bone, to nurse Mary Jane of three . . . [12]

Thackeray is not so much at home when he invites us to visit the new industrial northerly town of Newcome. The visit, we are told in advance, will be brief, and we are to see little of the chief interest of the place:

> My design does not include a description of that great and flourishing town of Newcome, and the manufactures which caused its prosperity; but only admits of the introduction of those Newcomites who are concerned in the affairs of the family which has given its respectable name to these volumes.
>
> Thus in previous pages we have said nothing about the Mayor and Corporation of Newcome, the magnificent bankers and manufacturers who had their places of business in the town, and their splendid villas outside its smoky precincts; people who would give their thousand guineas for a picture or a statue, and write you off a cheque for ten times the amount any day; people who if there was talk of a statue to the Queen or the Duke, would come down to the Town All and subscribe their one, two, three hundred apiece (especially if in the neighboring city of SLOWCOME they were putting up a statue to the Duke or the Queen)—not of such men have I spoken, the magnates of the place; but of the humble Sarah Mason in Jubilee Row—of the Reverend Dr. Bulders the Vicar, Mr. Vidler the apothecary, Mr. Puff the baker—of Tom Potts the jolly reporter of the "Newcome Independent," and—Batters, Esq., the proprietor of that journal—persons with whom our friends have had already, or will be found presently to have, some connection. And it is from these that we shall arrive at some particulars regarding the Newcome family, which will show us that they have a skeleton or two in *their* closets, as well as their neighbours.

When later he says:

> I could go on giving you interesting particulars of a hundred members of the Newcome aristocracy. . . . [13]

we have little doubt that he could, though it is by the thousand that he gives us interesting particulars of the London aristocracy. We suspect, however, that he might be hard put to it to give us a hundred about its plebs—rather, of course, because they are northern than that they are plebs: as Hannay observed.

> He was . . . too honest to draw fancy pictures of classes with whom he had never lived.[14]

In the period of writing his great novels, and on several occasions earlier, he bears some resemblance to his own Captain Fitz-Boodle, whose papers he invented in 1842, and who is still on his legs in 1860:

> Captain Fitzb—dle, who belongs to a dozen clubs, and knows something of every man in London;[15]

—by "man" he means "gentleman"—or his own Tom Eaves, the gossip who

> knew all the great folk in London, and the stories and mysteries of each family;[16]

—by "each family" he means "each great family." Thackeray's commentary cannot be considered of topical importance for his times. By and large it shows him to be still virtually living in the eighteenth century. We have only to remember that *Culture and Anarchy* was published six years after his death to see the old-fashionedness of his social sense, and the feebleness of his concern with the changes that mattered most. A lack of up-to-date interest in such things appeared a grave deficiency in the mid-nineteenth century, even in a novelist, seeming graver still after the advent of George Eliot, in whose novels, as Brownell noted, there was the very "taste of science," and the taste of most other intellectual interests as well. The strength of Thackeray's mind lay in other quarters, as Fitzjames Stephen well noted. His instance was the character of Warrington:

> Warrington is represented as being a man of great originality—full of powerful thought, scholarship, and knowledge of various kinds; but we have none of the powerful thought, or scholarship, or knowledge, produced in the book; still less are any incidents introduced to give scope to them.

And so to the positive side:

> We certainly get the impression that Warrington was a man of vigorous understanding; but we get it from learning that he behaved in the commonest affairs of life as such a man might be supposed to behave, not from any description of the remarkable things which he did.[17]

The inferences drawn by Thackeray's imagination were often sound, for all their slender basis in the sort of knowledge that the intellect can give an account of. In making the commentary of the novels, as distinct from the personages, there was more opening for thinking than Thackeray could always take advantage of. George Eliot, who learnt from him how to place commentary in the novel, had more penetrating political comments to place. When it came to politics the political animal was for Thackeray little more than another name for the moral animal.[18]

The moral interests of his novels are brilliantly served by that part of society given most attention in them. Thackeray would not have allowed himself to specialize on a part, even to the extent he did, if it had imperiled any universality on the plane that mattered to him first and foremost—the plane of human nature and morals. Like Wordsworth and Pope, he believed that we have all of us one human heart, but he did not effectively share Wordsworth's further belief that the heart shows itself best when there is least artificiality. Rather he shared the belief of Pope that it is the contrast between the heart and civilization that best reveals the cardiac condition:

> Bare the mean Heart that lurks beneath a Star[19]

and how much more is the meanness apparent. To have the Pretender is to make this contrast—whether or not out of invented matter does not concern me:

> The heir of one of the greatest names, of the greatest kingdoms, and of the greatest misfortunes in Europe, was often content to lay the dignity of his birth and grief at the wooden shoes of a French chambermaid, and to repent afterwards (for he was very devout) in ashes taken from the dustpan;

and to draw this generalization:

> 'Tis for mortals such as these that nations suffer, that parties struggle, that warriors fight and bleed. A year afterwards gallant heads were falling . . . whilst the heedless ingrate, for whom they risked and lost all, was tippling with his seraglio of mistresses in his *petite maison* of Chaillot.[20]

To have the vicious Lord Steyne is to have the opportunity of belitting him with his titles:

> . . . the Most Honourable George Gustavus, Marquis of Steyne, Earl of Gaunt and of Gaunt Castle, in the Peerage of Ireland, Viscount Hellborough, Baron Pitchley and Grillsby, a Knight of the Most Noble Order of the Garter, of the Golden Fleece of Spain, of the Russian Order of Saint Nicholas of the First Class, of the Turkish Order of the Crescent, First Lord of the Powder Closet and Groom of the Back Stairs, Colonel of the Gaunt or Regent's Own Regiment of Militia, a Trustee of the British Museum, an Elder Brother of the Trinity House, a Governor of the White Friars, and D.C.L.[21]

To have Colonel Newcome is to have that interesting thing, a contrast of manners because of the return from long absence abroad. To have the Sedleys is to have people who are high enough to come down in the world. To have the Reverend Charles Honeyman is to be able to write:

> I fancy Saint Peter of Alcantara, and contrast him with such a personage as the Incumbent of Lady Whittlesea's chapel, May Fair.
>
> His hermitage is situated in Walpole Street let us say, on the second floor of a quiet mansion, let out to hermits by a nobleman's butler, whose wife takes care of the lodgings. His cells consist of a refectory, a dormitory, and an adjacent oratory where he keeps his shower-bath and boots—the pretty boots trimly stretched on boot-trees and blackened to a nicety (not varnished) by the boy who waits on him. The barefooted business may suit superstitious ages and gentlemen of Alcantara, but does not become May Fair

> and the nineteenth century. If St. Pedro walked the earth now with his eyes to the ground he would know fashionable divines by the way in which they were shod. Charles Honeyman's is a sweet foot. I have no doubt as delicate and plump and rosy as the white hand with its two rings, which he passes in impassioned moments through his slender flaxen hair.
> . . . By his bedside are slippers lined with blue silk and worked of an ecclesiastical pattern, by some of the faithful who sit at his feet. . . . Purses are sent to him—pen-wipers—a portfolio with the Honeyman arms—yea, braces have been known to reach him by the post (in his days of popularity), and flowers, and grapes, and jelly when he was ill, and throat comforters, and lozenges for his dear bronchitis. In one of his drawers is the rich silk cassock presented to him by his congregation at Leatherhead (when the young curate quitted that parish for London duty), and on his breakfast-table the silver tea-pot, once filled with sovereigns and presented by the same devotees. The devoteapot he has, but the sovereigns, where are they?
> What a different life this is from our honest friend of Alcantara, who eats once in three days![22]

Again, how little there would have been to seize on had Mrs. Newcome—Sophia Alethea Newcome—been denied a palette of expensive colors:

> When his father married, Mr. [later Colonel] Thomas Newcome, jun., and Sarah his nurse were transported from the cottage where they had lived in great comfort to the palace hard by, surrounded by lawns and gardens, pineries, graperies, aviaries, luxuries of all kinds. This paradise, five miles from the standard at Cornhill, was separated from the outer world by a thick hedge of tall trees, and an ivy-covered porter's-gate, through which they who travelled to London on the top of the Clapham coach could only get a glimpse of the bliss within. It was a serious paradise. As you entered at the gate, gravity fell on you; and decorum wrapped you in a garment of starch. The butcher-boy who galloped his horse and cart madly about the adjoining lanes and common, whistled wild melodies (caught up in abiminable play-hourse galleries), and joked with a hun-

> dred cook-maids, on passing that lodge fell into an undertaker's pace, and delivered his joints and sweet-breads silently at the servants' entrance. The rooks in the elms cawed sermons at morning and evening; the peacocks walked demurely on the terraces; the guinea-fowls looked more quaker-like than those savoury birds usually do. The lodge-keeper was serious, and a clerk at a neighbouring chapel. The pastors who entered at that gate, and greeted his comely wife and children, fed the little lambkins with tracts. The head-gardner was a Scotch Calvinist, after the strictest order, only occupying himself with the melons and pines provisionally, and until the end of the world, which event he could prove by infallible calculations, was to come off in two or three years at farthest. Wherefore he asked should the butler brew strong ale to be drunken three years hence; or the housekeeper (a follower of Joanna Southcote), make provisions of fine linen and lay up stores of jams? On a Sunday (which good old Saxon word was scarcely known at the Hermitage), the household marched away in separate couples or groups to at least half a dozen of religious edifices, each to sit under his or her favourite minister, the only man who went to Church being Thomas Newcome, accompanied by Tommy his little son, and Sarah his nurse, who was I believe also his aunt, or at least his mother's first cousin. Tommy was taught hymns very soon after he could speak, appropriate to his tender age, pointing out to him the inevitable fate of wicked children, and giving him the earliest possible warning and description of the punishment of little sinners. He repeated these poems to his stepmother after dinner, before a great, shining mahogany table, covered with grapes, pine-apples, plum-cake, port-wine, and Madeira, and surrounded by stout men in black, with baggy white neckcloths, who took the little man between their knees, and questioned him as to his right understanding of the place whither naughty boys were bound. They patted his head with their fat hands if he said well, or rebuked him if he was bold as he often was.[23]

And so on. If Thackeray had limited himself to "the short and simple annals of the poor" he might not have seen less humanity but he would have foregone the spectacle of men who have access to materials adequate for the thorough display of their natures.

Notes

[1] *Roscoe,* II, 266.

[2] Perhaps in the sense of "compromises."

[3] *Pendennis,* Ch. LXI.

[4] *Ibid.,* Ch. V, "What sometimes happens in Our Street."

[5] This poem is written in the style of those of the "Hedge Schoolmaster", published in the Dublin *Nation* as part of the campaign for repealing the legislative union between Great Britain and Ireland (see Charles Gavan Duffy's *Young Ireland,* 1880–3, I, 164 and 243, which reproduces Thackeray's verses and his drawing as originally published in the *Nation* of 13 May 1843–the date in the title of the poem shows the poem to be prophetic). Lord Lowther, then Postmaster-General, had angered the Irish nationalists by accepting the tender of a Scottish coach-builder for the Dublin mail-coaches, a stroke of economy which would have thrown Irish coachmakers out of work. Thackeray's poem may have been written more for the sake of friendship than of politics—the owner of the Dublin coach-building firm was the "Mr. P[urcel]" of *The Irish Sketch Book,* ch. II, by whom Thackeray had been entertained. In that same book Thackeray had shown some contempt for the nationalists. Duffy points out that in the end he came to respect their leaders, if not the principles they advanced.

[6] *Pendennis,* Ch. XLVI.

[7] *Ibid.,* II, 274.

[8] E.g. "Caricatures and Lithography in Paris" and "Meditations at Versailles" in *The Paris Sketch Book.*

[9] I have failed to trace the source of this quotation.

[10] *Pendennis,* Ch. XXXVI.

[11] *Ibid.,* Ch. I.

[12] *The Newcomes,* Ch. LIII.

[13] *Ibid.,* Ch. LV.

[14] D. Hannay, *Studies on Thackeray* (London, 1869), p. 6.

[15] *Lovel the Widower,* Ch. IV.

[16] *Vanity Fair,* Ch. XLVII; cf. *Philip,* Ch. XL.

[17] "The Relation of Novels to Life," included in *Cambridge Essays, contributed by Members of the University. 1855,* p. 161.

[18] For a summary of Thackeray's interests in politics see John W. Dodds, *Thackeray: A Critical Portrait* (1941), pp. 211 ff., who concludes:

> To say . . . that Thackeray was not interested in the political currents of his time is to do an injustice to his active and inquiring mind. It would be foolhardly, however, to declare that his political opinions were always pertinent or ever really profound. In politics he was always more or less the big, beaming, enthusiastic outsider, with liberal instincts and

a judgment guided by a warm and sympathetic heart rather than by a clear political head. The best that Thackeray had to say to his generation cut across political lines and went much deeper than party affiliations.

[19] *Imitations of Horace,* Sat. II, i, 108.

[20] Book III, Ch. IX.

[21] *Vanity Fair,* Ch. LXIV.

[22] *The Newcomes,* Ch. XI.

[23] *The Newcomes,* Ch. II.

19.

John Holloway

Hardy's Major Fiction

The deepening and harshening pessimism of Hardy's later novels has been stressed often enough in the past. All that need be done here is to remind readers of how it is usually located in two particular aspects of his work: first, his "philosophical" asides ("the President of the Immortals, in Aeschylean phrase, had ended his sport with Tess" will be enough in illustration of this familiar story; the phrase itself will need re-examination later) ; and second, his apparently growing preoccupation with problems of marriage. One should perhaps add that to see this second issue as the product of difficulties in Hardy's own married life is very uninformative. Much more to the point are the divorce cases (the Parnell case being the best known) which became national sensations in the later 1880's and early 1890's; and besides this, the important influence of Ibsen, at least in the case of *Jude the Obscure*.

Recent criticism of Hardy has also emphasized something else: a special part of his connection with the southwest of England. An earlier generation of writers on Hardy underestimated this. Amiably if innocently equipped with haversack and large-scale map, they cycled over Wessex and noted Hardy's faithful geography, or his intimate and affectionate knowledge of rural occupations and customs. More recently, the stress has

Reprinted from *Jane Austen to Joseph Conrad*, edited by Robert Rathburn and Martin Steinmann, Jr., by permission of the author and Routledge & Kegan Paul Ltd, London, and University of Minnesota Press.

fallen on Hardy as one who registered the impact upon rural England of a great historical change, which went to the very roots of life. One cause of this was the swift and decisive decline in British agriculture which followed almost instantaneously on the completion of the railroad links to the American Middle West in about 1870. The other, less spectacular but in the long run much more far-reaching, was the industrial revolution in agriculture. This was progressing steadily in the later years of the century, and has even now far from completed its radical transforming work. As symbol of this second force, one might take a pair of incidents from Hardy's own work. In *The Mayor of Casterbridge* (1886) the new mechanical seed-drill which is to replace the methods in use since the time of the Anglo-Saxons is for sale in the marketplace. Someone has still to buy and use it. In *Tess of the D'Urbervilles,* only five years later, the mechanical harvester dominates and controls the whole scene of the cornstacking (Ch. 48) and reduces the tired, dazed human beings who serve it to mere automatons. The contrast is no proof of how rural life was changing; but as an illustration it is vivid.

Modern criticism of fiction often seems at its weakest in trying (or failing) to consider the forces in a book which unify it from beginning to end. This weakness is perhaps the result of a certain uneasiness which (for reasons obvious enough) often shows itself when the critic turns his attention to the plot. Yet such attention is necessary if the pervasive unifying drives of the work are to be located; and certainly the full seriousness and import of Hardy's major novels will be concealed from the reader who fails to apprehend their plots: plots, that is, not as mere summarizable sequences of events, but as the central unifying and significating forces of the books. These I hope now to approach.

The first step in that approach is not difficult, for it is taken simply by combining the two more or less familiar points from which this discussion started; by seeing Hardy's deepening and harshening gloom as not a mere self-ingraining philosophical bias, but rather as something in most intimate relation to his vision of the passing of the old rhythmic order of rural

England. Once the novels are seen from this point of view, they suggest a surprising development in Hardy's thought. They suggest not just a growing preoccupation with the rural problem, nor even a growing sense that an earlier way of life was inevitably vanishing. They suggest something more disquieting: a gathering realization that that earlier way did not possess the inner resources upon which to make a real fight for its existence. The old order was not just a less powerful mode of life than the new, but ultimately helpless before it through inner defect.

When one is arguing that a thought or an attitude comes increasingly into focus in a writer's work, it is always easy to claim too much and hide too much; yet in the present case the change looks convincingly steady. *The Return of the Native* (1878) has a half-tragic ending in its present form; and Hardy's original intention seems to have been to have made it more tragic rather than less so. Yet throughout the book, the stress falls on the revitalizing power of rural life, and on how its vitality is intrinsically greater than that of modernity. Eustacia and Wildeve, and at first Clym too, are alienated from it: indeed, this very alienation lies behind their ostensible successes (the marriages, for example). But because of the alienation, the successes are ill-placed and precarious, they are the successes of those who have lost the soundness, the inner strength, the power to choose and to achieve wisely which belongs to men whose life is in harmony with their world. By contrast, Venn the reddleman suffers reverses, but they do not impair his integrity; his vitality runs submerged, but it runs with the tide of life. The gambling scene on the heath is fantastic enough, but it tellingly conveys this. Moreover, the whole rural ambience can ultimately assert a greater vitality than the city life from which Clym has come. As he gives himself to it, he is regenerated from a basic source. By the end, Egdon has triumphed, even if on its own stern terms. The renegades have been destroyed or won over: even if Venn had never married Thomasin, the faithful would have been in possession. The novel resolves in an assertion of the old order, its regenerative austerity, its rewarding unrewardingness.

The next novel is very different. Henchard is the only major figure in *The Mayor of Casterbridge* (1886) who stands integrally for the traditional qualities. Farfrae is an agriculturalist, but of the new kind: he prospers by chemistry, machinery, and bookkeeping and elementary economics. His traditional songs are partly a social accomplishment, neither sincere nor insincere; his kindliness and even his amorousness are conventional. Henchard's daughter Elizabeth-Jane is turning into a cultivated young lady (I would sooner overrate than underrate Hardy's own educatedness, but I cannot help seeing something of importance in his seeming assurance here that education could without loss be self-education). Lucretta is entirely *déraciné*. On these premises, contrast with *The Return of the Native* is vivid. From beginning to end Henchard's course is downward. Whenever his older way of life meets the new, it is defeated. Step by step, he comes to work for the man whom he once employed, and in the end he feels himself driven away to his death; while those who were once his laborers work the new, harder (and easier) way, for a shilling a week less than they had had from him.

Yet, although this relentless decline of Henchard's is (as we take its meaning) what unifies the book, Henchard still stands above the others in what might be called psychic virtue. In the conventional sense, he is both less moral than they, and more so. He is violent and a liar and in one sense intensely selfish, but his generosity is true magnanimity, and he has reserves of affection and humility that they quite lack. The essential is something else, though: that his whole nature, good or bad, is centered upon a deep source of vital energy. The rich stream of life still issues from life's traditional order. It does not bring success, but it brings greatness and in a sense goodness. Farfrae prospers through *skill* which the new mode of life has impersonally taught him; Henchard is able to struggle on, though defeated, not because of what he has learned but because of what he *is*. He blocks out something like the full contour of the human being.

That Henchard should stand out as a human rather than a man was surely part of Hardy's intention. His lack of interest in "womankind" is stressed more than once, and we are reminded of how Marty South is also in a sense made sexless at the end of *The Woodlanders* (1887). But to turn to *The Woodlanders* is to find that Hardy has now moved further still. Marty South and Giles Winterborne do not display, like Henchard, a defeated strength. On the contrary, they leave the impression of debility. So far as goodness itself goes, they are, to be sure, alone in having contact with it: "You was a good man, and did good things." But the springs of goodness are now no longer the springs of strength. Rather the opposite. Such vitality as there is lies on the other side, in the self-assurance and plausible fluency of Fitzpiers, or the passionate sensuousness of Felice. Grace Melbury has a thwarted contact, anyhow, with the traditional order: but what it does for her is chiefly to make her impassive and acceptant.

In *Tess of the D'Urbervilles* (1891), Hardy moves further. Tess is "a pure woman," admittedly; but this is not the feminine counterpart to Henchard's "A Man of Character." It is not Tess's sexual misadventures which impugn her as a woman of character, and Hardy is indeed at pains to show, in the later part of the book when she resists the now twice-reprobate Alec, that she is comparatively faithful and steadfast. But she has a weakness nearer her center: an alienation, a dreaminess which Hardy depicts unsuccessfully in the ride at night when she tells her young brother that we live on a "blighted" planet (and becomes so engrossed that she causes a fatal injury to the horse), and which he depicts again, this time with brilliant success, at Talbothay's dairy when she tells Dairyman Crick how "our souls can be made to go outside our bodies when we are alive" (Chs. 4 and 18). Again, this incident is nodal in the book, and I must return to it. For the present it is enough to say that its nodality is stressed by Hardy, in that he makes this the moment when Angel Clare first gives Tess any special notice.

This dreamy unreality in Tess is no personal quirk. It results from her heredity, and is reflected in both her parents. Moreover, Hardy is at pains to stress that among country folk, degeneration of an old stock is common enough. The stock is in decline. It seems a positive disparagement of the old order. The contrast with Henchard is revealing. Quietly but clearly, Hardy indicates that in Tess there is something self-destroying. So there was, in a sense, in Henchard. Yet how differently does the stress fall, provided that the reader follows only the contours created by the author!

Tess of the D'Urbervilles also dwells, quite for the first time, upon another unattractive side of rural life. This is what appears in the barrenness and crippling toil of life on the upland farm of Flintcomb-Ash. Hardy links his picture to contemporary agricultural realities—the farm belongs to an absentee landlord—but the essential things which make life hard on it are those which have made the rural life hard since the beginning: stony soil, cold wind, rain, snow, callous masters—things that can be found in the Wakefield *Second Shepherds' Play* as easily as in *Tess*. Should this be in doubt, it may be confirmed from *Jude the Obscure* (1896). In fact, there is something like a parallel here to the double indictment of *Tess*. Jude Fawley is "crazy for books. . . . It runs in our family . . . ." Later, when the now adult Jude sees a stone-mason's yard and glimpses for a moment that happiness for him lay only in a life like that, Hardy passes decisive judgment upon bookish tastes in laborers' families. A still clearer parallel with *Tess,* however, is Hardy's insistence in this novel upon the essential harshness of rural life. "How ugly it is here," thinks Jude, as he drives off the rooks from the brown, featureless arable of the upland. This is in part an ironical judgment upon Jude. Hardy is at pains to stress the rich human associations of the scene. Yet some of these associations are themselves associations of human unhappiness; and the whole chapter goes far to endorse Jude's revulsion from the drab landscape and the inevitable greed and callousness of the farmer. Nor are this revulsion, and the inescapable grounds tending to justify it, incidentals. They initiate the whole train of events. Jude's quest for learning is to escape from a life of grinding toil that he could not but wish to escape. And what are the compensations of rurality, as they now appear? Only Arabella, whose work is to wash the innards of the newly slaughtered pig, and whose attractions take their force from brutal humor, coarse sensuality, and a rooted tradition of deceit.

This discussion of the later novels is not by itself, of course, anything like the whole truth about them. It virtually ignores Hardy's rich and intimate contact with the rural tradition in every book before *Jude,* and his profound dependence upon, and loyalty to, its characteristic virtues. It ignores these matters because they have often been discussed elsewhere, and its concentration upon Hardy's growing sense of weakness in the country world must be taken in the context of Hardy criticism as it now stands. Yet it remains true that in these later works the essence of plot, the distinctive trajectory of the narrative, is the steadily developed decline of a protagonist who incarnates the older order, and whose decline is linked, more and more clearly, with an inner misdirection, an inner weakness.

Two of the novels stand out as inviting a closer scrutiny, if we wish to see how this kind of movement lies at the heart of unity and meaning. These are *The Mayor of Casterbridge,* and *Tess of the D'Urbervilles. Jude the Obscure* clearly has another kind of concern; and *The Woodlanders,* surprisingly enough, proves largely to have it as well. Indeed, there is a sense in which this novel has a much looser organization than the other late ones. Deep and powerful as its awareness of rural life undoubtedly is (one cannot keep from mind the pictures of Giles spattered all over with his apples and their juice), yet much at the center of this work pursues another concern. Grace's response to Fitzpiers' infidelity, and the gradual rebirth of her affection for him, are not Wessex products. The novel resolves itself by amiably decanting these two characters into the middle-class urban life of the Midlands. The psychological change that we see in Grace is barely connected with Hardy's rural interests; and that, I think, is why the whole episode of their reconciliation is treated with a lightness and even something of a gentle half-ironical detachment that distinguishes the book clearly from *Tess.* At one point Hardy brings the difference out starkly through a metaphor. This occurs when Grace, running swiftly through the wood to meet Fitzpiers, just misses the man-trap (which is in itself, by the way, another scrap of evidence for the view that Hardy was beginning to dwell on the harsher side of country life). Her destiny is to evade, though barely, the issues of life in their brutal sharpness. All the man-trap does is whisk her skirt off: in Hardy's making this the occasion of her being reconciled to Fitzpiers we are to see, I think, that the whole sequence has about it something of the essentially trivial. Tess turns back to Angel over her rush-drawing labor in the snow-laden barn, as she comes to grasp her case, and

Angel's, in terms of the plainest, the essential relations between women and men as human animals. We are in a much different world, a world that has not skipped over the waiting man-trap. For these reasons, among others, it is *The Mayor of Casterbridge* and *Tess* that best warrant further questioning. They are the novels which have a single-minded organization along our present line of thought.

The word "theme," now the most hackneyed of clichés in criticism, is also one of its bugbears. An essay, a philosophical discourse, even a collection of different pieces, all these may equally well have a theme, or several themes. The word has no necessary connection even with imaginative literature, let alone with the narrative forms of it, and is therefore a standing temptation to the critic to overlook the whole narrative dimension. But almost always, the narrative trajectory is what makes a novel a novel and what makes any particular novel the novel it is. Only within the framework of this central drive can the real significance of the detail (incident, imagery, metaphor, local contrast) be grasped at all. Examples may be needed here; let us revert to *The Woodlanders*. To connect, say, Giles Winterborne's meeting with Grace while he holds up his apple tree in the market-place merely with "the theme of rural fertility," or Marty South's selling her hair with "the commercial theme," would be grotesquely uninformative. The significance of both these incidents, prominently placed at the outset of the narrative, is that the two characters are made to carry out, at the start, ritual gestures by which they formally (though unwittingly) surrender their essential strength. From this point out, we know what kind of character we are to watch, we are put on the track of the path their lives must take.

A tree also embodies the essential strength of Marty's father. In an aberration from his proper rural life, he wants it cut down. When this is done, he dies. As for Marty's hair, Hardy invests this with almost talismanic virtue. While Felice wears it as her own, her luck prospers. Toward the end of the book, her secret comes out. At once she loses her power over Fitzpiers, and almost immediately after she meets her death. Similarly with the contrast between how Grace meets Winterborne (under the flowering apple tree in his hand) and how she first meets Fitzpiers (he has bought the right to dissect her old nurse's body after she is dead, and Grace goes to buy it back). These meetings are no mere specimens of a theme, but exact pointers to a narrative movement; and they come at the start of the relation and show what its significance is, and what (if pursued) it will bring. For Grace to progress with one is to pursue the forces of life, with the other to pursue those of death. Similarly with the incident where Marty helps Giles to plant the young trees (Chapter 8). This does not merely take up the theme of rural order; it exactly indicates how Marty is Giles's proper strength and counterpart. His trees will flourish if he chooses her to help. When he turns elsewhere, we know what he has done. But all these details have significance within the frame of the basic narrative movement of the book, a movement which, as it takes its shape out of them, reciprocally determines what meaning they shall have.

"From beginning to end," it was suggested above, "Henchard's course is downward. Whenever his older way of life meets the new, it is defeated." It is this narrative movement in the book which embodies Hardy's deepest interests and the essence of his moral insight. But there is more to be said about the exact nature of the struggle and the downward movement, as he envisages it; and it is at this point that such matters as incident and imagery can take their proper and proportionate place in our awareness of the whole work. For it seems that Hardy has employed a single basic metaphor through which to embody the war between Farfrae and Henchard; local incidents and metaphors have their allotted place within it; and in spite of the recurrent suggestion that Henchard (like Old Hamlet) is "a man, take him for all in all," the basic metaphor through which Hardy sees the struggle between Farfrae and him, is that of a struggle between a man and an animal. This begins with the animal in possession of its territory. Henchard arrived on the scene during, as it were, the prehistory of the narrative. Now he is in occupation at Casterbridge. Farfrae is passing through on his way to emigrate. As the novel pursues its course, Farfrae takes possession. It is his rival who thinks to emigrate. But intead he is persuaded to live in his old home, now occupied by Farfrae; and like an animal, he becomes domesticated. "Henchard had become in a measure broken in, he came to work daily on the home premises like the rest." Later he is likened to a "netted lion," or to a lion whose fangs have been drawn. When he describes how Farfrae, now mayor, as he himself once was, forced him away on the occasion of the royal visit, he says, " . . . how angry he looked. He drove me back as if I were a bull breaking fence. . . . "

Several of the incidents of the book enter into this sustained metaphor. Henchard and Farfrae fighting in the cornstore is, in a sense, animal against man: it is very like the earlier fight in the barn between Henchard and the bull. The parallel extends even to Farfrae's "wrenching Henchard's arm . . . causing him sharp pain, as could be seen from the twitching of his face," and Henchard when he "wrenched the animal's head as if he would snap it off. . . . The premeditated human contrivance of the nose-ring was too cunning for impulsive brute force, and the creature flinched." Finally, at the end of the novel, Henchard crawls away, like a wounded beast, to die in an empty hovel that is more like an animal's hole than a place for men. His final instructions for how he is to be buried are not appropriate for *felo-de-se*: they are appropriate for the burial of an animal.

Henchard's character, moreover, is that of a beast; in the true, not the townee, sense of that word. His immense natural energy, his simplicity, his having no skill of any kind save that of hay-cutting, and his liabilty to enslavement above all through a disabling, yearning, dog-like need for human affection, all these features of his nature make their contribution. There is no need to remind readers that Henchard is not *simply* an animal. Far from it. At no point does metaphor become literal truth. But it is through this metaphor that we must see the struggle which constitutes the narrative and the unity of the book, and which predominantly defines its significance. Indeed, nothing but awareness of this metaphor will fully bring out the issues between old and new that are involved, or the length to which Hardy pursues them. "My furniture too! Surely he'll buy my body and soul likewise!" Henchard says at one point. (One cannot but—though it is an unhappy touch—see the caged singing-bird which Henchard brings Elizabeth-Jane at the end as a wedding present, and which he leaves behind when he goes away to die, as linking with this idea of his giving up "body and soul" together.) Yet even this is insufficient to bring out the lengths to which Hardy pursues his central conflict. Henchard is more than enslaved, he is *tamed*. That is something far more thoroughgoing. It is the measure of what Hardy sees as at issue.

Tess of the D'Urbervilles also has unity through a total movement; and the nature of this may also largely be grasped through a single metaphor. It is not the taming of an animal. Rather (at least for a start) it is the hunting of one. Several remarks and incidents in the book make this explicit, notably Tess's letter to her absent husband when he has deserted her: "I must cry out to you in my trouble—I have no one else. . . . if I break down by falling into some dreadful snare, my last state will be worse than my first." So does the night she spends in the wood with the wounded pheasants: strongly reminiscent, of course, of her earlier night in a wood, when she fell into the snare set for her by Alec. Throughout, Tess is harried from place to place at what seems like gradually increasing speed. Even the very start of her relation with Alec is relevant: "the handsome, horsey young buck" drove up early in the morning in his gig to fetch her. At the end, it is especially clear. When the hunt is over, Tess is captured on the sacrificial stone at Stonehenge, the stone where once, like the hart at bay, the victim's throat was slit with the knife. With these things in mind, Hardy's much-abused quotation from Aeschylus ("the President of the Immortals, in Aeschylean phrase, had ended his sport with Tess) takes on a new meaning and aptness.

Yet Tess's career represents more than a hunt. What this is, can again be summed up in a metaphor, one to which we are almost inadvertently led, if we attempt to summarize. That Hardy should have divided his book into "phases" is itself, perhaps, an indication of the field in which his mind was partly working: the word was good nineteenth-century currency in history and natural history, and Carlyle was fond of it. "Phase Three" is entitled "The Rally." In it, Tess strikes out for new country. She leaves the snug and familiar environment of the "Vale of the Little Dairies," surmounts the challenge of barren Egdon Heath which lies across her path, and enters a new territory, the "Vale of the Great Dairies," where life runs upon a basically different pattern. To this she almost completely adapts herself: so much so, that she finds a mate in Angel Clare, and almost succeeds in—there is only one word to use—in germinating.

This word is less odd than it seems at first. Hardy lays great stress on the rich, blossoming fertility of Tess's whole environment during this period, and also stresses, discreetly but with great force, her own richly sensuous nubility, her genuine bond, in the truest sense, with the milch cows and the lush blossoms where the fruit is setting.

The rally fails. Tess has to abandon her favorable environment, and is forced on to a harsh upland soil where existence is more difficult. She struggles not at the level of reproduction, but for mere survival. She is resistant, though, and for a long time she does survive. But her strength is shaken when her family is finally driven off the soil; and in the end, what Darwin called sexual selection begins to work contrariwise to natural selection. Tess gives up the struggle. She is driven out of her natural habitat altogether, and goes to live, kept like a pet, with Alec in Sandbourne.

Here, I think, is the second, bigger metaphor, embracing the first, through which Hardy embodies his central fictional movement. The central train of events demands description in Darwinian terms: organism, environment, struggle, adaptation, fertility, survival, resistance—and one more: Hardy has envisaged an individual life at the depth of, and to the length of, the ultimates for a species—establishment at one end, and at the other, extinction.

Many of the incidents in the book bring this total movement into focus. For example, Hardy provides the reader with an index to it by two scenes, one at the beginning and one at the end. In the first, Angel looks back down the road and sees the village girls in white, dancing in springtime on the green: Tess, still integrated with them, stands by the hedge. In the other, he looks back after what he thinks is their final parting, over bare, open countryside and an empty road: "and as he gazed a moving spot intruded on the white vacuity of its perspective. It was a human figure running." It is Tess, now alienated and isolated. Tess and her family take refuge in the family vault (Chapter 52). In terms of the hunt metaphor, they have been run to earth; and this parallels the sleep-walking scene (Chapter 37) when Angel lays Tess in the open tomb: within the larger movement there is a recurrent smaller pattern. Tess at the dairy says that "our souls can be made to go outside our bodies" if we "lie on the grass at night and look straight up at some big bright star." (This is exactly what she does at the end of the book, on her fatal last night on Salisbury Plain.) Meanwhile, Dairyman Crick was balancing his knife and fork together "like the beginning of a gallows." Most striking of all, Hardy reinvites us to register the total movement of Tess's career, in all its integration, by an ingenious and vivid résumé of it, toward the close of the book. He does this through the final days that Tess and Angel spend together—partly a psychological fugue, partly a kind of total recall, partly both. Leaving her sin with Alec behind her, she rejoins Angel, and the rich woodland of the first two days together corresponds to the rich vale of the dairies. The empty manor house they sleep in corresponds to the ancient house where their marriage was so nearly consummated before. Barren Salisbury Plain corresponds to the uplands of Flintcomb-Ash. The scene at Stonehenge corresponds both to Tess in the vault, and to the moment when she hung on the wayside cross to rest and looked like a sacrificial victim. Her whole tragic life is mirrored in little at its close.

To notice things of this order is to realize, in effect, that Hardy's novels (like many others) need a special mode of reading. The incidents in them which strike us as improbable or strained or grotesque invite (this is not to say that they always deserve) the kind of response that we are accustomed to give, say, to the Dover Cliff scene in *Lear*. Admittedly, Hardy has local failures; but incidents like these are intrinsically at one remove from the probable and the realistic. Almost, it is necessary for them to be unrealistic in order that their other dimension of meaning, their relevance to the larger rhythms of the work, shall transpire. Again and again, it is those larger rhythms which finally expand into the total movement of the novel, transmitting the author's sense of life, the forces that operate through it, the values that chart it out and make it what it is.

From what has so far been said, a new reason may perhaps be advanced as to why Hardy gave up fiction. It is both the strength (because of the integrity that it brought) and the limit of his achievement, to have seen the source of life-creating strength for human beings as being connected always with a certain limited context, the traditional rural order. As time passed, he lost confidence in the strength of this order to resist and survive, and in part, even seems more and more to have regarded the element of drabness and harshness in rural life as not a product of change and modernity, but intrinsic. This being so, he had no position to which to retreat. He does not seem ever to have viewed human nature as itself ineradicably vital, as possessing an innate power to transform, from its own resources, its waste land into a fertile one. To say this is not necessarily to make a point against him. He may very well have been right in thinking that the human species, like others, wilts out of its natural habitat and communal order. It is merely to recognize that by the middle 1890's, Hardy's course in fiction had become one that he could neither retrace, nor pursue.

20.

Herbert Read

Charlotte and Emily Brontë

Heredity is a factor which we cannot neglect in considering the course of any human life, but in ascribing any importance to it, we should be careful to distinguish rather sharply between intelligence or mental development, which is the product of natural selection in the race and education in the individual, and what for want of another word we must call genius, which, when it is of any value, is intelligence directed into personal and wayward channels. It is merely the instrument of genius—the brain considered as a muscle—that is susceptible to hereditary influences. The rest is the product of environment and chance—particularly of the psychological events introduced into life by human relationships.

When we have to reckon with any degree of historical remoteness, heredity becomes a very obscure influence, and the observed facts, in a case like that of the Brontë family, are far too unreliable and unsystematic to be of much use. We see two human strains, themselves the products of incalculable forces, which unite and give issue to genius. The process, one can persist in believing, is as natural as a chemical combination, but it is impossible to reduce it to an equation. We can at the best only point to tendencies and characteristics in the parent stock and hazard that these are some of the elements responsible—and these are but vague, obvious features which it would be difficult to use with any scientific precision.

In the case of the Brontës we have, on the one side, a stock of somewhat barbarous origin, culminating in a man of determination and capability, a man who "early gave tokens of extraordinary quickness and intelligence." Patrick Brontë had opened a public school at the age of sixteen, and at the age of twenty-five was still ambitious enough to proceed to Cambridge, where he took his degree after four years' study. Mrs. Gaskell's rather picturesque description of his passionate nature has been discredited in some of its details, but enough authentic evidence remains to evoke for us a grim puritanical mask, expressing, even while it repressed, the fires beneath. Mrs. Brontë brought characteristics which were of a more ordinary nature, though perhaps no less essential to the result. She was intelligent, placid, and ailing. Her delicate constitution passed to her children, and perhaps this factor, more than any other, determined their neurotic tendency. A neurosis, however, generally needs more than ill health for its inducement: it needs a psychic shock of some kind, and perhaps the mother provided this also by her early death in 1821, when Charlotte was but five and Emily three years old. The strong instinctive link between mother and child is never thus abruptly broken without unseen compensations and reverberations. The enormous body of childish writings still existing in Charlotte's case, but until recently withheld for its lack of literary qualities, may conceivably be of great significance from this point of view. I will merely suggest that we have in Charlotte's seemingly endless fictive evocations of the Duke of Wellington a fantasy of a kind made familiar to us by the researches of psychoanalysts. "Charlotte's little stories," writes Mr. Shorter,

> "commence in her thirteenth year, and go on until she is twenty-three. From thirteen to eighteen she would seem to have had one absorbing hero—the Duke of Wellington. Whether the stories be fairy tales or dramas of modern life, they all alike introduce the Marquis of Douro."[1]

Interpretations of such a fantasy as this might differ: Adler would see in it an unconscious attempt on the part of the neurotic weakling to free herself from a feeling of inferiority[2] by the creation of a compensating ideal of superiority; Jung would find the unconscious origin of such a hero fantasy quite simply in a longing for the lost mother, whereas Freud would probably treat it as the sublimation of a repressed love for the father. But whatever interpretation is adopted, a sense of inferiority, of incompleteness, is seen as the essential character of the neurosis underlying the fantasy.

In the case of Emily the same causes produced a "masculine protest" of a more complex kind, showing, indeed, the typical features of what I think we must, with the psychoanalyst, regard as some kind of psychical hermaphroditism. The outward expression of this state was evident enough. In her childhood the villagers thought her more like a boy than a girl. "She should have been a man: a great navigator!" cried M. Heger, despite his horror of her intractability. Charlotte refers to "a certain harshness in her powerful and peculiar character." "Stronger than a man, simpler than a child, her nature stood alone." Yet Emily was not given to expressing herself by outward speech or action; she was somber and reserved—was, in fact, of a shy, introspective cast; from which clue the psychologist will realize how much deeper and more powerful must have been the masculine assumptions of her mind. These found their fit expression, in due course, in *Wuthering Heights,* whose very peculiar merits show that mingling of the strong and the sweet which some critics make the criterion of all great works of the imagination, and which, in her case, was but the direct expression of her nature.

We might pass further, in illustration of our point, to the cases of Anne and Branwell. The former as an example of religious melancholy, and the latter as an example of disintegrated personality, offer familiar characteristics: they are true to type. But consideration of them is much less important, because it does not bear on a creative artist of much significance. It is sufficient to observe that though all four cases present very diverse symptoms, they are all traceable to the one cause: the early rupture of the maternal bond of affection and protection, the intolerance of a stern, impassive father, the formation of inferiority complexes in the children, and the consequent compensations by fantasy.

What it is now necessary to emphasize strongly, in concluding this psychological excursus, is that art is a triumph over neurosis; that though it originates in a neurotic tendency, it is a coming-out-against this tendency; and that in the case of the three sisters the sublimation was achieved. Their art is not neurotic in kind; no art is. It is only when we search for causes and origins (as we have a perfect right to do) that we discover the neurosis; in the final effect, according to the measure of its success, all is health and harmony.

In dealing with these psychological questions we have, I think, emphasized the kind of environment that leaves the deepest mark on the formation of character and genius. But we are left with the environment of place, of locality. This influence is most in question in the case of Emily, that "nursling of the moors," and indeed her poems show, I think, the most intense rendering of the embodied presence of nature that anywhere exists in English literature.

> The earth that wakes one human heart to feeling
> Can centre both the worlds of Heaven and Hell.

In these two lines she reaches a climax in her philosophy of nature, and shows a depth of emotional perception which was not exceeded even by Wordsworth.

But the immediate influence of natural scenes differs from this general evocation of the spirit of nature. There is about the moors of Yorkshire, where they yet remain, a quality that works strongly on the senses. Their sparseness and loneliness drive you to an intimacy with whatever life does exist there; a small thing like the scent of bog-myrtle can kindle a keen emotion. There is a severity in the unrelieved reach of gradual hill country; the eye drifts into distant prospects, seeks the skyline that is not a line, but a subtle merging of tones; the human mind *is* perhaps heard more distinctly in this inorganic stillness—only when, however, it has learned to think, and to express its thoughts. The moors, like any other local endowment, are merely material for observation and perception, and if into their confines there happens to enter a mind of exceptional dimensions, this mind will use its environment to some purpose.

Such was the case with Emily Brontë. Charlotte, writing that eloquent and penerating Preface to the second edition of *Wuthering Heights,* expresses this fact with all her rhetorical force:

> *Wuthering Heights* was hewn in a wild workshop, with simple tools, out of homely materials. The statuary found a granite block on a solitary moor; gazing thereon, he saw how from the crag might be elicited a head, savage, swart, sinister; a form moulded with at least one element of grandeur—power. He wrought with a rude chisel, and from no model but the vision of his meditations.

We should note how objective the attitude of the artist is made. A more facile conception would have imbued the statuary with the moor's savage elements, and made the image but the reflection of an entranced imagination. But the vision of her meditations was the product of an applied mind; and that this fixed itself mainly on a rustic scene was but the result of chance limitations—limitations, however, which we do not regret, since they drove that vision so deeply into the heart of the subject.

A far more effective factor, both in the case of Emily and of Charlotte, was what we might call quite simply education, but which resolves, upon deeper analysis, into the personal influence of Constantin Heger. In Charlotte's case it seems that this aggressive intellect—masculine, fiery, compact—came opportunely to occupy the stronghold of the unconscious evacuated by the Duke of Wellington, whose luster had no doubt waned with the growth of experience and intelligence. From the psychological point of view, that is all that need be said of a personal relationship which has been the subject of much speculation; though the intense nature that the hero worship was to assume, before the end of Charlotte's stay in Brussels, was, as I shall make out later, a determining experience in her life.

The immediate importance of this contact was its purely literary consequences. Charlotte and Emily learned the meaning of style—and style not in the English sense of picturesqueness, but in the French sense of clarity and brevity. Spirits that were romantic, or at any rate Celtic, submitted to the discipline of a strictly Latin mind—Latin in its scepticism, its dryness, and its dignity. Mrs. Gaskell printed a *devoir* of Charlotte's corrected by M. Heger, where the process may be seen in action. In the simple and halting French then at Charlotte's command we already experience the peculiar force and vividness of her impressions; but the corrections and marginal comments of M. Heger are the precepts, not of a schoolmaster, but of a master of the art of writing. "He told me," relates Mrs. Gaskell,

> that one day this summer [when the Brontës had been for about four months receiving instruction from him] he read to them Victor Hugo's celebrated portrait of Mirabeau, "mais, dans ma leçon je me bornais à ce qui concerne *Mirabeau Orateur*. C'est après l'analyse de ce morçeau, considéré surtout de point de vue du fond, de la disposition, de ce qu'on pourrait appeler *la charpente* qu'ont été faits les deux portraits que je vous donne." He went on to say that he had pointed out to them the fault in Victor Hugo's style as being exaggeration in conception, and, at the same time, he had made them notice the extreme beauty of his "nuances" of expression. They were then dismissed to choose the subject of a similar kind of portrait. This selection M. Heger always left to them; for "it is necessary," he observed, "before sitting down to write on a subject, to have thoughts and feelings about it, I cannot tell on what subject your heart and mind have been excited. I must leave that to you."

When Charlotte finally left the Heger institute at Brussels, some eighteen months after the composition of the *devoir* referred to, the intense desire to write, which had been hers since childhood, assumed a more definite urgency. It was not merely that she had perfected, under the Professor's care, the methods of self-expression; she had also endured a nervous crisis of an indefinite nature but of a deep effect. She herself (in a letter to Miss Wooler in 1846) described her state as *hypochondria*:

> I endured it but a year and assuredly I can never forget the concentrated anguish of certain insufferable moments,

> and the heavy gloom of many long hours, besides the preternatural horrors which seemed to clothe existence and nature, and which made life a continual walking nightmare. Under such circumstances the morbid nerves can know neither peace nor enjoyment; whatever touches pierces them: sensation for them is suffering.

Mrs. Gaskell pictures some of the circumstances of this period. Charlotte had been left during the *grandes vacances* in the great deserted pensionnat, with only one teacher for a companion.

> This teacher, a French-woman, had always been uncongenial to her; but, left to each other's sole companionship, Charlotte soon discovered that her associate was more profligate, more steeped in a kind of cold, systematic sensuality, than she had before imagined it possible for a human being to be; and her whole nature revolted from this woman's society. A low nervous fever was gaining upon Miss Brontë. She had never been a good sleeper, but now she could not sleep at all. Whatever had been disagreeable, or obnoxious, to her during the day, was presented when it was over with exaggerated vividness to her disordered fancy. . . . In the daytime, driven abroad by loathing of her companion and by the weak restlessness of fever, she tried to walk herself into such a state of bodily fatigue as would induce sleep. . . . The shades of evening made her retrace her footsteps—sick for want of food, but not hungry; fatigued with long continued exercise—yet restless still, and doomed to another weary, haunted night of sleeplessness.

During one such anguished progress, she found herself before a confessional in Ste. Gudule's, and, her strong Protestant prejudices succumbing to what she calls "an odd whim," she abandoned herself to that psychopathic consolation. "I was determined to confess," she writes to Emily. "I actually did confess—a real confession." The vivid use she made of the incident, in *Villette*, is only the most obvious record of this spiritual climax; the complete pathological phase (where sensation, as she says, was suffering) constituted, I think, the fundamental experience upon which she built her whole conception of imaginative reality.[3]

I have here used an epithet, "imaginative," which it is

necessary to use at all times with care and generally to avoid. It is one of those epithets that normally cloak a lack of thought or a failure of analysis. Nevertheless, I think it will be found, when reduced to its definite limits, to connote a certain process in the mind of the creative writer for which no other more suitable term can be used. The merely descriptive distinction between the fancy and the imagination, which has so long served in the sphere of literary criticism, is no longer adequate. It is not based on any corresponding psychological distinction; and even when the elements of fancy are excluded, we are left with no clear boundaries within which we can confine the activities of the imagination. It is merely a distinction, as Pater pointed out, between degrees of intensity. It would not, however, serve any useful purpose to import into literary criticism the purely technical conception of the imagination current in the old psychology, however precise such a use might be. We merely want a more definite understanding of the way in which ideas and images are associated in that abnormal manner we term imaginative. It was in the capture of such states of excitement that Wordsworth quite rightly saw the function of the poet. And although in the case of fiction the plane of conception is different, being more relative, less absolute—a detailed construction of dramatic events rather than a generalized expression of states of consciousness or thought—nevertheless, the psychological mechanism is the same. True imagination is a kind of logic; it is the capacity to deduce from the nature of an experienced reality, the nature of other unexperienced realities. Upon the depth and totality of the original experience will depend the reach and validity of the imaginative process. If the process is kept to a quasilogical rigidity, it may be observed that merely one kind of experience, sufficiently realized, will suffice for an almost unlimited progression of imaginative analogies: the one experience will be ballast enough to carry the author through any fictive evocation of feelings and actions. The case of Dostoevsky is very illustrative of this truth; and the life of Charlotte Brontë is well worth consideration precisely because the process, the logic, is there seen so uncontaminated by subsidiary influences.

Experience alone does not, of course, make the poet or novelist; it merely qualifies him. It must be united with a previous disposition to create an imaginary world, the origin of which, as I have suggested, is to be found in psychological factors at work during infancy and adolescence. Charlotte early had "the desire (almost amounting to illness) of expressing herself in some way,—writing or drawing."[4] At school she developed a talent, under the guise of play, of "making things out." "This habit," one of her school friends relates,

> 'of making out' interests for themselves that most children get who have none in actual life, was very strong in her. The whole family used to 'make out' histories, and invent characters and events. I told her sometimes they were like growing potatoes in a cellar. She said, sadly, "Yes! I know we are!"

The greater bulk of the unpublished Brontë manuscripts seems to consist of an elaborate "cycle" of stories and poems, written over a long period of years and concerned with the politics and chivalry of a kingdom imagined in every detail. To revert to the old antithesis, these were work of idle fancy; but when bleak disillusionment was added to the already sufficiently bleak existence of these children, when expression became a more serious necessity as an escape from emotional agitations too strong to be repressed with impunity, then the mere mechanism of literary expression was ready at their command.

This is to put the matter on its deterministic level; it is perhaps of more profit to note the conscious reactions of Charlotte to these emotional and mental transitions. There are two points to notice: her theory of the relation of experience to imagination; and the evolution, at her hands, of the analytic method in fiction. The best expression of the first point was elicited during Charlotte's brief correspondence with G. H. Lewes—a literary encounter very characteristic of the period and about which an effect of exquisite comedy lurks. On 6th November 1847 she wrote in reply to a friendly letter of Lewes's, dictated by his enthusiasm for *Jane Eyre*:

> You advise me, too, not to stray far from the ground of experience, as I become weak when I enter the region of fiction, and you say, "real experience is perennially interesting, and to all men." I feel that this is also true; but, dear sir, is not the real experience of each individual very limited? And if a writer dwells upon that solely or principally, is he not in danger of repeating himself, and also of becoming an egotist? Then, too, imagination is a strong, restless faculty, which claims to be heard and exercised: are we to be quite deaf to her cry, and insensate to her struggles? When she shows us bright pictures, are we never to look at them, and try to reproduce them? And when she is eloquent, and speaks rapidly and urgently in our ear, are we not to write to her dictation?

In reading this passage we must remember that Charlotte writes conscious of what she could but regard as a salutary lesson in the strategy of authorship: this was the complete failure of her first novel, *The Professor*, in which, as Mrs. Gaskell says, "she went to the extreme of reality, depicting characters as they had shown themselves to her in actual life." And in the letter to Lewes already quoted, Charlotte herself confessed:

> When I first began to write, so impressed was I with the truth of the principles you advocate, that I determined to take Nature and Truth as my sole guides, and to follow their very footprints; I restrained imagination, eschewed romance, repressed excitement; over-bright colouring, too, I avoided, and sought to produce something which should be soft, grave, and true.

But the publishers would have none of it, and the convenient theory of art for art's sake not being yet a part of the literary consciousness, she had decided to modify her virtuous course. She abandoned the mere transcript of experience and adopted the imaginative process I have tried to define.[5] It is here that we must realize the essential strength of her character and genius; a weaker writer would have had recourse to the less intense forms of imaginative activity; but Charlotte, driven, perhaps, by subconscious forces, determined, in her own phrase, to be "her own woman." She determined to see justly rather than to feel kindly; and when she was almost agonized by the suggestion, emanating from the *Quarterly,* but eagerly repeated even by the kind of people she herself thought nice, that *Jane Eyre* was a "wicked book," even then she had the courage of her magnificent retort: "I am resolved not to write otherwise. *I shall bend as my powers tend.*"

Her powers resided in her intuitive logic, though she rather tended to mask the incidence of her faculty. "We only suffer reality to *suggest,* never to *dictate,*" she writes to her old school friend; and some years later, with *Villette* fresh from her pen, she even went so far as to enunciate this slightly insincere maxim: "I hold that a work of fiction ought to be a work of creation: that the *real* should be sparingly introduced in pages dedicated to the *ideal.*" This hardly tallies with her own criticism of *Villette*: "I greatly apprehend that the weakest character in the book is the one I aimed at making the most beautiful; and, if this be the case, the fault lies in its wanting the germ of the *real*—in its being purely imaginary." We have in this latter statement, self-analyzed and self-confessed, the whole secret of her strength. Her practice of fiction resolves always into a nucleus of experience and the growth, from this nucleus, of an imaginative organism "given off," as in nature, cell by cell, with inexorable continuity.

Combined with this process, a part of its mechanism, was the gift of analysis. Some years before she began to write, even before her education at Brussels, she was aware of her capabilities in this direction. She warned a rejected suitor, who wished to become her "friend," that

> it has always been my habit to study the character of those amongst whom I chance to be thrown. . . . As for me, you do not know me: I am not the serious, grave, cool-headed individual you would suppose: you would think me romantic and eccentric; you would say I was satirical and severe.

The two faculties of her writing are clearly foreshadowed here: imagination and analysis. There is no need to enlarge upon this second quality; it is so obviously her distinction. The consistency of its exercise—as, for example, in the character of Madame

Beck—is perhaps for her date a matter for wonder. She herself remarks of Balzac: "By-and-by I seemed to enter into the mystery of his craft, and to discover, with delight, where his force lay: is it not in the analysis of motive, and in a subtle perception of the most obscure and secret workings of the mind?" But at the time of her first introduction to Balzac's work, her own gift was already fully formed. I find no evidence anywhere that she knew the work of Stendhal, or the solitary masterpiece of Benjamin Constant; but she introduced into English literature the very qualities of psychological observation and analysis by which these writers had instituted a new epoch in the literature of France.

The influence she exercised on the development of the English novel was more profound than is often acknowledged: it is *Villette,* more than any work of Thackeray or George Eliot, that we must recognize as the pioneer of an extension of the province and function of the novelist's art only completely worked into the tradition of the English novel by Meredith and Henry James. To her contemporaries this revolutionary element in her work was quite evident, and though they did not stop to consider its real nature, they disliked it strongly because it was strange. Open-minded critics of the stamp of Lewes and Thackeray were willing to acknowledge the power and originality of her art, but the more average minds of the time experienced a sense of shock, deepening to outrage when it gradually became evident that the mysterious Currer Bell belonged to the gentler sex. The particular charge, first raised against *Jane Eyre,* but repeated in the case of *Shirley,* was one of "coarseness." What her accusers meant by their term cannot be very vivid to our modern consciousness: all they meant would, I think, easily be included in our concept "realism." But even Mrs. Gaskell, who by no means shared all the prudery of her age, thought it necessary to apologize for this lapse on the part of her heroine; and did so in these curious sentences:

> I do not deny for myself the existence of coarseness here and there in her works, otherwise so entirely noble. I only ask those who read them to consider her life,—which has been openly laid bare before them,—and to say how it could be otherwise. She saw few men; and among these

> few were one or two with whom she had been acquainted since early childhood,—who had shown her much friendliness and kindness,—through whose family she had received many pleasures,—for whose intellect she had a great respect, —but who talked before her, if not to her, with as little reticence as Rochester talked to Jane Eyre. Take this in connection with her poor brother's sad life, and the outspoken people among whom she lived,—remember her strong feeling of the duty of representing life as it really is, not as it ought to be,—and then do her justice for all that she was, and all that she would have been (had God spared her), rather than censure her because circumstances forced her to touch pitch, as it were, and by it her hand was for a moment defiled. (*Life*, ch. xxvi.)

Charlotte herself could not comprehend the charge; and her unconsciousness of the very existence of what her critics so plainly realized, brings before us in all its uniqueness the amazing quality of *innocence* which distinguishes, not only her own work, but that of her sisters also. It is because the art was so innocent that it is so real. One can only account for the phenomenon by the unparalleled isolation of their lives. Though from an early age they devoured every scrap of literature that came within their reach, it is doubtful if anything of a directly inspiring kind ever came their way before Charlotte's and Emily's departure for Brussels. At Haworth they seem to have been confined to a diet of newspapers, sermons, and the Bible; and at Brussels, though in the matter of style and composition their reading there had incalculable influence, yet it seems certain that, with the possible exception of Hoffmann and Rousseau, it did not include anything that could form a model for their own efforts. At any rate, whatever the explanation, it is certain that when the three sisters solemnly and in unison sat down to compose their first serious novels, they did so without any prepossessions. They are the least influenced and most original geniuses in the whole history of the English novel. What Charlotte in her Introduction to *Wuthering Heights* wrote of the others, was equally true of herself:

> Neither Ellis nor Acton was learned: they had no thoughts of filling their pitchers at the well-spring of other minds;

> they always wrote from the impulse of nature, the dictates of intuition, and from such stores of observation as their limited experience had enabled them to amass.

It is this quality of innocence that gives to *Wuthering Heights* its terrible and unique intensity. If I have written of Charlotte to the neglect of Emily, it is not that for one moment I make the mistake of attaching more importance to her. It is merely that in the case of Charlotte the evidence is so much more ample. The psychology of Emily is at once less complex and more profoundly hidden. She is one of the strangest geniuses in our literature, and her kinship is with Baudelaire and Poe. It is not merely that her imagination traverses the same somber shadows, but also like these two anguished minds, she is for ever perplexed by the problem of evil—"conquered good and conquering ill." Her absorption in metaphysical problems has no parallel in the poetry of her age, and in her "Last Lines" rises to an intensity of emotional thought not surpassed in the whole range of English literature. Yet this same mind was capable of the purest lyrical utterance—in which, however, the sense of mortality seems to linger:

> Fall, leaves, fall; die, flowers, away;
> Lengthen night, and shorten day!
> Every leaf speaks bliss to me,
> Fluttering from the autumn tree.
>
> I shall smile when wreaths of snow
> Blossom where the rose should grow;
> I shall sing when night's decay
> Ushers in a drearier day.

Emily Brontë's poetry, which is at once explicit and profound, with sense finely annealed to cadence, is the most essential poetry ever written by a woman in the English tongue. Her mind, far more daring than Charlotte's, soared above particular creeds and attained in a few momentary manifestations those universal forms of thought common only to minds of the first order. Her best poems suffer, at present, by being bound up with much that is juvenile and occasional in kind. *Wuthering*

Heights remains, the towering rock of Charlotte's metaphor, extremely definite, completely achieved, and of an amazing unity of tone.

We are left with one other element, common to Emily and Charlotte, which needs a word of notice. A certain lack of reticence had shocked the ruck of their Victorian critics; a smaller and a rarer band were disturbed by the evident rapture. It fell to Harriet Martineau, economist, moralist, agnostic, and a very typical representative of her age, to bring this criticism to a head. Despite a friendship she had formed for Charlotte, she had felt bound to air her misgivings in *The Daily News*, and in a review of *Villette* had insisted that Charlotte made love too general and too absorbing a factor in women's lives, protesting against the assumption that "events and characters are to be regarded through the medium of one passion only." Charlotte demurred, but Miss Martineau, indomitable and pitiless, wrote to her:

> I do not like the love, either the kind or the degree of it; and its prevalence in the book and effect on the action of it, help to explain the passages in the reviews which you consulted me about, and seem to afford *some* foundation for the criticisms they offered.

Charlotte retired abashed; she had but followed "the impulses of nature and the dictates of intuition." And about this very book she had written to her publisher: "Unless I am mistaken, the emotion of the book will be found to be kept throughout in tolerable subjection." Emotion in subjection—that is the very definition of art! And because Miss Martineau did not realize this, she has become a curious paleolithic dummy, an Aunt Sally ready for our modern ironists, whilst Charlotte still lives in her books with all the directness of a real personality.

But it is not Miss Martineau who was destined to stand as antitype to the Brontës: a subtler and finer antagonist had been in the field for some time. It speaks a good deal for Charlotte's critical perception that she realized the implications of Miss Austen's talent as soon as she became aware of it, rather late in her life, and, though only in the privacy of her correspondence with her publisher, she then defined the limitations of that talent in terms which still remain unanswerable. In a letter written in 1850 she says:

> She does her business of delineating the surface of the lives of genteel English people curiously well. There is a Chinese fidelity, a miniature delicacy in the painting. She ruffles her reader by nothing vehement, disturbs him by nothing profound. The passions are perfectly unknown to her; she rejects even a speaking acquaintance with that stormy sisterhood. Even to the feelings she vouchsafes no more than an occasional graceful but distant recognition—too frequent converse with them would ruffle the smooth elegance of her progress. Her business is not half so much with the human heart as with the human eyes, mouth, hands, and feet. What sees keenly, speaks aptly, moves flexibly, it suits her to study; but what throbs fast and full, though hidden, what the blood rushes through, what is the unseen seat of life and the sentiment target of death—this Miss Austen ignores.

The justice of that analysis remains, to confront the present sophisticated rage for Jane Austen. But it also remains the statement of an extreme position, the weakness of which would have been exceedingly patent to the precise sensibility of the author of *Pride and Prejudice*. If she had lived long enough she might have criticized *Jane Eyre* in terms of almost exact contradiction. The psychologist does not venture to take sides in such a pitched battle, but resorts to his theory of types, and sees here the dry bones of his structure take on perfect flesh. It would be difficult to discover a more exact illustration of the main distinction he draws between faculties directed inwards, to the observation of feeling, and faculties directed outwards, to the observation of external things. The psychologist must halt at this distinction, unless he suggests, as a scientific ideal, some harmony or balance of these tendencies. But the critic must pursue the matter to a judgement. It will not, for that purpose, suffice to identify the ordered conception of objective facts with the classical spirit, or the research of passion with the romantic spirit—though it is tempting in this case to think of Jane Austen, as a typical (though rare, because feminine) embodiment of classicism, and Pater seized on *Wuthering Heights,* in preference to any work of Scott's, as the "really characteristic fruit" of the spirit of romanticism. That only proves once more the inadequacy of these outworn shibboleths, since from another point of view *Wuthering Heights,* with its unerring unity of conception and its full catharsis of the emotions of pity and terror, is one of the very few occasions on which the novel has reached the dignity of classical tragedy. And, in the other case, it would be hard to concede the full meaning of classicism to Jane Austen's universe of undertones.

We return to Charlotte's phrase—emotion in subjection—and contend that this is the only normal sense in which the classical spirit should be endured. The rest is pedantry, academic closures, and the "literature of our grandfathers." To apply the distinction to Jane Austen is hardly fair: she belongs to the spirit of comedy, which has never been easily classified, always existing as a free and detached criticism of life and literature. Jane Austen, in essentials, takes her place with Congreve, if with anybody in English letters; and maybe, after all, in making her the antitype to the Brontës we are but displaying the old discordant masks side by side. Is it an equal opposition? Well, not quite. Charlotte Brontë is again the critic—"Miss Austen being, as you say, without 'sentiment,' without *poetry,* maybe *is* sensible, real (more *real* than *true*), but she cannot be great." And that might be said equally well of Congreve, or of any representative of the comic spirit. It is a question of attitude. It is, finally, a question of courage—of throwing into the attempt for truth not only intelligence, spirit, faith, but also feeling, emotion, self.

Notes

[1] Clement Shorter: *The Brontës, Life and Letters* (London, 1908), p. 72.

[2] There are many direct betrayals in Charlotte's correspondence of this deeply-felt sense of inferiority. The following passage from the reminiscences of her school friend, Mary Taylor, is significant:

> She always showed physical feebleness in everything. She ate no animal food at school. It was about this time I told her she was very ugly. Some years afterwards I told her I thought I had been very impertinent. She replied: "You did me a great deal of good, Polly, so don't repent of it."

[3] In considering this period of her life, though I ignore, I do not deny what the four letters from Charlotte to Constantin Heger, published by *The Times* in 1913, are a sufficient proof of: the importance of her feelings for Professor Heger in the causation of this pathological state. There can be no question of the existence, in her mind, of an appalling conflict between the strength of her emotion and the considerations—social, moral, and religious—which caused her to hide, even from herself, the nature of this emotion. The result was a decided "complex," and I should be disposed to agree with a psychologist who identified her whole neurotic condition at this period with such a specific repression. I do not consider the *cause* of her state too closely because all I am concerned with is its effect upon her creative mind.

[4] Mrs. Gaskell's account of conversations with Charlotte. See *Life,* Chap. XXVII.

[5] It is interesting to note her own subsequent and detached opinion of the qualities which, nevertheless, did result from her first method. In a letter to W. S. Williams dated 14th December 1847, she writes:

> A few days since I looked over *The Professor.* I found the beginning very feeble, the whole narrative deficient in incident and in general attractiveness. Yet the middle and latter portion of the work, all that relates to Brussels, the Belgian school, etc., is as good as I can write; it contains more pith, more substance, more reality, in my judgment, than much of *Jane Eyre.* It gives, I think, a new view of a grade, an occupation, and a class of characters—all very commonplace, very insignificant in themselves, but not more so than the materials composing that portion of *Jane* Eyre which seems to please most generally.

21.

Phyllis Bartlett

The Novels of George Meredith

In the autumn of 1960 two questions were raised in the pages of *The Times Literary Supplement*: how Victorian are the novels of George Meredith; and how many of them should a Cambridge undergraduate, or by implication any educated person, be expected to read? The questions were sparked by a front-page article on the English curriculum at Cambridge that quoted disparagingly a sentence from the first chapter of F. R. Leavis's *The Great Tradition* in which Dr. Leavis sets George Eliot and Henry James in "the great tradition," "above the ruck of Gaskells and Trollopes and Merediths." In the next issue of *The Times Literary Supplement* Mr. Andor Gomme placed Meredith among "the more Victorian Victorians" and said that surely one of his novels is enough for any student to read. Mr. W. J. Lucas replied by reminding us that neither Meredith's reputation as an immoral novelist nor his championship of the progress of women marks him as one of "the more Victorian Victorians." Morever, Mr. Lucas asked, what one novel is the student supposed to read? One cannot know Meredith from any single novel. "It is sad," wrote Mr. Lucas, "to see a great novelist treated with such coarse naïvety." Mr. Gomme returned to the fray, ceding the point of "the more Victorian Victorians," but

Reprinted by permission of the author, the editor and Longmans-Green, London, from *Review of English Literature,* Vol, 3, No. 1 (January, 1962), 31–46.

insisting that either *The Egoist* or *Beauchamp's Career* will suffice for the three-year reading span of an undergraduate.

Leaving the Cambridge undergraduate to his one novel by Meredith and the strictures of Dr. Leavis, who would probably think that even the one was a waste of time, let us ask why many people who have passed beyond the baccalaureate feel perfectly content with their ignorance of Meredith. I am thinking of the educated readers who will have been freshly reassured by Mr. Gomme that: "As Forster and James both said, the life in Meredith is faked; and the famous poetic imagery only serves for a time to obscure the want of a true living centre." I write from the point of view of one who finds many living centers in Meredith's novels and contend that the educated apathy toward them is a direct inheritance from the fine writers who were brought up on Meredith, enjoyed him, learned from him, and then—in going their own necessary, creative ways—partly rejected him. I say "partly" because when such big names as Forster and James are linked in a simple sentence of condemnation, this judgment is only part of the record. Two voices were there when speaking of Meredith. To be selective, let us hear them in the records of Henry James, E. M. Forster, and Virginia Woolf.

The first voice of Henry James would have been enthusiastic if it had been heard because as a boy of seventeen he read *Evan Harrington* as it was coming out serially in *Once a Week* (1860). His father sent the magazine to him when he was at school in Bonn and he "rioted" in *Evan Harrington* as well as in the German classics during the season that he later said attuned him to the life of letters. James's second, negative voice is heard in the oft-quoted letter to Edmund Gosse on the "unspeakable *Lord Ormont*" (August 22, 1894) and is the passage that Mr. Gomme was presumably thinking of. After finishing the first volume of *Lord Ormont and his Aminta* James exploded to Gosse: "I doubt if any equal quantity of extravagant verbiage, of airs and graces, of phrases and attitudes, of obscurities and alembications, ever *started* less their subject, ever contributed less of what the reader needs to know. All elaborate predicates of exposition without the ghost of a nominative to hook themselves to; and not a difficulty met, not a figure presented, not a scene constituted—not a dim shadow condensing once either into audible or into visible reality—making you hear for an instant the tap of its feet on the earth." James would never have uttered such a blast publicly, for he and Meredith were friends, in a remote, rather respectful, fashion, and indeed he ended his outburst to Gosse: "There is another side, of course, which one will utter another day." Desmond MacCarthy accounted for that other side in a "Literary Causerie" of 1926 that opens, "Meredith is not worn just now." Classifying Meredith with other poet-novelists, MacCarthy praised Meredith's heights "at moments of tragic significance, of exultation, of profound happiness, he is supreme. As a novelist he is no artist, but, as Henry James once said to me, he does the best things best." (Incidentally, James had his trough too. In 1927, a year after MacCarthy had said that Meredith was out of fashion, Orlo Williams declared in an essay on *The Ambassadors*: "The house that James built is apparently in ruins. Nobody reads him now. . . .")

Virginia Stephen, as a child of ten, had won the heart of her father's great friend Meredith and, when young, had read *Harry Richmond* with "careless rapture," but at the age of forty, her voice was uneasy. She was writing about Percy Lubbock's *The Craft of Fiction* (1921) and what he had to say about Meredith's only first-person novel, *Harry Richmond.* The thought of reading this novel again to study its art appalled her. In one comment on Lubbock's book, she wrote that to read *Harry Richmond* again would be a "dangerous experiment"; in a second thought, she admitted that the only way one could face a second reading of a long Victorian novel by such a "master" as Meredith would be in order to trace its methods, because if we were once able to understand the methods, we would have the novel "whole" as we have *Hamlet.* Virginia Woolf set the reading time for *Hamlet,* five hours, as a norm for an English reader, and that is probably the stretch for her best novels. "That *Hamlet,*" she wrote, "is a work of art goes without saying; but that *Harry Richmond* is a work of art has to be said for the first time." Between 1922 and 1928, when Mrs. Woolf wrote an essay for Meredith's centenary, she had evidently undertaken the experiment of re-reading *Harry Richmond,* for she wrote acutely about the novel. She found that it seems easy and conventional, in the Dickens tradition of autobiographical narrative, until it moves into the world of Richmond Roy and the Princess Ottilia, "the world of fantasy and romance, where all holds together and we are able to put our imagination at the writer's service without reserve. That such surrender is above all things delightful: that it adds spring-heels to our boots: that it fires the cold scepticism out of us and makes the world glow in lucid transparency before our eyes, needs no showing, as it certainly submits to no analysis." Mrs. Woolf suggested that a "prolonged diet" of Russian fiction in neutral translation and "the convolutions of psychological Frenchmen, may have led us to forget that the English language is naturally exuberant, and the English character full of humours and eccentricities. Meredith's flamboyancy has a great ancestry behind it; we cannot avoid all memory of Shakespear." Virginia Woolf continued to respond warmly to Meredith's prose, even when there was no ceremonious occasion involved. In her *Diary*, on March 27, 1937, she remarked of the same novel that had so bedeviled Henry James:

> I began *Lord Ormont and his Aminta* and found it so rich, so knotted, so alive and muscular after the pale little fiction I'm used to, that, alas, it made me wish to write fiction again. Meredith underrated. I like his effort to escape plain prose. And he had humour and some insight too—more than they allow him now.

E. M. Forster's two voices about Meredith are heard within a few pages of *Aspects of the Novel* (1927), written as Forster himself noted when Meredith was "rather in the trough of a wave." Forster objected to Meredith because "The really tragic in scenery and life was hidden from him" and because "most of the social values are faked." These are arbitrary remarks, yet the two damaging pages on which they appear are enough for Dr. Leavis, who abruptly disposes of Meredith in *The Great Tradition*: "As for Meredith, I needn't add anything to what is said about him by Mr. E. M. Forster, who, having belonged to the original *milieu* in which Meredith was erected into a great master, enjoys peculiar advantages for the necessary demolition-work." But Forster did not consider that he had demolished Meredith in his brilliantly written passage of derogation, for his voice of praise follows immediately: "And yet he is in one way a great novelist. He is the finest contriver that English fiction has ever produced, and any lecture on plot must do homage to him." Forster paid his homage:

> Meredith's plots are not closely knit. Incident springs out of character, and having occurred it alters that character. People and events are closely connected, and he does it by means of these contrivances. They are often delightful, sometimes touching, always unexpected. This shock, followed by the feeling, "Oh, that's all right," is a sign that all is well with the plot: characters, to be real, ought to run smoothly, but a plot ought to cause surprise.

Forster gave as examples the horse-whipping of Dr. Shrapnel in *Beauchamp's Career* and the "concealed emotion" of Laetitia Dale within "the admirable plot of *The Egoist,*" so that when she says, "No" to Sir Willoughby's proposal of marriage in "the great midnight scene" the reader is astonished. "This is one of the countless examples in which either plot or character has to suffer, and Meredith with his unerring good sense here lets the plot triumph."

Having listened to Henry James, Virginia Woolf, and Forster, I now propose to examine some of the obstacles that are supposed to impede our reading of Meredith's thirteen novels. (I am not including the two early fantasies, *The Shaving of Shagpat* and *Farina.*)

One obstacle is supposed to be his "cleverness." This was the most frequent pejorative used by the reviewers during Meredith's lifetime, and there is no denying that Meredith was clever. E. M. Forster has taught us something about his cleverness in contriving plot. More disputable is the cleverness of Meredith's wit. From his earliest days, Meredith loved to invent epigrams; they dropped from him as he talked and walked, and many went into notebooks. Some of these epigrams were too good to waste, and Meredith found two ways of using them in his fiction.

One way, of course, was to put them in the mouths of clever

people, such as Adrian, the wise youth, in *The Ordeal of Richard Feverel,* and Diana, in *Diana of the Crossways.* The conversation of these characters when talking to other intelligent people is made of the same stuff as high comedy, although the subject is usually serious. These witty conversations often demand extraordinary attention, but they are worth attending to because the talk is not talk for talk's sake only; it moves into action. Furthermore, the reader of Meredith must learn to distinguish between wise wit and superficial wit. On reading *The Egoist* one is bound to be annoyed by the repetition of Mrs. Mountstuart Jenkinson's epigram that: "Sir Willoughby has a leg" and her description of Clara as "A dainty rogue in porcelain," but it is all right that we become bored with Mrs. Mountstuart, for she is a gossip and a busybody, who although she confounds the county aristocracy with her wit is not intended to confound the intelligent reader. Indeed, Mrs. Mountstuart loses in her big pretence of understanding Clara's character.

The other way in which Meredith used epigrams was in what the newest of Meredith scholars, Norman Kelvin, has called "tutelary books." In *Richard Feverel,* "The Pilgrim Scrip," written by the embittered Sir Austin Feverel before the immediate action of the novel, is often quoted as expressive of Sir Austin's pride and his distrust of women. "The Book of Egoism" in *The Egoist* is Meredith's own summing-up of a problem that preoccupied him and that he had to fight in himself as well as in Sir Willoughby. The opening chapter of *Diana of the Crossways,* entitled "Of Diaries and Diarists touching the Heroine," introduces us to Diana by means of entries in fictitious diaries "beginning with the second quarter" of the nineteenth century. Through this means Meredith measures Diana's wit and gives her the now famous statement that "Sentimental people. . . . fiddle harmonics on the strings of sensualism." Forster remarked that: "As far as characters go, Meredith plays with his cards on the table," and in this opening chapter of *Diana* he spread out all these cards; as he said at the end of the chapter, "the froth" is "out of the bottle." From that point on the shocking incidents must do their work. In an elaborate framework for his last completed novel, *The Amazing Marriage,* Meredith used for a fourth time a tutelary book, but he used it sparingly. The first three chapters of this novel are narrated in the *persona* of Dame Gossip as Chorus, and she reappears at intervals. Dame Gossip is not unintelligent and she has made researches into the subject of the novel. She tells us that the father of the heroine, Carinthia Kirby, and of the heroine's older brother Chillon, the Old Buccaneer, had written a book called "Maxims for Men" that made her shudder, it was so manly. Carinthia, throughout the novel, is shown to have lived by her father's standards. She was determined and invincible.

The device of the social commentator, Dame Gossip, in *The Amazing Marriage* seems an unnecessary complication in method, though Meredith probably intended her as a simplification over his own manner of narrating. He certainly did not intend the device to be an act of "literary playfulness," for he was upset by having been adversely accused of such playfulness in *One of Our Conquerors,* thinking that a novelist might have an occasional right to such pleasures. Even so, he felt that *The Amazing Marriage* would be free from this charge. Since the first sentence of *One of Our Conquerors* has been cited as an example of an unattractive "literary playfulness," let us have it:

> A gentleman, noteworthy for a lively countenance and a waistcoat to match it, crossing London Bridge at noon on a gusty April day, was almost magically detached from his conflict with the gale by some sly strip of slipperiness, abounding in that conduit of the markets, which had more or less adroitly performed the trick upon preceding passengers, and now laid this one flat amid the shuffle of feet, peaceful for the moment as the uncomplaining who have gone to Sabrina beneath the tides.

The mode of this sentence is indeed jocose, as Victor Radnor's spirit was genial on this April day when he lost an idea in his fall on London Bridge, yet every part of the sentence foretells the novel. The financial "Conqueror" would never have become the public success that he was if he had not had the native liveliness here displayed in his countenance nor if he had not adopted a mask to match his countenance, here symbolized by the waistcoat that was sullied by his fall. His pride in fresh waistcoats is alluded to in the very last pages of the novel when he and his wonderful, unwedded wife Nataly visit his dying, elderly, wedded wife, Mrs. Burman; and in his bath the night of that memorable visit he remembers the fall on London Bridge and how he had not seen in it a signification of "a moral fall, fully to the level of the physical" in maintaining his scheme for fashioning the greatest country house in England, a scheme ruined by his daughter, "who had saved him from fall further." An excess of ambition was ultimately his calamitous slip, and the "sly strip of slipperiness" is not specifically identified with orange peels or outside leaves of cabbages since the slipperiness symbolizes the false values which trip men in the capitalized Market of the City as well as in the lower-case market of foodstuffs. Victor Radnor's moment of peace forecast the peace that his death brought him on the penultimate page of the novel. Even the concluding simile of this first sentence, that Victor was "peaceful for the moment as the uncomplaining who have gone to Sabrina beneath the tides," is significant. It is playful, certainly, but not idly so. Sabrina, the pure nymph of *Comus,* was the Roman name for the river Severn that rises in Montgomeryshire, Wales. Victor Radnor's middle name was indeed "Montgomery"; he had "clear-water eyes," and he had deserted his wedded wife for the love of his Nataly, as the legendary King Locrine had deserted his wife for the love of the nymph Sabrina. Thus this one castigated sentence could not be more deeply weighted with significant paradox, tension, and ambiguity, for those who worship these gods. Over and over again, Meredith's sentences would yield this kind of fruit to the "body-snatchers," "the unworthy nibblers at the body of a great master" from whom Sir Osbert Sitwell wishes to save him. In 1891 one reviewer, the poet Lionel Johnson, reported that he had read *One of Our Conquerors* "three or four times" and found that in these readings "the book grows upon the reader, the apparent confusion disappears, the intricacies of style become intelligible, and the whole greatness of design is evident." This was the kind of study Mrs. Woolf was to recommend thirty years later.

In addition to hostile indictments of Meredith's cleverness, as displayed in his witty or playful style, a large roadblock to the reader's sympathy has been erected by many critics in their objection to Meredith's editorial intrusiveness. He was no God of creation, like Flaubert and Joyce, remaining "above his handiwork, invisible, refined out of existence, indifferent, paring his fingernails." Rather, Meredith forever entered the lists on the side of life. When he does this playfully, he will be objected to by those who cannot bear a playful tone or who are ignorant of his allusions. Take, for instance, the Hippogriff in *Sandra Belloni*. In this early novel about an entrancing young singer, first called *Emilia in England* (1864), the intrusive novelist doubles himself by introducing a capitalized Philosopher. In the last third of the novel the Philosopher makes brief and infrequent appearances, but is nevertheless conspicuous because he analyzes the maddened state of a sentimentalist, the enamoured Wilfrid Pole, in terms of one who has mounted the beast Hippogriff, "the foal of Fiery Circumstance out of Sentiment." Guy B. Petter has explained that Meredith took this beast from Ariosto's *Orlando Furioso* in which the "Hippogriff is a type of Love; an erratic and preposterous creature, who will lead you in the paths of error and destruction . . . " The Philosopher in *Sandra Belloni* explains that those who are truly passionate, like the heroine Emilia, never mount him. None of this allegorical explanation is really necessary, for Wilfrid's actions tell us all we need know about him, and the Hippogriff might well have been cut out if Meredith had ever revised the novel, as he did *Evan Harrington*. Meredith was fully aware that there was too much of the Philosopher in *Sandra Belloni*. In a brief Chapter VLIV he says he is loath to continue his partnership with the fellow "who first set me upon the building of THE THREE VOLUMES, it is true, but whose stipulation that he should occupy so large a portion of them has made them rock top-heavy, to the forfeit of their stability." The Philosopher "promises that when Emilia is in Italy he will retire altogether; for there is a field of action, of battles and conspiracies, nerve and muscle, where life fights for plain issues, and he can but sum results." This promise predicates the epic novel *Vittoria*.

Although Meredith never again used an allegorical beast, he retained the prerogative of telling his readers what kind of characters they were going to meet and what was wrong about the social *milieu* in which the action took place. His social analysis is often written in an ironic vein, as when in *Beauchamp's Career* he imagines an England governed by what we have come to call a Brains Trust or Eggheads.

> Conceive, for the fleeting instants permitted to such insufferable flights of fancy, our picked men ruling! So despotic an oligarchy as would be there, is not a happy subject of contemplation. It is not too much to say that a domination of the Intellect in England would at once and entirely alter the face of the country. We should be governed by the head with a vengeance: all the rest of the country being base members indeed; Spartans—helots. Criticism, now so helpful to us, would wither to the root: fun would die out of Parliament, and outside of it: we could never laugh at our masters, or command them: and that good old-fashioned shouldering of separate interests, which, if it stops progress, like a block in the pit entrance to a theatre, proves us equal before the law, puts an end to the pretence of higher merit in the one or the other, and renders a stout build the safest assurance for coming through ultimately, would be transformed to a painful orderliness, like a City procession under the conduct of the police, and to classifications of things according to their public value: decidedly no benefit to burly freedom. None, if there were no shouldering and hustling, could tell whether actually the fittest survived; as is now the case among survivors delighting in a broad-chested fitness.

This is not the "literary playfulness" previously discussed but sound satire written in a traditional mode with a completely contemporary glance at the survival of the fittest in brawn rather than brain. Meredith's own view of the future of the race was that the fittest to survive would posses a happy balance of blood, brain, and spirit, a thesis lyrically argued in "The Woods of Westermain."

Meredith's use of the intrusive novelist, so often objected to, is indeed just about his only traditional device, inherited from Fielding and Thackeray, and retained, as Walter Allen has pointed out, by E. M. Forster who is, in his novels, "a man telling a story in his own voice . . . His is the most personal style . . . since Meredith's, to whom he owes much . . . ." These personal voices have been out of fashion in mid-twentieth-century criticism but are persuasively supported by Professor Kathleen Tillotson who has given us an excellent analysis of exactly what Thackeray's own voice does for *Vanity Fair* and who devoted her inaugural lecture as Hildred Carlile Professor of English in the University of London to this topic. In this lecture, "The Tale and the Teller," Professor Tillotson observes that "in all modern novels" there is always one character missing:

> the narrator in person. There is no one there who stands outside the story and says "I," who explains how he knows what he is telling us, who addresses the reader, who discourses, confides, cajoles, and exhorts. We are unbidden guests, there is no welcome, no hospitality—the social context embracing us as readers has gone.

Professor Tillotson feels that we have suffered a loss in these vanished hosts and justly attributes the "rejection of the teller" to "the unconscious assumption of our time that drama is the dominant form, other modes aspiring towards its condition, whereby narrative as such loses its status. When the critic objects that the author's voice "destroys the illusion," it is surely dramatic rather than narrative illusion that he has in mind; in narrative illusion, the teller has a rightful place." I quite agree with Professor Tillotson's thesis and suggest that we can widen our range of pleasure by ceasing to apply Stephen Dedalus's words on the dramatic mode to narrative writing.

As recently as the winter of 1961, C. P. Snow, arguing on the assumption that *War and Peace* is probably the greatest of all novels, has had much the same thing to say about the teller of tales. His thesis is that the stream of consciousness technique has narrowed the range of the novel but that whatever net the critics set for the novelist the big fish, like Tolstoi, will slip past it. Snow's argument in favor of the "reflective intelligence" in the fabric of the novel is strong. Although Meredith does not figure in his list of truly great novelists, Snow's essay on "Science, Politics and the Novelist, or the Fish and the Net" recovers for us an interesting memory of the eighteen-nineties. He writes: "I remember G. H. Hardy telling me that, at Trinity in the 90's, in one of the most brilliant critical groups that England has ever thrown up, it was possible to argue that Tolstoi might be within touching distance of George Meredith, but that no one else possibly could be."

The last block I shall mention as supposedly in the way of our enjoyment of Meredith's novels is his lack of a tragic view of life. We have already heard E. M. Forster raise this objection, and it is perfectly true that, unlike Hardy, Meredith did not feel tragedy in landscape. It is not true, however, that his vision was limited to Surrey; it embraces the Rhineland, the Welsh mountains, Venice, Normandy, London, and the Alps—always the Alps for his aspiring characters for whom, although their homes may be in Surrey, the Alps are where they would like to be at times of discontent or hope.

As for his characters, Meredith well understood the nature of suffering and there are many ordeals in his novels in addition to those of Lucy and Richard Feverel; there is also the stuff out of which tragedy could be made. Indeed it can be argued that Nataly, the lovely heroine of *One of Our Conquerors,* is a tragic heroine. Meredith's thesis about tragedy, as he had learned it from his first marriage, is explicitly stated in the famous lines from "Modern Love":

> in tragic life, God, wot,
> No villains need be; passions spin the plot,
> We are betrayed by what is false within.

In the long list of Meredith's heroines and fewer heroes, some are innately incapable of falsity: one thinks of Lucy Desborough who was the victim of the falsities of the Feverel men; her death was a lesson to them. One thinks of Nevil Beauchamp, honorable, brave, and politically committed, whose death was a lesson to no one but was the simple result of his own characteristics. He, who was an excellent swimmer and who had already saved lives, would not have thought twice before diving to the rescue of drowning boys. Both of these deaths are examples of the incident that shocks, but of which we say, after the shock, it is just right. But, since neither Lucy nor Beauchamp is "false within," their deaths are calamitous rather than tragic. Other heroes and heroines have to learn the ways of honor, as Harry

Richmond did. When a genuine heroine like Diana commits a false deed, she very nearly dies for shame; Diana is tragic as well as witty. But it is part of Meredith's optimism about the human race that men and women of power and intelligence have the capacity to learn and to recover from their tragic experiences. When they welcome the buffets of the southwest wind again or go for a long swim, we know they are all right.

This power of Meredith's heroes and heroines to recover their mental health and vitality after damaging experiences brings me to the third part of this essay: a statement of some of the reasons, seldom mentioned nowadays, why those of us who enjoy reading him feel good about his work in retrospect as well as while reading it. Siegfried Sassoon expressed this feeling perfectly in the concluding sentences of his book, *Meredith* (1948), where he wrote that Meredith

> is the poet of nature in action and the joy of earth. At any season of the year he stands the test of being thought about when one is out of doors. For the outdoor element in him has the oxygen of aliveness in it. I was once asked what I meant by saying that I liked Meredith though I couldn't always enjoy what he wrote. I was too young then to frame the answer which has since become apparent to me. It is that the idea of Meredith means a sense of being fully alive. To be at one's best is to be Meredithian.

This simple statement of Sassoon is perhaps the best tribute ever paid to Meredith, though much the same thing was said by Robert Louis Stevenson, by the French, ethical critic, Ramon Fernandez, and by Sir Osbert Sitwell. The spirit of having "come through" pervades most of Meredith's novels, not all of them, and the achievement seems much the same as that which D. H. Lawrence was always looking for, except that the achievement of freedom together with union is in Meredith celebrated with joy. It is with "the deep power of joy" that Meredith sees "into the heart of things."

What is the nature of these characters who have the stamina to "come through"? I name only the most memorable: Evan in *Evan Harrington*, Emilia, later named Vittoria, in the two novels *Sandra Belloni* and *Vittoria*, Harry in *Harry Richmond*, Clara in

The Egoist, Diana in *Diana of the Crossways,* the daughter Nesta in *One of Our Conquerors,* Aminta in *Lord Ormont and his Aminta,* and Carinthia in *The Amazing Marriage.* These eight are entirely different in chemical composition. One would never confuse them. Yet one knows them by their essences, by their fundamental qualities rather than by the peculiarities which, as MacCarthy said, "make them that person and not another." I should say that each of these characters exactly fulfils the hope that Lawrence had for his principal characters in *The Rainbow* and *Women in Love* when he wrote to Edward Garnett about an early version of the material from which these two novels sprang (June 5, 1914). In this letter Lawrence sticks up for his psychology in terms of the physiology of matter. He warns Garnett:

> "You mustn't look in my novel for the old stable *ego* of the character. There is another *ego,* according to whose action the individual is unrecognisable, and passes through, as it were, allotropic states which it needs a deeper sense than any we've been used to exercise, to discover are states of the same single radically unchanged elements."

Meredith's favored characters are of this elemental sort.

It is the men and women with "the old stable *ego* of the character" who may be described as "flat," which is what they should be in comedy. Forster wrote in *Aspects of the Novel* of the advantage of flat characters, saying that Proust abounds in them and that Russian novels would profit by them. He used the Countess in *Evan Harrington* as a good example. "We do not remember what the Countess did or what she passed through." What is clear is her figure and the formula that surrounds it, namely, "Proud as we are of dear papa, we must conceal his memory." The Countess is the kind of character, Forster said, who keeps a book stable, so that it will always be the same when we turn back to it. Meredith's triumps in this *genre* are, I should say, the Countess who makes a career of hiding the fact that her father was a tailor; Roy Richmond, the great swaggering, romantic imposter who was the father of Harry Richmond; and the Egoist himself, Sir Willoughby Patterne. If it is protested that the hero of a novel should not be flat, I should answer that in some of the novels the titular hero is not heroic and does not reach his goal. There is behind him a more quiet and more honorable man, a pro-heroine hero, I call him, like Vernon Whitford in *The Egoist*. He is the one who will either marry the heroine or help her to find useful work in the world, for not all of Meredith's novels are marked by altars at the end.

In conclusion, I return to W. J. Lucas's question in *The Times Literary Supplement*: if a person were to read only one of Meredith's novels, which should it be? I cannot answer the question because no one of them, not even the most renowned, gives any impression of his variety. In 1865, while writing *Vittoria*, Meredith said in a letter:

> Much of my strength lies in painting morbid emotion and exceptional positions; but my conscience will not let me so waste my time. Hitherto consequently I have done nothing of mark. But I shall, and "Vittoria" will be the first indication of it. My love is for epical subjects—not for cobwebs in a putrid corner; though I know the fascination of unravelling them.

Let us suppose a reader, following the lead in this letter, who might choose to read *Vittoria* as his one Meredith novel. He would have chosen a good one, praised by the historian, G. M. Trevelyan, as "not only a great prose poem on an epic moment in human affairs but a detailed and accurate analysis of a people and of a period." Even so, *Vittoria* is unique among Meredith's novels and cannot be taken as characteristic of his work. *The Adventures of Harry Richmond* may also be called epic, but only in Fielding's sense; it is an unforgettable comic prose epic that makes not a bad man good but a good man wise, and the wisdom that Harry gains is, significantly, his insight into the nature of tragedy. He came to see that his father Roy instead of being comic was "a tragic spectacle." To "the rest of the world he was a progressive comedy," but Harry had come to chafe "at his unteachable spirit, surely one of the most tragical things in life." So that perhaps Fieldings' formula should be modified into a tragicomic prose epic to describe the *genre* of

Harry Richmond. Meredith's only other historical novel beside *Vittoria, The Tragic Comedians,* is, as the title suggests, a tragicomedy, but it is not epic in construction or scope; rather, it endeavors to penetrate the characters of the German Social Democrat Ferdinand Lassalle and of Helene von Dönniges, and it is dramatic in the sense that it sticks to a single plot.

Or, let us suppose that among Meredith's novels one might read only *The Egoist* and thereby be led to suppose that Meredith's novels were all written to support the arguments of his "Essay on Comedy." Again the reader would be wrong; *The Egoist* is the only novel that truly supports the famous Essay, although three more of the thirteen novels are written largely in the comic mode. *Rhoda Fleming,* not previously mentioned, is almost unrelievedly somber, a bid to win serious attention for the currently popular subject of the plight of the fallen woman. This is another novel that stands alone in Meredith's work and that is something of an embarrassment, for it is a poor successor to Scott's *Heart of Midlothian* and Eliot's *Adam Bede.* Meredith's interest in fallen women had really been exhausted with his first novel, *Richard Feverel,* and he seems in *Rhoda Fleming* to have been flogging what for him was a dead horse. One could go on and on criss-crossing between the thirteen novels to prove easily that no one is a pattern for any other one. Meredith was a serious experimenter in the art of the novel and, except for the now unpopular device of the intrusive narrator and the lugubrious theme of *Rhoda Fleming,* his novels read like the least rather than the most of the Victorians.

Moreover, for better or worse, and I take it for better, he is a tonic writer. I agree with Edward Sackville-West and a number of other contemporary critics that Meredith has much to say to a debilitated people, all the more because he understood "morbid emotions."

22.

L. C. Knights

Henry James and the Trapped Spectator

I

In even the most persistent admirers of Henry James admiration is tempered by serious qualifications. It is not altogether a superficial view that, regarding James as primarily a satirist—destructive—sees something unsatisfactory about the positives he offers, and I suppose that most readers would agree with F. R. Leavis when he speaks[1] of "some failure about the roots and at the lower levels of life." "He came to live in his art—and not the less so for living strenuously—the life of a spiritual recluse; a recluse in a sense in which not only no novelist but no good artist of any kind can afford to be one." It is easy—too easy, we shall see—to account for this sense of isolation, for the impression—more marked of course in the later novels—that there are bars between the artist and necessary kinds of experience, by referring to James's upbringing, his early environment, and the mode of life he adopted. There was, to start with, the influence of Henry James, Senior, behind whom, in spite of his cosmopolitan ease and enlightenment, one senses the Genteel Tradition.

> What was marked in our father's prime uneasiness in presence of any form of success we might, according to our lights, propose to invoke was that it bravely . . . dispensed with any suggestion of an alternative. What we were to do instead was just to *be* something, something unconnected

Reprinted from *Explorations* by L. C. Knights by permission of the author and Chatto & Windus Ltd., London.

> with specific doing, something free and uncommitted, something finer in short than being *that,* whatever it was, might consist of.

It was sufficient for the sons "to be liberally 'good,' " and although they owed their father a great deal it may be questioned whether he did not too successfully cultivate in his second son the faculty of detachment. And "detachment," Henry James was to note, was even more markedly the result of "the experience of Europe." After the four years spent in Europe whilst James was in his early adolescence, the family was "insidiously, fatally disconnected," and some of the most interesting passages in *Notes of a Son and Brother* describe their "almost distressfully uninvolved and unconnected state." In America of the 1860's—the modern America that was just taking shape—the Jameses found nothing to connect on to. Whatever was not business didn't exist: "Disconnected from business we could only be connected with the negation of it, which had as yet no affirmative, no figurative side." Henry James stood it for some years, and then in 1875—when he was thirty-two—left America for good.

Even as readers of the novels we need to know these facts, and we need to know too the thesis which Mr. Van Wyck Brooks —more consistently than anyone else—has evolved in *The Pilgrimage of Henry James* to explain James's development in terms of his uprooting. According to Mr. Brooks, James drew his strength as a novelist from the land that, after all, he knew best: he is the painter of the American scene in a certain phase of its development; he is "the historian and the poet" of those Americans who, "released from the compulsions of poverty and custom, . . . become aware of a thousand requirements for which the world about them offers no scope," and who—at home or abroad—pay the penalty of their divided state. James settled in England (the thesis continues) but he never became at home there, and his persistent attempts to acclimatize himself only served to sap his genius. "In adapting himself to this world he was to lose his instinctive judgment of men and things; and this explains his "virtuosity of vision" . . . the gradual decomposition, more and more marked the more his talent grew, of his sense of human values." James had strayed so far from his natural world that the tree of knowledge had withered and died in his mind." As the source of his inspiration recedes he becomes more and more "the watcher from afar," unable "to conceive a major moment" or to "go behind his characters," preoccupied with technical devices which are "simply rationalizations of his exiguities."

Now no one would wish to deny James's achievement in his handling of "the American theme"—an achievement which, ranging from the magnificent satire of *The Bostonians* to the lighter, but still serious, comedy of *The Reverberator,* includes successes of such different kinds as *Washington Square, Daisy Miller,* and *Four Meetings.* But one may guess that it is simply the requirements of his thesis that lead Mr. Brooks to balance his justifiable enthusiasm for the novels and stories of James's first period—the period, that is, in which he devotes most attention to the American theme—with such sweeping disparagement of the products of the second. It is one thing to suggest, as Mr. Leavis does—and this simply in qualification of his discerning praise—that "something went wrong with James's development"; it is quite another thing to assert, as Mr. Brooks asserts, that "those for whom formal significance . . . is not the cardinal virtue of prose literature, for whom the world of fiction is to be judged by the vitality, the depth, and the variety of its content, will never be satisfied with the novels of the later James." So many objections to this comprehensive indictment come to mind. The later novels contain sustained passages of lively, concrete writing which are sufficient proof that vitality has not altogether departed: one can point to the satiric verve of the portrait of Sarah Pocock in *The Ambassadors* and of Mrs. Lowder in *The Wings of the Dove,* or to the crisp skill of the dialogue in *The Awkward Age,* dialogue which is "witty" and "dramatic" but which firmly defines James's attitude towards his characters and—without explanatory asides—shows them up for what they essentially are. And one could point to a good many other signs of life. But what I wish to do in this paper is simply to take up Mr. Brooks's remarks about "the avid eye," "the watcher from afar," and to examine a few of the ways in which James treats the subject of the man or woman who, for some reason or another, is merely a watcher, unable to participate freely and fully in human experience. This may prove a way of disengaging elements of real value in James's later work, and—a secondary point—it may throw some light on the old question concerning the relation between the artist's "life" and his successful work.

II

One way of approaching the subject is to observe that Henry James's "villains" have one characteristic in common: they all, in some way, *use* other people. They may prey on others for their money, but James is not much interested in common robbery, and usually their predatoriness takes forms that are less obvious and more gross. They make excessive demands for sympathy and try to absorb their victims' life into their own, as Olive Chancellor attempts to absorb Verena Tarrant in *The Bostonians;* they are "primed with a moral scheme of the most approved pattern" which—like the representatives of Woollett in *The Ambassadors*—they apply as a universal yardstick; or—like the relatives of Owen Wingrave—they demand a course of conduct that cuts across the essential nature of the individual; or they display a gross insensitiveness to the feelings of others, like the crude young reporter in *The Reverberator* or the cultivated literary gentleman of *The Aspern Papers.* As these references indicate, the "villainy" that James is interested in is rarely simple wickedness; it is quite often an unholy righteousness, and it is no accident that in the phrase "the brutality of her good conscience" from *The Middle Years,* turns up again as "a high brutality of good intentions" in *The Spoils of Poynton.* The context of the second of these—a passage describing Mrs. Gereth's relations with Fleda Vetch—is worth quoting (James's judgment of the relationship is of course given by the metaphors):

> There were ways in which she could sharply incommode such a person, and not only with the best conscience in the world but with a high brutality of good intentions. One of the straightest of these strokes, Fleda saw, would be the dance of delight over the mystery she, terrible woman, had profaned; the loud, lawful tactless joy of the explorer leaping upon the strand. Like any other lucky discoverer she would take possession of the fortunate island. She was

> nothing if not practical: almost the only thing she took account of in her young friend's soft secret was the excellent use she could make of it. . . . She had no imagination about anybody's life save on the side she bumped against . . . Mrs. Gereth had really no perception of anybody's nature.

Few novelists have so fully explored the recesses and refinements of egotism as Henry James, and his egotists—whether they are calculating or frivolous or insensitive or armed with righteousness—are condemned because, as moral parasites, they thwart the free development of another's life.

In *The Portrait of a Lady,* for example, Gilbert Osmond marries Isabel Archer for her money, but the use she has for him is not of course merely a matter of pounds and shillings.

> The real offense, as she ultimately perceived, was her having a mind of her own at all. Her mind was to be his—attached to his own like a small garden-plot to a deer-park. He would rake the soil gently and water the flowers; he would weed the beds and gather an occasional nosegay. It would be a pretty piece of property for a proprietor already far-reaching. He didn't wish her to be stupid. On the contrary, it was because she was clever that she had pleased him. But he expected her intelligence to operate altogether in his favour, and so far from desiring her mind to be a blank he had flattered himself that it would be richly receptive. He had expected his wife to feel with him and for him, to enter into his opinions, his ambitions and his preferences.

When Isabel finally realizes that she has been *used*—"an applied handled hung-up tool, as senseless and convenient as mere wood and iron"—the full consciousness of her plight is put before us in a single brilliant chapter.

> She had taken all the first steps in the purest confidence, and then she had suddenly found the infinite vista of a multiplied life to be a dark, narrow alley with a dead wall at the end. Instead of leading to the high places of happiness, from which the world would seem to lie below one, so that one could look down with a sense of exaltation and advantage, and judge and choose and pity, it led rather downward and

> earthward, into realms of restriction and depression where the sound of other lives, easier and freer, was heard as from above.
>
> There were certain things they must do, a certain posture they must take, certain people they must know and not know. When she saw this rigid system close about her, draped though it was in pictured tapestries, that sense of darkness and suffocation of which I have spoken took possession of her; she seemed to be shut up with an odour of mould and decay.

I have referred especially to this chapter of *The Portrait of a Lady* because it indicates so clearly what was, in various forms, one of James's main preoccupations—a preoccupation with the plight of the trapped creature. Isabel Archer is trapped by Osmond just as Nanda Brookenham in *The Awkward Age* is trapped by the greedy gossiping crew who surround her. But there are other stories in which this preoccupation takes a different form. They produce a kindred sense of suffocation, of being in some way shut off from the free enjoyment of living, but in them the central character is not trapped by others but by "circumstances" or by something in his own nature or his own past history. In these stories our immediate interest is not so much in a series of relations, in the action and reaction of personalities; it has shifted almost entirely to the consciousness of the trapped spectator of life.[2]

One of the strongest feelings evoked in that long meditation of Isabel Archer's is a feeling as of being buried alive, and the strength of the book comes largely from the evoked contrast of the heroine's "fund of life"—"her delighted spirit"—and the "cold obstruction" that thwarts it. This is a feeling that runs through James's work from first to last. We find it in *The Princess Casamassima,* in which the hero, Hyacinth Robinson, "was liable to moods in which the sense of exclusion from all he would have liked most to enjoy in life settled on him like a pall . . . *he* was above all out of it"; and we sense something similar in *The Ambassadors* when Strether—exhorting Little Bilham to "live, live all you can!"—realizes that he himself has "missed the train." When this sense of exclusion is presented, not as the result of human machinations but as inherent in a character's situation, it is only too easy to assume that James—"insidiously, fatally disconnected" as he knew himself to be—is interested solely in presenting the excluded, the caged and thwarted consciousness as a kind of personal relief, and that the reader is invited merely to share a narrow though intense range of feeling.

The assumption, however, would be misleading. In the Preface to *The Lesson of the Master* James remarks that, "The strength of applied irony" is

> in the sincerities, the lucidities, the utilities that stand behind it. When it's not a campaign, of a sort, on behalf of something better (better than the obnoxious, the provoking object) that blessedly, as is assumed, *might* be, it's not worth speaking of. But this is exactly what we mean by operative irony. It implies and projects the possible other case, the case rich and edifying where the actuality is pretentious and vain.

This is something to keep in mind when examining those stories in which our immediate interest is in the consciousness of an apparently "detached" spectator or of an observer in whom the sense of exclusion operates—*The Sacred Fount, In the Cage, What Maisie Knew, The Beast in the Jungle,* or *The Ambassadors.* We should look for the value of each of these not merely in the representation of the trapped state of mind (which may or may not represent James's personal predicament) but in the projection of "the possible other case, the case rich and edifying"; we should seek, that is, *the sense of life* that is released by the story of frustration. In other words, our fundamental concern (as distinguished from the immediate interest I have mentioned) is not simply with the nature of the "speculative thread," the "mental reactions" of the central character, but with the quality of *James's own* "moral vibrations" as these inform each novel as a whole. "The question comes back thus, obviously" (I am quoting from the Preface to *The Portrait of a Lady*), "to the kind and degree of the artist's prime sensibility, which is the soil out of which his subject springs," although, the passage continues, "one is far from contending that this enveloping air of the artist's humanity—which gives the last touch to the worth of his work—is not a widely and wondrously varying element; being on one occasion a rich and magnificent medium and on another a comparatively poor and ungenerous one."[3] And the moral of this is simply that the value of James's of "detached" or "excluded" observers of life—the extent to which their irony does succeed in projecting "sincerities and lucidities," in releasing, in short, a sense of life—is something to be determined by the methods of literary criticism. This may seem a platitude, but it is a platitude which discussions about James, some portions of his Prefaces and—occasionally—his practice tend to obscure.

III

At this point it seems necessary to draw together the threads of a rather discursive paper. What I have tried to say is this:—From an early period James was interested in persons whose free and normal development—the development that, given their endowment, one might have expected—is thwarted by the egotism of others. As he grew older that preoccupation was joined (though never entirely superseded) by another—a preoccupation with the plight of the creature trapped not by others but—shall we say?—by Fate; and some of his most notable stories present the trapped, the caged, the excluded consciousness. Since it was in his later period too that James developed the technical device of "seeing" his stories through the eyes of one of his characters, the critic is presented with two different but related opportunities for going astray. He may regard the central consciousness as merely "detached" (as in *The Sacred Fount,* in which the narrator is a mere observer and James isn't interested in him except as a detective device), without realizing that it may be itself the central point of interest (as it is in *What Maisie Knew*). On the other hand, he may concentrate on the evoked sense of exclusion from experience, without realizing that it is the vitality, the qualities making for life, that the reader has most reason to be grateful for. To expose and establish those qualities is the main business of criticism.

Two examples may make these contentions clear. *In the Cage* (1898) concerns a young woman employed as telegraphist in the postal department of a Mayfair grocery store. She is literally, as well as figuratively, "caged," and the question James posed himself was "what it might 'mean,' " wherever the admirable service was installed, for confined and cramped and yet considerably tutored young officials of either sex to be made so free, intellectually, of a range of experience otherwise quite closed to them."

> It had occurred to her early that in her position—that of a young person spending, in framed and wired confinement, the life of a guinea-pig or magpie—she should know a great many persons without their recognizing the acquaintance. . . . Her function was to sit there with two young men—the other telegraphist and the counter clerk; to mind the 'sounder' which was always going, to dole out stamps and postal-orders, weigh letters, answer stupid questions, give difficult change, and, more than anything else, count words as numberless as the sands of the sea, the words of the telegrams thrust, from morning to night, through the gap left in the high lattice, across the encumbered shelf that her fore-arm ached with rubbing. This transparent screen fenced out or fenced in, according to the side of the narrow counter on which the human lot was cast, the duskiest corner of a shop pervaded not a little, in winter, by the poison of perpetual gas, and at all times by the presence of hams, cheese, dried fish, soap, varnish, paraffin, and other solids and fluids that she came to know perfectly by their smells without consenting to know them by their names.

In this position she employs her curiosity—the spare mental energy not absorbed by her work—to speculate on the "outside" lives of some of her more frequent customers, using as clues the telegrams which they lavishly commit to her. "The amusements of captives," James remarks, "are full of a desperate contrivance," and another of this young woman's amusements is to establish something which might be called a personal relationship with some of those whom she serves—a relationship so slight, however, that it is measured by her sticking on the stamps for those she likes and merely pushing them across to the peremptory. Her attention is particularly engaged by two handsome products of the leisured class—Lady Bradeen and Captain Everard—who are engaged in an "affair" which, since the woman is married, involves some element of danger. Lady Bradeen spends most of her time away from Mayfair, so it is through her lover's innumerable telegrams that the telegraphist is able to keep track of the relationship, and it becomes of the greatest importance to her that the Captain shall give some sign of recognizing the devotion—the speed and intelligence—with which she handles his business. On one occasion when she has contrived to meet him "outside," the Captain declares that he does recognize it, and her fantasy soars to the level of half-formulated desire:

> It was more and more between them that if he might convey to her he was free, with all the impossible locked away into a closed chapter, her own case might become different for her, she might understand and meet him and listen.

It is at this pitch of devotion and delusion that she has an opportunity of doing the aristocratic pair a genuine service, by recalling the contents of a telegram that has gone astray; but when Captain Everard, relieved of his anxiety, hurries out of the post office her share in the relationship is abruptly ended.

> And without another look, without a word of thanks, without time for anything or anybody, he turned on them the broad back of his great stature, straightened his triumphant shoulders and strode out of the place.

Since one critic, whom Mr. Van Wyck Brook quotes apparently with approval, has remarked that, "Reading *In the Cage* was like watching Henry James watching through a knot-hole somebody who was watching somebody else through a knot-hole," it may not be out of place to say that to watch through a knot-hole is exactly what the reader isn't required to do. It isn't a question here of detective work, of sifting clues and piecing together evidence in order to come at "the truth" concerning Captain Everard and Lady Bradeen. The ups and downs of that couple are purposely left vague, only the main lines are established, and James indicates again and again that, however much the telegraphist may divine, her guesses are only guesses: they have a subjective rather than an objective reference. The purpose of the story is, in short (the Preface is explicit), to display the mind of the telegraphist. The various pressures that reduce the girl to guessing, that determine the form of her fantasies, are vividly created. There is the pressure of her own and her mother's period of poverty.

> when, as conscious and incredulous ladies, suddenly bereft, betrayed, overwhelmed, they had slipped faster and faster down the steep slope at the bottom of which she alone had rebounded. Her mother had never rebounded any more at the bottom than on the way; had only rumbled and grumbled down and down, making, in respect of caps, topics and 'habits', no effort whatever—which simply meant smelling much of the time of whisky.

There is the pressure of the solid presence and limiting imagination of her betrothed, Mr. Mudge, a rising young man in the grocery trade, who offers her the snug prospect of a "sweet little home." And there is the pressure of her friend, Mrs. Jordan, the "reduced" widow of a clergyman, who "does the flowers" in the houses of the well-to-do, and whose intimations of the higher life provide a setting for adventures read of in novels. That these persons, and to some extent the telegraphist herself, are presented ironically in no way detracts from the seriousness of James's theme. (His intensely *moral* concern is explicit in the opening paragraph of Chapter V where the lives of "the two nations" are contrasted.) If James is to be blamed for anything it can only be for a misleading phrase in the Preface, where he speaks of the "solution" depending on the girl's "winged wit." "The action of the drama is simply the girl's 'subjective' adventure—that of her quite definitely winged intelligence; just as the catastrophe, just as the solution, depends on her winged wit." The "solution" is not, as this might suggest, the solution of Captain Everard's perplexities; it is simply the telegraphist's recognition—her final acceptance—of the bleakness of reality. Mrs. Jordan has just announced the death of Lady Bradeen's husband and her approaching marriage to the Captain:

> They sat there together; they looked out, hand in hand, into the damp dusky shabby little room and into the future, of no such very different complexion, at last accepted by each.

> There was no definite utterance, on either side, of Mr. Drake's position in the great world [Mrs. Jordan is to marry Lady Bradeen's butler], but the temporary collapse of his prospective bride threw all further necessary light; and what our heroine saw and felt for in the whole business was the vivid reflexion of her own dreams and delusions and her own return to reality. Reality, for the poor things they both were, could only be ugliness and obscurity, could never be the escape, the rise.

One does not need to peep through a knot-hole to observe that caged consciousness; it is firmly and lucidly presented, and the reader is made to feel the full weight of the circumstances that mould it.

The Beast in the Jungle (1903) may also serve to show that in James's later period subtlety is sometimes far from being evidence of evasiveness, hesitancy, or scrupulosity. It is the story of a man, John Marcher, trapped and made impotent—reduced to being a mere spectator of life—by an obsession, the belief, namely, "that experience will be marked for him, and whether for good or for ill, by some rare distinction, some incalculable violence or unprecedented stroke." The only person to whom Marcher confides this secret is a woman, May Bartram, whom he persuades to watch with him—to watch, that is, for the spring of the lurking beast in the jungle. It is May Bartram, who first sees the truth concerning Marcher and who, offering him an opportunity to recognize and respond to her love, offers him also the chance to escape his doom. He, however, remains fixed in his obsession—never thinks of her "but in the chill of his egotism and the light of her use"—and when she dies, assuring him that the beast *has* sprung and begging him not to seek further illumination, it is only over her grave that he can persuade himself that he has lived at all. It is there, on one of his periodic visits to the cemetery, that illumination finally comes to him. The occasion is the passing of an unknown mourner whose glimpsed face shows the marks of inconsolable grief, and whom Marcher is surprised to find himself looking after with envy.

> The sight that had just met his eyes named to him, as in letters of quick flame, something he had utterly, insanely

> missed, and what he had missed made these things a train of fire, made them mark themselves in an anguish of inward throbs. He had seen *outside* of his life, not learned it within, the way a woman was mourned when she had been loved for herself: . . . Now that illumination had begun, however, it blazed to the zenith, and what he presently stood there gazing at was the sounded void of his life. . . . The name on the table smote him as the passing of his neighbour had done, and what it said to him, full in the face, was that *she* was what he had missed. . . . The fate he had been marked for he had met with a vengeance—he had emptied the cup to the lees; he had been the man of his time, *the* man, to whom nothing on earth was to have happened. . . . It was the truth, vivid and monstrous, that all the while he had waited, the wait itself was his portion.

In summary the story may appear unimpressive. Bul all that an admirer needs to do is to indicate the subtle firmness with which James presents his "case," to demonstrate, that is, the mode which he establishes for the telling. Things are "seen" largely through the eyes of Marcher, but the seeing is flecked with unobtrusive irony so that we are aware of two views—Marcher's, and that of James himself—existing simultaneously.

> He had thought himself, so long as nobody knew, the most disinterested person in the world, carrying his concentrated burden, his perpetual suspense, ever so quietly, holding his tongue about it, giving others no glimpse of it nor of its effect upon his life, asking of them no allowance and only making on his side all those that were asked. He hadn't disturbed people with the queerness of their having to know a haunted man, though he had had moments of rather special temptation on hearing them say they were forsooth 'unsettled'. If they were as unsettled as he was—he who had never been settled for an hour in his life—they would know what it meant. Yet it wasn't, all the same, for him to make them, and he listened to them civilly enough. This was why he had such good—though possibly such rather colourless—manners; this was why, above all, he could regard himself, in a greedy world, as decently—as in fact perhaps even a little sublimely—unselfish. Our point

> is accordingly that he valued this character quite sufficiently to measure his present danger of letting it lapse, against which he promised himself to be much on his guard. He was quite ready, none the less, to be selfish just a little, since surely no more charming occasion for it had come to him. 'Just a little', in a word, was just as much as Miss Bartram, taking one day with another, would let him.

"His concentrated burden," "his perpetual suspense," "a haunted man"—these phrases, and a good deal besides, represent Marcher's view. James only allows himself a few asides—" 'Just a little,' in a word, was just as much as Miss Bartram, taking one day with another, would let him"—but these are sufficient to give an angle on Marcher's attitude towards himself, on his egotism, his calculated unselfishness,[4] and on his exalted view of his own refinements, even when we are given what are apparently his own thoughts: "A man of feeling didn't cause himself to be accompanied by a lady on a tiger hunt." And the two points of view—the subjective and the objectively critical—not only alternate swiftly and with almost unnoticed transitions, they are often presented simultaneously:

> The real form it [their relationship] should have taken on the basis that stood out large was the form of their marrying. But the devil in this was that the very basis itself put marrying out of the question. His conviction, his apprehension, his obsession, in short, wasn't a privilege he could invite a woman to share: and that consequence of it was precisely what was the matter with him. Something or other lay in wait for him, amid the twists and the turns of the months and the years, like a crouching beast in the jungle.

Almost every word, there, bears the double burden. And the advantage of this method is that it enables James to present Marcher's case with a degree of sympathy—for the theme is a common human feeling, though isolated and magnified, and the reader is made to share Marcher's horror—and at the same time to give a detached and penetrating analysis of the ravages of an obsession.

There is no need for further illustration of what is not, after all, an uncommon Jamesian method. What this account of *The Beast in the Jungle* is intended to bring out is the sureness, the relevance and coherence of the minute particulars of the style—of James's art. For when I said that *In the Cage* and *The Beast in the Jungle,* in common with other stories of "trapped spectators," released "a sense of life," I hadn't in mind merely the explicit sense of opportunities missed, as when Marcher realizes that his "escape" would have been to love May Bartram—"then, then he would have lived"—or when Strether reviews his life in Gloriani's garden. The "life" that is in question is simply the extension and refinement of consciousness, of that intelligence which, in Santayana's words, is "the highest form of vitality." One would like to attempt a definition of "intelligence" and to relate it to James' style which, at its best, is a medium for projecting the immediate awareness if not of "opposite and discordant" qualities at all events of varied and (in most minds) contradictory impulses, so that the reader's consciousness is enlarged to admit a new relationship. But perhaps enough has been said to establish what should be an obvious truth: that "the amount of felt life" informing *any* work is in exact correspondence with the "art," that it depends entirely on the fullness and fineness with which the subject is presented.

This, in turn, suggests the dangers inherent in the attempt to find a simple "explanation" of an author's work in terms of his life. When we read those novels and stories of Henry James in which the preoccupation I have illustrated is present, it is impossible to avoid a reference to James himself, whose "almost distressfully uninvolved and unconnected state" is dwelt on in *Notes of a Son and Brother,* a state which was not to be a mere accident of the early years. But to the same measure that the art succeeds the personal reference becomes irrelevant. *In the Cage* and *The Beast in the Jungle* may be personal in inspiration ("My attested predilection for poor sensitive gentlemen," James says when prefacing the latter, "almost embarrasses me as I march"), but in them the personal motive serves only as the spring which releases the achieved work of art.

Of course James was isolated—and he knew it; but it is ridiculous to speak as if his plight were peculiar and unrelated to a more general predicament. It wasn't merely that he saw more clearly than anyone else, and recorded in his Prefaces, the increasing gulf between the artist and the public of common readers, he sensed also the forces that, in his time, were making for "the awful doom of general dishumanization." [5] And in his apprehension of the isolation of the individual

> —I have heard the key
> Turn in the door once and turn once only—

he showed himself the first of the "modern" novelists.

Notes

[1] In an article in *Scrutiny* (March, 1937).

[2] This point needs to be stressed since Mr. Brooks has made it a reproach to James that in his later work he tends to "see" his story "through the opportunity and sensibility of some more or less detached, some not strictly involved, though thoroughly initiated and intelligent, witness or reporter" (James's words). Mr. Brooks seems to regard this device as evidence of "the evasiveness, the hesitancy, the scrupulosity of an habitually embarrassed man" (*The Pilgrimage of Henry James*). What he fails to notice is that, in most of the stories he mentions, the "observer" is not really "detached." He—or she—may be detached inasmuch as he is unable to influence the course of the action, but in other ways he is passionately committed. *His* reaction to persons and events is precisely what we are required to feel, so that to present the story as it appears to him is not at all a mere mechanical device for reporting. As James says in the preface to the volume containing *What Maisie Knew,* "The just remark for each of these small exhibited lives is . . . that they are actively, are luxuriously lived. The luxury is that of the number of their moral vibrations, well-nigh unrestricted—not that of an account at the grocer's." But there are a few stories that justify Mr. Brooks's strictures.

[3] 'There is, I think, no more nutritive or suggestive truth in this connexion than that of the perfect dependence of the "moral" sense of a work of art on the amount of felt life concerned in producing it. The question comes back thus, obviously, to the kind and the degree of the artist's prime sensibility, which is the soil out of which his subject springs. The quality and capacity of that soil, its ability to "grow" with due freshness and straightness any vision of life, represents, strongly or weakly, the projected morality. That element is but another name for the more or less close connexion of the subject with some mark made on the intelligence, with some sincere experience. By which, at the same time, of course, one is far from contending . . . etc.—Preface to *The Portrait of a Lady.*

[4] "He was careful to remember that she had also a life of her own, with things that might happen to *her,* things that in friendship one should likewise take account of." And, "It was one of his proofs to himself, the present he made her on her birthday, that he hadn't sunk into real selfishness. It was mostly nothing more than a small trinket, but it was always fine of its kind, and he was regularly careful to pay more for it than he thought he could afford."

[5] Preface to *The Altar of the Dead.*

23.

Graham Greene

Henry James: The Private Universe

The technical qualities of Henry James's novels have been so often and so satisfactorily explored, notably by Mr. Percy Lubbock, that perhaps I may be forgiven for ignoring James as the fully conscious craftsman in order to try to track the instinctive, the poetic writer back to the source of his fantasies. In all writers there occurs a moment of crystallization when the dominant theme is plainly expressed, when the private universe becomes visible even to the least sensitive reader. Such a crystallization is Hardy's often-quoted phrase: "The President of the Immortals . . . had ended his sport with Tess," or that passage in his preface to *Jude the Obscure*, when he writes of "the fret and fever, derision and disaster, that may press in the wake of the strongest passion known to humanity." It is less to find such a crystallization in the works of James, whose chief aim was always to dramatize, who was more than usually careful to exclude the personal statement, but I think we may take the sentence in the scenario of *The Ivory Tower*, in which James speaks of "the black and merciless things that are behind great possessions" as an expression of the ruling fantasy which drove him to write: a sense of evil religious in its intensity.

"Art itself," Conrad wrote, "may be defined as a single-minded attempt to render the highest kind of justice to the visible universe," and no definition in his own prefaces better describes the object Henry James so passionately pursued, if the word visible does not exclude the private vision. If there are times when we feel, in *The Sacred Fount,* even in the exquisite *Golden Bowl,* that the judge is taking too much into consideration, that he could have passed his sentence on less evidence, we have always to admit as the long record of human corruption unrolls that he has never allowed us to lose sight of the main case; and because his mind is bent on rendering even evil "the highest kind of justice," the symmetry of his thought lends the whole body of his work the importance of a system.

No writer has left a series of novels more of one moral piece. The differences between James's first works and his last are only differences of art as Conrad defined it. In his early work perhaps he rendered a little less than the highest kind of justice; the progress from *The American* to *The Golden Bowl* is a progress from a rather crude and inexperienced symbolization of truth to truth itself: a progress from evil represented rather obviously in terms of murder to evil *in propria persona,* walking down Bond Street, charming, cultured, sensitive—evil to be distinguished from good chiefly in the complete egotism of its outlook. They are complete anarchists, these later Jamesian characters, they form the immoral background to that extraordinary period of haphazard violence which anticipated the first world war: the attempt on Greenwich Observatory, the siege of Sidney Street. They lent the tone which made possible the cruder manifestations presented by Conrad in *The Secret Agent.* Merton Densher, who planned to marry the dying Milly Theale for her money, plotting with his mistress who was her best friend; Prince Amerigo, who betrayed his wife with her friend, her father's wife; Horton, who swindled his friend Gray of his money: the last twist (it is always the friend, the intimate who betrays) is given to these studies of moral corruption. They represent an attitude which had been James's from very far back; they are not the slow painful fruit of experience. The attitude never varied from the time of *The American* onwards. Mme de Bellegarde, who murdered her husband and sold her daughter, is only the first crude presentation of a woman gradually subtilized, by way of Mme Merle in *The Portrait of a*

Lady, into the incomparable figures of evil, Kate Croy and Charlotte Stant.

This point is of importance. James has been too often regarded as a novelist of superficial experience, as a painter of social types, who was cut off by exile from the deepest roots of experience (as if there were something superior in the Sussex or Shropshire of the localized talent to James's international scene). But James was not in that sense an exile; he could have dispensed with the international scene as easily as he dispensed with all the world of Wall Street finance. For the roots were not in Venice, Paris, London; they were in himself. Densher, the Prince, just as much as the redhaired valet Quint and the adulterous governess, were rooted in his own character. They were there when he wrote *The American* in 1876; all he needed afterwards to perfect his work to his own impeccable standard was technical subtlety and that other subtlety which comes from superficial observation, the ability to construct convincing masks for his own personality.

I do not use superficial in any disparaging sense. If his practice pieces, from *The Europeans* to *The Tragic Muse*, didn't engage his full powers and were certainly not the vehicle for his most urgent fantasies, they were examples of sharp observation, the fruits of a direct objective experience, unsurpassed in their kind. He never again proved himself capable of drawing a portrait so directly, with such command of relevant detail. We know Charlotte Stant, of course, more thoroughly than we know Miss Birdseye in *The Bostonians*, but she emerges gradually through that long book, we don't "see" her with the immediacy that we see Miss Birdseye:

> She was a little old lady with an enormous head; that was the first thing Ransom noticed—the vast, fair, protuberant, candid, ungarnished brow, surmounting a pair of weak, kind, tired-looking eyes. . . . The long practice of philanthropy had not given accent to her features; it had rubbed out their transitions, their meanings. . . . In her large countenance her dim little smile scarcely showed. It was a mere sketch of a smile, a kind of instalment, or payment on account; it seemed to say that she would smile more if she had time,

> but that you could see, without this, that she was gentle and easy to beguile. . . . She looked as if she had spent her life on platforms, in audiences, in conventions, in phalansteries, in seances; in her faded face there was a kind of reflexion of ugly lecture-lamps.

No writer's apprentice work contains so wide and brilliant a range of portraits from this very early Miss Birdseye to Mrs. Brookenham in *The Awkward Age*:

> Mrs. Brookenham was, in her forty-first year, still charmingly pretty, and the nearest approach she made at this moment to meeting her son's description of her was by looking beautifully desperate. She had about her the pure light of youth—would always have it; her head, her figure, her flexibility, her flickering colour, her lovely, silly eyes, her natural, quavering tone, all played together towards this effect by some trick that had never yet been exposed. It was at the same time remarkable that—at least in the bosom of her family—she rarely wore an appearance of gaiety less qualified than at the present juncture; she suggested for the most part the luxury, the novelty of woe, the excitement of strange sorrows and the cultivation of fine indifferences. This was her special sign—an innocence dimly tragic. It gave immense effect to her other resources. . . .

The Awkward Age stands formidably between the two halves of James's achievement. It marks his decision to develop finally from *The American* rather than from *The Europeans.* It is the surrender of experience to fantasy. He hadn't found his method, but he had definitely found his theme. One may regret, in some moods, that his more superficial books had so few successors (English literature has too little that is light, lucid, and witty), but one cannot be surprised that he discarded many of them from the collected edition while retaining so crude a fiction as *The American*, discarded even the delicate, feline *Washington Square*, perhaps the only novel in which a man has successfully invaded the feminine field and produced work comparable to Jane Austen's.

How could he have done otherwise if he was to be faithful to his deeper personal fantasy? He wrote of "poor Flaubert" that

> he stopped too short. He hovered for ever at the public door, in the outer court, the splendour of which very properly beguiled him, and in which he seems still to stand as upright as a sentinel and as shapely as a statue. But that immobility and even that erectness were paid too dear. The shining arms were meant to carry further, the outer doors were meant to open. He should at least have listened at the chamber of the soul. This would have floated him on a deeper tide; above all it would have calmed his nerves.

His early novels, except *The American*, certainly belonged to the outer court. They had served their purpose, he had improved his masks, he was never to be more witty; but when he emerged from them again to take up his main study of corruption in *The Wings of the Dove* he had amazingly advanced: instead of murder, the more agonizing mental violence; instead of Mme de Bellegarde, Kate Croy; instead of the melodramatic heroine Mme de Cintré, the deeply felt, subjective study of Milly Theale.

For to render the highest justice to corruption you must retain your innocence: you have to be conscious all the time within yourself of treachery to something valuable. If Peter Quint is to be rooted in you, so must the child his ghost corrupts; if Osmond, Isabel Archer too. These centers of innocence, these objects of treachery, are nearly always women: the lovely daring Isabel Archer, who goes out in her high-handed wealthy way to meet life and falls to Osmond; Nanda, the young girl "coming out," who is hemmed in by a vicious social set; Milly Theale, sick to death just at the time when life has most to offer, surrendering to Merton Densher and Kate Croy (apart from Quint and the Governess the most driven and "damned" of all James's characters); Maggie Verver, the unsophisticated "good" young American who encounters her particular corruption in the Prince and Charlotte Stant; the child Maisie tossed about among grown-up adulteries. These are the points of purity in the dark picture.

The attitude of mind which dictated these situations was a permanent one. Henry James had a marvellous facility for covering up his tracks (can we be blamed if we assume he had a reason?). In his magnificent prefaces he describes the geneses of his stories, where they were written, the method he adopted, the problems he faced: he seems, like the conjurer with rolled sleeves, to show everything. But you have to go further back than the anecdote at the dinner-table to trace the origin of such urgent fantasies. In this exploration his prefaces, even his autobiographies, offer very little help. Certainly they give his model for goodness; he is less careful to obliterate *that* trail back into youth (if one can speak of care in connection with a design which was probably only half-conscious if it was conscious at all). His cousin, Mary Temple, was the model, a model in her deadly sickness and her high courage, above all in her hungry grip on life, for Milly Theale in particular.

> She had [James wrote of her] beyond any equally young creature I have known a sense for verity of character and play of life in others, for their acting out of their force or their weakness, whatever either might be, at no matter what cost to herself.... Life claimed her and used her and beset her—made her range in her groping: her naturally immature and unlighted way from end to end of the scale. ... She was absolutely afraid of nothing she might come to by living with enough sincerity and enough wonder; and I think it is because one was to see her launched on that adventure in such bedimmed, such almost tragically compromised conditions that one is caught by her title to the heroic and pathetic mask.

Mary Temple then, whatever mask she wore, was always the point of purity, but again one must seek further if one is to trace the source of James's passionate distrust in human nature, his sense of evil. Mary Temple was experience, but that other sense, one feels, was born in him, was his inheritance.

It cannot but seem odd how little in his volumes of reminiscence, *A Small Boy and Others* and *Notes of a Son and Brother,* Henry James really touches the subject of his family. His style is at its most complex: the beauty of the books is very like the beauty of Turner's later pictures: they are all air and light: you have to look a long while into their glow before you discern the most tenuous outline of their subjects. Certainly of the two main figures, Henry James, Senior, and William James, you learn nothing of what must have been to them of painful importance: their sense of daemonic possession.

James was to draw the figure of Peter Quint with his little red whiskers and his white damned face, he was to show Densher and Kate writhing in their hopeless infernal sundering success; evil was overwhelmingly part of his visible universe; but the sense (we get no indication of it in his reminiscences) was a family sense. He shared it with his father and brother and sister. One may find the dark source of his deepest fantasy concealed in a family life which for sensitive boys must have been almost ideally free from compulsions, a tolerant cultured life led between Concord and Geneva. For nearly two years his father was intermittently attacked by a sense of "perfectly insane and abject terror" (his own words); a damned shape seemed to squat beside him raying out "a fetid influence." Henry James's sister, Alice, was a prey to suicidal tendencies, and William James suffered in much the same way as his father.

> I went one evening into a dressing-room in the twilight to procure some article that was there; when suddenly there fell upon me without any warning, just as if it came out of the darkness, a horrible fear of my own existence. Simultaneously there arose in my mind the image of an epileptic patient whom I had seen in the asylum, a black-haired youth with greenish skin, entirely idiotic, who used to sit all day on one of the benches, or rather shelves against the wall, with his knees drawn up against his chin, and the coarse grey undershirt, which was his only garment, drawn over them enclosing his entire figure. . . . This image and my fear entered into a species of combination with each other. *That shape am I,* I felt potentially. Nothing that I possess can defend me against that fate, if the hour for it should strike for me as it struck for him. There was such a horror of him, and such a perception of my own merely momentary discrepancy from him, that it was as if something hitherto solid within my breast gave way

> entirely, and I became a mass of quivering fear. After this the universe was changed for me altogether. I awoke morning after morning with a horrible dread at the pit of my stomach, and with a sense of the insecurity of life, that I never knew before.... It gradually faded, but for months I was unable to go out into the dark alone.

This epileptic idiot, this urge towards death, the damned shape, are a more important background to Henry James's novels than Grosvenor House and late Victorian society. It is true that the moral anarchy of the age gave him his material, but he would not have treated it with such intensity if it had not corresponded with his private fantasy. They were materialists, his characters, but you cannot read far in Henry James's novels without realizing that their creator was not a materialist. If ever a man's imaginaion was clouded by the Pit, it was James's. When he touches this nerve, the fear of spiritual evil, he treats the reader with less than his usual frankness: "a fairy-tale pure and simple," something seasonable for Christmas, is a disingenuous description of *The Turn of the Screw*. One cannot avoid a conviction that here he touched and recoiled from an important inhibition.

It was just because the visible universe which he was so careful to treat with the highest kind of justice was determined for him at an early age that his family background is of such interest. There are two other odd gaps in his autobiographies; his two brothers, Wilky and Bob, play in them an infinitesimal part. To Miss Burr, the editor of Alice James's Journal, we owe most of our knowledge of these almost commonplace, almost low-brow members of a family intellectual even to excess. To Wilky "the act of reading was inhuman and repugnant"; he wrote from his brigade, "Tell Harry that I am waiting anxiously for his "next". I can find a large sale for any blood-and-thunder tale among the darks." From his brigade: that was the point. It was the two failures, Wilky and Bob, who at eighteen and seventeen represented the family on the battlefields of the Civil War. William's eyesight was always bad, and Henry escaped because of an accident, the exact nature of which has always remained a mystery. One is glad, of course, that he escaped the obvious effects of war: Wilky was ruined physically, Bob nervously; both drifted in the manner of wartime heroes from farming in Florida to petty business careers in Milwaukee; and it is not improbable that the presence of these ruined heroes helped to keep Henry James out of America.

Is it possible that through Wilky and Bob we can trace the source of James's main fantasy, the idea of treachery which was always attached to his sense of evil? James had not, so far as we know, been betrayed, like Monteith, like Gray, like Milly Theale and Maggie Verver and Isabel Archer, by his best friend, and it would have taken surely a very deep betrayal to explain an impulse which dictated *The American* in 1876 and *The Golden Bowl* in 1905, which attached itself to the family sense of supernatural evil and produced his great gallery of the damned. It takes some form of self-betrayal to dip so deep, and one need not go, like some of his modern critics, to a "castration complex" to find the reason. There are psychological clues which point to James having evaded military service with insufficient excuse. A civil war is not a continental squabble; its motives are usually deeper, represent less superficial beliefs on the part of the ordinary combatant, and the James family at Concord were at the very spot where the motives of the North sounded at their noblest. His accident has an air of mystery about it (that is why some of his critics have imagined a literal castration, and one needs some explanation of his almost hysterical participation in the Great War on the side of a civilization about which he had no illusions, over whose corruption he had swapped amusing anecdotes with Alice. It will be remembered that in his magnificent study of treachery, *A Round of Visits,* Monteith's betrayer, like all the others, was a very near friend. "To live thus with his unremoved, undestroyed, engaging, treacherous face, had been, as our traveller desired, to live with all of the felt pang." His unremoved face, the felt pang: it is not hard to believe that James suffered from a long subconscious uneasiness about a personal failure.

This, then, was his visible universe: visible indeed if it faced him daily in his glass: the treachery of friends, the meanest kind of lies, "the black and merciless things," as he wrote in the scenario of *The Ivory Tower,* "that are behind great possessions." But it is perhaps the measure of his greatness, of the wideness and justice of his view, that critics of an older generation, Mr. Desmond MacCarthy among them, have seen him primarily as a friendly, rather covetous follower of the "best" society.

The sense of evil never obsessed him, as it obsessed Dostoyevsky; he never ceased to be primarily an artist, unlike those driven geniuses, Lawrence and Tolstoy, and he could always throw off from the superfluity of his talent such exquisite amiable fragments as *Daisy Miller* and *The Pension Beaurepas*: satire so gentle, even while so witty, that it has the quality of nostalgia, a looking back towards a way of life simple and unreflecting, with a kind of innocence even in its greed. "Common she might be," he wrote of Daisy Miller, "yet what provision was made by that epithet for her queer little native grace." It is in these diversions, these lovely little marginalia, that the Marxist critic, just as much as Mr. MacCarthy, finds his material. He was a social critic only when he was not a religious one. No writer was more conscious that he was at the end of a period, at the end of the society he knew. It was a revolution he quite explicitly foresaw; he spoke of

> the class, as I seemed to see it, that had had the longest and happiest innings in history . . . and for whom the future wasn't going to be, by most signs, anything like so bland and benedictory as the past. . . . I cannot say how vivid I felt the drama so preparing might become—that of the lapse of immemorial protection, that of the finally complete exposure of the immemorially protected.

But the Marxists, just as much as the older critics, are dwelling on the marginalia. Wealth may have been almost invariably connected with the treacheries he described, but so was passion. When he was floating on his fullest tide, "listening" as he put it, "at the chamber of the soul," the evil of capitalist society is an altogether inadequate explanation of his theme. It was not the desire for money alone which united Densher and Kate, and the author of *The Spoils of Poynton* would no more have condemned passion than the author of *The Ambassadors* would have condemned private wealth. His lot and his experience happened to lie among the great possessions, but "the black and merciless things" were no more intrinsically part of a capitalist than of a socialist system: they belonged to human nature. They amounted really to this: an egotism so complete that you could believe that something inhuman, supernatural, was working there through the poor devils it had chosen.

In *The Jolly Corner* Bridon, the cultured American expatriate, returned to his New York home and found it haunted. He hunted the ghost down. It was afraid of him (the origin of that twist is known to us. In *A Small Boy* James has described the childish dream he built his story on). He drove it to bay in its evening dress under the skylight in the hall, discovered in the "evil, odious, blatant, vulgar" features the reflection of himself. This was what he would have been if he had stayed and joined the Wall Street racket and prospered. It is easy to take the mere social criticism implied, but I have yet to find socialist or conservative who can feel any pity for the evil *he* denounces, and the final beauty of James's stories lies in their pity: "The poetry is in the pity." His egotists, poor souls, are as pitiable as Lucifer. The woman Bridon loved had also seen the ghost; he had not appeared less blatant, less vulgar to her with his ruined sight and maimed hand and million a year, but the emotion she chiefly felt was pity.

> "He has been unhappy, he has been ravaged," she said.
> "And haven't I been unhappy? Am not I—you've only to look at me!—ravaged?"
> "Ah, I don't say I like him *better*," she granted after a thought. "But he's grim, he's worn—and things have happened to him. He doesn't make shift, for sight, with your charming monocle."

James wasn't a prophet, he hadn't a didactic purpose; he wished only to render the highest kind of justice, and you cannot render the highest kind of justice if you hate. He was a realist: he had to show the triumphs of egotism; he was a realist: he had to show that a damned soul has its chains. Milly Theale, Maggie Verver, these "good" people had their escapes, they were lucky in that they loved, could sacrifice themselves like Wilky and Bob, they were never quite alone on the bench of desolation. But the egotists had no escape, there was no tenderness in their passion and their pursuit of money was often no more than an interest, a hobby: they were, inescapably, themselves. Kate and Merton Denscher get the money for which they'd schemed; they don't get each other. Charlotte Stant and the Prince satisfy their passion at the expense of a lifetime of separation.

This is not "poetic justice"; it was not as a moralist that

James designed his stories, but as a realist. His family background, his personal failure, determined his view of the visible universe when he first began to write, and there was nothing in the society of his time to make him reconsider his view. He had always been strictly just to the truth as he saw it, and all that his deepening experience had done for him was to alter a murder to an adultery, but while in *The American* he had not pitied the murderer, in *The Golden Bowl* he had certainly learned to pity the adulterers. There was no victory for human beings, that was his conclusion; you were punished in your own way, whether you were of God's or the Devil's party. James believed in the supernatural, but he saw evil as an equal force with good. Humanity was cannon fodder in a war too balanced ever to be concluded. If he had been guilty himself of the supreme egotism of preserving his own existence, he left the material, in his profound unsparing analysis, for rendering even egotism the highest kind of justice, of giving the devil his due.

> It brought Spencer Brydon to his feet. 'You "like" that horror—?'
> 'I *could* have liked him. And to me,' she said, 'he was no horror, I had accepted him.'

"I had accepted him." James, who had never taken a great interest in his father's Swedenborgianism, had gathered enough to strengthen his own older more traditional heresy. For his father believed, in his own words, that "the evil or hellish element in our nature, even when out of divine order . . . is yet not only no less vigorous than the latter, but on the contrary much more vigorous, sagacious and producive of eminent earthly uses" (so one might describe the acquisition of Milly Theale's money). The difference, of course, was greater than the resemblance. The son was not an optimist, he didn't share his father's hopes of the hellish element, he only pitied those who were immersed in it; and it is in the final justice of his pity, the completeness of an analysis which enabled him to pity the most shabby, the most corrupt, of his human actors, that he ranks with the greatest of creative writers. He is as solitary in the history of the novel as Shakespeare in the history of poetry.

PART IV Prose

24.

Robert Kimbrough

Calm Between Crises: Pattern and Direction in Ruskin's Mature Thought

In the spring of 1870, after the excellent reception of his first lecture as the first Slade Professor of Fine Arts at Oxford, John Ruskin wrote to his mother, "I really think the time has come for me to be of some use."[1] Six months earlier, upon enthusiastically accepting his appointment to the new chair, Ruskin had written to his friend Sir Henry Acland, "The last ten years have ripened what there was in me of serviceableness, and chastised much of my hasty stubborn and other foolish, or worse, faults. . . . For instance, I now recognize in Tintoret faults before entirely hidden from me, because I can now measure him by standards I then [when finishing *Modern Painters*] knew not, and because my own character is more formed."[2]

Such calm self-criticism would have seemed strange coming from the still maturing, impetuous author of *Modern Painters* and *The Stones of Venice*.[3] However, Ruskin had turned fifty in 1869; his famous books on art were ten years behind him; and in the 1860's he had been busy forming his ideas on ethics and sociology. By 1870, his marriage was a thing forgotten; for a number of years he had been reconciled to Rose La Touche's refusal; and, although his father was dead, his mother was still alive. After 1870 Ruskin was to be distracted by his many and varied projects as well as to be troubled by his frequent and prolonged mental breakdowns. But coming just as his thought was reaching full maturity, the Oxford appointment afforded Ruskin an opportunity to "sum-up" before an intelligent audience. It should not be surprising, then, that he said his In-

Reprinted by permission of the author and the editor from *Transactions of the Wisconsin Academy of Sciences Arts & Letters,* Vol. 49 (1960), 219–227.

augural Lectures on Art were "the most important piece of my literary work done with unabated power, best motive, and happiest concurrence of circumstance."[4]

A return to academe is not very dramatic. It is hardly so biographically engaging as Ruskin's earlier turn from art to ethics after *The Stones of Venice* and the last volumes of *Modern Painters*. Yet for those whose interest is either in the main Victorian writers as prophets and thinkers or in main Victorian habits of mind, this later turning point in Ruskin's life ought to prove much more significant. Ruskin believed that the Slade Professorship was his first responsible position; hence, he wrote his Inaugural Lectures with a new self-conscious care and seriousness.[5] As a result here can be found a convergence of the diverse movements of Ruskin's thought, early and late; here more cogently than elsewhere he adjusted and corrected previous ideas at the same time that he introduced new ones. The lectures, thus, attained a consistency not usually associated with Ruskin and in them for the first time can be seen how his ideas on morality, art, and ethics follow one upon another.

(This statement should not be taken to mean that Ruskin was consistent in the way that a philosopher tries to be consistent, nor does it imply that Ruskin was conscientiously any more logical than is the average well-educated man. Yet it does rest on the assumption that a high native intelligence educated by experience brings to a true maturity a sound basis upon which thought can be analyzed, refined, and built. Needless to say, insight and reflection can work together productively without knowing how or caring why.)

This study, then, will attempt to show the general pattern and overall direction of Ruskin's mature thought as expressed in his Inaugural Lectures on Art. Although it will emphasize his final ideas on art and ethics, his basic philosophy of life will have to be suggested first because for Ruskin art and ethics "are founded on the same primal order."[6] Then, because Ruskin's social schemes simply did not work, it will be helpful to see where his ideas on ethics went astray, so that we may view his last years of frustration and distraction with somewhat fuller understanding. But above all, analysis of the interrelationship of Ruskin's thought on man, art, and ethics may stand as an *exemplum* to major ideas and moods which run throughout the Victorian period.

I

Ruskin's general philosophy was "moral"; his writings are crowded, and perhaps clouded, by the repetition of the words *moral, morals,* and *morality*. The *NED* attests that each of these words has escaped, historically, constant or single definition, and Ruskin's writing is a perfect example of the fact because he, like all of us, used the words loosely. But we can see that he understood their basic significance when he said that morality is "*an instinct in the hearts of all civilized men*" which enables them to "acknowledge, instinctively, a relation of better and worse, and a law respecting what is noble and base."[7]

The human ability to distinguish good from bad, and to choose correctly or wrongly is, of course, the traditional humanistic concept which allows reason to become operative as the guiding force in life. But Ruskin did not believe in the Aristotelian idea of warring passions or in the Christian idea of the recurring curse of original sin. With him, as with Wordsworth and the intuitional philosophers, man was born fundamentally good and pure: "There is no black horse in the chariot of the soul. . . . They [the human instincts] are all good" (88). Hence, *goodness*, not reason, was for Ruskin the basic human attribute which gives meaning to and actuates morality. And it must be noted that for Ruskin who was no professional philosopher the words *good, noble, courageous, gentle,* and *great* were synonymous.[8]

With Ruskin as with Socrates and a myriad of others, the first step in morality was to "know thyself." However, because of his basic assumption concerning the nature of man, he adapted that humanistic *dictum* to: "the first thing we should want to know [is], what stuff we are made of—how far we are . . . good, or good for nothing." And the way to find out is to apply this test: if you knew beyond doubt that you would die in seven days and had no knowledge of, or belief in, an hereafter of any sort or condition, then, "the manner in which you would spend the seven days is an exact measure of the morality of your nature." If your natural goodness were strong, you would, first, "set your affairs in order" and, then, provide "for the future comfort ... of those whom you loved," because, in support of goodness, man has two main instincts, powers, or energies through which goodness is enlarged: "the energies of Order and of Love." This test, then, defines Ruskin's basic philosophy of innate human goodness supported and enlarged by an exercise of the instincts for order and love, for the test "will mark to you the precise force, first of your absolute courage [i.e., basic goodness], and then of the energy in you for the right ordering of things, and the kindly dealing with persons."

Because this definition of morality might seem abrupt and limited, I should like to quote at some length what Ruskin said further about the "energies of Order and of Love" in practice:

> Now, where those two roots are set, all the other powers and desires find right nourishment, and become, to their own utmost helpful to others and pleasurable to ourselves. And so far as those two springs of action are not in us, all other powers become corrupt or dead; even the love of truth, apart from these, hardens into an insolent and cold avarice of knowledge, which unused, is more vain than unused gold.
>
> These, then, are the two essential instincts of humanity: the love of Order and the love of Kindness. By the love of order the moral energy [of goodness] is to deal with the earth, and to dress it, and keep it; and with all rebellious and dissolute forces in lower creatures, or in ourselves. By the love of doing kindness it [goodness] is to deal rightly with all surrounding life. And then, grafted on these, we are to make every other passion perfect; so that they may every one have full strength and yet be absolutely under control.[9]

Thus Ruskin's philosophy of life was: know that you are basically good, pure, and noble and that, by following the laws of love and obeying the laws of universal order, you may become Good, Noble, and Great. As Ruskin said in 1883 in a sentence which he called the heart of his moral philosophy, morality begins, and consists "to the end, in truthful knowledge of *human power* and *human worth* [i.e., the moral attribute of goodness]; in respect for the natural claims of others [i.e., love]; and in the precision and thoroughness of our obedience to the primal laws of probity and truth [i.e., order]."[10]

II

Ruskin's philosophy of art follows easily from his general philosophy simply because an artist is a man. For Ruskin, the picture is the measure of the artist, and to adapt Milton's version of the classical maxim, he who would be a great artist, ought himself to be a true picture. That is, to be great, art must be "the work of *manhood* in its entire and highest sense"; it must be *"the expression of a mind of a God-made great man."*[11]

But to be a good man is one thing and a great artist is another. The connecting point, as Ruskin had early discovered, is the creative imagination of the artist.[12] Hence his definition of the imagination is just as basic to his philosophy of art as was his definition of goodness to his moral philosophy. What ties the two areas of inquiry together is the fact that the imagination is the "highest faculty of the human mind" which sees "the eternal difference between good and evil" (52–53). Because it is morally grounded in goodness the imagination was to follow the moral energies of order and love. The pull of order on the imagination leads to art created, as Aristotle said, "in accordance with true reason"[13]; the pull of love leads to *harmony* and *beauty* (55, 90, 207–209, and 298). Thus the artistic imagination contains highly refined Aristotelian reason which sees *truth* through order, and a sharply defined instinct for *beauty* because "beauty is exactly commensurate with the imaginative purity of the passion of love" (90). Imagination, then, is both "noble and truthseeking" (242).

But how does an artist with a noble and truthseeking imagination actually go about creating *beauty* and *truth?* Again with echoes of "know thyself," Ruskin said that "the first morality of a painter, as of everyone else, is to know his business"

(81). As a result he naturally must first have the "skill" of painting what his morally rooted imagination has seen in the order of life. Then he must subdue subjective emotion to the discipline of external form, because only through form can the "truth" of life be shown (95 and 265–71). The artist has to pierce through flux and appearance to imitate the permanent order and essential forms of nature. *Not* by proceeding now in the subjective manner of *Modern Painters* but only by being guided by the Aristotelian principle of imitation can the artist relate "the utmost ascertainable truth respecting visible things" (46). Once truth is obtained, "the laws and forms of beauty" will follow (55).

The *law* of beauty is "harmony" and comes into painting because the artist has mastered total morality and the skill of orderly painting (95–96 and 297–98). And the *form* of beauty takes its definition from the natural result of a good man's skillful and harmonious creation; that is, beauty "is what one noble spirit has created, seen and felt by another of similar or equal nobility" but possibly lacking the artist's creative imagination (209). In summary, then, fine art is that "which demands the exercise of the full faculties of the heart and intellect"; for the heart with its energy of love leads to beauty, and the intellect with its instinct of order leads to truth (46). Such exercise of the moral energies of love and order calls for imagination, but to have imagination the artist "must have the right moral state first" (73).

III

At the end of his work on *The Stones of Venice* Ruskin decided that it was impossible for an artist to have the moral state conducive to the creation of art unless the nation in which he lived was itself moral; by the time he had finished *Modern Painters*, he realized that the art of England was not so fine as he had first thought. Hence, in 1860 he turned his attention to the ethical state of the English people with the hope of correcting the cause of artistic decadence, and by the time he had assumed his Oxford chair, he had worked out his ethical philosophy.

In his moral philosophy Ruskin thought Everyman was basically good; in this ethical philosophy, he believed that all men had an instinct for work, which he called variously *duty, industry, useful energy,* and *useful action* (40, 87, 93, 264). Realizing that people might doubt this ethical instinct, Ruskin asked, "Does a bird need to theorize about building its nest? . . . All good work [i.e., moral, human work] is essentially done that way."[14] Man can do good work, or "noble deeds," instinctively because along with the moral attribute of goodness, God gave man the ethical attribute of industry (116). In fact He reinforced this instinct after the fall with the commandment that man must work; thus it is doubly true that "life without industry is guilty" (93). But by obeying God's will men can enlarge their instinct for industry, which in turn will teach them the laws of eternal righteousness and mercy. As a result, just as the end of morality was a man apt "for the right ordering of things, and the kindly dealing with persons," so also the end of all men's useful work will be a society full of justice and brotherly love. Work is the way, for "all things lovely and righteous are possible for those who believe in their possibility, and who determine that, for their part, they will make every day's work contribute to them"; Ruskin's credo led him to see in the future "an Ecclesia of England" (117). But Victorian England was not a "lovely and righteous . . . Ecclesia"; it was ugly and evil.

Surveying the scene, Ruskin concluded, as had Carlyle, that " 'the triumphs of modern industry' . . . do not seem to produce nobler [i.e., better, greater] men and women" (xxvii) because the industrial revolution had led some of the people to live in the folly of *"imagining that they can subsist in idleness upon usury"* (40). Believing that the "general productive and formative energy, of any country, is an exact exponent of its ethical life" and that living on capital income, or "usury," was not productive, he was sure that he had found the reason why the ethical state of England was not good (39).

But Ruskin was Victorian enough to find hope for England in a bit of dated racism. He believed that the "instinct for beauty" was inherited, but only within races with a noble "ethic" (36, 79). Because they have the instinct for beauty, these races show that they are in some "kind of moral health"; therefore, for them "*absolute* artlessness . . . is impossible; they have always, at least, the art by which they live—agriculture or seamanship; and in these industries, skillfully practiced, you will find the law of their moral training" (84). Agriculture and seamanship skillfully practiced, in contrast to "usury," are "productive"; hence, they reveal moral health and contribute to the betterment of the ethical state of a nation. Because the English was one of those races so blessed with the "instinct for beauty," there was hope for England (40–41); however it lay not in the industrial revolution, but in the "elementary practice of manual labor" (264). For Ruskin, then, the function of ethics was to cultivate and nurse the basic ethical attribute of industry in the English people.

Having no doubt in his ethical philosophy Ruskin set about to put it into practice. By his test of morality, a man whose affairs were in order, and who dealt kindly with others was moral. The beginning of social morality, then, was simple; it lay "*in getting our country clean, and our people beautiful*" (107). Ruskin was sure that cleaning up the country would put order into English society, and that giving the people beauty would teach them the instinct of love (108–15). Once order and love were in society, "agriculture by hand, then, and absolute refusal or banishment of unnecessary igneous forces," would insure the proper environment for the instinct for industry to develop which, in turn, would lead to fine art [i.e., refined morality] and a just and merciful nation (114 and 89–90). When the triumphs of the industrial revolution were banished or curtailed, every man's work would have to be "productive," and Ruskin's ethical theory would become reality. However, the industrial growth of England continued, and although he never gave up his ethical scheme, Ruskin became more and more disillusioned.

IV

Ruskin's idea of work as a means of ethical salvation was as old as Genesis and as new as *Sartor Resartus*. But Ruskin was frustrated in his ideas for the same reason as was Carlyle.

Neither had a sense of history which was sufficient to cope with the fact and reality of an industrialized England. But unlike Carlyle, Ruskin's moral response to human suffering made him persist in his dreams. Although his road building scheme and his St. George's Guild could not succeed in Victorian England, the moral and ethical thought behind them is a tribute to Ruskin's determination not to be caught up in the philosophic relativism and economic rationalism of his time.

The failure of his theories stems from the fact that, when Ruskin started *Modern Painters,* he believed in the efficacy of the landscape feeling, the Wordsworthian impulses from the vernal wood which taught that each man was basically good. But, after finishing Volume V and *The Stones of Venice,* when he knew that there was evil in society, he turned to ethics without looking back to individual men as the cause of evil. Morally corrupting evil was an external, and the way to destroy it was by external means. In itself, his moral philosophy was not too "wrong-headed." If each man looks inward, believes he is good, and wills to improve his goodness by following a positive, constructive discipline and by living in love and charity with his neighbor, the end is no different than if each man finds both good and evil within his soul, but wills to follow goodness only, by always choosing aright. However, not all men are good, or choose to be good. Hence when Ruskin's basic philsophy is extended to the philosophy of art, it is only a partial, incomplete theory simply because not all great painters have been good men. When extended to ethics, it is mere fantasy.

The ethic of a country is the sum of the moralities of all men. The populace is not a single, noble *tabula* which will be good if you erase the evil impressions which it has received and give it only kind and orderly impressions. The moral fibre of each man's *tabula* varies. All men may be capable of good, but not all men will be good just because they work with their hands, and live in beautiful houses and orderly towns. Because there is no single formula for social salvation, ethics cannot be legislated. Progress to complete social morality must be as slow as it takes to reach and teach each man, first, individual morality, and, then, his ethical responsibility.

The heart of Ruskin's fallacy is best seen when he discussed

Plato's image of the chariot: "There is no black horse in the chariot of the [individual] soul," but when "Plato uses [the chariot] as an image of moral government," "it is among the most beautiful pieces of mysticism to which eternal truth is attached" (88). How the black horse appeared in society was, indeed, a piece of mysticism for Ruskin, because there was no evil in the people who made up society. If the people were good, then the evil horse in society which Ruskin wished to whip away was made of straw.

Ruskin was frustrated in his ideals because he never saw the basic contradiction in his jump from morality to ethics. Unfortunately, it is easier for us to see the frustration and contradiction than it is to see the ideal for which Ruskin was aiming. We call him inconsistent; yet few men have been more consistent in their love of their fellow men and in their dedication to understanding and correcting the evils that abound in modern society. His failings were not a lack of intelligence and moral sensibility, even though he may have lacked the rational objectivity to comprehend fully what was going on around him. I think it not amiss to see Ruskin caught in the rebound from Wordsworthian, intuitional romanticism that moves through the Victorian period and that leads to the reawakened interest in classical humanism so clearly discernible in the twentieth century, in France and America as well as in England. If we should ever make a full return from basically romantic to basically classic premises of taste and judgment, Arnold may be the most important writer in England advocating the change, but Ruskin well may be the most important figure exemplifying the transition itself. For example, we have already noted his final advocacy of Aristotelian imitation of external form as interpreted through right reason. Furthermore, the disillusionment which Ruskin experienced during the last quarter of the century is perhaps another instance of how he was a child of his period. Thus, if we find that a major source of his dejection came from the philosophical dilemma which arose out of his switch from morality and art to ethics, perhaps the present analysis of Ruskin's attempt to synthesize his ideas may shed light on a major source of the general Victorian pessimism.

In any case the Inaugural Lectures on Art allow us to see

for the first time how Ruskin's mature ideas on morality, art, and ethics all follow one upon another. To overlook this period of calm between crises needlessly complicates and confuses any study of Ruskin and his ideas. Perhaps students of Ruskin would do well in the future to keep in mind that he is reported to have said, "I have taken more pains with the Oxford Lectures than with anything else I have ever done, and I must say that I am immensely disappointed at their not being more constantly quoted and read" (xxii).

Notes

[1] Letter dated 16 February 1870, *The Works of John Ruskin . . .* eds. E. T. Cook and Alexander Wedderburn, 39 vols. (London, 1903–12), XX, xlviii. Further quotations are from this edition which will be cited as *Works.*

[2] Letter dated 19 August 1869, *Works,* XX, xix–xx. See also Wm. Hardman, *A Mid-Victorian Pepys: the Letters and Memoirs of Sir William Hardman,* ed. S. M. Ellis (London, 1923), p. 95, and E. T. Cook, *Works,* XX, xlviii.

[3] For an excellent account of the development of Ruskin's maturing thought, see Francis G. Townsend, *Ruskin and the Landscape Feeling: a Critical Analysis of His Thought During the Critical Years of His Life,* 1843–56, Illinois Studies in Language and Literature, XXXV, No. 3 (Urbana, 1951).

[4] *Works,* XX, 13. See also, pp. xviii–xlix for E. T. Cook's account of Ruskin's pleasant and dedicated first years at Oxford.

[5] See his comments, *Works,* XX, 47, 49, 60 n., 61 n., *et passim.* Citations in the text will be from Vol. XX which contains these lectures and *Aratra Pentelici,* the fall lectures, which will be used to clarify and support the spring lectures.

[6] *The Laws of Fesole* (1879), *Works,* XV, 467.

[7] *Works,* XX, 49, 268. See also *Val D'Arno* (1873), *Works,* XXIII, 131, where Ruskin repeats this view when summarizing his moral philosophy, and where he quotes Carlyle and Kant on the "miracle" of man's instinctive feeling for right and wrong. (The italics here and throughout the quotations are Ruskin's; when revising his works, he emphasized what he believed were his most important ideas.)

[8] Cf. The usage in Bertram Morris, "Ruskin on the Pathetic Fallacy, or How a Moral Theory of Art May Fail," *The Journal of Aesthetics and Art Criticism,* XIV (December, 1955), 248–66.

[9] *Works,* XX, 85–88. Ruskin said in 1877 that the passages here summarized and quoted were central to all his writings on morality (*Works,* XVIII, 204).

[10] The 1883 Preface to *Modern Painters,* II, *Works,* IV, 6. See also, *Works,* XX, 91–93, and *The Bible of Amiens* (1884), *Works,* XXXIII, 173.

[11] *The Stones of Venice, Works,* XI, 201: *Modern Painters,* III, *Works,* V. 189.

[12] See Van Akin Burd, "Ruskin's Quest for a Theory of the Imagination," *Modern Language Quarterly,* XVII (March 1956), 60–72.

[13] *Works,* XX, 45. Ruskin quoted the Greek from Aristole's definition of art in *Ethics,* vi. 4; I have used the editors' translation. Ruskin's new respect for Aristotle and imitation in contrast to his earlier contempt in *Modern Painters* is seen best in his lecture on "Likeness," *Works,* XX, 272–300.

[14] *Sesame and Lilies* (1865), *Works,* XVIII, 167.

25.

Herbert J. C. Grierson

Thomas Carlyle

In the *Tractatus Theologico-Politicus* Spinoza points to an interesting distinction between the manner in which the Hebrew Prophets announce their religious and political judgments and that of the Christian prophets, notably St. Paul. The former spoke as if all that they declared had been imparted to them by God; in their menaces and exhortations they were obeying the irresistible commands of God. They had reached these truths by no conscious process of reasoning. They were revealed to them as indisputable truths, sometimes to the accompaniment of a vision, as when Isaiah saw the Lord sitting upon a throne and about Him the Seraphim, or the similar visions of Ezekiel. "For the most usual thing with the prophets is to testify everywhere that they speak according to the edict of God: thus saith the Lord." "And this seems to have been the case not only in public pronouncements of the prophets, but even in epistles which contained revelations, as seems evident from the letter written by Elijah to Jehoram: And there came a writing to him from Elijah the prophet saying: Thus saith the Lord, the God of David thy Father." The nature of the vision, the style in which they record their judgments, vary with the personality and experience of the prophet, but they have all in common this reference to a source which is not the operation of their own minds.

Reprinted by permission of The British Academy, London, from the *Proceedings of the British Academy,* Vol. 26 (1940), 3–27.

It is not the same with the epistles of the Apostles. On the contrary, in 1 Corinthians vii. 40, "Paul speaks according to his own opinions," and Spinoza goes on to give other examples of Paul speaking not as a Hebrew prophet but as a teacher: "For the apostles everywhere reason, so that they do not seem to prophesy but to dispute." Leaving to individual conviction the question of supernatural inspiration, Spinoza undoubtedly indicates a radical distinction between the Hebrew and the Greek mind, but also between individual minds neither Hebrew nor Greek even if the direct reference to a revelation is not claimed. The difference is that between the writer whose thoughts are developed by a conscious process of reasoning and the writer who reaches his conclusions by what we call intuition, whose imagination brooding over the course of things, or the flow of consciousness within, reaches and declares the findings which he, no more than those to whom or for whom he speaks, can trace the steps by which they have been attained to and which are accepted, if accepted at all, by a similar intuitional response:

> Hear the voice of the bard!
> Who present, past and future sees:
> Whose ears have heard
> The Holy Word
> That walked among the ancient trees.

"And they were astonished at his doctrine: for he taught them as one that had authority, and not as the Scribes."

But if the distinction which Spinoza emphasizes indicates a difference between certain types of mind, it corresponds also, if one takes a broader view of the Hebrew and Greek literature, to a difference between the topics on which the chief interest is centered. Of natural science the Hebrew Scriptures as represented from Genesis to Malachi tell us nothing. Indeed the progress of natural science has in the modern world been often hampered and checked by the necessity of conciliating, or explaining away, notions derived from accepting as scientific the simple and naive statements of writers to whom scientific inquiry was unknown. "But here it is first to be noted that the Jews make no mention of secondary or particular causes, not paying any attention to them, but for the sake of religion and piety or (as the phrase usually goes) devotion they recur always to God." (Spinoza.) The creation of the world in six days, with that of the sun and the moon as intermediate events, the waters above the firmament, the standing still of the sun that "hasted not to go down about a whole day" that Joshua might defeat the Amorites, the great fish in which Jonah sojourned three days and three nights—these beautiful myths, or poetic hyperboles, or charming stories were to prove troublesome obstacles to many minds beginning to feel the necessity of scientific inquiry and evidence. But Greek thought began in these physical inquiries in which the Hebrew mind took no interest, content to refer everything direct to God and His great purpose. The significance of Thales "is to be found in the fact that he dealt with the problem of the origin of things, which primitive man treats mythologically, on a purely physical basis from which all anthropomorphic ideas have been exercised." (Wicksteed, *Dante and Aquinas.*) The significance of Socrates is that he transferred to moral questions the method of physical inquiry. He generalized and distinguished not in the physical but in the moral world. "He sought out the common underlying conception of justice . . . which makes one man call a thing 'just' while another calls the very same thing 'unjust,' though perhaps they both have the same general idea of what justice means." But in this sphere the starting-point is an intuition, the intuition of what is "just" latent, more or less, more or less express, in every man's mind. The field of natural science has nothing to teach us of justice, of morality, or of spiritual religion. "For," as Bacon says,

> if any man shall think by view and inquiry into these sensible and material things to attain that light whereby he may reveal unto himself the nature or will of God, then indeed is he spoiled by vain philosophy: for the contemplation of God's creatures and works produces (having regard to the works and creatures themselves) knowledge, but having regard to God, no perfect knowledge, but wonder which is broken knowledge.

Indeed, it seems to be the fact that spiritual religion, as we find it in the Hebrew prophets, took its rise in rebellion against natural religion, religions which sought means to propitiate the powers which are behind the forces of nature, the causes of rain and earthquakes and other phenomena disturbing to the life of man, their cruelties and sensualities. "There is no natural religion." (Blake.) And Goethe and Huxley are at one in declaring that it is as man rises above the natural that he enters the sphere of morality and religion. One may of course, as the Hebrew Prophets and Psalmists did, and we shall find Carlyle doing also, by faith believe or declare that the God of Abraham and Isaac, the God of Righteousness, is also discernible in nature, the beauties of nature as we see them around us, and even in all that fills the *espaces infinies qui nous effraient*. But such a poetic extension of faith is most easily maintained by averting our eyes from the darker side of nature, red in tooth and claw.

The prophetic type of mind, as Spinoza describes it, works not through the logical, analytic intellect but through the imagination.

> For we may without scruple affirm, that the prophets do not apprehend the revelations of God except by the power of imagination. That is, by the mediation of words or images and those either real or imaginary; . . . therefore, the prophets apprehended the revelations of God, since by the power of the imagination there is no doubt that they could apprehend many things which are beyond the limit of the intellect. For from words and images far more ideas can be composed than from those principles and notions on which our whole natural knowledge is builded.

It is just so that Blake speaks of the poetic genius: "if it were not for the poetic or prophetic character the philosophic and experimental would soon be at the ratio of all things, and stand still, unable to do other than repeat the same dull round over again." The imagination is the instrument of the prophetic mind and its sphere the ethical and religious, taking these as different aspects of one experience, or it may be more justly as different levels of the same consciousness.

But the prophets may err when they too call in the intellect and from their vivid intuitions deduce consequences, predictions for the truth of which it may be necessary to institute careful, scientific inquiry. The Hebrew Prophets were convinced that their people suffered for their sins in being conquered by the Assyrians. That may be; but it would also be necessary to inquire whether there were not at work great social and national forces which would have involved, in any case, the absorption of such smaller countries as Israel and Judah in the great empire of Assyria or Egypt. Even the wickedness of his people to which the prophet attributes their suffering may be relative. It was to the moral superiority of Florence that the success of Savonarola was due. Probably the sins of Israel and Judah were not more, were rather less, than those of the peoples whom the prophets include in their denunciations of doom.[1]

That Thomas Carlyle thought himself and was a prophet to his age is evident in the purpose and character of everything he wrote—autobiography as one may call *Sartor,* if it is also more, biography, history, essays on the social questions of the day. The late H. D. Trail, indeed, pronounced magisterially in 1896 that Carlyle was neither prophet nor ethical doctor but simply a great master of literature. All the problems which had troubled him seemed to Trail to have solved themselves. But he was in too great a hurry. The mills of God grind slowly. Much water of a very troubled kind has flowed under the bridge since 1896, and the problems of democracy and industry are very much alive today if some of them have found a partial solution, and that not always in the manner in which Carlyle anticipated. And some of his prophecies have come true. Democracy has been rejected by more than one people and the outcome is far from clear. If my predecessor in this lecture could speak of Hobbes as "the father of totalitarianism," a French author can write of Carlyle as "un précurseur du National Socialisme." Indeed two sentences from the opening paragraphs of Mr. Gooch's lecture are not inapplicable to Carlyle. "Living in an age of civil turmoil he mistook a distressing phenomenon for an incurable disease." If one substitutes social or industrial for civil that is in part true of Carlyle's demand for heroic remedies. "Order was heaven's first law and no price too high to obtain it. Anarchy was a ferocious animal." To Carlyle, too, order seemed worth even the sacrifice of liberty, was the most evident aspect of justice. To extend the suffrage to the working classes was, with a Jew at the helm, to shoot Niagara, to add to the forces making for anarchy and chaos. Fear, though it is the most constant attendant on, is not the wisest counsellor in political crises. Disraeli's daring confidence in the good sense and conservative instincts of the English people has not proved entirely mistaken.

If we understand by prophet "foreteller," then Carlyle was, of course, not the only prophet of his day. It was an age of prophets in that sense, as he himself declares in his first contribution to the *Edinburgh Review,* his first protest against the mechanical spirit of the age, which is to be his enemy throughout. (*Signs of the Times,* 1829). Catholic emancipation was a fact, reform of Parliament was a growing threat, and

> "therefore day after day, and in all manner of publications, the most lugubrious predictions are set forth. The King has virtually abdicated; the Church is a widow without jointure; public principle has gone; private honesty is going; society in short is fast falling in pieces,"

which is very much how Wordsworth and Southey felt. "At such a period," he goes on,

> "it was to be expected that the rage of prophecy should be more than usually excited. Accordingly the Millenarians have come forth on the right hand and the Millites on the left. The Fifth-Monarchy men prophesy from the Bible, and the Utilitarians from Bentham."

But it is not as one of these many forecasters of the probable course of events that I claim Carlyle as a prophet. It is that his approach to the questions of the day is that of the Hebrew Prophets; that the cast of his mind is that which Spinoza indicates, one in which the imagination predominates, whose judgments are a reaction to what his imagination presents with poetic vividness; and I might add that, like other prophets, his intellectual deductions from these vividly presented intuitions sometimes go astray. Like the Hebrew prophet Carlyle is a preacher of righteousness, of justice as between classes, employer and employed. He is a preacher of righteousness and his medium is a vivid imagination, not the logical ratiocination of a Bentham or James Mill. His method as an historian is a fascinating combination of often minute research with vivid presentation of the results. His method is specially clear in the *Frederick,* because there his feelings are not so deeply engaged as in the *French Revolution* or the *Cromwell.* He assembles his details, a map, a description of the country, a dry business document, some sentences from a letter, etc., and all with a view, not to a broad generalization in the manner of Gibbon, but to the presentation of as vivid a picture as he can achieve of what men of that day saw passing under their eyes. The *French Revolution* is a sequence of highly colored pictures of definite incidents—the procession of the States-General, the taking of the Bastille, the march to and from Versailles, the flight and capture of the King, etc. In *Cromwell,* though the flow of the narrative is broken by letters and speeches, and these he edits with comments as if he were hearing them delivered, his method is the same—to derive from letters, journals, newspaper reports the details which he fits into a picture as of a contemporary event of which his readers are to be eyewitnesses:

> And so the soldiers stand to their arms, or lie within reach of their arms all night; being upon an engagement very difficult indeed. The night is wild and wet; 2nd September meaning 12th by our calendar; the Harvest Moon wades deep among clouds of sleet and hail. Whoever hath a heart for prayer, let him pray now, for the wrestle of death is at hand. Pray—and withal keep his powder dry! And be ready for extremities, and quit himself like a man. Thus they pass the night, making that Dunbar Peninsular and Brock Rivulet long memorable to me. We English have some tents; the Scots have none. The hoarse sea moans bodeful, swinging low and heavy against whinstone bays; the sea and the tempests are abroad; all else asleep but we—and there is one that rides on the wings of the wind.

An event thus evoked from the past has for Carlyle something mysterious about it:

> Read in the extinct old pamphlets, and ever again obstinately read, till some light rises on them, you do at last

> obtain small glimmerings of distinct features here and there which coalesce into a kind of image for you; and some spectrum of the Fact becomes visible; rises veritable, face to face on you, grim and sad in the depth of the dead Time.

The Fact—that is what appeals to Carlyle. It was and therefore it is in a sense that is not true of any fiction.

But it is not my aim, nor am I the person, to pronounce on the worth of Carlyle's work as history. But it is in the same imaginative vivid manner that he contemplates and presents the social, industrial confusion of his own day. He does not reach conclusions by the logic of Bentham or Mill. For logic he has a considerable contempt:

> Consider for example the general fashion of Intellect in this era. Intellect, the power man has of knowing and believing, is now nearly synonymous with Logic or the mere power of arranging and communicating. Its implement is not Meditation but Argument. Cause and Effect is almost the only category under which we look at and work with all Nature. . . . Our favourite philosophers have no love and no hatred, they stand among us not to do, nor to create anything, but as a sort of Logic-mills to grind out the true causes and effects of all that is done and created.

"This is not a religious age. Wonder indeed is on all hands dying." The truth, the religious truth of which he is in quest, comes from the fullest vision of nature and the human heart to which he can attain. It is to give to men who lack such vision and the power to attain to it, and to the intuitions which such a vision quickens, that the Hero as prophet arises, or, in the sphere of action, the Hero as King; and the two have at times been one—Moses, Mahomet. What I wish therefore to consider is the nature and value of Carlyle's vision of the life of his own day and the intuitions which that vision inspired, and especially of his conception, so far as he could make it clear to himself, of the relation between Right and Might, his reading of the problem of the Book of Job and of Ecclesiastes, the interval between the way in which our sense of justice would demand that things should happen and the way in which they actually do go. The works on which I shall specially rely are *Sartor Resartus, Past and Present, Latter Day Pamphlets* with such an overflow from these as *Shooting Niagara.*

Carlyle was thirty-three when he wrote *Sartor,* and had come through much deep water, physical ill health (at least nervous dyspepsia, a troublesome if not a dangerous complaint), a struggle not yet over to find how to earn his bread and deliver his message, a difficult courtship, and marriage with a woman as electric as himself. The book was begun as a novel, autobiographical and satirical. It became an imaginative picture of the life of his day as he saw it around him and felt its reactions within, life social and religious. It is a work of the imagination throughout. What is not autobiographical, and parts of this, might be described as a series of metaphors—the metaphor of clothes with its subdivisions, Aprons, Adamitism, Church-Clothes, Old-Clo' in Monmouth Street, and such other metaphors as the Centre of Indifference, the Eternal No, the Everlasting Yes, Dandyism and Drudgism with the metaphors of the whirlpools and the electric machines.

The metaphor of clothes was, of course, an old one. Biblical, Shakespearian (in *King Lear*). Swift had elaborated it with satirical, misanthropical purpose. To Burke it bore a profound significance as he contemplated the disappearance in the Revolution of "all the pleasing illusions which made power gentle and obedience liberal."

> All the decent drapery of life is to be rudely torn off. All the superadded ideas furnished from the wardrobe of a moral imagination, which the heart owns and the understanding ratifies as necessary to cover the defects of our naked shivering nature, and to raise it to dignity in our own estimation, are to be exploded as a ridiculous and absurd and antiquated fashion.

For Carlyle the metaphor has value (1) satirically, a satire ranging from the fashionable novels of Bulwer and Disraeli to the creeds and ritual of religions; (2) socially, for if Burke laments the disappearance of the decent drapery of life, Carlyle seeks consolation in the belief that new garments are ever being woven afresh.

"Ever as the ashes of the Old are blown about, do organic filaments of the New mysteriously spin themselves"; and finally (3) the metaphor has its deepest significance metaphysically, religiously, and here Carlyle's imagination is quickened or supported by what he knew of German transcendental philosophy, the distinction which Kant had renewed (for it was already in Plato) between the phenomenal and the real, what appears and what is:

> Nay, worst of all, two quite mysterious world-embracing Phantasms Time and Space, have ever hovered round him perplexing and bewildering: but with them also he now resolutely grapples, these also he victoriously rends asunder. . . . Here therefore properly it is the Philosophy of Clothes attains to Transcendentalism. . . . But deepest of all illusory Appearances for hiding wonder, as for many other ends, are your two grand fundamental world-enveloping Appearances, Space and Time . . . and of these the most wonderful is Time: Know of a truth that only the Time-Shadows have perished and are perishable: that the real Being of whatever was, and whatever is, and whatever will be *is* even now and for ever. This, should it unhappily seem new, thou mayest ponder at thy leisure; for the next twenty years or the next twenty centuries; believe it thou must, understand it thou canst not.

Religion, what to think of the universe in which we find ourselves, and the social problem, the "condition of the people" question, are the two foci of Carlyle's interest as a prophet, as they were those of his Hebrew predecessors. Of the three chapters in which he outlines the religious reactions of Teufelsdroeckh in his years of despondency, the crucial one is the *Everlasting No*. He never really got beyond that (nor, I think, receded from it), for in the *Everlasting Yea,* when he sees in Nature the "living Garment of God" he does not get beyond that Wonder which Bacon has said is all that Nature can reveal of the spirit which informs its majestic operations. It is in the *Everlasting No* that he rises above nature, above the world to which as an animal he belongs. Nature knows nothing of Justice or Injustice.

"The everlasting No had said: Behold thou art fatherless, outcast, and the Universe is mine, the Devil's. . . . My whole Me now made answer: 'I am not thine, but Free and forever hate thee.' "[2]

That he felt and knew from within his whole Me. Anything that goes beyond it is matter of Faith. "Effected it will be," he writes, thinking of justice to the working classes, "unless it were a demon that made the Universe: which I for my part do at no moment . . . in the least believe." The Moral Law within, the Starry Heavens above, it is faith alone which can link them;

> Thou dost preserve the stars from wrong
> And the most ancient heavens through thee are fresh and strong.

And Carlyle's faith was often sorely tried.

But the quest of justice, what it is and how to be secured, especially in the relation between employer and employed, the injustice of whose relations was manifest and yet that injustice had the support, not only of personal interest but of economic doctrine that posed as an exact science, is the inspiration and the end of all that Carlyle wrote. Whatever one may think of Carlyle's conclusions, the aberrations of his last angry pamphlets, his passion for order at the expense of liberty, his vindication of might by some ultimate belief in right in the long run, one will do him injustice if one ignores the fact that this, justice, was his goal. The human spirit is enclosed in a troublesome and decaying tenement. Something of the temper and training of the individual is traceable, Spinoza declared, in the Hebrew prophetic utterances. Did Jeremiah suffer from nervous dyspepsia? Carlyle did, and the unhappy reactions of his alimentary canal affected his outlook on life: and not that alone, the ecclesiastical prejudices of a Scot, his peasant nature and upbringing, his exclusion from any more active career of usefulness than that of a writer of books. But his theme is always the same, and it is that of the Hebrew prophets. "If men and nations suffer it is because they have gone astray." "Do justly, and love mercy; and walk humbly with thy God." But what is justice is not always apparent nor always in accordance with our presuppositions. And mercy must not be identified with the pampering of scoundrels and the encouragement of idleness in white men or black. All must work; but it is equally clear that no society is in a healthy condition in which there is not work for able-bodied and intelligent citizens. To walk humbly with thy God is to accept the Universe as it is ordered, recognizing that our happiness is not God's primary concern:

> Foolish soul! What act of legislation was there that *Thou* shouldst be happy. A little while ago thou hadst no right to *be* at all. What if thou wert born and predestined to be unhappy! Art thou nothing other than a Vulture that fliest through the Universe seeking after something to eat and shrieking dolefully because carrion enough is not given thee? Close thy Byron, open thy Goethe.

And the Goethe he is thinking of is the proclaimer of the truth: "Entbehren sollst du, sollst entbehren."

Carlyle's direct treatment of the problems of his own day is mainly contained in the tracts, as they might be called, which followed the *French Revolution–Chartism* (1839), *Past and Present* (1843), and the angrier pamphlets which followed the *Cromwell, Latter Day Pamphlets* (1850), *The Nigger Question* (1853), *Shooting Niagara and After* (1867). In all of them the imagination is his instrument, the vivid picture he conceives and presents rather than the logical arguments of Bentham or Mill or Bagehot. For speculation and logic he professes no respect: Logic is good but it is not the best."

> "Often by some winged word, winged as the thunderbolt is, of a Luther, a Napoleon, a Goethe shall we see the difficulties split asunder, and its secret laid bare; while the irrefragable with all his logic tools, hews at it, and hovers round it, and finds it on all hands too hard for him."

(*Characteristics.*) "Yea, friends, not our Logical, Mensurative faculty, but our imagination is king over us; I might say Priest and Prophet to lead us heavenward: or, Magician and Wizard to lead us Hellward." (*Sartor.*) "Wouldst thou plant for Eternity, then plant into the deep infinite faculties of man, his Fantasy and Heart." (*Sartor.*) And it was the picture he presented of a strong capable man in the twelfth century bringing order out of debt and disorder in a monastery, and the chaos of the industrial world of the nineteenth century with the cash-nexus as the only tie between employer and worker that made *Past and Present* to so many a prophetic work. "I think the effect of Carlyle's *Past and Present,*" said so unlikely a person as Sir Stafford Northcote in 1844, " . . . upon me has been to unsettle any opinion, if ever I had any, on political subjects."

Of the remedies he suggested, Carlyle had no monopoly: education, emigration, etc. Where he differed from his fellow reformers was in his rejection of democracy, extension of the franchise, his appeal to the masters themselves to become the leaders, to take the place of the landed aristocracy who had given themselves up to preserving and shooting game and cared for nothing but the defence of the corn laws. Carlyle's distrust of democracy and the ballot-box was, of course, not that of the privileged classes whose interests were threatened. It was in part a revolt of the imagination as he looked out over the chaotic masses of uneducated workers English and Irish, but mainly had its source in his conviction that the advocates of the extension of the franchise were believers in what he detested, a mechanical social order. Supported by Ricardian economics and Benthamite political science the doctrine found support from both the main reform parties, Whig and Radical. One must remember what Carlyle understood by Radicalism when, himself a radical in one sense of the word, he denounced it as represented even by Mill's *London Review*: "Hide-bound Radicalism is to me a well-nigh insupportable thing . . . a breath as of Sahara and the Infinite Sterile comes from its every page." Mill's *Liberty* (1859) seemed to him an entirely pernicious book:

> In my life I never read a serious, ingenious, clear, logical essay with more perfect and profound dissent from the basis it rests on and most of the conclusions it arrives at. . . . Mill has the student's worst prejudices. He views Society as a kind of debating club for the reception or the rejection of new ideas after boundless babblement.

For the Radicals of the day differed from the Whigs only in that they wished to carry the extension of the suffrage further. The reform of 1832, which the working class had supported so passionately, left them out, simply transferred power from the landed classes to the great industrialists. Break down these limitations, cried the Radicals, e.g. Hume and Place, and give everyone the vote, and with mechanical certainty the desired reforms will work themselves out.

It was this idea of a mechanical development of society which Carlyle detested. His appeal was to the governing classes to awake to a sense of their responsibility, to the industrialists to abandon the pursuit of wealth for its own sake and establish between employer and worker something other than a purely cash-nexus, the tie of just treatment, an adequate wage and security of employment:

> For under all the wild and divergent cries of Chartists, and the wild inarticulate souls of suffering men and women, lies a demand for justice. But what is justice, or what are the rights of man? Who can say? He were an Oedipus and deliverer from sad social pestilence who could resolve us fully.

"If you ask me," Burke had written, "what a free government is, I answer that for any practical purpose it is what the people think so." Of justice Carlyle might or would have said much the same. Liberty and justice are best known to most of us by their absence. We know when we are *not* free. We know when we are being treated with manifest injustice; and this was what the mass of the British working people were convinced of under the system of *laissez-faire,* a doctrine of liberty which worked out as liberty for the employing and commercial classes to exploit those who could not defend their liberties. But the solution for Carlyle was not to be found in further emancipation of the people as voters. The cure must come from above. Democracy at the best could only be a passing phase, a temporary slack tide, or a wild welter, the waters moving hither and thither till a leader appear to direct the flow:

> Democracy is by the nature of it a self-cancelling business: and gives in the long run a short result of *zero*. Where no government is wanted save that of the parish constable, as in

> America with its boundless soil, every man being able to find work and recompense for himself, democracy may subsist: not elsewhere except briefly as a swift transition towards something other and further.

(That stage is over in America now.) It is the mind which must direct in society as in a ship, and the skill to rule belongs only to the few, it may be to the one man, an Oliver Cromwell or a General Francia. Universal suffrage leads nowhere. "Can it be proved since the beginning of the world there was ever given a universal vote in favour of the worthiest man or thing?"

It was in the same direction as Carlyle that Milton moved in the seventeenth century, as his early confidence in the Long Parliament and the English people failed him, and he rallied to Cromwell and the Army, if always with reserves. "Nothing is more agreeable to the order of nature or more for the interest of mankind than that the less should yield to the greater, not in numbers but in wisdom and virtue."

> Liberty hath a sharp and double edge, fit only to be handled by just and virtuous men, to bad and dissolute it becomes a mischief unwieldy in their hands, neither is it given but by them who have the happy skill to know what is grievous and unjust to a people and how to remove it wisely: what good laws are wanting and how to frame them substantially, that good men may enjoy the freedom which they merit and the bad the curb which they need.

These are the words of Milton. They might have been those of the author of *Past and Present* when he appealed to the new aristocracy of Captains of Industry to recognize their responsibilities and what is just in the claims of the worker to an adequate wage and security of employment. In the *Latter Day Pamphlets* Carlyle grows as scornful and angry as does Milton in his references to the greed and ambition of presbyterian divines or the corruptions of Parliament. Milton's hopes based on Cromwell were disappointed, and so were Carlyle's on Peel. The question how the best are to be found, those who have the happy skill, the Hero, remained a problem.

Carlyle's faith in the hero, the great man, the savior of

society, had more than one source. It supplied the vacancy left by the decay of his early faith, though how deeply the Christian religion, the personality of Christ, had ever appealed to him is not made clear either by his own words or the evidence of his biographers. We know that his parents were pious, that he had intended to enter the ministry, but had read Gibbon and cut himself completely adrift. "Young man, your day is over." The doctrine of the hero had a root also in his dramatic interest in human nature which made him a lover of such poetry as that of Homer, of Shakespeare, of Burns. Like Dr. Johnson, he preferred biography to any other kind of reading. But it had also a root, perhaps a partly hidden root, in his confidence in himself. Carlyle's frequently recurring complaint that no place had been found in the rule of his country for a Robert Burns was also a complaint that for Thomas Carlyle no other means of serving his country and fellow men had been found but the writing of books. "Carlyle," wrote Emerson, "has a hairy strength which makes his literary vocation a mere chance and which seems very contemptible to him. . . . He is not mainly a scholar, like most of my acquaintances, but a very practical Scotsman such as you would find in any saddler's or iron-dealer's shop." In the conduct of his life he was at the opposite pole from a shuffler and self-deceiver like Coleridge; as a thinker from a transcendentalist like Emerson. He would have been glad in 1848 to succeed Buller as Chief Commissioner of the Poor Law. If there is any meaning in Democracy, it is, he maintained, just this, that every man should find a place in the social organism, *la carrière ouverte aux talents*. This was not to be effected by the ballot-box, but it might be by giving to the king, that is, his prime minister, the power to choose his ministers, not alone from those who had secured a seat in the legislature, but wherever he could find a suitable person. We have done so in the emergency of war. In America the complete severance of executive and legislature has not proved an entire success. In part one might argue that what Carlyle had in view is met by the growth of a highly qualified civil service selected without reference to political party.

I have not the time nor do I think it entirely worth while to discuss all the aspects of the doctrine of the hero. I would rather consider how far Carlyle's warnings and forecasts have been justified by the course of events in this country since his time. De Tocqueville early indicated that the "great danger of developing democracy lay in the fact that it favoured equality but suppressed freedom"; and he found that the best corrective to this tendency in English-speaking countries had been the training in self-government afforded by the growth of local government. There is something to be said, though neither Milton nor Carlyle would have accepted it, in the late Sir Henry Campbell-Bannerman's statement that "self-government is better than good government." It has its roots in, and is to some extent the guarantee of, the essential freedom which is not without its disadvantages and yet is, De Tocqueville says, as the air we breathe, "the pleasure of speaking, acting and breathing without restraint, under no master but God and the law." But to Carlyle, looking round on the condition of the working classes under the doctrine of *laissez-faire,* it seemed that a serf like Wamba in *Ivanhoe,* with his food and shelter secure, was in a more enviable situation than an English or Irish worker with all his boasted freedom. And there is much to be said for the position. Is the condition of a slave, if he have a status and is secured of his livelihood and that of his family, worse than that of the worker of Carlyle's day when, as Scott describes it, "a man can assemble 500 workmen one week and dismiss the next, without having any further connexion with them than to receive a week's work for a week's wage, nor any further solicitude about their future fate than if they were so many shuttles?" It was not because he lost sympathy with the condition of the people, the workers, that Carlyle moved away from the Radicals but because he had no other hope. Anything was better than the state of men and women regarded and treated as flotsam and jetsam on the turbid sea of *laissez-faire,* of supply and demand. Yet a Radical like Place could see no other escape except the Malthusian one of a reduction of the birthrate. That the worker could improve his position by his own endeavor or the use of the ballot-box seemed to Carlyle impossible. Yet that is what has happened. Many of the things which Carlyle demanded for the workers in *Past and Present* have, in whole or in part, been secured by their own action in the field of politics, and by no gift of a benevolent Führer. For no government, however benevolent in intention, can be trusted for long to do justice to any class that is not in a position to make itself formidable, if not by the ballot-box, by some other method often more troublesome. That is the justification of democracy, despite all its deficiencies. If, indeed, the choice lay between a perfect dictatorship administering our affairs efficiently and yet leaving us sufficient freedom of thought and criticism, and on the other hand, democracy with all its evils—its tendency to become plutocracy, its stump oratory, general elections, inefficient ministers always a possibility and often a fact—we might prefer a dictatorship. Modern dictatorship can allow no such freedom of thought and speech as might live even under the inefficient rule of Louis XVI or of a Czar. Nor can we be sure of the dictator's wisdom and efficiency. To be immune from criticism is to take great risks. "The wish of those writers," said Bagehot, speaking of such prophets as Carlyle, Comte, Frederic Harrison, etc., "is very natural. They wish to organize society, to erect a despot who will do what *they* like, work out *their* ideas; but any despot will do what he himself likes, and will root out new ideas ninety-nine times for once that he introduces them." "Every class of society that brought the present government of Germany into power," so say many students of recent history, "has been disappointed." Every advance in the dignity of men and women, of efficiency in this or that direction, education, social welfare, etc., has been sacrificed to the one end of efficiency for war.

In Milton and Carlyle alike, it seems to me, what failed them was faith, faith in God and in their fellow men, and the two seem to be inextricably interwoven. Neither of them could believe that a people was capable of finding and following a leader uncompelled, if they felt, however confusedly, that he was to be trusted, and that he respected their essential liberties. The fall of Cromwell and failure of the rule of Saints and Major-Generals was to Milton and Carlyle alike the great tragedy of English history. The English people, it seemed to Milton, had passed through the fire to perish in the smoke. "Oliver is gone," cries Carlyle, "and with him English Puritanism. . . . The Genius of England no longer soars sunward . . . the Genius of England much like a greedy ostrich intent on provender and a whole skin mainly, stands with its other extremity sunward; with its ostrich-head stuck into the readiest bush of old church tippets, King-cloaks or whatever sheltering fallacy there may be, and so awaits the issue," etc. But surely so complete a failure implies some fault on the side of the government as well as the people. A government that does not rely on force alone must rest on at least consent. Burke has well stated the essential relation between government and people; "Government gave the impulse," he writes in *Letters on a Regicide Peace*. "As well may we fancy that of itself the sea will swell, and that without winds the billows will insult the adverse shore, as that the gross mass of the people will be moved and elevated and continue by a steady and permanent direction to bear upon one point without the influence of superior authority or superior mind." But he states the other side equally well in his *Letters to the Sheriffs of Bristol*: "In effect to follow, not to force the public inclination; to give a direction, a form, a technical address, and a specific sanction to the general sense of the community is the true end of the legislature." That such a relation between the people as he knew them and any democratically elected government could be achieved, for any wise and beneficent purpose, Carlyle could not bring himself to believe. Yet even in his own day he had before his eyes a striking instance of just such leadership, and acceptance of leadership by a free, democratically ruled people, when Abraham Lincoln, without the aid of secret police or concentration camp or suppression of criticism carried the northern states through a prolonged and bloody war.

Carlyle's distrust of democracy in any form, his unreadiness to believe that any people could find and accept such leadership as secured responsibility on the one side and willing consent on the other, made him almost necessarily willing to accept, and ready to justify, rule based frankly on power, even on conquest —a Cromwell and a Frederick. From the outset he had clearly seen that the relation of right to might was a problem not easy of solution, that justice conceived abstractedly offered no solution for many of the problems of internal government on the one hand and the relation between nations on the other. But it is absurd or unjust to suggest that Carlyle ever came to such an identification of right with might as is frankly accepted by a Nietzsche or Hitler or Stalin. In the words of a Lenin: "The scientific concept dictatorship means nothing more nor less than power which rests on violence, which is not limited or restricted by any absolute rules." The essence of right is just that it is *not* might, that the idea has its source in the recognition by *homo sapiens* (it is unknown to the beasts), that there are things he will not do, and that not because another desire is stronger than that which prompts to the act, but because something within himself, his practical reason, says with authority that he ought not to do what he can do. "No man at bottom," Carlyle contends,

> means injustice; it is always for some obscure distorted image of a right that he contends. . . . Could a man own to himself that the thing he fought for was wrong, contrary to fairness and the law of reason, he would own also that it thereby stood condemned and hopeless: he could fight for it no longer. But there is something else that a man needs to know besides what is right, or he believes to be right, viz. what he can do. Nay, independently of right, could the contending parties get but accurately to discern one another's might and strength to contend the one would peaceably yield to the other and to Necessity: the contest in this case too were over.

Right and Necessity—it is the capacity to perceive both of these clearly, what one ought to do limited by what one can do, that constitutes the "Seeing eye," the Hero in the sphere of action, the Hero as King. To see both aright is not given to all Kings. One or other tends to dominate, but both must be there or the end will be, in the long run, disaster. Carlyle's whole-hearted admiration for Cromwell proceeded from his belief, right or wrong, that he not only had the seeing eye for what could be achieved, but that his goal was righteousness, to do the will of God. In Frederick the balance inclined the other way. He had the eye for the fact, the cause and effect. "A veracious man he was at all points; not even conscious of veracity but had it in the blood of him; and never looked upon mendacity but from a very great height indeed." But by "mendacity" Carlyle meant apparently what Plato calls the lie in the soul, self-deception; for he admits that in his diplomacy Frederick was not "superstitiously veracious." But he never deceived himself: "No salvation but in the facts. Facts are a kind of divine thing to Frederick; much more so than to common men, that is eventually what Religion I have found in him."

But the question of the relation of might to right concerns more often the choice of means than of ends. It is possible for most of us to find "some distorted image of a right" in what he, be it Cromwell or Frederick or Lenin or Hitler, is aiming at. Most often the question is really: Does the end justify the means? Carlyle had no great esteem for the abstractly righteous—the Catos, Falklands, Lafayettes. Still, on what ground of right can one justify Cromwell's execution of the King, his dismissal of the Parliament to which he owed his power? Frederick had a certain claim to Silesia, but had he the right to invade it on the plea that he was acting for the Empress, and half conquer it before war was formally declared—and we have seen similar outrages in our time?

It is a difficult question, and Carlyle could only fall back on the belief in the ultimate justice of the universe, of God. In the long run justice must be victorious. Dr. Johnson loved the University of Salamanca because, when asked by the Pope whether it was just to conquer America, that University said NO. Carlyle could not accept so abstract a finding: "Conquest is a fact often witnessed, conquest which seems mere wrong, and force everywhere asserts itself as a right among men.[3] . . . Yet if we examine it we shall find that in this world no conquest would ever become permanent which did not show itself beneficial to the conquered as well as to the conquerors." That is a sweeping statement. What is "the long run"? It may be that Silesia benefited, as he says, more under Prussian than under Austrian rule. But the effect of the conquest of the peoples of Central Asia by the Nomadic tribes has been, in the long run, the complete demoralization of the conquered peoples. "What a tragic fate for an enslaved people. Although its lowest degradation is already behind it, how long yet will it be the object of universal and not unnatural contempt, while the former oppressor, void of all humane feeling, a professional murderer and cattle-thief, remains as a hero and ideal superman." (*Camb. Med. History*.) It would be more just, I venture to think, to recognize that war is the product of a phase in the growth of civilization, a phase to which it is only too easy to revert, in which the value of justice as a cement of society is but partially realized, if it ever will be by men as they are. In *Physics and Politics* Bagehot contends that war is a necessary stage in the evolution of civilization, in which on the whole the better conquers the less fit. But it is a phase which must be passed through. Military virtues soon become a danger to all further development. True civilization began in Greece when force was to a growing extent superseded by discussion. Rule by discussion—that was Mill's faith. Carlyle's abhorrence, rule by babblement. And yet it is by discussion and all that it implies that we have made the most precious and enduring advances in a civilized life—precious because they come to us without the loss of self-respect that accompanies the best of gifts which come as a concession from our masters, enduring because discussion tends to secure consent. Democracy seems to depend on two things—freedom of discussion and the acceptance of, the consent to, the will of the majority. The minority continues free to advise and often to modify the proposals of those in power, and may itself come into power. But if it rebels, whether by force, or the refusal of taxes, or the general strike, then we are on our way to rule by force, for there is one thing which the majority of men will prefer even to liberty, namely security. One must live before one can live well, and liberty is a condition not of mere life but of the good life.

A prophet, I maintain, Carlyle was to his generation, the most potent voice of the spirit in reaction against a mechanical view of society, against a too great faith in the findings of an economic science which claimed infallibility, which claimed to have discovered the laws governing both the production and the distribution of wealth. His friend and enemy J. S. Mill, who, Carlyle complained to Espinasse, in conversation used to insist on "having everything demonstrated," came to recognize in his *Autobiography* "the proper distinction between the laws of the Production of Wealth, which are real laws of nature, dependent on the properties of objects, and the modes of its distribution which, subject to certain conditions, depend on human will." Macaulay, too, in his speeches modified the extreme faith in *laissez-faire* which he had announced with so entire confidence in his review of Southey's *Colloquies on Society*. But as a prophet I feel that Carlyle lost the faith which gives inspiration to what the prophet says. It is not only that he grows angry. He ceased, Espinasse complains, to give close study to the problems. There is a measure of *a priori* judgment in his pronouncements on the subjects with which he deals in the *Latter Day Pamphlets.* "He says over and over," Emerson complained, "for months, for years, the same thing." It is true of what he writes also. "He is terribly earnest but never serious—that is, never *in earnest*" was the judgment passed on him by G. M. Hopkins. The difference is not at once obvious but is, I think, real. Carlyle is "in earnest" up to the writing of *Past and Present* because he believes he can persuade those he is appealing to. In what came later his manner is as "earnest" as ever, even more so, but it has lost the note of hope and conviction. If one has come to regard one's fellow men with "abhorrence mingled with pity," one may be willing to hail any dictator who can secure order and find work for all. Faith, Hope, Charity—the three great religious virtues—are all, it would seem, necessary to the prophet who would, like Lincoln, lead his people through a terrible crisis to a better world. Faith and Hope carried Lincoln through the war. Of the Charity which might have healed the wounds America was deprived by his assassination.

Notes

[1] See II Esdras iii. 27–36. "And so thou gavest thy city over into the hands of thine enemies. Are their deeds then any better that inhabit Babylon, that they should therefore have the dominion over Sion?" etc.

[2] To the doctrine of the *Everlasting No* he recurs in a later work, never to that of the *Everlasting Yes:* "The evidence to me of God—and the *only* evidence, is the feeling I have, deep down in the very bottom of my heart, of right, truth and justice. . . . Whoever looks into himself must be aware that at the center of things is a mysterious Demiurge who is God and who cannot in the least be adequately spoken of in any human words."

[3] "Force everywhere asserts itself as a right among men." What do those words mean? It cannot be with Nietzsche that the strong man has the right to exercise his might at the expense of others for his own sake. That is to take the meaning out of the word "right." If it mean anything it seems to me it is this: Might, physical or mental, is capable of rendering real service to men, and it is right that if possible this should find an outlet. Whether that which it seeks or takes is right is often difficult to decide *a priori*. One must to some extent judge by the result.

26.

Basil Willey

Newman and the Oxford Movement

Forty years ago, when I was an undergraduate at Oxford, voices were in the air there which haunt my memory still. Happy the man who in that susceptible season of youth hears such voices! they are a possession to him for ever. No such voices as those which we heard in our youth at Oxford are sounding there now. Oxford has more criticism now, more knowledge, more light; but such voices as those of our youth it has no longer. The name of Cardinal Newman is a great name to the imagination still; his genius and his style are still things of power. But he is over eighty years of age; he is in the Oratory at Birmingham; he has adopted, for the doubts and difficulties which beset men's minds today, a solution which, to speak frankly, is impossible. Forty years ago he was in the very prime of life; he was close at hand to us at Oxford; he was preaching in St. Mary's pulpit every Sunday; he seemed about to renew what was for us the most national and natural institution in the world, the Church of England. Who could resist the charm of that spiritual apparition, gliding in the dim afternoon light through the aisles of St. Mary's, rising into the pulpit, and then, in the most entrancing of voices, breaking the silence with words and thoughts which were a religious music—subtle, sweet, mournful?

Reprinted from *Nineteenth Century Studies* (1955), pp. 73–101 by permission of the author, Columbia University Press, New York and Chatto & Windus Ltd., London.

So spoke Matthew Arnold in 1883, introducing his American discourse on Emerson; such, in general, has been the prevailing estimate of Newman in England, and no one has stated it more memorably. In that passage of cadenced prose, so akin in spirit and tone to Newman's own manner, Arnold has given us a Newman who, like the dreaming spires and moonlit gardens of Oxford, has become a symbol of lost youth and lost causes. "Somewhere or other I have spoken of those 'last enchantments of the Middle Age' which Oxford sheds around us, and here they were!" The story of the Oxford Movement has been often told, and it is no part of my intention to repeat it here. But our account of the nineteenth century, though pretending to no exhaustiveness, would be out of proportion without some attention to its significance. I propose, therefore, to enquire briefly how far Newman's thought and work belong to the main line of nineteenth century development. I shall suggest that he was no mere spell-binder, beckoning his hearers with mysterious gestures into an enchanted garden of the spirit, but a seer through whose prophesyings some of the deepened insights of the age found utterance: insights none the less "advanced" because of their "reactionary" coloring.

What was it that gave to the "Movement Party" in its early years its joyous, exuberant energy, its militant self-confidence, its sense of leadership? This kind of *élan*, so clearly marked in the early stages of the Oxford Movement, and echoing throughout Newman's many retrospects of its history, is usually only given to a party which knows and feels that it holds the clue to a contemporary problem, and can minister to the special needs of its time; it is not the "note" of a merely romantic or antiquarian craze. Something must have been rotten in the state of Protestantism for a Catholic movement started by a few academic clergymen to have attracted so much attention, and to have become known so soon "to the police in Italy, and the backwoodsmen of America."[1] The movement was, in fact, a part of that great deepening of seriousness, that impulse to come to grips with history, with the unseen, and with the fundamentals of the general human plight, which showed itself also as the French Revolution, as Romanticism and as Evangelicalism. That other and older Oxford Movement, the Methodist, had begun with the same glow and warming of the heart, but occurring in the eighteenth century it had had other tasks to perform, and could melt the spiritual ice-pack by reaffirming the old Protestant certainties. Tractarianism, if only because it followed the revolutionary and romantic upheavals, was bound to be more scholastic dogmatic and ecclesiastical—in a word, more "Catholic." To unprotestantize the English Church was a project so wildly paradoxical, so flatly opposed to ingrained national prejudice, that at any previous time since the Reformation it could not have been entertained without risk of bloodshed. The significant thing about the period we are now considering is that then, in a country where Popery had so long been abhorred and tabooed, it began to be possible to listen to popish arguments—at first perhaps with a guilty joy as in tasting forbidden fruit, and then with exhilaration in finding the fruit medicinal after all. Newman habitually speaks of the movement as spontaneous in its origin, not contrived; it was "in the air," it was a "spirit afloat," a "spiritual awakening of spiritual wants." "There has been for some years," he wrote in 1839, "a growing tendency towards the character of mind and feeling of which Catholic doctrines are the just expression"; opinions long obscured begin to be revived, and capivate by their seeming novelty, but still more by the "touching beauty, loftiness of idea, and earnestness of character which they evidence or require."[2] Scott, Southey, Coleridge, and Wordsworth have all contributed something towards this climatic change, though they are to be counted rather as "indications of what was secretly going on in the minds of men, than as causes of it." When a historical situation has for long enough been undermined and riddled, it only needs the unimaginable touch of time and of genius to send it toppling; such, in a sense, was the condition of Protestantism in the England of Newman's prime. So he could write "the spirit of Luther is dead; but Hildebrand and Loyola are still alive"; so he could say, in one of his first sermons: "I do not shrink from uttering my firm conviction that it would be a gain to the country were it vastly more superstitious, more bigoted, more gloomy, more fierce in its religion than at present it shows itself to be." Slowly, as the mists of controversy and illusion begin to clear, the forms of the two real spiritual antagonists come into view, and are discerned to be those of Catholicism and Rationalism. The battle is on, and it lies between these two; all alleged intermediaries—all evangelicalisms, Erastian establishments, liberalisms or latitudinarianisms are things of straw, without life or cohesion. When these real opposites meet, "then, indeed, will be the stern encounter, when two real and living principles, simple, entire, and consistent, one in the Church, the other out of it, at length rush upon each other, contending not for names and words, or half views, but for elementary notions and distinctive moral characters."[3]

Newman always remembered and kept July 14, the day of Keble's Assize Sermon of 1833, as the starting point of the Tractarian Movement. That Sermon was a protest against interference by a secularized Parliament in matters spiritual, and the movement has accordingly been regarded as political in its origin. As Hurrell Froude pointed out, the House of Commons in Hooker's time had been a Synod of the laity of the Church of England, and for that reason alone could Hooker tolerate its interference in spiritual concerns. But now, after the Reform Bill and the repeal of the Test and Corporation Acts, the true situation of the Church became apparent; its liturgy, its articles, and its status could be altered, as its Bishops would be appointed, at the will of a parliamentary majority which might be non-Anglican or even non-Christian. So, in one sense, the original impulse of the movement might be expressed in Froude's exclamation: "let us give up a *national* Church and have a *real* one." Or again, Newman himself has said that its object was "to withstand the liberalism of the day." But the movement was only political and antiliberal because it was primarily spiritual; its deepest concern was with the invisible world, not with politics or the obsolete; its driving power, a hunger and thirst after righteousness, an effort towards true sanctity. Newman's influence over his Oxford hearers was due to no ritual practices or popish affectations—he wore a black gown, and used no incense and no eastward position: it was due to "the wonderful charm of his mysterious and almost unknown personality."[4] When men passed him on an Oxford pavement, and whispered "Look, that's Newman!," it was with reverence towards a "spiritual apparition"—for Newman had the air of one whose converse has been in heaven, as indeed it had. He was opposed to Erastianism, then, and he was opposed to liberalism, because both these things struck at the spiritual life: Erastianism by enslaving its divine guardian, and liberalism by destroying its dogmatic foundation. Looking back in later years upon the past, he names, as the party's "great and deadly foe, their scorn and their laughing-stock," "that imbecile, inconsistent thing called Protestantism." It was Protestantism which, by rejecting Papal authority, had subjected the Church to the State; it was Protestantism which, by exalting Scripture and "private judgment," had opened the way to schism and sect, and finally to infidelity; it was Protestantism which, by decrying asceticism and good works, and by rejecting so much of the ritual, symbolism, and practice that Catholicism had held conducive to holiness, had lowered the whole devotional life of the Church in England, and left it exposed and defenseless in its hour of greatest need. Above all, by watering down the doctrines of the Eucharist and of baptismal regeneration, by minimizing the authority of the priesthood, by turning the Bishops into civil servants, and by dismissing as "Romish" so many essential means of grace, it had left Christianity unprotected against those forces of unbelief which, as the nineteenth century drew on, were assembling for the destruction of all religion whatsoever. To the Tractarians Protestantism seemed weak and rotten not merely because it was aesthetically meager, but because it was worldly and unspiritual, and because it had no center of spiritual authority. Even its palmary efforts after holiness—its Methodism and Evangelicalism—were houses built upon sand: the sands of inward assurance and of private judgment. The Tractarians needed no Tübingen critics to teach them that the Bible, and the Bible alone, could not be the rule of faith; it was enough for them to know that the authority of Scripture rested upon the authority of the Church, and that the Bible existed to prove dogmas, not to supply or constitute them.

The strength of Tractarianism lay, then, in its diagnosis of the age as blighted by the upas-tree of worldliness, and of contemporary Protestantism as incapable of rescuing it from spiritual decay and death. The original plan of the Oxford men, long before it was borne in upon Newman that "the Church of Rome will be found right after all,"[5] was to un-Protestantize the Church of England without Romanizing it. "We are Catholics without the Popery, and Church-of-England men without the Protestantism," wrote Hurrell Froude in 1835.[6] "The Reformation was a limb badly set—it must be broken again in order to be righted."[7] "The spirit of lawlessness came in with the Reformation, and Liberalism is its offspring."[8] The ancient religion "had well nigh faded away out of the land, through the political changes of the last 150 years, and it must be restored. It would be in fact a second Reformation:—a better reformation, for it would be a return not to the sixteenth century but to the seventeenth."[9] Compare the Church of England now, in its decorous torpor, with the Church of the first centuries A.D. in all the "joyous swing of her advance!" It is not the old Reformation that can save her now, or restore her jubilant militancy. Nearly all the assumptions on which English Protestantism had unthinkingly rested for two centuries could now be represented as baseless. The "plain man's Bible"—but which plain man? and who gave the scriptural books their canonical authority? "Justification by Faith only"—then has moral effort no intrinsic worth? has the old Christian ethical and ascetic ideal no value in the sight of God? And is not the Church of England, in fact, deficient precisely in the "note of sanctity"? "Must it not be owned that the Church of England saints, however good in essentials, are with a few rare exceptions deficient in the austere beauty of the Catholic ἦθος?"[10] "The State Church"—but we are united to the State as Israel was to Egypt, and "if the State will but kick us off we may yet do in England"![11] The alleged "purity" of the Church as opposed to "Romish corruptions?"—but what is the "pure" state of any living organism: the embryo or the adult? the seed or the flower? It needed all Newman's knowledge of the early Church, and all his argumentative subtlety, to show in a lengthy work how "corruptions" may be distinguished from genuine "developments." The Reformers of the sixteenth century were not the men they have been taken for; they were often timeservers and politicians rather than prophets or saints. Froude scorned Jewell for calling the Mass a "cursed, paltrie service," for laughing at the Apostolical Succession, for denying the Lord's Supper to be a means of grace as distinct from a pledge of remembrance, and for saying that the only "Keys of the Kingdom" are instruction and correction, and that the only way they open the Kingdom is by touching men's consciences.

> Really I hate the Reformation and the Reformers more and more, and have almost made up my mind that the rationalist spirit they set afloat is the ψενδοπροφήτης of the Revelation.[12] I shall never call the Holy Eucharist "the Lord's Supper," nor God's Priests "ministers of the word" or the Altar 'the Lord's table,' etc. etc.; innocent as such phrases are in themselves, they have been dirtied. . . .Nor shall I even abuse the Roman Catholics *as a Church* for any thing except excommunicating us.[13]

As long as Newman retained his Englishman's suspicion of Rome as corrupt, crafty, and idolatrous—a "stain upon my imagination," he later called it—he continued to believe in the possibility of a *Via Media*: an English Catholic Church like that of Laud, apostolic, yet free from "the practical abuses and excesses of Rome." If we were tied to the Reformation, then Anglicans might well be forced towards Rome, but fortunately (or should we not rather say providentially) the Church of England is not implicated in the conduct and opinions of the Reformers. It might have been so, but happily Henry VIII wanted only as much doctrinal and liturgical change as would enable him to steal church property and usurp church government; Edward VI died young, and Elizabeth liked the old ritual. All this might "even suggest the idea of a Design to prevent the English Reformation from proceeding in any point to express contradiction of Antiquity."[14] We may thus legitimately interpret the formularies of the Church of England, "in all essentials, conformably to the doctrine and ritual of the Church Universal."[15] It was to prove just this that Newman wrote Tract xc (1841). The Prayer-Book might breathe the spirit of Catholicism, but the Thirty-nine Articles seemed stubbornly Protestant: were they really so? His thesis was that the Articles do not oppose Catholic teaching, and but partially oppose Roman dogma; they for the most part oppose only the "dominant errors of Rome." To the argument that the Articles were composed *against* Rome he replies that it was only so in a political sense; had Elizabeth "a conscience against the Mass"? The only "popery" then opposed was the Papal Supremacy, and the Articles were even drawn up in the hope of gaining the Papists. This Tract, this attempt to put a Catholic construction upon the Articles, was grounded, says Newman, upon the belief that "the Articles need not be so closed as the received method of teaching closes them, and ought not to be for the sake of many persons. If we will close them, we run the risk of subjecting persons whom we should least like to lose to the temptation of joining the Church of Rome." In truth the attempt was hopeless; the new ("reformed") bottles would not stand the old wine. The earlier Tracts had appealed to English ecclesiastical patriotism, but No. xc outraged Anglican susceptibilities, and the attacks upon it showed how far the movement had forfeited the support of average Churchmen. How hopeless was the attempt, Newman has nowhere shown more clearly than in the *Lectures on Difficulties Felt by Anglicans in Catholic Teaching,* addressed to his former associates from the further side of the Rubicon. To illustrate the antagonism of the English Bishops towards the very party which had toiled to uphold their spiritual authority, he quotes from episcopal Charges such phrases as these:

> 'It is impossible not to remark upon the subtle wile of the Adversary; it has been signally and unexpectedly exemplified in the present day by the revival of errors which might have been supposed buried for ever.'
> 'Those who sit in the Reformers' seat are traducing the Reformation.' They are 'walking about our beloved Church, polluting the sacred edifice, and leaving their slime about her altars.'[16]

Well might Newman mourn that "it is not at all easy (humanly speaking) to wind up an Englishman to a dogmatic level."[17] It became clear that there were but two alternatives, "the way to Rome, and the way to Atheism: Anglicanism is the halfway house on the one side, and Liberalism is the halfway house on the other." He became more sure that England was in schism than that Roman "additions" were not true "developments" of the primitive Christian doctrine. Speaking later, from his post-conversion vantage-point, he could show how impossible it was for the Anglican Church to be "wound up" to the

Catholic level without denying its own nature and ceasing to be itself. The Church of England has perhaps been a bulwark against worse things, and historically it has "diluted the virulence of Protestantism." But it is no real Church at all; it is a mere department of Government, dependent on the civil power; its Prayer-Book is authorized by an Act of Parliament passed two centuries ago; its cathedrals are "the spoils of Catholicism." The Privy Council has decided (in the Gorham case) that a clergyman may hold whatever views he likes on Baptismal Regeneration; what, then, is to hinder the national will from sliding down the slippery slope into Arianism and finally Atheism? Protestants may rejoice over the Gorham judgment, but in their blindness they do not see that to weaken a *part* of the dogmatic structure is to weaken the *whole*.

> What though the ritual categorically deposes to the regeneration of the infant baptized? The Evangelical party, who in former years had the nerve to fix the charge of dishonesty on the explanations of the Thirty-nine Articles, put forward by their opponents, could all the while be cherishing in their own breasts an interpretation of the Baptismal Service, simply contrary to its most luminous declarations.[18]

Ah well, "may not the free-born, self-dependent, animal mind of the Englishman choose his religion for himself?" The Establishment has life indeed, but not Catholic life; it is the life of a nation, of a state, which is irretrievably Erastian and Protestant in sentiment. But the very first principle of the movement was ecclesiastical liberty—antagonism to the Royal Supremacy, to the Establishment as such. On this principle depended, for the Tractarians, the preservation of dogma, of the sacraments, ceremonial observances, practical duty, counsels of perfection; without it, what could prevent the sacrifice or rationalization of dogma? Without it, the time could easily come when a man would fraternize with Unitarians, and "pronounce his butler to be as able to give communion as his priest." "Establishment" principles "destroyed the supernatural altogether, by making emphatically Christ's Kingdom a Kingdom of this world." The Establishment "keeps back those doctrines which, to the eye of faith, give real substance to religion." Are you going to be lulled into acquiescence, he asks the Anglo-Catholics, with the daily and weekly routine of comfortable unreality? No! You must secede! The Church of England has always been an imposture; now, it is a mere wreck. Don't be afraid to leave the sinking ship; in so doing, you will be weakening nothing divine. Such as the State is, will the State Church ever be. Where is its authority to be found? Whose teachings unmistakably declare its doctrines? Driven from Prayer-Book and Bible, first upon the Anglican divines, and thence upon the Fathers, it seeks in vain for the authoritative principle which resides in Rome alone. The established Church *is* the nation (not in Arnold's favorable sense), and therefore you cannot use it to resist the nation, which is "on its way to give up revealed truth."

In much of this book of Newman's we can see an oblique self-justification; there is a tension in his mind between triumph and regret. At rare moments this resolves itself in one of those moving and tender passages which bring us close to his inmost self, and give us a glimpse into the hiding places of his personal power. He pauses, for example, and asks, is there then no such thing as Grace working savingly in the heart? and has not this Grace worked inwardly through the offices and devotions of the Church of England? No one, no Catholic, will deny it, and least of all Newman himself:

> Why should I deny to your memory what is so pleasant in mine? Cannot I too look back on many years past, and many events, in which I myself experienced what is now your confidence? Can I forget the happy life I have led all my days, with no cares, no anxieties worth remembering; without desolateness, or fever of thought, or gloom of mind, or doubt of God's love to me and providence over me? Can I forget,—I never can forget,—the day when in my youth I first bound myself to the ministry of God in that old church of St. Frideswide, the patroness of Oxford? nor how I wept abundant, and most sweet tears, when I thought what I then had become; though I looked on ordination as no sacramental rite, nor even to baptism ascribed any sacramental virtue? Can I wipe out from my memory, or

> wish to wipe out, those happy Sunday mornings, light or dark, year after year, when I celebrated your communion-rite, in my own church of St. Mary's; and in the pleasantness and joy of it heard nothing of the strife of tongues which surrounded its walls? When, too, shall I not feel the soothing recollection of those dear years which I spent in retirement, in preparation for my deliverance from Egypt, asking for light, and by degrees gaining it, with less of temptation in my heart, and sin on my conscience, than ever before? O my dear brethren, my Anglican friends! I easily give you credit for what I have experienced myself."[19]

Yes, God's grace may be available to individuals everywhere, even to pagans. But is it *safe* to rely entirely even upon the felt, inward evidence of God's presence and favor? "It is quite impossible to conclude," he says, "that a certain opinion is true, or a religious position *safe* [my italics], simply on account of the confidence or apparent excellence of those who adopt it." If it were possible, then we must admit that there are finer examples of Christian character, and on that principle safer positions, to be found outside the national Church than within it—above all John Wesley, and the Methodists generally. "Personally I do not like him [Wesley]," he adds,

> if it were merely for his deep self-reliance and self-conceit; still I am bound, in justice to him, to ask, and you in consistency to answer, what historical person in the Establishment, during its whole three centuries, has approximated in force and splendor of conduct and achievements to one who began by innovating on your rules, and ended by contemning your authorities?[20]

What, too, of Elizabeth Fry? or Howard? "Even old Bunyan" is "more Apostolical than you." And consider the death of Dr. Arnold:

> Does the extreme earnestness and reality of religious feeling, exhibited in the sudden seizure and death of one who was as stern in his hatred of your opinions as admirable in his earnestness, who one evening protested against the sacramental principle, and next morning died

> nobly with the words of Holy Scripture in his mouth—does it give any sanction to that hatred and that protest?[21]

The answer to that rhetorical question will not be unanimous. Newman is here maintaining a delicate position: he cannot deny the workings of grace in non-Catholics, but he has to deny that they come through the operation of non-Catholic ordinances. Now the Catholic ordinances are divinely appointed for the salvation of sinners, therefore it is precarious to rely on direct access to the divine source.

The magnetism of Newman, wrote J. A. Froude in *The Nemesis of Faith* (1849), "took us all his own way; all, that is, who were *not Arnoldised*" [my italics]. With W. G. Ward in mind, we might add that it also attracted some who were. Arnold and Newman, indeed, may be taken to symbolize the two conflicting trends in nineteenth century religious thought: Arnold, ethical and liberal, aiming at the promotion of goodness by Christian gentlemen; Newman, mystical and dogmatic, aiming at the production of saints by an infallible Church. We have seen how Arnold condemned the exaltation of the sacerdotal caste, and rejected as trivial "all this stuff about the True Church"—all, in fact, that to Newman seemed vital. Arnold accused the Tractarians of teaching old error instead of new truth, and of exalting Church and Sacrament above Christ himself. Newman would reply that error is always renewing itself, while truth is ever the same; and that we do no dishonor to Christ by holding that we can only know Him fully through the Church and the ordinances which He instituted, and through which His spirit is mediated. Arnold accepted the spirit of the age, and believed that, in so far as it was searching for truth, it could be Christianized; Newman dreaded and resisted it, believing that the spirit of enquiry was in its very nature destructive of faith in the unseen, and that, unless checked, it must inevitably lead to atheism. It was, and is, commonly said of the Tractarians that they were reactionary dreamers, out of touch with their times, caring little about the "condition of England question," ignoring modern science and modern criticism, and in general "substituting unrealities for realities." F. D. Maurice, who believed that the Kingdom of Christ, though transcending this world, could and must be made to include it, commented thus on the Oxford Tracts:

> To me they are, for the most part, more unpleasant than I quite like to acknowledge to myself or others. Their error, I think, consists in opposing to the spirit of the present age the spirit of a former age, instead of the ever-living and acting Spirit of God, of which the spirit of each age is at once the adversary and the parody.[22]

To Newman this distinction would have been meaningless; his concern, as he said, was not with the obsolete, but with the invisible. Truth, divinely communicated, attested and guarded, belongs to no age more than another—it must remain for ever the same; while the unregenerate nature of fallen man tends at all times towards error and denial. If Newman was unmoved by the specific challenges of his own century, it was because he saw in them merely the reincarnation of early heresies, over which the Catholic Church had triumphed centuries ago. After he had wound his dangerous way, "with anxious eyes and a beating heart," through the dreary mazes of Arianism, Sabellianism, Nestorianism and the rest, how could nineteenth-century rationalisms alarm or even interest him, save as new sproutings from the age-old hydra of misbelief? Newman's view of history was apocalyptic, and not—like that of most of his contemporaries —progressive; he did not view it as a linear forward movement towards light and truth. Where others saw, and rejoiced in, a progress along the ringing grooves of change, he saw simply light amid the encircling gloom: the Word that was with God and was God, coming incarnate into the darkness, bringing light, grace, and truth which the darkness apprehended not.

If we then, like Arnold and others, ask how it was possible for a mind so trenchant as Hurrell Froude's, so subtle, profound and imaginative as Newman's, or so sceptical and logical as Ward's, to attach, in that enlightened age, such high, such supreme importance to "externals," "forms" and dogmas, which the *Zeitgeist* had interpreted and rationalized away—if we ask this, the reply must be that they believed what many only professed and others denied, and were "not afraid of inferences."[23]

Accept the view of history and of fallen humanity taken by Newman or Ward, and the inferences follow in an unbroken series. To the average Englishman and Churchman of the time—to a man like Kingsley, for example—it was so shocking to hear proclaimed, as vital truths, doctrines long regarded as exploded superstitions, so disturbing to find the charges of ignorance and inconsistency retorted upon themselves, that one explanation alone seemed possible: these Catholics were crafty priests who did not, could not, mean or believe what they said. I will not enter here upon the details of the Kingsley-Newman controversy, but the famous passage in the *Apologia* introducing the "General Answer to Mr. Kingsley"[24] is so revealing, and so pertinent to the question we have just raised, that it must be summarized at this point. Newman is dealing with the Protestant suspicion that the Catholic creed is "set up in inevitable superstition and hypocrisy," and its upholders intellectually dishonest. He lifts us straight up to the highest level of spiritual vision, and from this vantage-point interprets for us the vast and tragic panorama of existence:

> Starting then with the being of a God (which, as I have said, is as certain to me as the certainty of my own existence . . .), I look out of myself into the world of men, and there I see a sight which fills me with unspeakable distress. The world seems simply to give the lie to that great truth, of which my whole being is so full; and the effect upon me is, in consequence, as a matter of necessity, as confusing as if it denied that I am in existence myself. If I looked into a mirror, and did not see my face, I should have the sort of feeling which actually comes upon me, when I look into this living busy world, and see no reflexion of its Creator.

Were it not for the voice within the conscience and the heart, the spectacle of the world would make him an atheist, pantheist, or polytheist; the sight is "nothing else than the prophet's scroll, full of 'lamentations, and mourning, and woe.'" To consider the world and the ways of man,

> the disappointments of life, the defeat of good, the success of evil, physical pain, mental anguish, the prevalence and

> intensity of sin, the pervading idolatries, the corruptions, the dreary hopeless irreligion, that condition of the whole race, so fearfully yet exactly described in the Apostle's words, "having no hope and without God in the world"—all this is a vision to dizzy and appal; and inflicts upon the mind a sense of profound mystery, which is absolutely beyond human solution.

It forces us to the inference, either that there is no Creator, or that man has been "discarded from His presence." "*If* there be a God, *since* there is a God, the human race is implicated in some terrible aboriginal calamity." So the doctrine of original sin becomes almost as certain as that God and the world exist.

> And now, supposing it were the blessed and loving will of the Creator to interfere in this anarchical condition of things—

is it not natural to suppose that He would use abnormal means, miraculous means? What must be "the face-to-face antagonist, by which to withstand and baffle the fierce energy of passion and the all-corroding, all-dissolving scepticism of the intellect in religious enquiries?" *Right* reason indeed, even unaided by revelation, can point to the saving truths, but reason as it acts habitually in fallen man tends "towards a simple unbelief in matters of religion." Today, outside the Catholic Church, things are tending with acceleration towards atheism:

> What a scene, what a prospect, does the whole of Europe present at this day! And not only Europe, but every government and every civilization through the world, which is under the influence of the European mind! Lovers of their country and of their race, religious men, external to the Catholic Church, have attempted various expedients to arrest fierce wilful human nature in its onward course, and to bring it into subjection. The necessity of some form of religion for the interests of humanity, has been generally acknowledged: but where was the concrete representative of things invisible, which would have the force and the toughness to be a breakwater against the deluge?

Religious "establishments" served their turn in Protestant countries, but now their crevices are "admitting the enemy"; education, the hope of world-peace, the optimism of the Great Exhibition era—all have failed to check the onrush. Even of the Bible the same must be said; it "does not answer a purpose, for which it was never intended"; no book, however divine, can by itself "make a stand against the wild living intellect of man."

Newman now proceeds to the last inference in this chain of impassioned argument: if the Creator has made provision for "retaining in the world a knowledge of Himself, so definite and distinct as to be proof against the energy of human scepticism"—supposing that this is so (and we cannot suppose otherwise), would it be surprising

> if He should think fit to introduce a power into the world, invested with the prerogative of infallibility in religious matters? . . . and, when I find that this is the very claim of the Catholic Church, not only do I feel no difficulty in admitting the idea, but there is a fitness in it, which recommends it to my mind. And thus I am brought to speak of the Church's infallibility, as a provision, adapted by the mercy of the Creator, to preserve religion in the world, and to restrain that freedom of thought, which of course in itself is one of the greatest of our natural gifts, and to rescue it from its own suicidal excesses . . . a working instrument, in the course of human affairs, for smiting hard and throwing back the immense energy of the aggressive intellect.

The force and momentum of Newman's rhetoric are spoilt by this compression, but I have given enough, I hope (and less would hardly have sufficed), to convey something of the sweep and coherence of his vision. Few, I think, after deeply pondering this passage, would be inclined to dismiss Newman as a reactionary dreamer, out of touch with his time; if he lacked interest in what was specifically of the nineteenth century, it was because he was a spectator of all time and all existence. What concerns him is not the local and the transient, but the perennial plight of fallen man. The solution which he proposed seemed to many, as it did to Arnold, "frankly impossible"; indeed, to the average Englishman, for whom Catholicism had long been an object of scorn and fear (associated with Guy Fawkes and hocus-pocus), it seemed preposterous. Yet in so far as Catholicism meant really believing what others only professed, and really using means of grace which others had abandoned or used as mechanical routine: in so far as it meant a return and a recall to spiritual first principles, it could again, as of old, form the advance-column in the holy war against the principalities and powers. The current of the Reformation had run its course, and its spent energies were losing themselves in the flats and shallows of worldliness and unbelief; could it be that Rome had been right all along? The question could never have been asked if Protestantism had not became moribund, and if Catholicism had not been exhibited, in the saintliness and visionary power of Newman and his associates, as a source—perhaps the only source?—of spiritual power, and as a discipline—perhaps the true one?—for the wayward will of humanity. No Protestant historian need deny that Catholicism, as Newman presented it, was both intellectually more coherent and imaginatively more alluring than what Protestantism had largely become; nor need he deny that unbelief could then be more effectually opposed by inflexible dogmatism than by the softened and blunted weapons of the Reformation. Protestantism, indeed, proved capable of new life, but it needed for its rejuvenation the challenges of Catholic asceticism and of scientific enquiry; it needed, too, a deepened understanding of the ground of faith and the nature of religious experience. It is because Newman contributed so largely to the deepening of that understanding that we may claim for him a place, not amongst the reactionaries or obscurantists, but amongst the light-bearers of the nineteenth century.

The Oxford Movement, as A. P. Stanley pointed out, may have owed some of "its exclusive peculiarities to an intense revolt against every kind of latitude," but it also derived "some of its most persuasive elements, not from those points in which it differs, but from those points in which it agrees, with the liberal and historical impulse which long preceded it."[25] There is, in particular, a remarkable consonance between the teachings of Coleridge and of Newman about Faith and Reason—an affinity so real that many have regarded Newman as Coleridge's disciple. This can hardly be, since Newman records that in 1835, when he had already "taken up all his distinctive positions," he read parts of Coleridge for the first time. But he significantly adds, "I am surprised how much I thought mine, is to be found there."[26] We have seen that for Coleridge Faith meant a commitment of the will to the insights of Reason, an acting-out of confidence in the reality of "things hoped for," and that in his view it sprang from our whole experience as moral and spiritual beings, not from the intellect in isolation. Coleridge, accepting Hume's view of faith but inverting its sense, had shown that faith was indeed incapable of rational "proof," but that on that very account it was unassailable by the "mere" reason; a faith which rested on demonstration would be either compulsory and mechanical, or would be exposed to disproof by other demonstrations. Faith, like Imagination, is alive and creative, ever *realizing* its own objects. This was Newman's position in the *University Sermons* and the *Grammar of Assent;* let us illustrate first from the *Sermons*. In No. IV, for example, on "The Usurpations of Reason," Newman says of "Reason" what Coleridge had said of "Understanding": he means by it "secular reason" or "the wisdom of this world" (Coleridge's "mind of the flesh"). It is not on this that faith is founded; Christ does not assume or expect intellectual ability in his hearers; the Bible makes no appeal to this faculty as a means of suasion. Faith may, indeed, encroach upon reason's legitimate sphere, as when men "apply such Scripture communications as are intended for religious purposes to the determination of physical questions. . . . This was the usurpation of the schools of theology in former ages, to issue their decrees to the subjects of the Senses and the Intellect."[27] The reverse happens, and has disastrously happened since the Reformation, when reason presumes to deal with matters belonging to religion and morals—when it works on "assumptions foreign and injurious" to religion. What Hume said in irony is most sober truth—"it is true as far as every important question in Revelation is concerned, and to forget this is the error which is at present under consideration." A Worldly-Wiseman discoursing on religion, whether for or against, is like a blind man lecturing on colors; the necessary assumptions of religion are supplied, not by reason, but by the moral sense, and by "spiritual discernment." Reasonings on "evidences" may be plausible, but they do not *convince*. The modern "usurpations" of reason have typically consisted, since the Reformation, in trying to make the proof of Christianity independent of its only true foundations: the Church and the Conscience—the external and internal witnesses. Scripture was set up in place of the first—with what results we know; Conscience was resolved into Utilitarian expediences, and increasing reliance was placed on "evidences from Nature." On this last point Newman repeats (without mentioning him) the declaration of Pascal, who, at a time when it was becoming the vogue in philosophic circles to look to Nature as the surest evidence of Nature's God, had seen that Nature only proves God to those who already believe in Him on other grounds. Evidences from Nature? Yes, says Newman: "beautiful and interesting to the believer in a God; but, when men have not already recognized God's voice within them, ineffective." In Sermon X he goes even further:

> It is indeed a great question whether Atheism is not as philosophically consistent with the phenomena of the physical world, taken by themselves, as the doctrine of a creative and governing Power. But, however this be, the practical safeguard against Atheism in the case of scientific enquirers is the inward need and desire, the inward experience of that Power, existing in the mind before and independently of their examination of His material world.[28]

The eighteenth century, "a time when love was cold," was the great Age of Evidences; but the history even of that age shows that when men do embrace the Gospel it is because it meets their needs, not because it convinces their minds; while, on the irreligious, evidences are always wasted. This tenth Sermon has significantly as its text: "Now Faith is the substance of things hoped for, the evidence of things not seen." Faith has to make its own objects real; it must realize them and make them substantial; it is not a mere believing upon evidence, or assenting to the conclusion of a chain of arguments. "Mere facts have no warmth," and reason, which deals with them, is cold and critical, not creative. Faith, like Coleridge's Imagination, is essentially vital, while objects and inferences, as such, are fixed and dead. It follows from that this faith, springing from the conscience, from an antecedent habit or predisposition, is content with proofs which from the point of view of reason are defective or insufficient; religious certainty cannot be had ready-made—it has to be hungered and thirsted after, and so *deserved*. On the level of reason, proofs *constrain* assent; on that of faith, love and purity *produce* it. Faith may be justified by reason without originating in it, just as reason may analyze motives without itself being a motive. Logical proofs are made for us by the nature of the mind; proofs of faith we must make for ourselves in the course of our struggle towards a holier life; faith arises out of the hunger and thirst after righteousness, and is part of its blessedness.

> A mutilated and defective evidence suffices for persuasion where the heart is alive; but dead evidences, however perfect, can but create a dead faith.[29]

Newman, feeling this theme to be vital to his defense of the believing temper in an unbelieving age, devoted very great attention to the process whereby "probabilities" are transmuted by faith into certainties. In the *University Sermons* he had already indicated his position, but the final distillation of his thought is to be found in the *Grammar of Assent* (1870). I do not propose to analyze this closely wrought book in any detail; it must suffice to indicate briefly how the earlier ideas are there developed. The main theme of the work is that religious truth is "proved," not by scientific demonstration, but by an accumulation of probabilities "sufficient for certitude." Even in matters of science and of everyday life we can and must assent to certain strong probabilities on evidence short of demonstration; in religion this is not only inevitable but essential.

> As in mathematics we are justified by the dictate of nature in withholding our assent from a conclusion of which we have not yet a strict logical demonstration, so by a like dictate we are not justified, in the case of concrete reasoning and especially of religious enquiry, in waiting till such logical demonstration is ours, but on the contrary

> are bound in conscience to seek truth and to look for certainty by modes of proof which, when reduced to the shape of formal propositions, fail to satisfy the severe requisitions of science."[30]

The distinction between "notional" and "real" assents, which is elaborated at the outset, corresponds to Keats's distinction between "axioms of philosophy" before and after they have been "proved upon the pulses," and to D. H. Lawrence's distinction between mental knowledge which is scientific—knowledge in terms of "apartness," and religious or poetic knowledge, which is knowledge in terms of "togetherness." The world of notions is "the dry and sterile little world the abstracted mind inhabits"; it is the world of catchwords, clichés, and unexamined assumptions—"progress," "liberalism," "civilization," "justification by faith only," "private judgment," "the Bible and nothing but the Bible." Most religion in England now, says Newman, is mere notional assent, and involves little beyond correct behavior, pious sentiments and a decent reverence for "sacred scenes." It is one thing, then, to accept a notion, and quite another thing to realize a fact; one thing to "acquiesce in an abstract truth," and quite another to give it "practical expression" in action. A "real" assent is one which is "felt in the heart, and felt along the blood," one which affects the imagination, and impels the will towards relevant action. Notional demonstrations cannot produce these results, and real assents therefore—religious beliefs above all—cannot be their outcome. Religious assent has always been enjoined upon us by revelation or by authority: "it never has been a deduction from what we know; it has ever been an assertion of what we are to believe."[31] It cannot be too emphatically stated, however, that Newman builds revealed religion upon the foundation of natural religion; the primary assumptions of religion are supplied by the Conscience. In our awareness of right and wrong, of good and bad, of a higher and a lower quality of living, in our sense of sin and failure, in our sense of obligation, in our yearnings after deliverance and a holier life—here, and not in brittle reasonings, lie the materials for a *real* apprehension of a Divine Sovereign and Judge. This apprehension is independent of Revelation or dogma; it is independent of theological formulations. That is not to say that dogma and theology are superfluous; on the contrary, being the intellectual expressions of religious experience, they strengthen and define it: "devotion falls back upon dogma as its intellectual stay." Theology is the notional formulation of what the experience seems to mean; "the firmest hold of theological truths," accordingly, "is gained by habits of personal religion." It is here that Newman makes the transition from natural to revealed religion, a transition rendered imperative for him by his wider vision of human nature in its fallen state, by his sombre and tragic view of our weakness and sinfulness. Conscience, the inner witness, can become feeble through neglect, and almost fade away; on the other hand, it can be strengthened and illuminated. Starting from the belief in God, we are predisposed to assent to the probability that God will have provided some extraordinary means to redeem us, and to define and clarify the dim conception of Himself which is all that Nature affords. The probability that a revelation has been vouchsafed deepens into certainty when, obedient to the heavenly intimation, we advance further and further towards sanctity.

> If religion is to be devotion, and not a mere matter of sentiment, if it is to be made the ruling principle of our lives, if our actions, one by one, and our daily conduct, are to be consistently directed towards an Invisible Being, we need something higher than a balance of arguments to fix and to control our minds. Sacrifice of wealth, name, or position, faith and hope, self-conquest, communion with the spiritual world, presuppose a real hold and habitual intuition of the objects of Revelation, which is certitude under another name.[32]

A real assent to the truths of natural religion, then, will lead to a real assent to those of revealed religion, and our sense of probability, our "illative" sense (which judges degrees of truth), will further lead us to acknowledge the Church to which, under His divine guidance, God has committed the tasks of preserving and interpreting the revelation. To reach this ultimate certainty, and the "triumphant repose" which it brings, we have but to begin obeying conscience; if we persevere—one step at a time—the kindly light will lead us on.

In this rejection, then, of the flimsy evidences which had satisfied a more superficial age, and in this disclosure of a deeper and firmer foundation for religious faith, Newman was carrying on the main, the vital task of the nineteenth century, the work which had been begun by Coleridge. Its importance can be appreciated even by those who cannot admit its necessary connection with the Catholic system with which, for Newman, it was all of a piece. We have seen how, in Newman's thought, assent to the dictates of conscience led on towards Catholic dogma. The pattern of this development is repeated, with even greater clarity of outline, in the life of his disciple W. G. Ward, and for this reason—but also because Ward moved from Arnoldism to Newmanism, and thus links our previous chapter with this—I will conclude with a few allusions to his biography.[33]

Ward (1812–1882), though not a Rugbeian, had in early life been deeply impressed by Arnold's high ethical earnestness, by this unworldiness, and by the note of reality in all his words and works. Arnoldism, "by its rejection or disparagement of all in religion which did not directly tend to bring the soul nearer to God and farther from sin," was to Ward a "wholesome antidote" to two kinds of formalism: the old Protestant religion of respectability, and the new romantic "antiquarianism." He trusted Arnold as a man of higher moral perception than himself. But Arnold was touched by the spirit of "free enquiry," and Ward soon began to ask himself how much doctrine would free enquiry really support? how much would it leave undamaged? He began to attend Newman's Oxford sermons, and the very first one he heard changed his life. He became convinced that the answer to his question was, *None*.

> When as time went on he came to feel that that very *minimum* of doctrine which was necessary as a support and sanction to the moral law must fade away before the consistent application of the latitudinarian intellectual principles, the question presented itself: May there not be after all some indissoluble connection between the plentitude of doctrine and the highest morality?[34]

Might not Church authority be a necessary, and a divinely appointed, external embodiment and safeguard of conscience? The principles of free enquiry and private judgment falsely assume that belief is the outcome of a balancing of pros and cons. Moreover, the Protestants, who claim this liberty, do not consistently employ it; they leave their own positions unexamined; they shrink from German biblical criticism; they fail to see that their arguments against Rome would, if rigorously applied, undermine their own faith, and probably theism itself. The true genesis of religious belief, as Newman taught Ward to see it, was in obedience to conscience:

> Obedience comes first, knowledge afterwards. It is by being pure in heart that we see God, not by seeing God that we become pure in heart. . . . He who learns the truth from argument or mere trust in men may lose it again by argument or by trust in men; but he who learns it by obedience can lose it only by disobedience.[35]

But we need an external guide to correct our private idiosyncrasies: we need the funded wisdom of the ages to give us the true sense of Scripture, we need a visible symbol of the unseen world—the unseen world which, alas! so often and so easily fades into seeming unreality. "An unseen Church would be a very sorry antagonist against so very visible a world." Ward read Froude's *Remains* in 1838, and noted with approval its clarity and above all its *thoroughness*; Froude, as we have seen, was not afraid of inferences. Arnoldism, by contrast, seemed to "stop short"; like the Protestantism of which it was a typical product, it took the first steps towards belief, but shrank from its "plenitude." It could accept the Incarnation, and the mystery of the Trinity, but not the developments of these doctrines— not the Eucharist, not the priesthood, not saints, not angels. Arnold substituted Porson and Hermann for the "prophetical office of the Church," and in interpreting Scripture he relied, not on Church tradition, but on his own private intuitions. Gradually, then, and especially as the storm over Tract xc moved to its climax, Ward began to see the whole corpus of Catholic doctrine and practice, not only as an organic and legitimate development from the origins which Protestantism also acknowledged, but as a necessary *succedaneum* to the spiritual life.

> "The more a person feels his deficiency in the apprehension of unseen things," he wrote to Pusey, "the more painfully he feels the want of "so consoling and impressive" an image of a visible Church, as even Rome displays; the more difficult he finds his contest with his old nature; the more he regrets that he has not been trained from the first in regular confession; the more he misses the practical rules of conduct in which Roman books of devotion abound, drawn from the stores, which they have retained, of traditional teaching; the more he misses the guidance of a priest carefully trained with a view to the confessional."[36]

In his book *The Ideal of a Christian Church* (1844), published the year before he entered the Roman Catholic Church (a book which has been called "Tract xc writ large"), Ward gave systematic expression to the insights he had by then attained. The aim of the Church is the personal sanctification and salvation of each believer; now, in the Church of England the general standard of Christian attainment was lamentably low. Moreover, the spirit of questioning and the reliance on private judgment, set in motion by Protestantism, lead eventually to scepticism; contemporary unbelief was implicit in the Reformation, and for this the only antidote is in Catholic principles. Existing religions, however, must be saved, not destroyed. How? by returning to fundamentals, and building up the Catholic life thereon. The starting-point with Ward, as with Newman, is the appeal to the facts of our moral experience; religious truth may be brought to life again by realizing its indissoluble connection with moral truth. The category "ought"—Kant's "Thou Shalt"—is a primary fact of our consciousness as moral beings; this sense of unconditional obligation, which is present with us all, points beyond ourselves to a region infinitely higher than the sensible world, and informs us of an unseen reality, the objective source of the moral imperative. An earnest man will cultivate an attitude of faith in this unseen reality; he will give "watchful and reverent attention" to the voice of conscience. This attitude of faith is distinguished from the Evangelical "sense of assurance"; the latter is passive and subjective, while the former involves effort to do God's will. In opposition to Luther, Ward argues that moral effort *has* intrinsic worth, and that the function of revealed religion is to develop, not to abrogate or supersede, natural religion. He finds in the Catholic Church this natural fulfillment; its credentials are established, above all, by its superior standards of sanctity. These insights lead the enquirer to expect

> some home in which this moral reality may have a secure rest and lodgment,[37]

and he will be inclined to seek this where there are Unity, Sanctity, Catholicity, Apostolicity. "The saints of the Church are the greatest witnesses to her divinity."

Wilfrid Ward, reviewing this argument, indicates as follows what is for us its most significant note:

> Religious belief is nowhere allowed to be normally the result of the impartial review of certain considerations, but is uniformly maintained to depend finally upon an insight given by a special course of action.[38]

We may round this off by a quotation from W. G. Ward himself—it is a deliverance which might well have come from Coleridge (or Kant):

> Knowledge of phenomena is obtained by the intellect, knowledge of realities by the conscience; knowledge of phenomena by inquiry, knowledge of reality by obedience. . . . the one pursuit tends to pride, the other indispensably requires and infallibly increases humility.[39]

Critics of the Oxford Movement, then as now, attended too exclusively to its "objectionable" and "Romanizing" manifestations, and failed to appreciate that the "Catholicity" of men like Newman and Ward was no piece of fastidious or wanton Romanticism, but an organic outgrowth from their searching critique of religious foundations. After even so perfunctory a hearing as we have here allowed these men, how woefully superficial seem the strictures of Arnold or Stanley!

> A dress, a ritual, a name, a ceremony . . . objects so pitiful that if gained ever so completely they would make no man the wiser or the better. [Arnold]

> It is curious to look back upon the trivial elements which produced so much excitement. . . . The apostolical succession, the revival of obsolete rubrics, together with one or two Patristic tendencies, such as the doctrine of reserve and of mysticism, were the staple of their teaching.
>
> [Stanley][40]

The fact is, on the contrary, that Newman and Ward, led by a profound spiritual instinct, placed religion on a surer basis than any afforded by scriptural fundamentalism or evangelical "assurance." The perennial strength of Catholicism was never more strikingly displayed than when, by-passing the new scriptural criticism and forestalling scientific agnosticism, it showed itself—what popular Protestantism in general certainly was not—invulnerable to both. "Religious belief is nowhere allowed to be normally the result of the impartial review of certain considerations"—to take up this ground was indeed to perfect strength in weakness; it was indeed to steal the enemy's thunder: for the impossibility of extracting religion out of "candid" enquiry on the level of reason was the commonest topic of unbelievers. To the other part of their teaching, that the moral foundation must needs sustain a Catholic superstructure, that the path of consistent sanctity must inevitably lead to Rome, a non-Catholic cannot accord the same praise. The fascination, the compulsive power of Rome were and are irresistible exactly in proportion to the weakness or degeneracy of alternative disciplines. Others than Catholics could learn, and learn from Catholicism itself, to ground their faith upon "an insight given by a special course of action"; to deserve, by purity of heart, the vision of God. They could, and can, do this without ceasing to honour, and even to envy, those to whom the Catholic solution is *not* "frankly impossible."

Notes

[1] Cardinal Newman, *Difficulties Felt by Anglicans in Catholic Teaching* (London, 1850), p. 86.

[2] Cardinal Newman, "State of Religious Parties," *British Critic,* XXV (April, 1839), 395 ff.

[3] *Ibid.*, p. 419.

[4] The phrase is Dean Stanley's.

[5] Cardinal Newman, *Apologia* (London, 1913), p. 121. (References are to Everyman edition.)

[6] Hurrell Froude, *Remains,* I (London, 1838), 404.

[7] *Ibid.*, p. 433.

[8] *Apologia,* pp. 180–181.

[9] *Ibid.*, p. 63.

[10] Froude, *Remains,* p. 395.

[11] *Ibid.*, p. 302.

[12] *Ibid.*, p. 389.

[13] *Ibid.*, pp. 394–395.

[14] *Ibid.*, p. xxiii (Preface).

[15] *Ibid.*, p. xxi.

[16] Newman, *Difficulties,* pp. 97–99.

[17] *Apologia,* p. 190

[18] Newman, *Difficulties,* p. 20.

[19] *Ibid.*, pp. 71–72.

[20] *Ibid.*, p. 80.

[21] *Ibid.*, p. 81.

[22] *Life of F. D. Maurice,* I, p. 17.

[23] Hugh Rose's phrase about R. H. Froude.

[24] *Apologia,* pp. 215 ff.

[25] A. P. Stanley, "The Oxford School," *Edinburgh Review,* CLIII (April, 1881), 309.

[26] H. F. Davis, "Was Newman a Disciple of Coleridge?" *Dublin Review* (October, 1945), 171.

[27] *Oxford University Sermons* (London, 1872), p. 59.

[28] *Ibid.*, p. 194.

[29] *Ibid.*, p. 200.

[30] Cardinal Newman, "An Essay in Aid of a Grammar of Assent," *Grammar of Assent* (London, 1870), p. 407.

[31] *Ibid.*, p. 93.

[32] *Ibid.*, p. 230.

[33] Wilfrid Ward, *W. G. Ward and the Oxford Movement* (London, 1890).

[34] *Ibid.*, p. 74.

[35] *Ibid.*, p. 77.

[36] *Ibid.*, p. 183.

[37] *Ibid.*, p. 259.

[38] *Ibid.*, p. 257.

[39] *Ibid.*, p. 258.

[40] *Ibid.*, p. 374.

27.

Charles Richard Sanders

Lytton Strachey's Conception of Biography

"Human beings are too important to be treated as mere symptoms of the past. They have a value which is independent of any temporal processes—which is eternal, and must be felt for its own sake." These two sentences, embedded in the well-known Preface to *Eminent Victorians,* must always be the starting point and a constant point of reference in any discussion of Strachey's conception of biography. The basis of all good biography must be, he firmly held, the humanistic respect for men—men in their separateness as distinct from lower creatures and in their separateness apart from economical, political, ethical, and religious theories; men in their separateness as distinct from one another, men as individuals, various, living, free. It has been well said that Strachey wrote with "a glowing conviction that character is the one thing that counts in life" and with a realization that individual human beings, however simple they may appear, are enigmatical, complex, and compact of contending elements.[1] Each person carries his secret within him, and the biographer is one who has the gift for discerning what it is.[2] Hence individual human beings are not only highly important; they are also highly interesting. The puzzle which the biographer has to solve in dealing with ordinary people is fascinating enough; but when the subject is a great man, the biographer works with his problem in an atmosphere of intense excitement, for about all great men there is something wondrous and incredible.[3]

Reprinted by permission of the author and the Modern Language Association of America from *PMLA,* Vol. 66, No. 4 (June, 1951), 295–315.

To lose interest in human beings and the sense of their importance was to Strachey a sure sign of literary decadence, not merely in the biographer, but in the novelist and dramatist as well. Fanny Burney could have become a much greater novelist if she had not turned away from an honest treatment of characters in order to give her attention to various other matters which had engaged her interest.[4] And it was a great pity that Shakespeare's later plays, full of glorious poetry as they were, revealed this same kind of decadence. In them, the dramatist turned his back on "the stupendous creations in character" in his great tragedies and contented himself with a method in which character served merely as a "miserable prop" for the "gorgeous clothing of his rhetoric."[5] He allowed words, which had been his servants, to dominate him completely. "Shakespeare, certainly, knew what he was doing; and yet, in the end, those little creatures were too much for him. . . . In Shakespeare's later works character has grown unindividual and unreal; drama has become conventional or operatic; the words remain more tremendously, more exquisitely alive than ever—the excuse and the explanation of the rest. The little creatures had absolutely fascinated their master; he had become their slave."[6] On the other hand, when the reader discovered the real thing—individual human character—there could be no doubt in his mind about its relative importance: " . . . what makes Sterne immortal is not his sentiment, nor his indecency, not asterisks, but his Mr. Shandy and his Uncle Toby."[7]

Only art could show a Mr. Shandy, an Uncle Toby, a Hamlet, or an Iago active and alive on the printed page or in the theater. Only art could make "created" or imaginary characters live before us. Moreover, and the fact had been too often overlooked, only art could make real people who had once lived, who had had their place in time, awaken and become alive again for us to see. Only art could show us what they had really been in their very essence. History, therefore, was art. And biography was art—"the most delicate and humane of all the branches of the art of writing."[8] What Strachey has said about history can be applied with equal force to his conception of biography. "It is obvious that History is not a science: it is obvious that History is not the accumulation of facts, but the relation of them. Only the pedantry of incomplete academic persons could have given birth to such a monstrous supposition."[9] The biographer must so exercise his art that he will convince the reader that he understands the motives of his characters and "the actual conditions of their lives." "No study of a man can be successful unless it is vital; a portrait-painter who cannot makes his subject live has very little reason for putting brush to canvas."[10]

There are plenty of examples in English of how *not* to practice the art of biography. Some of these were older works; others were new ones which Strachey came to grips with as a reviewer for the *Spectator* and other journals in the years from 1903 onward. Such works convinced him that England was very much in need of a great biographical tradition like that of the French. "The art of biography seems to have fallen on evil times in England. We have had, it is true, a few masterpieces, but we have never had, like the French, a great biographical tradition."[11] The seventeenth-century Samuel Butler's characters, for instance, "after the manner of Theophrastus," were "curiously unreal to us, and this effect is heightened by his method of vituperative caricature. . . . And, in addition, their very wealth of matter proves a stumbling block. The mind is overburdened by the serried succession of ideas, the immense accumulation of images."[12]

Edmund Gosse's biography of Sir Thomas Browne had the very great merit of an entertaining style but suffered from two major faults: failure to adhere to a proper principle of selection and lack of a clearly defined point of view. Browne's works were not the kind which, if they were to be understood, required the biography of the author as a commentary. Browne was very much unlike Byron in this respect. "The Glasgow merchant who read through *Don Juan* and asked at the end whether the author was a married man was surely in need of some enlightenment."[13] But for writers like Browne "it is sufficient to know that they have lived."[14] Gosse's book, therefore, "would have gained if it had told us a little more about Sir Thomas's style and a little less about his sons." And, unfortunately, "Mr. Gosse is apparently so anxious to be impartial, to look at things from every point of view," that it is at times difficult to discover his own point of view.[15]

Strachey found G. C. Macaulay's *James Thomson* much

longer than the subject justified and faulty in its style. "Most readers will probably be of opinion that Messrs. Macmillan have been a little overgenerous in allowing to James Thomson, the author of 'The Seasons,' a place in their well-known series of representative 'English Men of Letters.' Thomson was certainly not a great poet. . . . Nor is there anything worthy of particular record in the history of his life, which passed, without incident and without romance, in easy independence among congenial friends and patrons. It can hardly be doubted that a concise writer could say all that need be said upon the subject of Thomson in a magazine article of a dozen pages." And even if such length were deserved, Macaulay's style, which consisted of "copious paraphase interspersed with copious quotation," was certainly not a happy one.[16]

Strachey's review of Andrew Lang's *Sir Walter Scott,* published in the *Speaker,* 20 October 1906, was almost savage. Not anyone's reputation, he said, could be enhanced by Lang's book. Lang seemed to have brought "neither care, nor diligence, nor attention" to his work. His style was slovenly, "shapeless and invertebrate stuff." And the whole book was filled with "a mass of affectation which would have made Scott's gorge rise."[17]

George Paston's biography *Lady Mary Wortley Montagu and Her Times* had some of the same faults—and others. Strachey deplored "its slipshod writing, its uninstructed outlook, its utter lack of taste and purpose." It was a "bulky" book, "unwieldy and pretentious." It was "a fair specimen of the kind of biographical work which seems to give so much satisfaction to large numbers of our reading public. Decidedly, 'they order the matter better in France,' where such a production could never have appeared."[18]

Such a work as H. Noel Williams' *The Women Bonapartes,* in two volumes, was simply dull.[19] And Austin Brereton's *The Life of Henry Irving,* also in "two large volumes," with its superficiality, its unreality, its failure to evaluate its materials, its eulogistic tone, and its complete lack of psychological insight, could provide an excellent object lesson in how biography should not be written.

> . . . the interest of these two large volumes lies almost entirely in their record of outward facts; and the result is that,

> to the ordinary reader, they can hardly fail to be disappointing. Mr. Brereton has made no serious attempt to draw a picture of the man. He has been content to fill out his work with an immense number of quotations from contemporary Press notices—quotations which, curious though they may be as documents in the history of taste, throw only a confused light upon Irving's artistic methods, and produce an atmosphere of superficiality which strikes the reader as altogether out of place in a biography intended to be definitive. Indeed, the total impression made by the book is not only singularly superficial but singularly unreal. As one turns over Mr. Brereton's pages, one finds oneself transported into a strange world of limelight, attitudes, splendor, and endless applause,—a world all scarlet carpets and waving palms and lovely ladies, where after-dinner speeches are the only form of utterance, and nothing is drunk except champagne. The very headlines of the chapters form a kind of triumphant procession—"Tribute of the Press," "Chicago Conquered," "A Great Reception," "Compliments Galore," "A Brilliant Audience," "A Memorable Season," "An Honor from Germany," "Appears at Archbishop's House"—the mind grows bewildered by the catalogue. "The supper was a very elaborate affair," etc. But, if we are to believe Mr. Brereton, the supper always was very elaborate, the guests always the most distinguished, and every moment proud. One looks in vain for a record of intellectual effort and development, for expressions of noble thought or profound feeling, for any of those manifestations of original and unmistakable genius which occur so often in the private lives of truly great men. It almost seems as if the stage had crossed the footlights and enveloped the whole of Irving's existence, so that the best account of it was in truth to be found in the contemporary notices of the Press[20]

In the Preface to *Eminent Victorians* Strachey gave a clear and concise summary of the faults which he had found in many English biographies:

> . . . we have had no Fontenelles and Condorcets, with their incomparable *éloges*, compressing into a few shining pages the manifold existences of men. With us, the most delicate

> and humane of all the branches of the art of writing has been relegated to the journeymen of letters; we do not reflect that it is perhaps as difficult to write a good life as to live one. Those two fat volumes, with which it is our custom to commemorate the dead—who does not know them, with their ill-digested masses of material, their slipshod style, their tone of tedious panegyric, their lamentable lack of selection, of detachment, of design? They are as familiar as the *cortège* of the undertaker, and wear the same air of slow, funereal barbarism. . . . To preserve, for instance, a becoming brevity—a brevity which excludes everything that is redundant and nothing that is significant—that, surely, is the first duty of the biographer. The second, no less surely, is to maintain his own freedom of spirit. It is not his business to be complimentary; it is his business to lay bare the facts of the case, as he understands them. That is what I have aimed at in this book—to lay bare the facts of some cases, as I understand them, dispassionately, impartially, and without ulterior intentions.

Modern English biographers could learn much, Strachey believed, not only from Fontenelle and Condorcet, but from other writers, French, English, and even Russian, and from some writers who were not biographers. The study which Strachey made of Racine, reflected in the brilliant essay published in the *New Quarterly* for June 1908, was of incalculable value in preparing him to be a biographer. In Racine's plays he found three of the qualities which he admired most in biography: an unfailing sense of reality, selection made in accordance with true judgment, and psychological insight of a very high order. Racine's art might be declared "the sublimed essence of reality, save that, after all, reality has no degrees." It was as a psychologist that Racine had achieved his most remarkable triumphs; his concern had been primarily with "the mystery of the mind of man." It provided him with a principle of selection. "Every art is based upon a selection, and the art of Racine selected the things of the spirit for the material of its work. . . . When Racine is most himself, when he is seizing upon a state of mind and depicting it with all its twistings and vibrations, he writes with a directness which is indeed naked, and his sentences, refined to the utmost point of significance, flash out like swords, stroke upon stroke, swift, certain, irresistible."[21]

Saint-Simon was likewise one from whom Strachey was willing to learn much. In him a concentrated psychological insight and a rare vitalizing power were associated with great skill in selection. "It is upon the inward creature that he expends his most lavish care—upon the soul that sits behind the eyelids, upon the purpose and the passion that linger in a gesture or betray themselves in a word. The joy that he takes in such description soon infects the reader. . . . Nor in spite of the virulence of his method, do his portraits ever sink to the level of caricatures. His most malevolent exaggerations are yet so realistic that they carry conviction. . . . he never forgot, in the extremity of his ferocity, to commit the last insult, and to breathe into their nostrils the fatal breath of life."[22] There is certainly much here to suggest Strachey's own biographical method. Strachey had great admiration for Clarendon, "who had the advantage of drawing from the life," as a prose portrait-painter but, even so, maintained that "his fine and sympathetic studies" fell far below "the fiery presentments of Saint-Simon" and "the brilliant profiles of La Bruyère."[23]

Among English biographers not only Clarendon but also John Aubrey deserved praise. Brief biography was not the only kind, as Boswell had clearly demonstrated, but Aubrey had shown early what could be done through the art of brevity. "He was accurate, he had an unfailing eye for what was interesting, and he possessed—it was almost inevitable in those days—a natural gift of style. . . . A biography should either be as long as Boswell's or as short as Aubrey's. The method of enormous and elaborate accretion which produced the *Life of Johnson* is excellent, no doubt; but, failing that, let us have no half-measures; let us have the pure essentials—a vivid image, on a page or two, without explanations, transitions, commentaries, or padding. This is what Aubrey gives us."[24]

As for Boswell himself and as for Johnson the biographer, from the beginning to the end of his life Strachey found them both irresistible. No greater mistake could be made than to assume that Strachey rebelled against the Boswellian conception of biography or against Boswell's methods. It was not Boswell that he objected to; it was the Boswellian technique after it had fallen into the less skillful hands of those who had perverted it—into the hands of those who wrote the wearisome "two fat volumes" in the nineteenth and early twentieth centuries. But Boswell—and Johnson—were a perennial delight. "No one needs an excuse for re-opening the *Lives of the Poets;* the book is too delightful. It is not, of course, as delightful as Boswell; but who reopens Boswell? Boswell is in another category; because, as every one knows, when he has once been opened he can never be shut."[25] In *The Life of Johnson* there was to be found something which no mere compilation of facts possessed, "Boswellian artistry . . . that power of selection and evocation which clothes its object with something of the palpable reality of life."[26]

Strachey also admired Lockhart's *Life of Scott* and Carlyle's portraits from life.[27] Possibly he was impressed by the detachment and the slight suggestion of irony in Froude's treatment of the Carlyles. He certainly disapproved of Alexander Carlyle's angry references to Froude and stood ready to defend Froude's right to exercise his freedom of spirit.[28] Edmund Gosse's unsigned "The Character of Queen Victoria," published in the *Quarterly Review* in April 1901, only two or three months after the Queen's death, had not only skillful selection and good style but also remarkable objectivity in the light of its date. The footnotes of Strachey's *Queen Victoria* significantly contain a number of references to this article. Gosse's *Father and Son* (1907) also had qualities which Strachey admired: judicious selection, a definite point of view, and an excellent style. Like Strachey, Gosse kept before his eyes the best French models of biography. Strachey knew Gosse in later years and did not greatly respect him. He believed that Gosse was too often careless in his handling of facts. It is possible, however, that Strachey owed more to Gosse than he himself realized.[29]

It is certain that he admired greatly and owed much to the great Russian novelist Dostoyevsky. He read Constance Garnett's translations of *The Brothers Karamazov, The Idiot,* and *The Possessed* when they were published in 1912 and 1914 and reviewed them in the *Spectator*. Strachey's taste was never exclusively classical, and his enthusiasm was almost unbounded for Dostoyevsky's rich, Gothic complexity, his genius for filling his pages with concentrated, burning human passion, and his psychological profundity. He was amazed at "the wonderful intensity and the subtlety of Dostoyevsky's psychological insight" and declared, "Here, no doubt, lies the central essence of his genius."[30]

There was at least one early twentieth-century biography in two large volumes to which Strachey gave high praise. It was Logan Pearsall Smith's *The Life and Letters of Sir Henry Wotton,* which he reviewed in the *Spectator* for 23 November 1907. Here was a copious work abounding in good things. In it were to be found fresh and significant materials which Smith by diligent research had unearthed "among the manuscript collections of our great country houses." Smith's and Issac Walton's lives of Wotton supplemented one another neatly. Smith gave the facts; Walton "preserved all the fragrance of the subject and very few of the facts." But Smith's work was no mere compilation of facts; his pages, "in spite of the weight of learning at the back of them, are eminently readable, for they are full of stirring narrative and vivid description, and they are informed throughout with a sympathy and a distinction such as it is a rare pleasure to find." The review, one of Strachey's best, provides clear evidence that Smith's biography made Wotton live for Strachey, for in it Strachey sketches Wotton's life and character with an economy, a sharpness, and an eye for the picturesque detail which suggest his later profiles.[31]

The survey which we have made above of Strachey's pronouncements concerning various faulty and admirable biographies leaves little doubt as to what characteristics he believed the good biography should have. It should be based on the facts. It should be art, with judicious selection, good structure, and good style. It should make its subject live again before the eyes of the reader. It should be written from a definite point of view. It must be the product of a free mind, bound only by considerations of impartiality and justice. And, as to length, it must be either long or short; it must either use the Boswellian art which produced a life-size portrait, or it must use the art of brevity, the art of the profile. The two arts must be kept separate: to try to find the halfway ground between the two was to court disaster.

To what extent did Strachey realize his ideal in his own

biographies? With regard to part of the answer his readers have been in agreement. They have agreed that both the longer and the shorter works have been highly readable, with excellent style, proportion, and structure. They have agreed that the author has consistently dominated his materials, maintained his own point of view, and exercised his own freedom of mind and spirit. They have agreed too that Strachey possessed a rare gift for breathing life into his subjects.

When one pauses for a moment to consider just how Strachey succeeded in making his subjects live again, one cannot avoid noting his strong preference for the dramatic method and the consistency and skill with which he used it. It should be noted that throughout his life he was writing not only biographies but also poems and plays, most of which are still preserved in manuscript. He took delight in writing dramatic criticism, in seeing plays, in acting in them. Virginia Woolf has gone so far as to say that his biographies are the product of a frustrated dramatist.[32] Possibly so, but if so his unusual interest in the drama and the marked degree to which the dramatic instinct was developed in him served him well as a biographer. For in Strachey's conception of biography the subject is not merely written about. Rather, the main character and all those persons significantly related to him are quick once more and act out again the various roles which life had formerly assigned to them. But although they are alive and active, they are now confined within the framework of art—art which excludes all the irrelevances, discerns and emphasizes whatever is truly significant, and controls the behavior of all those on the stage. Edwin Muir has discussed well the skill with which Strachey transferred the dramatic method to the purposes of literary biography:

> He went out in search not of great figures and noble characters, but of human nature, and he always found it. Having found it, he set it out in his own terms. All his characters passed through his eighteenth-century workshop, and emerged in the ironically appropriate costumes he had devised for them. They emerged, if not in their own shape, then in some shape which revealed it. For the time being their author's puppets, they played over again the game which they had played far more intensely, sometimes in

> tears and agony, in the actual world. Mr. Strachey held the strings which moved this puppet play, and they were constantly being manipulated, but very rarely did we catch sight of them. The figures seemed to be going through the ballet of their own lives, a ballet simplified and stylized to the last detail; and it was only in the conventionalization of the costumes and attitudes that one recognized the choreographer.[33]

But Strachey's characters, stylized though they may be, are not mere puppets in a dumbshow; they talk. And the words which they utter are, in the main, the very words which they once said or wrote. As important as their actions are, it is through their words that we get to know them best. Strachey believed that people in actual life may be reasonably successful in concealing their real nature as long as they do not talk. But let them once open their mouths, and soon we know them for what they are—know far more than they wished to reveal and usually far more than they realize that they have revealed.[34] It is thus with the characters in Strachey's biographies. Their own words, skillfully selected and put in quotation marks, betray them and become a mocking echo of what they really were.

The question remains as to whether Strachey in making his characters live again and in compelling them to re-enact their lives on a stage of his own devising was able to deal with them in accordance with his own ideal of justice and in accordance with the accepted biographical facts. The prerogative of selection which was necessary to him as a literary artist was one certain to throw temptations in the way of anyone who exercised it. Did he succeed in resisting the temptations? Those who have attacked him during his lifetime and later say that he did not.

One such critic was Sir Edmund Gosse. Although it is true that, roughly classified, Gosse and Strachey both belong to the school of biography which reacted against the Victorians, Gosse found *Eminent Victorians* in general and its portrait of Lord Cromer in particular too much for him. Only a few weeks after Strachey's book appeared, he wrote a letter of protest to the *Times Literary Supplement.* In it he conceded that the book had been received "publicly and privately with a chorus of praise" and that the author possessed "wit and vigor." But he regretted that Strachey had used his gifts in "a pyrotechnical display of satire. He reduces the demigods of our youth to the Gog and Mogog of Bartholmy Fair. It is very amusing, and gratifying to those who grudge the dead their prestige. But even what is sparkling should be just. The late Lord Cromer is the object (among others) of Mr. Strachey's sardonic humor, and as Mr. Strachey is being accepted as an oracle, Lord Cromer's friends can but expostulate." Strachey's representation of Cromer was "a caricature, and not a good-natured one . . . our friend is hardly to be recognized." Furthermore, Strachey was unfair to indicate that Cromer was ignorant of the East in his efforts to administer colonial affairs, for actually there was nothing in which Cromer took more interest than in the East. Gosse admitted that Strachey wrote "with extreme ability and in a most attractive style" but warned, "It is therefore all the more important to check his statements before they are crystallized into history."[35]

In his prompt reply to this letter Strachey did not retreat one inch. Gosse, he said, had written as a friend of Cromer. He himself had made "a detached examination of Lord Cromer's published writings and public acts." Although Cromer may have talked with his friends intimately and confidentially, the evidence showed that "the temper" of his mind was "essentially secretive, cautious, and diplomatic." As for the East (and here Strachey must have been conscious of his own father and of generations of his family who in unbroken succession back to the time of Lord Clive had distinguished themselves in India), possibly Cromer had manifested an interest in Eastern administrative questions. "But Eastern administrative questions are not the East." In ending, he returned with additional emphasis to the importance of the principle of detachment in biography. "My description of Lord Cromer is not a full-length portrait; it is an incidental sketch of the Sir Evelyn Baring of 1884. Nobody could regret more than I do that it should seem to Mr. Gosse, and others of his friends, to be a bad likeness, but the fact in itself does not appear to be a sufficient reason for thinking that it is. Unfortunately, in this world, it is not always a man's friends who know him best."[36]

If Sir Edmund Gosse objected to Strachey's Lord Cromer, Miss Rosalind Nash in an article published in the *Nineteenth*

Century for February 1928 objected fully as much to his Florence Nightingale. Like Gosse, she insisted that her objection rested upon a basis of fact. She was, she said, very well acquainted with Sir Edward Cook's biography of Florence Nightingale, was herself conversant with Miss Nightingale's papers which Sir Edward had used in the life, and had also known Miss Nightingale, her parents, and other relatives, "I think I may say well, from my childhood in the 'sixties and 'seventies until their death." Then Miss Nash proceeded to give a fairly long list of errors which she had found in Strachey's work. We may note a few of them. The dog was not Florence's dog but the shepherd's, not a pet but a valuable working dog. Florence did not apply elaborate splints to it but ordinary hot-water fomentations. Further, "it is difficult to think of dainty Parthe 'tearing up dolls.'" Mr. Nightingale did not suggest that a husband might be advisable; the mother was the matchmaker. The room in which Florence Nightingale died was not gloomy; it was full of light. And as for Strachey's main point, not demoniac fury, but calm persuasiveness characterized Florence Nightingale. "Sir Edward Cook's *Life* disposed of the mythical figure, and left in its place a very human personality. But the *Life* was not for the many, and Mr. Strachey could not resist the temptation to go a step further. What fun, he seems to have said to himself, to turn the saint into a fiend! . . . Is the result biography?"[37]

Queen Victoria seems to have proved itself generally satisfactory to those who have insisted that biography should be entirely faithful to the facts. *Books and Characters*, as we have seen, with its studies of Racine and Beddoes, did much to give Strachey a reputation for directing attention to deserving writers who had been neglected and for rescuing important facts that had been forgotten. But with the publication of *Elizabeth and Essex* in 1928, there were new indictments of Strachey's scholarship. The most important of these was made by G. B. Harrison, an acknowledged authority in the field of Elizabethan history and literature. Harrison admired Strachey's portrait of the Queen herself; she "lives most vitally," he said. Strachey's Bacon, too, was praiseworthy—"dissected with especial skill." Essex he found much less convincing. Essex, he observed, was a man of action:

and Strachey did not understand him. Furthermore, Strachey failed to give the stories which he could have given to explain the great popularity of Essex. Neither did he show one very important side of Essex. "Essex was over-sensitive to laughter; and he often made himself ridiculous." Whereas Strachey indicated that Essex destroyed Lopez from a motive of patriotism, actually he destroyed him out of revenge: Lopez had once made the Queen and others laugh at him. Harrison questioned such suppressions and manipulations as "privileges denied to the pedestrian scholar." The bibliography at the end of the book, he added, was "disturbing to the creeping critic—the pedant—who reads such things; for it omits at least five of the most important sources for the life of Essex."[38]

Even André Maurois, who admired Strachey greatly and owed much to him, found him "in some instances a shade nastier than is really fair," and said that we sometimes get tired of "the plucking of dead lions by the beard."[39] Leonard Bacon has declared that Strachey was temperamentally unfitted to practice the art of the historian. "Unless truth was piquant or dramatic, unless a fact could be forced, by fair means or foul, into the strait jacket of his ironic preconception, or made to lend color to one of his superb imaginative paintings, he was fully capable of ignoring it, in favor of something more poignant and more legendary."[40] Edgar Johnson has likewise said that Strachey's "most reprehensible fault as a responsible biographer" was that he did not hesitate to manipulate either facts or documents to secure a more striking effect." According to Johnson, Douglas Southall Freeman in 1936 described Strachey as "one of the most pernicious influences in modern biography."[41]

On the other hand, Strachey's command over facts and respect for them have greatly impressed some of the commentators on him. Claude W. Fuess has described Strachey as "a scholar of remarkable industry, who examined sources with assiduity and discretion."[42] F. L. Lucas praised his "restraint and intellectual honesty" and spoke of him as one who "wrote fastidiously and little, but read enormously."[43] Some of Strachey's friends who knew him best say that he seemed to be reading constantly and that he almost always had a book in his hand.[44]

Undoubtedly, also, the long thesis which Strachey wrote at Cambridge between 1903 and 1905—a thesis dealing with extremely complicated and difficult questions concerning the charges against Warren Hastings—gave him valuable training in the techniques of historic research and a respect for the integrity of historic facts. It is noteworthy, furthermore, that throughout his life he battled for the principle of the uncorrupted text. It mattered not whether an editor's motive was to Bowdlerize or to improve by alteration, he had done what in Strachey's eyes was unpardonable if he had tampered with the text. When he himself in his last years edited the Greville *Memoirs,* most of the notes to which he completed before his death, he resisted every temptation to say spicy things in the footnotes. The spice, he seems to have assumed quite rightly, should all be Greville's. When he was reviewing an edition of Blake's poems as early as May 1906, he was unsparing in his condemnation of the editors, who, he said, had praised Blake's meter and then emended it. "This is Procrustes," Strachey wrote, "admiring the exquisite proportions of his victim." Blake's poems should have been left just as he wrote them; " . . . add a comma to the text of Blake, and you put all heaven in a rage."[45]

It cannot be maintained that Strachey admired scholarship but did not know what modern scholarship really was. One would be hard pressed to find a more clear and satisfactory statement of the nature of modern scholarship than Strachey gave in a passage dealing with the historian Mandell Creighton:

> Born when the world was becoming extremely scientific, he belonged to the post-Carlyle-and-Macaulay generation—the school of Oxford and Cambridge inquirers, who sought to reconstruct the past solidly and patiently, with nothing but facts to assist them—pure facts, untwisted by political or metaphysical bias and uncoloured by romance. In this attempt Creighton succeeded admirably. He was industrious, exact, clear-headed, and possessed of a command over words that was quite sufficient for his purposes. . . . In his work a perfectly grey light prevails everywhere; there is not a single lapse into psychological profundity; every trace of local colour, every suggestion of personal passion, has been studiously removed. In many ways all this is a great com-

> fort. One is not worried by moral lectures or purple patches, and the field is kept clear for what Creighton really excelled in—the lucid exposition of complicated political transactions, and the intricate movements of thought with which they were accompanied. The biscuit is certainly exceedingly dry; but at any rate there are no weevils in it.[46]

In the same spirit, shortly after the death of Sir Sidney Lee, Strachey commended his labors as editor of *The Dictionary of National Biography,* "one of the most useful books in existence, and the motto of which was: 'No flowers, by request.' "[47]

But the achievement of a Creighton or of a Sir Sidney Lee was far from adequate when tested in the terms of Strachey's ideal of history and biography. To him, true history and true biography must be art. And to be art they must deal with facts as they were interpreted and at times even transmuted by the imagination. Imaginative refraction, with its readjustment of line and its addition of color, was far different from mere willful distortion of fact. Strachey had far more in common with Macaulay than has perhaps been generally realized. He was greatly superior to Macaulay in intellectual subtlety and psychological insight; and although both used rhetoric, Strachey was much more successful than Macaulay in controlling rhetoric so that it would not become ostentatious. But, like Macaulay, he made errors of fact; he was very sure of his own mind and had very positive opinions; he disliked misty generalizations and philosophical obscurity; he read widely and constantly; and he studied and wrote history primarily for the sake of its appeal to the imagination. History and biography were for both drama with a story which marched, proudly and vigorously, and in which all the details were vivid, alive, significant. Macaulay spoke of the work of the historian being comparable to that, not of the ant, but of the bee. To Strachey also, history and biography were not the mere gathering of facts but, far better, a sweet distillation of their very essence.[48] It is significant that both held Thucydides in high admiration—Thucydides with his lucid order, his conciseness, his vividness, and his sure sense of the significant.

Actually, three years before he published his first book, Strachey stated the principle which would guide him in relating his scholarship to his art. He did so in his comments on Guglielmo Ferrero's *The Greatness and Decline of Rome,* which he reviewed for the *Spectator,* 2 January 1909:

> When Livy said that he would have made Pompey win the battle of Pharsalia if the turn of the sentence had required it, he was not talking utter nonsense, but simply expressing an important truth in a highly paradoxical way,—that the first duty of a great historian is to be an arist. The function of art in history is something much more profound than mere decoration; to regard it, as some writers persist in regarding it, as if it were the jam put around the pill of fact by cunning historians is to fall into grevious error; a truer analogy would be to compare it to the process of fermentation which converts a raw mass of grapejuice into a subtle and splendid wine. Uninterpreted truth is as useless as buried gold; and art is the great interpreter. It alone can unify a vast multitude of facts into a significant whole, clarifying, accentuating, suppressing, and lighting up the dark places with the torch of the imagination. More than that, it can throw over the historian's materials the glamor of a personal revelation, and display before the reader great issues and catastrophes as they appear, not to his own short sight, but to the penetrating vision of the most soaring of human spirits. That is the crowning glory of the greatest history—that of Thucydides, for instance, or Tacitus, or Gibbon; it brings us into communion with an immense intelligence, and it achieves this result through the power of art. Indeed, every history worthy of the name is, in its own way, as personal as poetry, and its value ultimately depends upon the force and the quality of the character behind it.[49]

But, remembering the strong objections of those who have insisted that some of Strachey's portraits do violence to the facts, one may still ask whether his conception of the art of biography is actually tenable and, from the point of view of the literary artist, practicable. The question is whether even the most gifted literary artist can have his cake and eat it too: can have his facts and still retain his personal point of view and his prerogative of exercising his own freedom of imagination and spirit. We know that he can in the drama and in the historical novel, for we remember Jonson's *Sejanus* and Thackeray's *Henry Esmond.* But we also remember Shakespeare's *Julius Caesar* and *Henry IV* and the novels of Scott, in which the dramatist and the novelist deal with facts very freely. May the biographer take the same liberties with facts as Shakespeare and Scott took? It is seriously to be doubted, for in history and biography facts are particularly stubborn, and rightly so. In them, facts are not subordinate to the purposes of art, as they may be in *Julius Caesar* and *Kenilworth,* but must be kept constantly in view as the solid substance of which art is the shaping and interpreting power. History and biography are the arts which master them but which preserve them in their proper integrity. It follows that they are extremely difficult arts. Strachey's main point was that to be mastered by the facts was not to write biography. He would certainly agree, on the other hand, that the biographer who has achieved art at the expense of the facts has failed to solve his problem. Did Strachey always succeed in solving it? Certainly not always, but the frequency with which he did succeed is remarkable when we consider the difficulty of his art in general and of some of his subjects in particular. He did succeed with his Manning and his Gordon, with almost all the portraits, both major and minor, in *Queen Victoria,* with such complex and difficult subjects as Cecil, Bacon, and the Queen in *Queen Elizabeth,* and with scores of other subjects which he has given us in delightful profiles. And where he has failed, he has simply failed, as I think he has with his "Dr. Arnold" and possibly with some of the other portraits which have been objected to. To admit as much is not to admit that his conception of biography was invalid but that he was not infallible as a literary artist. The real distinction of Lytton Strachey as a biographer is that he succeeded as often as he did and that his literary gifts were usually found working in close association with unusual learning.

One further point must be insisted upon. He wrote even his biographical failures as an artist, not as a reporter; and his works must be judged as portraits, not as photographs. A good photograph is a convincingly realistic copy; a good portrait has verisimilitude. A photograph which is not a likeness is altogether worthless; but a portrait may have a value independent of its subject. How much does it matter how faithfully Rembrandt represented his subjects or how closely Browning's portrait of the Lost Leader resembles Wordsworth? Strachey, however, aimed at verisimilitude and usually achieved it. Where he did not, he usually produced brilliant caricatures, as I think he did in his treatment of Dr. Arnold, Florence Nightingale, and Lord Cromer. And although Strachey aimed at portraiture rather than caricature, even unintentional caricature, if it is the work of an artist, may be worth something. Not only does the good caricature seize upon and emphasize through exaggeration the traits which the artist finds interesting and important, but it also has the great virtue of creating an interest in its subject and of arousing curiosity which may lead to investigation. Strachey's "Dr. Arnold" is both brilliant caricature and an invitation to read Stanley's biography of the Headmaster of Rugby. A highly intelligent friend of mine has made what I believe to be precisely the right approach to Strachey's "Florence Nightingale." She first read Strachey's treatment and found it delightful. She then read very carefully the sketch of Florence Nightingale in the *Dictionary of National Biography* and was greatly impressed by the difference between the impression that it made and that made by Strachey's work. Then she returned to Strachey and read him again—with even more pleasure than before.

Notes

[1] Arthur Waugh, "Mr. Lytton Strachey," a letter to the *Spectator,* CXLVIII (30 Jan. 1932), 146. John Russell's comment on Strachey in the following passage is excellent: "Other writers have used portraits to give pause to their narratives; but with Strachey the narrative is all portrait, and if we look into the eyes of his Voltaire or, more surprisingly, of his Prince Consort, we seem to see, reflected in their pupils, the gaze of their bland inquisitor. All the other facts of history are dimmed and thrust backward by this intense and continuous scrutiny of individuals."—"Lytton Strachey," *Horizon,* XV (February, 1947), 93.

[2] Preserved among Strachey's MSS are 88 numbered aphorisms which Strachey seems to have composed when he was still at Cambridge. Aphorism 32 reads: "The worst and best parts of us are the secrets we never reveal."

[3] The last clause is quoted almost verbatim from Strachey's Aphorism 63.

[4] "The Wrong Turning," *Independent* Rev., II (Feb. 1904), 169–73. In the same article Strachey objected to Burke's praise of the unreal characters in Fanny Burney's later novels: " . . . 'characters' Burke meant just what he should not have meant—descriptions, that is to say, of persons who might exist."

[5] "Shakespeare's Final Period," *Independent Rev.,* III (August, 1904), 405 ff.

[6] Strachey's Introd. to G. H. W. Rylands' *Words and Poetry,* rptd. in *Characters and Commentaries* (New York: Harcourt, Brace, 1933), p. 287.

[7] "The Wrong Turning." Strachey believed that Carlyle had many faults as a writer but that when he drew his "inimitable portrait-sketches" he was at his best: "Some New Carlyle Letters," *Spectator,* CII (10 April 1909), 577 ff. I have been able to identify this and a number of other unsigned reviews in the *Spectator* as Strachey's partly through the help of Mr. James Strachey, Lytton Strachey's brother and literary executor (who has very generously given me permission to quote from the unpublished MSS. and from these reviews, most of which have not been collected) and partly through access to the private file of the *Spectator* kindly granted to me by the present editor of that periodical, the Honorable H. Wilson Harris, M. P. For bibliographical information concerning the short writings which have been collected and some of the others, see my "A Chronological Check List of Lytton Strachey's Writings," *MP,* XLIV (February, 1947), 189–92.

[8] Preface to *Eminent Victorians.*

[9] "Gibbon," *Portraits in Miniature* (New York: Harcourt, Brace, 1931), p. 158.

[10] "The Italian Renaissance," *Spectator,* CI (21 November, 1908), 838 ff. "It was Mr. Strachey's distinction in reinstating biography as an art to draw attention to the formlessness of literature generally. He did this in common with writers very unlike him, for whom he could have had little sympathy: with such writers as Mr. Joyce and Mr. Eliot"—Edwin Muir, "Lytton Strachey," *Nation and Athenaeum,* XXXVII (25 April 1925), 102. " . . . if Strachey was to influence biographical art dangerously, at least his influence was deliberate, and not a chance bomb thrown on the highway by a lunatic. He knew perfectly well what he was about, and announced his intentions as clearly in his Preface as Milton in his Foreword to *Paradise Lost*"—Guy Boas, *Lytton Strachey,* English Association Pamphlet No. 93 (November, 1935), p. 10. When the University of Edinburgh awarded Strachey the Order of Merit in literature, 20 July 1926, the citation read in part: "Mr. Strachey has blazed a trail through the thicket of this crowded epoch for which every future explorer passing that way will have reason to thank him. He is eminently worthy of our Order of Merit in the department of letters, if only for restoring to the delectable but almost forgotten art of biography its proper style, proportion, and attitude."

[11] Preface to *Eminent Victorians.*

[12] "The Author of 'Hudibras'," *Spectator,* CII (6 February, 1909), 224 ff. (a review of A. R. Waller's *Samuel Butler: Characters and Passages from the Notebooks*).

[13] "A New Book on Sir Thomas Browne," *Speaker,* 3 (February, 1906), p. 441.

[14] Ibid. Compare this passage from Strachey's review of Mary E. Coleridge's poems: "The greatest poetry is always impersonal. . . . The biographies of great poets are of interest merely from the historical and psychological point of view; so far as poetry is concerned they are, so to speak, works of supererogation; we could do very well without them. The voice of Homer will ring for ever in the ears of the world, though it be a voice and nothing more . . . . But there is

another kind of poetry, which . . . depends less on pure artistic achievement than on the power of personal revelation. . . . It is on this select and quiet shelf of the Muses that the late Miss Mary Coleridge's little volume of poems will find a place"—"The Late Miss Coleridge's Poems," *Spectator,* c (4 January, 1908), 19.

[15] "A New Book on Sir Thomas Browne."

[16] "The Poetry of Thomson," *Spectator,* c (14 March, 1908), 421–22.

[17] "Not by Lockhart," *Speaker* (20 October, 1906), pp. 82–83. Strachey also reviewed G. L. G. Norgate's abridgment to Lockhart's *Scott* in this article and was able to commend it as "simply what it pretends to be, a condensation of Lockhart's life. It is straightforward, ordinary, and (like all condensations) dull. But it is neither careless, nor affected, nor pretentious; it is an honest piece of work."

[18] Lady Mary Wortley Montagu," *Albany Review,* I (September, 1907), 708 ff. When Strachey reviewed George Paston's *Mr. Pope: His Life and Times* over two years later, he objected to its rambling structure but, despite its two volumes, praised its "easy, unaffected style."—"Alexander Pope," *Spectator,* CIII (20 November, 1909), 847–48.

[19] "Some Napoleonic Books," *Spectator,* CI (26 December, 1908), 1100–01. In the same review Strachey gave Joseph Turquan's *The Sisters of Napoleon* credit for being amusing. As for his opinion concerning the Bonapartes themselves, he wrote: " . . . the fundamental characteristic of the Bonaparte family was meanness. . . . Really, it is difficult to decide which was the more remarkable thing about Napoleon—his generalship or his lack of humor."

[20] "The Life of Henry Irving," *Spectator,* CI (26 December, 1908), 1104.

[21] I, 361–84. Here given the title "The Poetry of Racine," but collected with alterations as "Racine" in *Books and Characters* (New York: Harcourt, Brace, 1922).

[22] *Landmarks in French Literature,* Home Univ. Library (New York: Henry Holt; London: Thornton Butterworth, 1912), pp. 150–51.

[23] "The Author of 'Hudibras.' " In *Landmarks in French Literature* Strachey wrote that La Bruyère's character studies were "caricatures rather than portraits—records of the idiosyncrasies of humanity rather than of humanity itself" (p. 125). D. S. (Prince) Mirsky goes too far when he says that Saint-Simon, dealing with history and biography as a complex thing, is "the only author to whom Mr. Strachey is essentially indebted"—"Mr. Lytton Strachey," *London Mercury,* VIII (June, 1923), 175 ff.

[24] "John Aubrey," *Portraits in Miniature,* pp. 28–29 (first published in the *Nation and the Athenaeum,* XXXIII (15 September, 1923), 741–42). Cf. Strachey's much earlier comment on William Barry's *Newman:* "The author of this readable monograph writes in fetters and is quite aware of the fact." He "writes eloquently, occasionally rather too eloquently. But, on the whole, the book is a sound performance in every sense, and hits the happy medium between scrappiness and oppressive amplitude." "Cardinal Newman," *Spectator,* XCIII (1 October, 1904), Suppl., 457.

[25] "The Lives of the Poets," *Independent Review,* X (July, 1906), 108 ff. In the same article Strachey wrote: "It is sufficient for us to recognize that he [Johnson] is a mountain, and to pay all the reverence that is due."

[26] "A Sidelight on Frederick the Great," *New Statesman* (27 January 1917), pp. 397 ff. In the diary which Strachey, at the age of eighteen, kept for a while during 1898, when he was attending Liverpool College, he wrote that Boswell's *Johnson* was "the best biography ever written" and expressed his indignation over the poor format of a copy which he had recently examined. See also "James Boswell," *Nation* (London), XXXVI (31 January 1925), 609–10, a review of C. B. Tinker's *Letters of James Boswell.*

[27] See notes 7 and 17 and Harold Nicolson, *The Development of English Biography* (London: Hogarth Press, 1933), pp. 117, 143, 153. Nicolson maintains that Lockhart and Boswell, unlike Strachey, had no thesis but worked entirely through the inductive method.

[28] *Ibid.*, p. 143, and "Some New Carlyle Letters."

[29] Nicolson, *op. cit.* For Gosse's identification of himself as the author of the article on Queen Victoria in the *Quarterly Review* for April 1901, see his *More Books upon the Table* (London: Heinemann, 1923), pp. 3–10, where he speaks with some gratification of Strachey's borrowings from the article. E. F. Benson has written that Gosse in *Father and Son* was really the first to revolt against the Victorian method of biography. "It was Gosse who broke through that tradition of pious unreality. . . . Strachey undoubtedly followed Gosse, though without sacrificing one whit of his own originality" ("Strachey and Gosse," London *Sunday Times,* 4 Sept. 1932, p. 4). Strachey's antipathy for Gosse was partly personal and partly a feeling that Gosse's scholarship could not be trusted. On one occasion something by Gosse was published with his name misspelled "Goose." Henceforth to Strachey he was always "Goose Gosse."

[30] "Dostoievsky," *Spectator,* CIX (28 September 1912), 451–52. See also "A Russian Humorist," *Spectator,* CXII (11 April 1914), 610–11, where Strachey maintained that Dostoievsky had not only psychological insight but humor: ". . . and so it happens that, by virtue of that magic power, his wildest fancies have something real and human in them, and his moments of greatest intensity are not melodramatic but tragic." There is little evidence that Strachey was influenced directly by George Eliot, but his mother knew and admired her as a person and was enthusiastic about her novels; Strachey surely must have read them. He and his brothers and sisters grew up reading Henry James, and preserved among his MSS. is a short piece entitled "The Fruit of the Tree" (dated June 1901) which he wrote in imitation of James.

[31] "Sir Henry Wotton," *Spectator,* XCIX (23 November 1907), 821–22. Strachey also spoke here of the pleasure which he had received from reading Walton's *Reliquiae Wottonianae.* It must have pleased Strachey to find that one of the documents which Smith had unearthed was a letter from John Donne to Wotton, then British Ambassador at Venice, recommending to him his friend William Strachey, the biographer's ancestor and the author of one of the best early histories of the Virginia colony.

[32] "The Art of Biography," *Atlantic Monthly,* CLXIII (April, 1939), 506 ff. Some of Strachey's shorter plays were actually produced by the Bloomsbury group at Ham Spray House, his country home in Wiltshire; and at Charleston, the home of the Clive Bells in Sussex. His full-length play *The Son of Heaven* was enacted twice at the Scala Theater, London, on 12 and 13 July 1925, and was revived for three weeks in London in 1949.

[33] *Op. cit.,* pp. 103–104.

[34] Note Strachey's Aphorism 22: "We meet people about whom we cannot make up our minds; their features, their manners, and their dress might equally be those of a vulgar or a cultivated person, and observe as we may, we can find no detail of their appearance which is not as indeterminate as the rest; we search, we balance, we hesitate, we rack our imaginations, we are on the point of giving up in despair; when they speak, and we know at once that they are impossible."

[35] 27 June 1918, p. 301. Gosse had written an article entitled "Lord Cromer as a Man of Letters," published in the *Fortnightly Review* for March 1917 (collected in *Some Diversions of a Man of Letters* two years later). Ironically, much of what he said about Cromer can be applied to Strachey himself. Witness the following excerpts: "He would have been at home in the fourth quarter of the eighteenth century, before the French Revolution." "I have always found him amusingly impervious to ideas of a visionary or mystical order." "He himself hated mere eulogy, which he said had ruined most of the biographies of the world. . . . 'I don't want Mr. ———,' he would say, 'to tell me what I can learn for myself by turning up the file of the *Morning Post.* I want him to tell me what I can't find out elsewhere. And he need not be so very much afraid of hinting that his hero had faults, for if he had not had defects we should never have heard of his qualities. We are none of us perfect, and we don't want a priggish biographer to pretend that we are." Cromer was an intimate friend of St. Loe Strachey, editor of the *Spectator* and first cousin of Lytton Strachey. St. Loe Strachey once said that Cromer and Lytton Strachey were the best reviewers that he had ever had. Was there professional rivalry between the two, or could there have been an unpleasant meeting, say, in the *Spectator* office? For Gosse's condemnation of Hallam, Tennyson's life of his father as one of the worst "two-fat-volume" Victorian biographies, see *Some Diversions of a Man of Letters,* pp. 320–21.

[36] "The Character of Lord Cromer," a letter to the editor, *TLS* (4 July 1918), pp. 313–14. Consider in this connection Strachey's Aphorism 31: "Is it not true that a man's tables and chairs know more about him than his most intimate friends? When he is left alone, who can guess what words escape him? What gestures he gives vent to? What strange expressions come into his face? His looking-glass, perhaps, could tell us most. When he dies, those unfathomable depths are abolished, that multitude of secrets is extinguished, that whole vast universe of mysteries too mysterious to be revealed; and what do the friends about the bed know of all these things? It is the bed itself that knows." May we assume, then, that Strachey believed personal intimacy such as Johnson had with Savage, Boswell with Johnson, and Froude with Carlyle to be of little value to the biographer? Possibly so, since the ideal of detachment meant much to him. Certainly he chose his own subjects from the dead whom he could have never known. Yet much of the "private information" referred to in the notes to *Queen Victoria,* probably his best work, came from Lady Lytton, whom he visited frequently when he was writing this biography and who was one of Queen Victoria's Ladies-in-Waiting. For a friendly, conciliatory letter from Gosse to Strachey, dated 21 May 1922, see Evan Charteris, *The Life and Letters of Sir Edmund Gosse* (New York and London: Harper, 1931), pp. 464–65.

[37] "Florence Nightingale according to Mr. Strachey," *Nineteenth Century,* CIII (February, 1928), 258–65. Concerning two of Strachey's victims to whom I happen to have given some study I must say a word of defense. Dr. Arnold had a vigor and breadth of intellect and a human warmth which are entirely lacking in Strachey's caricature. And Julius Charles Hare, introduced as a minor character

in "Cardinal Manning," was not a fanatical Low Churchman, as Strachey represented him as being, but a scholarly Broad Church latitudinarian, thoroughly steeped in Plato and in British, French, and German liberal theology, a disciple of Coleridge, and the friend of F. D. Maurice and John Sterling.

[38] "Elizabeth and Her Court," *Spectator,* CXLI (24 November, 1928), 777. Cf. E. G. Clark, "Mr. Strachey's Biographical Method," *Catholic World,* CXXIX (May, 1929), 129–35; Christopher Hollis, "Elizabeth and Mr. Strachey," *Dublin Review,* CLXXXVI (January, 1930), 21–30; Edmund Wilson, "Lytton Strachey," *New Republic,* LXXII (21 September, 1932), 146–48. Max Beerbohm wrote in 1943 that *Elizabeth and Essex* was "a finely constructed work, but seems to me to be essentially guess-work." *Lytton Strachey,* Rede Lecture for 1943 at Cambridge University (New York: Alfred A. Knopf, 1943), p. 20. For an accusation that Strachey was guilty of both carelessness and deliberate falsification in his "Cardinal Manning," see F. A. Simpson, "Methods of History," *Spectator,* CLXXII (7 January, 944), 7–8. A similar attack, but with other points added to the indictments is made by James Pope-Hennessey in "Strachey's Way," *Spectator,* CLXXXII (25 February, 1949), 264. On the other hand, Desmond MacCarthy has written: "I believe that as time goes on *Elizabeth and Essex* will be rated much higher." "Lytton Strachey: The Art of Biography," *Sunday Times* (London), 5 November, 1933, p. 8. In 1947 a distinguished British historian told me that he had found *Elizabeth and Essex* to be essentially true, that he admired it very much, and that "Dr. Arnold" was the only one of Strachey's characterizations which seemed to him seriously distorted and unfair.

[39] "The Modern Biographer," *Yale Review,* N.S. XVII (January, 1928), 231 ff. Maurois also wrote here that Strachey was "a very deep psychologist" and was "the father and master of modern biography." A little later he wrote: "A biographer, such as Mr. Strachey, who has the power to diffuse through his record of facts the poetic idea of Destiny, of the passage of Time, of the fragility of human fortune, brings us in fact a secret comfort . . . . There is no such thing as progress in literature. Tennyson is not greater than Homer, Proust is not greater than Montaigne, Strachey is not greater than Boswell. They are different." *Aspects of Biography,* transl. S. C. Roberts (New York: D. Appleton, 1929), pp. 142, 203.

[40] "An Eminent Post-Victorian," *Yale Review,* N.S., XXX (Winter, 1941), 321–22. Bacon has also taken exception to Strachey's Cromer and suspects "some personal animosity" (p. 318).

[41] *One Mighty Torrent: The Drama of Biography* (New York: Stackpole, 1937), pp. 511, 520. But Johnson praised Strachey for insisting that the biographer must have a clear and definite point of view. "No portrayal of character can be purely objective, because our conception of a personality is the intersection between it and ourselves. Strachey's great achievement was that he forced this fact into the open. The author's point of view became explicit instead of being a muzzy, unacknowledged projection of his personality" (pp. 522–23). Among others who have attacked Strachey are James Truslow Adams and Hugh Kingsmill. Adams wrote: "Among the psychological school of biographers the unquestioned leader and by far the most influential practitioner is Lytton Strachey. . . . Strachey develops in his own mind a psychological character for his heroine and makes his selection of facts fit into this character . . . his influence has been little short of disastrous." "New Modes in Biography," *Current History,* XXXI (November, 1929), 258. Kingsmill was vehement in his dislike for Strachey. He first

parodied Strachey's style in "Joseph, from *Eminent Egyptians,*" *English Review,* LIV (April, 1932), 399–404; and then attempted to turn the tables on a biographer who had taken great liberties with Victorian subjects by having him annihilated in an imaginary passage by Carlyle: "Our Wart-School of Modern Portraiture I name Biographer Strachey and his apes, blasphemously scribbling for pence their *Acta Stultorum,* or Deeds of the Fools. As tho there were no other veracity about a Hero but his warts! As tho brave Oliver's monition to Court Painter Lely has been: 'Meddle not with my face! Paint my warts only'!" "Some Modern Light-Bringers Extinguished by Thomas Carlyle," *English Review,* LVI (January, 1933), 25–26.

[42] "Lytton Strachey," SRL, VIII (6 February, 1932), 501.

[43] "Lytton Strachey: An Artist in History," *Observer* (London), 24 January 1932, p. 5.

[44] "Private information.

[45] "The Poetry of Blake," *Books and Characters,* pp. 222–23. First published in the *Independent Review* (May, 1906).

[46] "Creighton," *Portraits in Miniature,* pp. 204–206. First published as "Mandell Creighton," N. Y. *Herald Tribune Books,* 26 May 1929, p. 6.

[47] "A Frock-Coat Portrait of a Great King," *Daily Mail* (11 October 1927), p. 10. A review of Lee's *King Edward VIII,* Vol. II.

[48] It is important to note his manner of reading here. His friend Desmond MacCarthy said that he was not a "a born scholar" and that "though he read immensely, lazily, attentively, he was not learned." "Lytton Strachey," *Sunday Times* (London), 24 January 1932, p. 8 An excellent obituary.

[49] "A New History of Rome," *Spectator,* CII (2 January 1909), 20–21.

PART V Criticism

28.

Leon Gottfried

Between Two Worlds: Matthew Arnold and Romanticism

Il y a dans la poésie toujours un peu de mensonge. L'esprit philosophique nous habitue à le discerner; et adieu l'illusion et l'effet.
—DIDEROT

I. Arnold and English Poetic Tradition

...I propose to consider here Arnold's relations with Romanticism first in connection with the poetic tradition available to him, secondly in terms of his own ambivalence of feeling towards Romanticism, then by discussing changing attitudes towards the relationship between truth and poetry in the nineteenth century, and finally by reviewing the judgment he passed on the English poetry of the first quarter of the nineteenth century.

...I should [first] like to consider...Arnold in his relation to a poetic tradition. Let me say at the very outset that I do not believe that a "tradition" has any real existence in the same sense that particular poets and particular poems have. Moreover, it is clear by the middle of the twentieth century that there is not one major poetic tradition, but rather there are many traditions, almost as many one might say rashly as there are important modern poets seeking to relate themselves to the literature of the past. For in any discussion of influence and tradition it is salutary to remember that a poet certainly is free to exercise some choice in his reading and studies, constructing, if he wishes, a "tradition" out of the most heterogeneous elements; Ezra Pound with his amalgam of Browning, Whitman, Propertius, Old English, Provençal, early Italian, and classical Chinese is a sufficient example. Nevertheless, a poet is born at a certain time and place; he goes to certain schools and reads certain books; and both his society and the very language he speaks are historically conditioned. This means that his personal choice, however free, is still not completely unlimited in its field of operation. There are limits to the "usable past" available to him.

What was this "usable past" for Matthew Arnold about the middle of the last century? I refer especially to English poetry and the English language, because it is my conviction that, except perhaps for true bilingual poets like Milton or Tagore, foreign influence, however strong, must always be in some sense secondary. The poet's raw material is his own language; foreign influence is only significant to the extent that the poet can transmute it, recreating and validating its effects in his own living language. The multifaceted problems of poetic translation are enough evidence for this, I believe. Arnold himself, though deeply affected by German and French writers, for example, was primarily concerned as a practising poet with what he felt were the inadequacies of English poetry, and his major purpose was to put English poetry on the right path. . . .

We may best approach the make-up of Arnold's "tradition" by seeing first what is omitted. Arnold's list of "our Chief poetical names" from the age of Elizabeth downwards includes Shakespeare and Milton, Spenser, Dryden, Pope, Gray, Goldsmith, Cowper, Burns, Coleridge, Scott, Campbell, Moore, Byron, Shelley, Keats, and Wordsworth. It is indeed strange, as Lionel Trilling comments, "that a roll of the great English poets does not include such names as Marlowe, Jonson, Donne, Marvell, Herbert, Vaughan, and Blake." And these are not all the significant omissions, while even among the names included by Arnold are several whose presence was merely conventional. Thus, Arnold could include Dryden and Pope in "a large and liberal first class among English writers," but he had no real sympathy with them as poets though he could treat them respectfully as men of letters. It is significant that in his essay on Johnson, he urged the reading of Pope, Addison, Dryden, and Swift for their historical interest. If we re-examine Arnold's list of "chief poetical names" with our attention on Arnold's own views of their usefulness to him, we shall get a fairly clear picture of his available tradition. Chaucer he excluded as "anterior" and for "other" reasons; that is, I suppose, because of linguistic and cultural differences and because of his alleged lack of high seriousness. Spenser's "fluid movement and liquid diction" he praised in passing, but there is no evidence that he took Spenser seriously, or thought he had much to offer a modern poet beyond some lessons in refinement of craft, already overemphasized by Keats, Tennyson, and their followers. Dryden and Pope are "classics of our prose," indispensable in their time and place but no longer useful, and Arnold praised the Romantics for rejecting the poetry between Milton and Wordsworth.[2] Such lesser lights as Goldsmith, Cowper, Campbell, and Moore named in his list may be put aside without comment. Scott's true glory was as a novelist; his verse, Arnold thought, was competent and enjoyable but unimportant. We are left, then, from the original list, with Shakespeare and Milton, Gray, Burns, Wordsworth, Coleridge, Byron, Shelley, and Keats. But Shakespeare, though an unparalleled genius, is dangerous as an influence. The Gray in whom Arnold is interested is essentially a minor Romantic, in spite of Arnold's opinion that Gray was saved from the worst poetic excesses of his time by his thorough knowledge of the Greeks.[3] Burns is at his best when he writes in Scottish of Scottish life—a foreign poet, and also a minor one. What remains is Milton and the great Romantics as the living tradition of read and reread poets who could form his attitudes towards the stuff of English poetry. These are the English poets, selected partly by the taste of the age and partly by conscious choice, whose work created the linguistic milieu in which Arnold formed his image of what had been successfully and relevantly accomplished in English verse; it is against this background that his own poetry should be placed.

Hence, we can see that Arnold was cut off by taste, opinion, and conditioning from most of the English poetry outside the Romantic tradition. The line of Shakespeare, Milton, and the Romantics was for him, as for most of his contemporaries, *the* tradition in English poetry, and even Shakespeare is suspect in proportion as he becomes subtle and "conceited." This background is an important limitation to the possibility of Arnold's rebellion against Romanticism and to the possible scope of his reform of English poetry. Recognizing this, Arnold sought help by turning to contemporary Europe and to the literature of the past. In modern Europe he found Goethe and Senancour valuable above all, but was also interested in George Sand, Maurice de Guérin, and Joubert; what is such a list but a roll call of Romantics, great and small? German critics, to be sure, do not regard Goethe as a Romantic. We must not underestimate his broad rationality and his humane classicism, but it still seems, from a modern and cosmopolitan point of view such as Santayana's, that Goethe's classicism is but one facet of his immensely energetic, many-sided, and limitless development of the self. His hero Faust is the very epitome of that restless, expansive individualism which we associate on the economic side with the bourgeois revolution, on the scientific with the human conquest of brute matter, and on the literary with Romanticism. It is true that Faust marries Helena, but their offspring Euphorion bears a striking resemblance to Lord Byron.

As for the literature of the past, Arnold tended to see that too, in part, through the filtering lens of Romanticism, although it was primarily in that literature that he sought an antidote for modern subjectivism and excessive richness and refinement of artistry. Medieval Europe offered such an antidote in Dante, whom Arnold greatly admired. True, Dante's civilization was second-rate from Arnold's point of view, but then so was Homer's,[4] and, after all Dante's accomplishment was enormous. In the clear and precise use of language Dante is unsurpassed; there is no clutter, no bombast, no decoration. His verse possesses all the virtues of great prose, combined with that fusion of symbol, object, and idea at the greatest intensity of imaginative power which marks the greatest poetry. Moreover, this power of fusion, this intensity, coupled with clarity in the texture of his verse, is amplified in the completeness of his architectonics. Perhaps more than any other work one can think of, Dante's *Divine Comedy* possesses the magisterial qualities of depth, comprehensiveness, grandeur, seriousness, and organization which Arnold demanded. In spite of all this, when we look at what Arnold had to say about Dante, we do not find that he selects his work as an example of the "literatures which in their day and for their own nation have adequately comprehended, have adequately represented, the spectacle before them." Instead, wearing the twin blinders of the Enlightenment's contempt for the age of jarring monks, and Romantic sentimentalizing of medieval spirituality, Arnold saw only a Romantic version of Dante as an other-worldly visionary: "the vital impulse of Dante's soul is towards reverie and spiritual vision. . . ." Dante, that is—and the whole tenor of the essay on "Dante and Beatrice" bears this out—is a more impassioned Senancour, a Senancour living at a time when belief in a spiritual order was still possible:

> . . . the task Dante sets himself is not the task of reconciling poetry and reality, of giving to each its due part, of supplementing the one by the other; but the task of sacrificing the world to the spirit, by making the spirit all in all, of effacing the world in presence of the spirit. . . .[5]

Arnold seems quite to overlook Dante's attitude of tough-minded, Christian realism, an attitude which brings Dante in some ways nearer than Arnold to the spirit of classical literature. In fact, Arnold's whole essay on Dante is a remarkable example of romanticizing under the guise of correcting another critic for doing so. In its lack of historic insight, its unconscious employment of contemporaneous assumptions, it smacks more of the Romanticism of the eighteenth century, however, than of the nineteenth. Arnold was too much a child of the Enlightenment to take the Middle Ages seriously; that epoch was too irrational, too unmodern.

In Athens during the age of Pericles he found what he wanted—a *modern* epoch with an *adequate* literature. There he found the wholeness, simplicity, order, and objectivity of the highest art for the moment achieving perfect balance with the critical intellect and profound moral insight. Yet even in his praise of classic art there is to be detected something of the tone of Wordsworth's "old, unhappy, far-off things,/And battles long ago" and of Keats's "a billowy main, / A sun, a shadow of a magnitude"; that is, he tends to be Romantic about the Classic. The tone is audible in Arnold's Preface to *Merope*:

> ... I am convinced, even in England, even in this stronghold of the romantic school, a wide though an ill-informed curiosity [exists] on the subject of the so-called classical school, meriting a more complete satisfaction than it has hitherto obtained. Greek art—the antique—classical beauty —a nameless hope and interest attaches, I can often see, to these words, even in the minds of those who have been brought up among the productions of the romantic school; of those who have been taught to consider classicalism as inseparable from coldness, and the antique as another phrase for the unreal. So immortal, so indestructible is the power of true beauty, of consummate form: it may be submerged, but the tradition of it survives: nations arise which know it not, which hardly believe in the report of it; but they, too, are haunted with an indefinable interest in its name, with an inexplicable curiosity as to its nature.

Arnold was capable of a different sort of perception of classical art when dealing with its "criticism of life" (see his comment on the *Iliad* below, but in his nostalgic yearning towards Greece, a yearning to be felt in the very rhythms of the passage just quoted, there is a definite Romantic element. And consequently the usefulness to him of Classicism as an antidote to Romanticism was limited.[6]

II. Arnold's Ambivalence

So far we have seen two kinds of limitations in Arnold which may justifiably be related to his derivation from the Romantic movement—first, a narrowness of taste that cut him off from a sizeable body of work in English of potential usefulness in his effort to reinstate the social utility of poetry, and second, a certain tendency to romanticize and hence to limit the medicinal effectiveness of the literatures of the past. Two ... limitations ... [may here be noted]: namely, Arnold's narrowing concept of the permissible emotional range of poetry to the exalted, the solemn, the melancholy, or the pathetic, and his inability to construct a new style adequate to his demands on poetry. These limitations, representing the negative side of Arnold's inheritance from the giants of the preceding generation, were particularly effective in preventing him from fulfilling his very highest ambitions for poetry because he was at the same time lacking in many of the positive attributes of Romanticism. He was deeply mistrustful of the craving for the infinite which Muirhead sees as the essential quality of Romanticism.[7] Above all he lacked the energy of the Romantics; he lacked their robust, expansive ego;[8] he lacked their faith in the imagination as the highest, truest, and the most creative way of knowing; he did not share in the slightest degree their nature animism; and he did not, consequently, believe in a special system of correspondence between nature and the mind of man. Of course, the five major Romantic poets [Wordsworth, Byron, Keats, Shelley, and Coleridge] did not all possess all these attitudes, or possess them all at once, or for ever. But in so far as we call them "romantic" (with Byron always the doubtful case in certain respects), we have in mind, among lesser things, some combination of them.

Arnold could not sustain the Wordsworthian faith in

> How exquisitely the individual Mind
> (And the progressive powers perhaps no less
> Of the whole species) to the external World
> Is fitted:—and how exquisitely too—
>
> . . .
>
> The external World is fitted to the Mind.

In its expression of this loss of faith and regret for the loss, Arnold's poetry reveals both his derivation from the Romantics and his reaction against them. As an antiromantic, he harped continually on the limitations imposed by a lawful but inscrutable universe upon the subjective demands and expectations of the self. But while Arnold's thought in his poetry is naturalistic, his feeling is thoroughly unclassical. Classical art recognized that the world was not made for man, but showed that man could achieve dignity in that world. In accepting with total clarity of vision this view of the relationship between man's aspirations and the rigorous limitations imposed by circumstance and natural law, classic art rises to tragic grandeur. Arnold, more than any other leading poet of his day, participated in such a vision of man.

But his feeling, instead of rising to tragic clarity, is one of disillusionment, and since this implies anterior illusionment, and unresolved regret, it is at the opposite pole from the tragic emotion. Arnold's disillusionment seems romantic when contrasted with the stern realism (Santayana's "naturalism") of pagan antiquity. Perhaps it would not be too much of a distortion to suggest that if Arnold was not a Romanticist, he nevertheless wished he could be, and that his melancholy attitude of lost and yearning disenchantment defined the nature of his own Romanticism.

Arnold's negative Romanticism, his self-pitying sense of the rigorous subjection of the ego to natural law, is reflected in his work and thought by a split between the reason and the imagination, symbolized by the characters of Empedocles and Callicles in *Empedocles on Etna*; this subjective split is complemented on the objective side by an equally firm division between man and Nature. Both dichotomies are caught up in the loss of faith in the imagination, the faith that had been so powerful a force in stimulating the creativeness of the Romantics. It is true that in the essay "Pagan and Medieval Religious Sentiment," Arnold, like the Romantics before him, urged the necessity of the "imaginative reason" in poetry, but the general drift of the essay is toward favoring the reason over the imagination. He nowhere shows interest in, or even awareness of, the profound and complex theories of Wordsworth and Coleridge on the imagination, or of their distinctions between imagination and fancy or between primary and secondary imagination. In short, for Arnold the concept of the imagination, in spite of a few instances of his using the word honorifically, has been stripped of most of the prestige it enjoyed among the Romantics, and has become almost synonymous with emotion, superstition, wish, and self-will.[9] Lacking the Romantic faith in man's ability to create reality, Arnold, like Aristotle, divides man's higher impulses between the intellectual and the moral—"the effort to see things as they really are and the effort to win peace by self-conquest."[10] The imagination, in turn, seems at times to have shrunk in Arnold's usage to the "false secondary power," not by which we multiply distinctions, but by which we invent mechanisms of escape from stern reality. Certainly Arnold was not always conscious of the extent to which he was depreciating the imagination, but it is visible there and in the turn at the end of *Celtic Literature,* amounting almost to a sleight of hand, by which he decisively elevates German intellectualism in poetry over the Celtic imagination of the great English geniuses.

The obverse side of Arnold's elevation of reason at the expense of the imagination may be seen in his attitude towards Nature; the latter attitude may indeed be the cause of the former. Defending what another critic had called Arnold's "week-end" attitude towards Nature, J. D. Jump points out that

> Arnold was not protected by private income, personal gift, sinecure, or legacy from the obligation of working for a living in the ordinary Philistine sense of the phrase. Because he knew it in his own life, Arnold presents in his verse the dilemma of many who in the modern world are compelled to live their lives in circumstances which fail to satisfy their natures, which distract them indeed from learning what those natures are, and which they must for their own well-being periodically elude. If Arnold's landscapes are commonly those of a week-ender—and the Georgian poets are indeed his enfeebled successors—at least he also knew and gave utterance to that unease which drives the week-ender to the countryside.[11]

This economic explanation merits consideration, but it does not go deep enough. Arnold could not feel "at home" in Nature for reasons more profound than this, and, given his temperament and beliefs, we cannot imagine that a well-timed legacy of £1000 a year would have substantially altered the situation. The main point to consider is that for Arnold, Nature was irrevocably *other* than man and limited him; its rigorous laws were firm barriers against man's egocentric, expansive tendencies. Hence, man can never be more than a "week-ender" in the physical universe. Here Arnold differs most profoundly from Wordsworth, Coleridge, Shelley, and Keats, who all, in their various ways, saw in the imagination a power creative of reality. True, Arnold reveals some kinship with them in the feeling of disillusion that accompanies his belief, and he is like them in deriving a philosophy from Nature. But his philosophy as expounded by Empedocles, and by Arnold speaking for himself in other poems, is a doctrine of discipline, limitation, self-control, and stoic resignation. Hence he is more in accord with Senancour and other continental Romantics who, in the words of a French critic, were "emmurés en eux-mêmes; le monde extérieur ne leur apporte ni réconfort ni chaleur."[12] It has been argued that science can fulfill a religious function by "enforcing belief in a real world which imposes limits upon human self-will."[13] Empedocles-Arnold would have agreed that science in fact fulfilled such a function, but from his position at the bleak terminus of Romantic faith he would not have thought of calling it religious. Starting from this dead end, there would seem to have been two paths open to him—that of Christianity or that of a thorough-going naturalism. Unable to choose, he bent his mightiest efforts towards a reconciliation of the two, and so ended his years impaled, but with a minimum of discomfort, upon both horns of the dilemma.

How did these conflicts affect his poetry? Arnold's critics are in substantial agreement that he was at his best when he was most romantic. Indeed, if Arnold was situated in relation to the Romantic tradition in the way I have described above, how should it have been otherwise? Caught in the conflict between rationalism and Romanticism, and expressing the emotional effect of this conflict with deep honesty, it was inevitable that his poetry should be most moving when it deals with the alienation and incompleteness of modern man in such poems as *Dover Beach, Obermann, Stanzas from the Grande Chartreuse, The Scholar-Gipsy,* and *Empedocles on Etna.* It was in this work, and not in his academic efforts to achieve classical serenity, that his poems truly represent, as in 1869 he said they did, "the main movement of mind of the last quarter of a century."[14] But also, since he recognized the inadequacy of disillusion as a philosophy for either life or art, it was inevitable that he should have agreed with Goethe, that "Klassisch ist das Gesunde, romantisch das Kranke."

III. Truth and Poetry

It was almost a necessary consequence that Arnold should have been unable to take poetry itself as seriously as most of the Romantics had done, in spite of his extravagant claims on its behalf. For in his feelings there was as deep a split between "truth" and "poetry" as there was between "science" and "religion," or "reason" and "imagination." To explore this hypostatization, we shall have to examine various meanings of "truth" in Arnold's thought.

In his 1865 preface to *Essays in Criticism,* Arnold personified truth as a mysterious Goddess "whom we shall never see except in outline," but even in outline only by supple and dialectical processes. Although he had learned much from such systematic thinkers as Aristotle and Coleridge, he had never acquired their passion for careful definition and for the rigors of logic; on the contrary, he frequently asserted his radical mistrust of abstract speculation and of systematic thought. We shall not expect to find, therefore, and do not find any consistent set of ideas in Arnold about so complex a concept as "truth," either as to its own nature or concerning the faculties and means by which we may gain apprehension of it. For this reason, any attempt to reduce his ideas and attitudes to logical order is bound either to fail, or to reveal that Arnold was more inconsistent than he perhaps really was. Basically, his approach to ideas, for all his sophistication, was homespun, empirical, and intuitive in the everyday rather than philosophical meaning of that term. For example, he argues that a man is better off to take the forms of religious expression "which have commended themselves most to the religious life of his nation" rather than battle for "his own private forms," for he may thus ensure to himself the "leisure and composure to satisfy other sides of his nature as well."[15] Again, in surveying Amiel's work, he acknowledges that his "sense for philosophy" is far from satisfying such a rationalistic critic as Frederic Harrison. "But," he continues, "I am too old to change and too hardened to hide what I think; and when I am presented with philosophical speculations . . . , I persist in looking closely at them and in honestly asking myself what I find to be their positive value."[16]

At the risk, therefore, of somewhat misrepresenting Arnold's studied vagueness, we may yet observe that when he speaks of "truth" or implies standards for its measurement, he is likely to mean one of three things. He may have in mind the sort of certitude that nineteenth-century materialism held up as "scientific truth," based on certain assumptions about the absolute truth of "laws of nature." By this standard, he rejects, for example, faith in miracles, although even here it should be noted that he is less concerned to prove that miracles do not happen, than that the temper of the times, the Zeitgeist, has rendered the whole question of miracles as obsolete as the problem of angels on a pinhead.[17] Secondly, under the influence of prevailing utilitarianism, he may make "truth" essentially synonymous with utility. This pragmatic approach is especially evident in his religious writings, where the "human truth" of Christianity is proved by its rich adequacy, when put to the test of practice, to man's needs. Finally, Arnold may employ still another notion of truth, namely, aesthetic or "poetic" truth. The appeal to this kind of truth is equally prominent in his defence of Christianity; it is a debatable question whether it or the pragmatic argument is the more important in his apologetics, but I am inclined to favor the aesthetic.

Inevitably, Arnold's pragmatic defense of Christianity encounters certain difficulties. After all, though such a test may prove religion useful, it cannot prove it true unless the terms are defined as synonymous. Measured by any absolute standard, the utility of religion may be just what makes one suspicious of the existential truth of its assertions. To be sure, in appealing to the modern notion of practical "verifiability." Arnold thought that he was providing his arguments on behalf of faith with a firmly scientific basis. But such a notion of "verifiability" is close to being a travesty of scientific operationalism. The scientist who develops a theory adequate to the data in his possession never loses awareness of the hypothetical and, by any absolutist standards, tentative nature of his "truth." Furthermore, when a scientific hypothesis is made subservient to any set of psychological needs or to any value system, it is at once in the gravest danger of losing its scientific validity; when it is treated as an absolute it has already lost its validity.

At the same time, scientific method and discipline teach wariness of those hypotheses which seem subjectively most "adequate," for they are most likely to be rationalizations. Hence a rigorous critical method was developed which, as it became part of the psychological set of the thinking portion of mankind, worked against acceptance of the pragmatic argument for religious truth. The louder it is asserted, "Religious truth is proved by its adequacy to man's needs; try it and see," the more surely the critical response is likely to become, "All that such adequacy really proves is that the religious view of life is manufactured out of those very needs." For in the sphere of religion, however latitudinarian, certain absolutes are demanded, and in effect created, by the very nature of faith. Job's cry, "Though He slay me, yet will I trust in Him," may be employed here as a touchstone. Such faith, beyond reason, in the existence of the Absolute is incommensurable with the provisional assent lent to any scientific theory whatsoever. And here was Arnold's difficulty, for he appears to have been incapable of appreciating the state of mind of those whose hunger for faith was such that the objective, material truth of a doctrine was a fundamental concern.[18]

While Arnold was rejecting all those parts of religion, such as miracles and the historical accuracy of the Scriptures, which were contradicted by modern science, he was also apparently aware of the defects of the pragmatic approach. Consequently, he makes his primary appeal to aesthetic standards of truth to establish the validity of religion. That is, religion may be "true" as a novel, play, poem, or any work of art is true—by embodying a satisfactory organization of responses to both externally given and inward data, facts, and feelings (Wordsworth's "impassioned expression on the countenance of all science"). Viewed in this way, religion is not explanatory, but expressive, hence exempt from corrosion by science. At a mythopoeic stage of civilization, with the universe taken as homocentric, there would be little difference between scientific and aesthetic truth, as data and responses are not sharply differentiated. T. S. Eliot has argued that the metaphysical poets of the early seventeenth century were the last to possess this "unified sensibility"; it may seem strange to think so, but perhaps from this point of view the Romantics were the heirs of the metaphysicals, representing a last desperate effort to reassert this fusion of thought and feeling in the face of what came to seem by Arnold's time the inevitable triumph of scientific standards of truth. The development of Keats's thought in his letters may be taken as an example of this effort; the whole letter to Reynolds of May 3, 1818, which contains the famous remark "axioms in philosophy are not axioms until they are proved upon our pulses," is a central document, as the remark itself is a summary expression of Keats's version of the fusion of thought and feeling which he sought.

But as the data came to be organized in ways which increasingly made of man a phenomenon or at most a mere observer, man found himself squeezed from the center of action, while science developed methods of analysis and criteria of certitude quite different from those of art. The word *satisfactory,* used above in the characterization of aesthetic truth, becomes crucial, for conceptual organizations which satisfy the demands of critical method are not the same as expressive organizations which satisfy our aesthetic sense of how things ought to be. The most obvious difference is in what is appealed to: scientific demonstration must meet standards which are somehow independent of me or of any man; these standards may "satisfy" me in so far as I accept them emotionally, but my acceptance is, one the other hand, quite irrelevant to their validity. But no such objective or self-subsistent standards are available for measuring artistic truth; in art assent is gained by methods analogous to persuasion, not demonstration. The futile efforts of Zola and the Naturalists to turn art into science and the work of art into a laboratory demonstration was a characteristic nineteenth-century expedient.

For the great Romantics, typically, poetry was an article of faith. They believed that its truth was on an equal footing with, if it was not indeed superior to, scientific truth. "What the imagination seizes as Beauty must be truth—whether it existed before or not," proclaimed Keats in an important letter of November 22, 1817. Both the psychology and the philosophy they accepted provided a rationale: since the mind itself was a plastic, shaping force, there did not exist a radical split between data and responses. Another way of putting this, in Wordsworthian terms, is that Nature is a living spirit infusing and infused by the human mind. Consequently, to have attributed artistic truth to religion would in no way have detracted for them from its truth in other senses. But for succeeding generations the matter was more difficult. Science was rapidly organizing itself into patterns which left no room for or were totally indifferent to human response (although this process had been going on since Bacon had banished final causes from scientific discourse). One understood these organizations or did not, but one's emotions regarding them were irrelevant except to another system of such organizations called psychology. Under these circumstances, what becomes of "aesthetic truth"? Not by canard or conspiracy, but merely because of the inevitable progress of science, the valuation placed on it diminished. And what becomes of religion? On the one hand there was the last-ditch effort to keep alive the belief in its scientific truth—fundamentalism. This seemed to Arnold not only hopeless, but undesirable, for then the highest expression of man's spirit (for it was in such humanistic terms that he conceived of religion) would become ossified in a set of dubious material facts. Pragmatism, on the other hand, is a struggle in quicksand which draws the struggler deeper. Arnold could flirt with this approach in his prose, but in his poetry where his intuitions were more certain he recognized its inadequacy, and sternly denied that the world was in any sense created to satisfy us; it has its laws, we have ours.

Thus, while Shelley, for example, could see poetry as the true organizer of the moral order and could somehow believe in its divine function (and Yeats wanted to study *Prometheus Unbound* as a sacred book), Arnold could not. He tried hard, to be sure. But where Shelley believed that he was describing what was, Arnold was pleading for what he hoped *might be.* Thus Shelley argued from a position of strength, Arnold from a position of weakness; Shelley fully believed in the truth of poetry as a fact of the universe, Arnold could not; Shelley defined, Arnold defended. Unlike the rebellious, passionate Yeats, Arnold was too much a willing child of his time for it to be otherwise. Beneath his aesthetic cloak, he was a believer in certitude. Science possessed certitude, but did not satisfy; poetry satisfied, but alas possessed no certitude.[19]

If aesthetic truth, which was necessary to support religion, was itself falling victim to scientific standards of certitude, if truth and poetry were coming to be virtual antonyms, as they are to this day in the popular cliché, what was Arnold to do? In his debate with Huxley over education ("Literature and Science"), Arnold again appealed to the standard of utility, this time to defend poetry; my respected ancestor the ring-tailed baboon, it seems, was born with a need for it. Now let us review the steps of the argument: First, science tells us that the statements of religion lack material truth; very well, religion still possesses aesthetic truth. But then aesthetic truth turns out to be usefulness. However, the actual or potential user who is needed to validate the standard of usefulness may fail to perceive that quality in what is offered unless it measures up to his standards of certitude, no matter how much he desires to believe. It may then be argued that he is missing a great deal, and he may even agree, but no logical argument is left to convince him of the *truth* of art or religion. The attempt to prove pragmatically the truth of either has not only failed, but it has opened the door to the possibility of all sorts of bad art (e.g., "socialist realism") or sentimental religion (e.g., "the power of positive thinking)." As far as art is concerned, there was only one more step to take in this direction, or rather in desperate opposition to it, and aestheticism took that step: art is supremely valuable because it is useless.

Actually, Arnold's aesthetic defense of religion and religious defense of poetry can be plausible if one does really conceive highly enough of poetry. But it has been only a rare spirit since the time of Shelley and the Romantics who has been capable of it, while prior to that time it was unnecessary.[20] Arnold tried to hold and to propagate such a conception, but couldn't succeed; in his own language, the Zeitgeist was against him. And it can scarcely be doubted that the breach in our society's attitude between "truth" and "poetry" is wider than ever, although faith in certitude is no longer a part of the critical method of advanced scientific thought. But because man still hungers, he feeds himself insatiably on what is neither aesthetically nor scientifically "true." In his flight from the twin demons of boredom and despair he voraciously consumes in alarming quantities the meretricious and the ersatz in the arts, and the soothing religiosity of popular "psychologists," weekly magazine preachers, and billboard slogans.

IV. Arnold and the Romantics

Finally, we must review Arnold's evaluation of the Romantic poets and movement. His ranking of the five poets is still controversial. For one thing, Blake has now, and quite properly, assumed his rank as one of the major poets of the period; probably my own opinion that he and Wordsworth share the supreme rank is fairly common. In taking up the five poets whom Arnold did deal with, we must recognize that the qualities he most highly valued were power and breadth of achievement. He badly underestimated Shelley, but, considering his critical premises, his view of Coleridge as a poet is quite understandable. Coleridge's significance as an intellectual force can hardly be overestimated, but as a poet his accomplishment, after all, was the production of a very few masterpieces on the basis of which he has his own special but minor place. Again, Arnold's relative ranking of Byron and Keats is in accord with his general principles, although of course other premises are defensible. This placement is certainly in opposition to much current opinion, but it is possible that our contemporary tendency to elevate Keats, the artist of profound genius but narrow accomplishment, over Byron, a lesser genius of ampler scope, is symptomatic of our own Romantic provinciality. At any rate, one formidable controversialist, F. R. Leavis, finds himself in complete agreement with Arnold's relative evaluation from first to last.[21]

Whatever personal attraction Arnold may have felt toward Romanticism, and whatever virtues he may have found in some of the poets, his lack of critical sympathy is evident from the way he used the term itself. Sometimes he was condescendingly affectionate, as in the delicately ironic panegyric on Oxford which he apostrophizes as an "adorable dreamer, whose heart has been so romantic!" and as a "queen of romance" steeped in sentimental moonlight, "so unravaged by the fierce intellectual life of our century." This tone is closely related to the momentary attraction of the cloister in *Stanzas from the Grande Chartreuse* or of the passion and charm of the impractical Celtic temperament, an attraction that Knowledge and Duty may permit or even momentarily encourage for the sake of "refreshment," but then must proscribe. In his notebook Arnold copied a sentence out of Pater's *Renaissance* characterizing the Romantic and Hellenic spirits: "The Romantic spirit—its adventure, its variety, its deep subjectivity; Hellenism—its transparency, its rationality, its desire for beauty."[22] This may be more of what Douglas Bush has referred to as "Romantic Hellenism," but there is no doubt which of these two spirits claimed Arnold's critical allegiance. His most definitely damning comment on the Romantic, calling it by name, is backed by the authority of Sainte-Beuve in a passage of *On Translating Homer*. There a remark of Ruskin's on a phrase from the *Iliad* elicits the following response:

> It reminds one, as, alas! so much of Mr. Ruskin's writing reminds one, of those words of the most delicate of living critics: 'Comme tout genre de composition a son écueil particulier, *celui du genre romanesque, c'est le faux.*' [Arnold's italics.] . . . It is not true, as a matter of general criticism, that this kind of sentimentality, eminently modern, inspires Homer at all. "From Homer and Polygnotus I every day learn more clearly," says Goethe, "that in our life here above ground we have, properly speaking, to enact Hell:"—if the student must absolutely have a keynote to the *Iliad*, let him take this of Goethe, and see what he can do with it; it will not, at any rate, like the tender pantheism of Mr. Ruskin, falsify for him the whole strain of Homer.[23]

I have omitted the details of the argument for they are not relevant here; the important thing to notice is Arnold's linking of "romantic," *le romanesque,* with words like *sentimentality* and *tender pantheism*. A quarter of a century later, Arnold still recalled Sainte-Beuve's words when he again referred to *le faux* as the special danger "of the romantic artist."[24]

Arnold's belief that falsity was the particular stumbling-block of the romantic artist was entirely consonant with his conviction that "the burst of creative activity in our literature, through the first quarter of this century" was premature, that the poetry it produced "did not know enough." For expressing a similar opinion, Maurice de Guérin is praised for judging "the romantic school and its prospects like a master." Since this poetry had its "source in a great movement of feeling, not in a great movement of mind," its inadequacy must eventually be recognized as the world pursues its relentless course of attempting to understand the real nature of things. In *Memorial Verses* and elsewhere, Arnold associated the period of the Romantics with other intellectually primitive ages—the Elizabethan, the medieval, and the pre-philosophic antique. Himself and his own times, on the other hand, he associated with the clear-eyed disillusion of a Lucretius and his epoch: "The infancy of the world was renewed with all its sweet illusions but infancy and its illusions must for ever be transitory, and we are again in the place of the Roman world, our illusions past. . . ."[25]

To *know*—that was the great impulse of the mid-Victorians. Literary England had travelled far from Wordsworth's "It is the hour of feeling." This intellectual bias is reflected in many other poets of the period and in a considerable body of critical opinion on the Romantics which was similar to Arnold's.[26] Consequently, Arnold's own critique of the Romantic movement was not startlingly independent, although it did not represent majority opinion.[27] The Romantics have not lacked defenders ready to point out Arnold's deficiencies of sympathy, understanding, or judgment. Jacques Barzun, for example, in *Romanticism and the Modern Ego,* deplores the fact that the Romantic poets' output should have come to us filtered through Arnold's "sentimental critical taste." He frankly blames Arnold for "our incomplete view of Byron and Wordsworth," for helping to create the legend of Shelley as an ineffectual angel, and for numerous other crimes against the reputations not only of the Romantics, but of Burns, Dryden, Pope, and Swift.[28] In a sense it is flattering to Arnold's own reputation to have so much power imputed to him, but surely we may wonder whether any one critic could have caused so much unmerited damage. Still, after allowance is made for exaggeration, some residue of justice remains in Barzun's indictment of Arnold. If we cannot ignore him in approaching the Romantics, we have certainly found it necessary to supplement and transcend him.

However, Arnold's services as a critic of the Romantics should not be forgotten. It was Arnold who helped not only to popularize Wordsworth, but who reminded an earnest generation that Wordsworth was, above all, a great poet. It was Arnold who, in his poetry and lectures *On the Study of Celtic Literature,* spoke out on behalf of Byron at a time when English taste had turned against him. It was Arnold, too, who saw and insisted on pointing out that there was something deeper and something stronger in Keats than the aesthetes or the perpetuators of the Johnny Keats legend could see. At the same time, Arnold made important discriminations. If he did not believe that the English Romantics possessed the towering stature that parochial English taste found in them, it is yet to his credit that he paid them the compliment of measuring them against the broad and ample standards of a European literature that included Homer, Sophocles, Virgil, Dante, Shakespeare, and Goethe. Finally, in Arnold's appraisal of the movement as a whole, he demonstrated his power to prophesy with considerable accuracy what taste would be a century later. Arnold's frankest and simplest expression of this evaluation is to be found in a letter he wrote to his brother Thomas on December 28, 1857

> A great transformation in the intellectual nature of the English, and, consequently, in their estimate of their own writers, is, I have long felt, inevitable. When this transformation comes the popularity of Wordsworth, Shelley, Coleridge, and others, remarkable men as they were, will not be the better for it.[29]

On the whole he was right. It has not been.

Notes

[1] *Matthew Arnold* (New York, 1949), p. 379.

[2] *Essays in Criticism* III (London, 1910), 208–209.

[3] *Ibid.*, p. 215.

[4] *Ibid.*, p. 68.

[5] *Ibid.*, pp. 43, 89. After saying of Dante that he effaces the world in presence of the spirit, Arnold seems to be inconsistent in reproving other critics for placing too much emphasis on the allegory in the *Divine Comedy*.

[6] Cf. Douglas Bush, *Mythology and the Romantic Tradition* (Cambridge, Mass.), p. 247. On this point, cf. D. G. James, *Matthew Arnold and the Decline of English Romanticism* (Oxford, 1961). I am pleased to acknowledge the

similarity of many of my conclusions in this chapter to those of Professor James in this recent (1961) publication of his Gregynog lectures, published since the present study was written.

[7] John H. Muirhead, *Coleridge as Philosopher,* p. 28.

[8] I do not mean the total ego in the psychological sense, but the more limited poetic ego or sense of self-as-poet and poet-as-seer.

[9] Cf. Bonnerot, *Matthew Arnold* (Paris, 1947), pp. 233–34, 264.

[10] *Culture and Anarchy* (London, 1910), p. 139.

[11] *Matthew Arnold,* p. 67. Jump is alluding to F. R. Leavis, who had traced the ancestry of the feebler sort of Georgian nature poetry to Matthew Arnold.

[12] Bonnerot, *Matthew Arnold,* p. 184. Cf. Beach, *The Concept of Nature in Nineteenth-Century English Poetry* (New York, 1936), p. 403, and H. F. Lowry's introduction to *The Letters of Matthew Arnold to Arthur Hugh Clough,* ed., H. F. Lowry (London, 1932), pp. 33–34.

[13] Fairchild, *Religious Trends,* III (New York, 1949), 229.

[14] *Letters,* II, 10. Cf. Jump, *Matthew Arnold,* p. 64 and Trilling, *Matthew Arnold,* p. 79.

[15] *Culture and Anarchy,* p. 15.

[16] *Essays in Criticism,* II, p. 308. Cf. a very striking passage from the preface to the first edition of *Essays in Criticism,* I (1895), later suppressed:

> . . . the truth is, I have never been able to hit it off happily with the logicians, and it would be mere affectation in me to give myself the airs of doing so. They imagine truth something to be proved, I something to be seen; they, something to be manufactured, I, as something to be found. I have a profound respect for intuitions, and a very lukewarm respect for the elaborate machine-work of my friends the logicians. I have always thought that all which was worth much in this elaborate machine-work of theirs came from an intuition to which they gave a grand name of their own. How did they come by this intuition? Ah! if they could tell us that. But no; they set their machine in motion and build up a fine showy edifice; glittering and unsubstantial like a pyramid of eggs; and then they say "Come and look at our pyramid!" And what does one find it? Of all that heap of eggs, the one poor little fresh egg, the original intuition, has got hidden away far out of sight and forgotten. And all the other eggs are addled!

Quoted by E. K. Brown, *Studies in the Text of Matthew Arnold's Prose Works* (Paris, 1935), p. 2.

[17] See *Literature and Dogma,* Chapter V.

[18] Cf. Alan Harris, "Matthew Arnold: The 'Unknown Years,'" *Nineteenth Century and After,* CXIII (1933), 500.

[19] Cf. Arnold's discussion in *Literature and Dogma* of *"Aberglaube."* He quotes from Goethe the maxim "der Aberglaube ist die Poesie des Lebens," then proceeds to comment: *"Extra-belief,* that which we hope, augur, imagine, is the poetry of life, and has the rights of poetry. But it is not science." *Literature and Dogma,* p. 70.

[20] Cf. Jacques Rivière, quoted and translated by Martin Turnell, *Jacques Rivière* (New Haven, 1953), p. 50: "If in the seventeenth century, anyone had taken it into his head to ask Molière and Racine why they wrote, they would probably have been able to answer: "To amuse people." It was only with Romanticism that the art of writing began to be thought of as a raid on the

absolute and its result a revelation. At this time literature garnered the heritage of religion and organised itself on the model of the thing it was replacing. The writer became a priest; the sole aim of his gestures was to produce in the host that literature had become 'the real presence.' The whole of nineteenth-century literature is a vast incantation towards the miraculous." Cited by William A. Madden, "The Divided Tradition of English Criticism," *PMLA*, LXXIII (1958), 78n.

[21] "Matthew Arnold," *The Importance of Scrutiny* (New York, 1948), p. 97.

[22] *The Note-books of Matthew Arnold,* ed. H. F. Lowry, K. Young, and W. H. Dunn (1950), p. 513.

[23] *Homer,* pp. 148–49.

[24] *Letters of an Old Playgoer,* ed. Brander Matthews (December 6, 1882) p. 24.

[25] C. B. Tinker and H. F. Lowry, *The Poetry of Matthew Arnold* (1950), p. 270.

[26] R. G. Cox, "Victorian Criticism of Poetry: The Minority Tradition," *Scrutiny,* XVIII (1951), 2–17. William A. Jamison, *Arnold and the Romantics* (Anglistica, vol. 10: Copenhagen, 1958), is primarily concerned with placing Arnold's criticism of the Romantics against its Victorian background.

[27] T. S. Eliot called it "startingly independent" in *The Use of Poetry* (Cambridge, Mass., 1933), p. 104.

[28] *Romanticism and the Modern Ego* (Boston, 1944), pp. 148–49.

[29] Lowe, "Two Arnold Letters," *Modern Philology,* LII (1955), 262–63.

29.

René Wellek

Walter Pater's Literary Theory and Criticism

Today Pater is under a cloud. He is no longer widely read, and he is dismissed as an "impressionistic" critic. T. S. Eliot gives him as the example of a type of criticism which he calls "etiolated." "This is not worth much consideration, because it only appeals to minds so enfeebled or lazy as to be afraid of approaching a genuine work of art face to face."[1] Eliot must be thinking of the famous passage on Mona Lisa, which has become the stock warning against "creative" criticism. The young smiling woman with a widow's veil is transformed into a *femme fatale,* "older than the rocks among which she sits; like the vampire, she has been dead many times."[2] In addition a passage from the Conclusion to *The Renaissance* is remembered: "To burn always with this hard, gemlike flame, to maintain this ecstacy, is success in life" (p. 236). It is often quoted as the summary of Pater's philosophy, an aesthetic hedonism or hedonistic aestheticism. Today few want to burn with such a gemlike flame, and those few are usually very young indeed.

But these two passages—too well known for the good of Pater's reputation—are not really representative either of his method or his philosophy. The Mona Lisa passage is quite isolated in Pater's work. It is a tour de force modeled, it has been shown, on such poems as Gautier's "Caerulei Oculi" or Swinburne's "Cleopatra" or on Swinburne's "Notes on Designs of the

Reprinted from *A History of Modern Criticism,* Vol. IV, 1956, by permission of the author and Yale University Press.

Old Masters in Florence," describing Michelangelo's female heads.[3] Nowhere else in Pater is there such a revery quite out of touch with the work of art itself. The fantasy contains, one should admit, one of Pater's and Gautier's favorite ideas: the hypothesis of the multiplicity of individuals in one individual, "the idea of humanity summing up in itself all modes of thought and life."[4] If we look for other examples of a metaphorical method of criticism, even on a small scale, we are hard put to find many in Pater's writings. I have noticed only four which are at all conspicuous. Morris' poem "The Defense of Guenevere" is described in an early essay, "Aesthetic Poetry" (1868), as "a thing tormented and awry with passion, like the body of Guenevere defending herself from the charge of adultery."[5] In the sonnets of Michelangelo, we are told, there is "a cry of distress," "but as a mere residue, a trace of the bracing chalybeate salt, just discernible, in the song which rises like a clear, sweet spring from a charmed space in his life" (*Ren.*, 85). The concluding paragraph of the essay on Lamb, the originator of the method,[6] compares him elaborately to the London of sixty-five years before.[7] The *Bacchae* of Euripides is described as "excited, troubled, disturbing—a spotted or dappled thing, like the oddly dappled fawn-skins of its own masquerade."[8] These are little marginal fancies or rhetorical flourishes, but one would give an entirely false impression of Pater's mind and method if one advanced them as typical.

Rather, Pater's theory of criticism stresses not only personal impression but the duty of the critic to grasp the individuality, the unique quality of a work of art. Pater never advocates the impressionistic theory of the "adventures of the soul among masterpieces," the "speaking of myself on occasion of Shakespeare," as it was formulated by Anatole France. Pater quotes Arnold, "To see the object as in itself it really is," and modifies that only by adding that the "first step in criticism" is "to know one's impression as it really is, to discriminate it, to realize it distinctly" (*Ren.*, viii). He paraphrases Goethe when he asks, "What is this song or picture, this engaging personality in life or in a book to *me*? Does it give me pleasure?" (*Ren.*, viii).[9] But this personal pleasure is merely the first step, the prerequisite of criticism. The critic must go beyond it: penetrate "through the given literary or artistic product, into the mental and inner condition of the producer, shaping his work."[10] Moreover, he must know how to communicate this insight to others. In practice, Pater looks for the "formula," the "virtue," the "active principle" (*Ren.* xi), the "motive" in a work—terms substantially the same as Taine's (*Ren.,* 76) "master-faculty" or Croce's "dominant sentiment." The "formula" for Mérimée is "the enthusiastic amateur of rude, crude, naked force in men and women wherever it could be found; himself carrying ever, as a mask, the conventional attire of the modern world."[11] The "motive" of all Michelangelo's work is "this creation of life—life coming always as a relief or recovery, and always in strong contrast with the rough-hewn mass in which it is kindled" (*Ren.,* 76). The "virtue," the "active principle" in Wordsworth is "that strange, mystical sense of a life in natural things, and of man's life as a part of nature" (*Ren.,* xi).

The whole essay on Wordsworth circles around this one problem: how to define this "intimate consciousness of the expression of natural things" (*Appr.,* 43), his sense for "particular spots of time" (*Appr.,* 46), his "recognition of local sanctities" (*Appr.,* 50). "By raising nature to the level of human thought he gives it power and expression: he subdues man to the level of nature, and gives him thereby a certain breadth and coolness and solemnity" (*Appr.,* 49). Pater puts Wordsworth in a framework of intellectual history: he speaks of the survival of ancient animism (*Appr.,* 47–48); he draws the parallel with pantheism in France which from Rousseau to Hugo sought the "expressiveness of outward things" (*Guardian,* 95). When he writes on the *Intimations Ode,* he alludes to the Platonic doctrine of reminiscence (*Appr.,* 55) and elsewhere quotes the anticipation of mood and doctrine in Henry Vaughan's "The Retreat."[12] He speaks of Wordsworth's drawing on old speculations about the *anima mundi,* the one universal spirit (*Appr.,* 55). He is certain that Wordsworth felt, as Pater probably did too, that "the actual world would, as it were, dissolve and detach itself, flake by flake," that "he himself seemed to be the creator, and when he would the destroyer, of the world in which he lived—that old isolating thought of many a brain-sick mystic of ancient and modern times" (*Appr.,* 55). Pater, in short, attempts to define the mood, the temper, the dominant quality of Wordsworth's personality and work, what he once calls "the fine mountain atmosphere of mind" (*Guardian,* 93). He uses the traditional methods of 19th-century criticism: historical, when he suggests the intellectual affinities; descriptive, evocative, when he recalls "the biblical depth and solemnity which hangs over this strange, new, passionate, pastoral world" (*Appr.,* 53); and evaluative, when he discriminates between the good and the inferior in Wordsworth. As to method, there is nothing new except insight and finesse, nor is there anything subjective in it except sympathy.[13] It is a"portrait" as good as anything in Sainte-Beuve.

Pater's essays vary greatly in quality. Some are only book reports or exercises in translation from the French which should never have been reprinted (the colorless piece on Octave Feuillet's *La Morte* was even included in *Appreciations*). Others are small noncommittal reviews written to recommend (rather tepidly) the publication of a friend or disciple: George Moore, Edmund Gosse, George Saintsbury, Arthur Symons, Oscar Wilde. But if we make the necessary discriminations, we are left with a handful of subtle studies, models of the art of the essayist and portraitist. The essays concerned with English literature treat of Shakespeare, the romantics and the Pre-Raphaelites. It is true that of the three essays on Shakespeare only one is really distinguished. The piece on *Love's Labour's Lost* tries to convey a sense of Shakespeare's joy in verbal artistry. "Shakespeare's English Kings" pursues the theme of the sad fortune of English kings as "conspicuous examples of the ordinary human condition" (*Appr.,* 186). But the essay on *Measure for Measure* takes an original view of the play. Contrary to the usual complaints about its "painfulness," Pater sees the play as the "central expression of Shakespeare's moral judgments" (*Appr.,* 171), of his "finer justice" (*Appr.,* 183), of his tolerance and insight into man's fatal subservience to circumstance and temptation. In substance, he anticipates the view of Wilson Knight and F. R. Leavis, though he makes concessions to the view that Shakespeare did not properly assimilate the old story. The preoccupation with the moral issues of the play, "those peculiar valuations of action and its effect which poetry actually requires" (*Appr.,* 184), supplies a ready refutation of the common cliché about Pater's amoral aestheticism.

The essay on Sir Thomas Browne is largely narrative and descriptive but conveys a clear image of Browne's mentality, though Pater was, I think, mistaken in saying that "Browne, in spite of his profession of boisterous doubt, had no difficulties with religion" (*Appr.*, 137).[14]

The companion piece to the Wordsworth essay, that on Coleridge, suffers somewhat from being pieced together from two parts: an older essay on "Coleridge's Writings,"[15] from which Pater dropped the passages on the theology,[16] and a much later piece on the poetry.[17] Pater's discussion of Coleridge's philosophy and criticism is unsympathetic because he objects to Coleridge's search for the absolute and is suspicious of German metaphysical aesthetics. In the section on poetry, Pater oddly enough ignores *Kubla Khan* and does not get beyond rather random comments on *The Ancient Mariner* and *Christabel*. His essay on Lamb is more unified and superior in perceptiveness and sympathy both for the criticism (which seems to Pater the "very quintessence of criticism" [*Appr.*, 111]) and for the general mood of the essays of Elia: the enchantment of distance, the poetry of things, the dark undercurrent of tragedy.

The Pre-Raphaelites were obviously near to Pater's mind and heart: his early essay on William Morris (1868) describes very well Morris' "sense of death" (*Sketches*, 19), though it argues obscurely for the "charming anachronisms" of Morris' *Death of Jason*, the Greek legend told as if it were by Chaucer. The superior essay on Rossetti defines well the fusion of the "material and the spiritual" (*Appr.*, 212), his knowing, like Dante, "no region of spirit which shall not be sensuous also, or material" (*Appr.*, 213). But one is less convinced by Pater's praise for his "quality of sincerity" (*Appr.*, 206), by which he means unconventionality, novelty, and originality.

Though ostensibly art criticism, *The Renaissance* (1873)[18] is really a very literary book. Pater's conception of the Renaissance is substantially that of Burckhardt (and Michelet). It is the age that makes the discovery of man, of his body and his senses; the age that accomplishes the revelation of antiquity. Pater makes much of the traces of paganism in the Middle Ages, the medieval Renaissance, with its spirit of rebellion and revolt, "its worship of the body" (*Ren.*, 24). Still, in the first essay, "Two Early

French Stories," he can do little beyond producing the passage from *Aucassin and Nicolette* where, to be with his mistress, Aucassin is ready to start for hell rather than heaven. In the next essay Pater picks Pico della Mirandola as an example of the desire for the reconciliation of paganism and Christianity, the syncretism of the Florentine Platonic Academy. He emphasizes again the Platonic tradition in Michelangelo's poetry, which he contrasts with Dante's as being based on "principles diametrically opposite" (*Ren.,* 86). Michelangelo appears as the "spiritualist," Dante as the "materialist" in the sense that he believes in the literal resurrection of the body (*Ren.,* 86). Michelangelo is pronounced neither baroque nor a precursor of the baroque (though Pater does not yet use these terms), but a kind of survivor in the new and incomprehensible world of the Counter Reformation. Italy is the center of the Renaissance, but with the exception of the sonnets of Michelangelo no Italian literature is discussed in Pater's highly selective series of studies.

The French Renaissance is the "aftermath, a wonderful later growth" (*Ren.,* xii). Ronsard and Du Bellay are characterized, one-sidedly, as having "elegance, the aerial touch, the perfect manner" (*Ren.,* 158). Pater, in this context, seems to depend on Sainte-Beuve, the early *Tableau de la poésie au XVIe siècle* (1828) and the very late essays on Du Bellay,[19] which Pater quotes. This view of Ronsard, the stress on "his exquisite faintness, a certain tenuity and caducity" (*Ren.,* 170), is repeated in the fictional evocation of the elderly man retired to a convent, in *Gaston de Latour*. Ronsard's feeling for nature is described as if it were Wordsworth's. "The rain, the first streak of dawn, the very sullenness of the sky, had a power, only to be described by saying that they seemed to be *moral facts*."[20]

Obviously one must not treat Pater's fiction precisely as criticism, but it is difficult not to touch on it, as whole chapters of *Marius the Epicurean* and *Gaston de Latour* are concerned with works of literature: with Apuleius' *Golden Ass,* the *Pervigilium Veneris,* the *Meditations* of Marcus Aurelius, Ronsard's poetry, the *Essays* of Montaigne, and the philosophy of Giordano Bruno. These discussions have a strange ambiguity, a double focus at it were. Pater does not describe *The Golden Ass* as a book; he traces the aesthetic and moral experience of his hero, and Marius, though ostensibly a Roman of the later Empire, is a thinly veiled Walter Pater passing through the same or analogous experiences. The *Golden Ass* is, in *Marius,* not just a particular book but a representative of all or any finely wrought art: it is something like Gautier's *Mademoiselle de Maupin.* It illustrates what Pater calls, with deliberate anachronism, "Euphuism"; it shows "jeweller's work," "curious felicity," the art of concealing art, the "labor of the file,"[21] the worship of the word that was Pater's. Although Pater alludes to "an unmistakably real feeling for asses" (*Marius,* I, 60) and translates the whole of the episode "The story of Psyche and Cupid," he loses sight of the text of the *Golden Ass.* Similarly Ronsard in *Gaston de Latour,* while a fictional figure with definite traits of the historical man, functions also as the representative of youth's enthusiasm for contemporary poetry, for "modernity," and of Pater's own enthusiasm for nature poetry of a kind found in Wordsworth, Keats, Tennyson, and the Pre-Raphaelites: poetry that reproduces "the exact pressure of the jay at the window; you could count the petals—of the exact natural number; no expression could be too faithful to the precise texture of things . . . the visible was more visible than ever before, just because soul had come to its surface" (*Gaston,* 54).

The book on the Renaissance concludes with an essay on Winckelmann (1867), who in Pater's mind "really belongs in spirit to an earlier age." By his "Hellenism, his life-long struggle to attain the Greek spirit, he is in sympathy with the humanists of a previous century. He is the last fruit of the Renaissance" (*Ren.,* xv). Winckelmann is seen in the light of Goethe's memorial tract and of Hegel's aesthetics; his life is told in the terms of Otto Jahn's short biography.[22] But the analysis of Winckelmann's position is rather vague and shows little knowledge of its complexities: this early essay, with its many close parallels to Hegel,[23] is still not quite emancipated from its sources, still impersonally reproductive in spite of Pater's marked sympathy for its hero.

"The aim of a right criticism is to place Winckelmann in an intellectual perspective, of which Goethe is the foreground" (*Ren.,* 226), says Pater, and thus implies that the Renaissance actually ends with Goethe. Goethe is for Pater not only the last of the classics, but the first of the romantics. He represents their union, "the union of the Romantic spirit, in its adventure, its variety, its profound subjectivity of the soul, with Hellenism, in its transparency, its rationality, its desire of beauty—that marriage of Faust and Helena, of which the art of the nineteenth century is the child, the beautiful lad Euphorion" (*Ren.*, 226–27). Pater, oddly enough if one considers chronology, speaks of the romantic school in Germany as "that movement which culminated in Goethe's *Goetz von Berlichingen,*" or couples the names of Goethe and Tieck as examples of romanticism. (*Appr.*, 243, 249).[24]

Pater looks at German romanticism through the eyes of Madame de Staël and Heine. He does not seem to know any of the texts, with the exception of one passage from Novalis (*Ren.*, 236), and he thought that "neither Germany with it Goethe and Tieck, nor England, with its Byron and Scott, is nearly so representative of the romantic temper as France, with Murger, and Gautier, and Victor Hugo" (*Appr.*, 249). Pater admired Hugo greatly, alluding to several of his novels (*Ren.*, 223; *Sketches,* 7; *Appr.*, 253–54) and comparing him with Michelangelo and Blake (*Ren.*, 74). It is obvious that he is deeply read in Gautier (*Appr.*, 253–54). He wrote a laudatory essay on Mérimée that shows some uneasiness about Mérimée's "exaggerated art: intense, unrelieved, an art of fierce colours. Terror without pity" (*Misc.*, 27–28). Pater's admiration for the weird and macabre Gothic extends from *Wuthering Heights* (*Appr.*, 242) to Wilhelm Meinhold's vulgar, sensational novels,[25] which Rossetti had made known in England (*Appr.*, 243). Pater's taste defines itself clearly as late romantic, a taste that does not exclude an appreciation for the ancients and the Renaissance.

Theoretically, Pater was less interested in the national variety of the romantic schools than in romanticism as an eternal, ever-recurring type. In the postscript to *Appreciations* he defines romanticism: "It is the addition of strangeness to beauty which constitutes the romantic character of art" (p. 246). Poe had quoted Bacon, in speaking of Ligeia: "There is no exquisite beauty without some strangeness," and Baudelaire had said: "Le beau est toujours bizarre."[26] But Pater is the first to add "strangeness" to a definition of romanticism. He enumerates other traits, such as curiosity, the new, the contemporaneous, the grotesque, and these he contrasts with the classical qualities of measure, purity, temperance, as he found them stated in Sainte-Beuve's famous lecture. Pater defines romanticism so broadly, as "a spirit which shows itself at all times, in various degrees, in individual workmen and their work" (*Appr.*, 257), that he can speak of the *Odyssey* as being "more romantic than Sophocles" (*Appr.*, 258). The term—like all such terms when they divide the whole world into two camps—has lost all precision and hence all usefulness.

Only now can we return to the passage about "burning with this hard, gemlike flame." Pater in the second edition of the *Renaissance* (1877) suppressed the Conclusion, because it was misunderstood as the advocacy of vulgar hedonism. He had been ridiculed under the name of Mr. Rose in W. H. Mallock's satirical novel, *The New Republic*,[27] and therefore thought it necessary to define and defend his position in many passages of *Marius the Epicurean* (esp. I, 144 ff.) before he again reprinted the Conclusion in later editions (3d ed. 1888). In *Marius* Pater tells us that hedonism means "Be perfect in regard to what is here and now," and not "let us eat and drink, for tomorrow we die" (I, 145). It is culture, *paideia*, "an expansion and refinement of the power of reception" (*Marius*, I, 147), "not pleasure, but fulness of life, and insight as conducting to that fulness" (*Marius*, I, 151). The association with the Epicurean style, the attempt of enemies "to see the severe and laborious youth [Marius] in the vulgar company of Lais" (I, 150) is a gross libel. I find no difficulty in recognizing the high-mindedness of Pater's ideal and in admitting that the pleasures he recommended are intellectual and aesthetic. In our context we need not argue the sufficiency of his doctrine as a rule of life. The point important for criticism is Pater's central experience of time. To him "our existence is but the sharp apex of the present moment between two hypothetical eternities" (*Marius*, I, 146). "All that is actual is a single moment, gone while we try to apprehend it" (*Ren.*, 235). Such a feeling for "the perpetual flux," the *panta rhei* of Heraclitus,[28] is the corollary of Pater's almost solipsistic sense of man's confinement within "the narrow chamber of the individual mind," "that thick wall of personality through which no real voice has ever pierced on its way to us." Man is a "solitary prisoner" with his own "dream of a world" (*Ren.*, 235). This basic conception —no doubt a psychological *datum* of the retiring, shy, and unloving man—must lead him to a theory that sees the highest possible value in the individual moment of aesthetic experience. "Art comes proposing to us frankly to give nothing but the highest quality to your moments as they pass, and simply for those moments' sake" (*Ren.*, 239). This highest quality concentrated in a moment, is, however, inconsistently interpreted as oriented toward an outward reality. Art, in these moments, presents us with the concrete variety of the world. This hedonism is a form of empiricism and sensationalism. Pater condemns philosophical and aesthetic abstractions and the world of Platonic ideas. "Who would change the colour or curve of a rose leaf . . . for that colourless, formless, intangible being—Plato put so high?" (*Appr.*, 68). Hence the "first condition of the poetic way of seeing and presenting things is particularization" (*Appr.*, 208). Poetry should be as "veritable, as intimately near, as corporeal, as the new faces of the hour, the flowers of the actual season" (*Gaston*, 52). Poetry is thus concrete and sensuous, almost imagistically so. But poetry in this moment must be also intense and hence charged with emotion, with personal emotion. Pater thus values—side by side with a poetry of images—the personal lyric. As emphatically as Leopardi, John Stuart Mill, and Poe, Pater declares lyrical poetry to be "the highest and most complete form of poetry" (*Ren.*, 137). Lyrical poetry, "which in spite of a complex structure often preserves the unity of a single passionate ejaculation, would rank higher than dramatic poetry." A play "attains artistic perfection just in proportion as it approaches that unity of lyrical effect, as if a song or ballad were still lying at the root of it" (*Appr.*, 203). *Richard the Second,* like a musical composition, possesses "a certain concentration of all its parts, a simple continuity," and *Romeo and Juliet* approaches to "something like the unity of a lyrical ballad, a song, a single strain of music" (*Appr.*, 202–203). Unity of impression follows from lyrical intensity as a criterion of good art. Pater can praise a poem of Browning[29] for the "clear ring of a central motive. We receive from it the impression of one imaginative tone, of a single creative act" (*Ren.*, 215). *Measure for Measure* is even considered as having "almost the unity of a single scene" (*Appr.*, 171). But precisely because their unity is a unity of impression, a lyrical moment, Pater refuses to follow Coleridge into identifying unity with organism. The organic analogy "expresses truly the sense of self-delighting, independent life which the finished work of art gives us: it hardly figures the process by which such a work is produced" (*Appr.*, 80–81).

If art is lyrical, emotional, intense, it must be "sincere." Pater often uses this term, as do other English critics, as a vague term of praise for successful art, for the tone of conviction in Browne, or even for "the grandeur of literary workmanship," the great style of Rossetti (*Appr.*, 210). But often sincerity means something more concrete to him, "that perfect fidelity to one's own inward presentation, to the precise features of the picture within, without which any profound poetry is impossible" (*Guardian*, 102). It thus is a term for faithfulness to the inner vision, for the success of the transformation of the intuition into expression. Often it is another term for personality, the "impress of a personal quality, a profound expressiveness, what the French call *intimité*, by which is meant some subtler sense of originality. . . . It is what we call *expression*, carried to its highest intensity of degree. . . . It is the quality which alone makes work in the imaginative order really worth having at all" (*Ren.*, 71–72). Pater finds such personality even in the pale terra-cotta reliefs of Luca della Robbia, and he "longs to penetrate into the lives" of the Florentine sculptors of the 15th century "who have given expression to so much power and sweetness" (*Ren.*, 63). But in spite of this statement and although the life of Winckelmann attracts him, Pater is not primarily interested in biography. He has to make some defense for the "loss of absolute sincerity" which Winckelmann suffered when he became a convert to Roman Catholicism in order to go to Rome (*Ren.*, 187). But his guess that there is "something of self-portraiture" in Shakespeare's Mercutio and Biron (*Appr.*, 168) is a quite isolated remark in Pater's work.

Still, Pater, with his lyrical pathos, must reject the theory of impersonality in art and especially as he meets it in Flaubert. "Impersonality in art, the literary idea of Gustave Flaubert, is perhaps no more possible than realism. The artist *will* be felt. His subjectivity must and will colour the incidents, as his very bodily eye selects the aspects of things" (*Sketches,* 79–80). Pater is deeply impressed by the objectivity of Flaubert and Mérimée, and temperamentally he is given to hiding his own personality. But he sees that Mérimée's "superb self-effacement, his impersonality, is itself an effective personal trait" (*Misc.,* 37).

Pater's preference for concrete, intense, sincere, personal poetry manages to include the criterion of unity, and unity (while it is not organic unity) is the fusion of matter and form. "The ideal of all art is . . . the point where it is impossible to distinguish form from the substance or matter" (*Appr.,* 37). Art is a constant effort to obliterate the distinction between form and matter, as "the matter is nothing without the form, the spirit, of the handling" (*Ren.,* 135). This is also the meaning of Pater's much misinterpreted dictum that "all art constantly aspires towards the condition of music" (*Ren.,* 135). This does not mean that all art should become music, or even like music. Music is the "typically perfect art . . . precisely because in music it is impossible to distinguish the form from the substance or matter" (*Appr.,* 37). Good poetry should aspire to such an identity, but with its own means, and the arts should and will remain separate, since "each art has its peculiar beauty, untranslatable into the forms of any other" (*Ren.,* 130). Still, in one context, Pater recommends what he calls, using a Hegelian term, an *Andersstreben,* "a partial alienation of each art from its limitations through which the arts are able, not indeed to supply the place of each other, but reciprocally to lend each other new forces" (*Ren.,* 134). Pater's endorsement of the union of the arts is thus very partial: even the frequent parallelisms between the arts, acknowledged by him, are drawn only as a "great stimulus to the intellect" (*Ren.,* 3) not as literal truths, and, in a concrete question, he can appeal to arguments drawn from Lessing's *Laokoon* for the distinction between poetry and painting (*Ren.,* 52).

So far Pater's concept of poetry and art is consistently romantic, lyrical, pastoral. Romantic also is the great role Pater ascribes to imagination. The office of imagination is "to condense the impressions of natural things into human form" (*Greek,* 32), to achieve "the complete infusion of the figure into the thought" (*Appr.,* 88), to be as it is in Coleridge, a "unifying or identifying power" (*Greek,* 29). Pater, however, ascribes no significance to Coleridge's distinction between imagination and fancy: this reduces itself to a difference "between the lower and higher degrees of intensity in the poet's conception of his subject" (*Guardian,* 93–94). Romantic also (though hardly reconcilable with his emphasis on the intense moment) is Pater's acceptance of the idea of an ideal world of poetry, "a new order of phenomena, a creation of a new ideal" (*Appr.,* 218) which we are to contemplate (and not merely enjoy), "behold for the mere joy of beholding" (*Appr.,* 62). This ideal world is often thought of as a "refuge," "a sort of cloistral refuge from a certain vulgarity in the actual world," and even compared, in its uses, to a religious "retreat" (*Appr.,* 18), or called "a refuge into a world slightly better–better conceived, or better finished–than the real one" (*Appr.,* 219). The ivory tower–the dream world of the poet, the theme of escape–is prominent in Pater.

But these romantic motifs are crossed and modified or even contradicted by Pater's intellectualistic strain: by his sense of art as craft and labor. He thought of "severe intellectual meditation" as the "salt of poetry" and argued that "without a precise acquaintance with the creative intelligence itself, its structure and capacities . . . no poetry can be masterly" (*Marius,* I, 126). He can even say that "the philosophical critic" (and here Pater himself is the philosophical critic) "will value, even in works of imagination seemingly the most intuitive, the power of understanding in them, their logical process of construction, the spectacle of a supreme intellectual dexterity which they afford" (*Appr.,* 81). Pater protests that with Schelling and Coleridge the artist "has become almost a mechanical agent: instead of the most luminous and self-possessed phase of consciousness, the associative act in art or poetry is made to look like some blindly organic process of assimilation" (*Appr.,* 80). Pater sees the particular task of his time as that of doing "consciously what has been done hitherto for the most part unconsciously, to write the English language as the Latins wrote theirs, as the French write, as scholars should write" (*Appr.,* 260–61). Only in the case of Wordsworth would he grant that the "old fancy which made the poet's art an enthusiasm, a form of divine possession, seems almost literally true" (*Appr.,* 41). But just this feeling that "the larger part was *given* passively" (*Appr.*, 41) explains the unevenness, the fitfulness, of Wordsworth's achievement.

On the question of style, however, Pater is not entirely on the side of labor and the search for the right word. The famous essay "On Style" (1889) consists of two rather abruptly joined parts: a defense of what could be called "ornate," "imaginative" prose, "the special art of the modern world" (*Appr.*, 11), and a discussion of Flaubert's view of style for which Pater draws not only on the *Correspondence* but also on Maupassant's Preface to *Lettres de G. Flaubert à G. Sand* (1884). Pater first defends a personal style aimed at transcribing not "the world, not mere fact, but the sense of it" (*Appr.*, 9–10). The beauties of such a style will be not exclusively "pedestrian." "It will exert all the varied charms of poetry, down to the rhythm which as in Cicero, or Michelet, or Newman, at their best, gives its musical value to every syllable" (*Appr.*, 11–12). The names mentioned are extremely diverse, and neither Cicero nor Michelet conform to Pater's own ideal style. Pater seems to have learned something from Newman but even more from Ruskin and De Quincey. In vocabulary, he recommends a sensible eclecticism which will not be afraid to assimilate the phraseology of pictorial art, of German metaphysics, or of modern science, but this eclectic vocabulary must be used with restraint, with an economy of means, a sense of difficulty overcome (*Appr.*, 17). His recommendation of a highly imaginative, rhythmic, personal prose drawing on a varied modern vocabulary is modified by his insistence on the classical virtue of restraint and a polished style achieved by intellectual labor. "In truth all art does but consist in the removal of surplusage" (*Appr.*, 19). This is a rule that would make havoc of many of those Pater would consider to be the greatest stylists. Pater's recommendation that a conscientious writer "be fully aware not only of all latent figurative texture in speech, but of the vague, lazy, half-forgotten personification" (*Appr.*, 20) and his conviction that in prose "structure is all important," that "mind is a necessity in style" are consistent with his stress on consciousness and labor. "Insight, foresight, retrospect," "design," "a true composition and not mere loose accretion," "constructive intelligence which is one of the forms of the imagination" (*Appr.*, 21–25) are variations on the same theme. But suddenly Pater sees the insufficiency of his intellectual criterion and begins to speak of "soul in style." He finds it in theological writings as diverse as the English Bible, the Prayer Book, Swedenborg's visions and the *Tracts of the Times.* Each of these writings has a "unity of atmosphere" rather than of design (*Appr.,* 26).

The essay switches then to an exposition of Flaubert's theory of style. Pater obviously admires Flaubert's "martyrdom" and toil and agrees with the doctrine of *le mot juste.* He sympathizes with Flaubert's struggle against "facile poetry, facile art–art facile and flimsy" (*Appr.,* 32), though he does look for a moment in another direction to recognize the "charm of ease" (*Appr.,* 31). "Scott's facility, Flaubert's deeply pondered evocation of 'the phrase,' are equally good art" (*Appr.,* 34). This concession to a taste opposite from his own is wrung from him reluctantly, with a hidden envy for the easygoing master. On the question of the impersonal style, however, Pater had to decide against Flaubert. Style *is* the man; the "essence of all good style is expressiveness" (*Misc.,* 67).[30] Expressiveness must not, however, be confused with subjectivity, with "the mere caprice, of the individual, which must soon transform [style] into mannerism" (*Appr.,* 36). The subjectivity must not only be faithful to the inner vision but widen it into something objective.

The essay concludes with a sudden *salto mortale.* Pater now draws a distinction between good and great art not according to form but according to matter:

> Thackeray's *Esmond,* surely, is greater art than *Vanity Fair,* by the greater dignity of its interests. It is on the quality of the matter it informs or controls, its compass, its variety, its alliance to great ends, or the depth of the note of revolt, or the largeness of hope in it, that the greatness of literary art depends, as the *Divine Comedy, Paradise Lost, Les Misérables, The English Bible,* are great art. Given the conditions I have tried to explain as constituting good art;—then, if it be devoted further to the increase of men's happiness, to the redemption of the oppressed, or the enlargement of our sympathies with each other, or to such presentment of new or old truth about ourselves and our relation to the world as may ennoble and fortify us in our sojourn here, or immediately, as with Dante, to the glory of God,

> it will be also great art; if, over and above those qualities I summed up as mind and soul—that colour and mystic perfume, and that reasonable structure, it has something of the soul of humanity in it, and finds its logical, its architectural place, in the great structure of human life. (*Appr.*, 38)

There could not be a fuller and more explicit revocation of Pater's earlier aestheticism. It is a recantation at the expense of any unified, coherent view of art. It gives up the earlier insight into the unity of matter and form, divides and distinguishes them again, and either introduces a double standard of judgment or shifts the burden of criticism to the subject matter. Pater ends in a dichotomy destructive of his own insights into the nature of art. It reminds one of the distinction drawn years laters by T. S. Eliot between art and great art, the latter to be judged by its conformity to orthodoxy and tradition, and of Tolstoy's distinction between good universal art and the highest art flowing from the love of God. *Les Misérables* appears on both Pater's and Tolstoy's lists among the great works of literature, and Pater's phrases about "the increase of men's happiness, the redemption of the oppressed, the enlargement of our sympathies with each other, the soul of humanity" imply that he had now accepted art as an agency of sympathy and even of humanitarianism. He had returned to the Church. In his last days he wrote an essay on Pascal, who interested him "as precisely an inversion of what is called the aesthetic life" (*Misc.*, 80).

It is true, however, that even in his last stage Pater preserved the fundamental critical insight of his time, the historical sense. In fact he seems to have accepted Christianity and specifically the Anglican Church out of this sense of history. He criticizes Amiel in 1886 for "shrinking from the concrete," for "his fear of the actual, in this case the Church of history" (*Guardian*, 33). "By failure, as we think, of that historic sense, of which he could speak so well, he got not further than the glacial condition of rationalistic Geneva" (*Guardian*, 33–34). The implication that Pater himself had reached a warmer place seems obvious. But Pater had come a long way before he could apply the historical sense to the purposes of apologetics. The late religious moment of Pater's career is hardly represented in his literary criticism. To analyze the concept of history in Pater we need to turn back to the earlier phases.

In his very first essay, he had criticized Coleridge for "the dulness of his historical sense" (*Sketches,* 110), for getting involved in difficulties "which fade away before the modern or relative spirit, which, in the moral world as in the physical traces everywhere change, growth, development" (*Sketches,* 114). "Truth is a thing fugitive, relative, full of fine gradations." Coleridge was mistaken when he "tried to fix it in absolute formulas" (*Appr.,* 72). Relativism applies also to art. "All beauty is relative" (*Ren.,* vii). Everything changes and passes, develops and progresses. Pater was pleased with the Darwinian theory. "The idea of development," he says approvingly, "is at last invading . . . all the products of mind, the very mind itself, the abstract reason; our certainty, for instance, that two and two make four. Gradually, we have come to think, or to feel, that primary certitude. Political constitutions, again, as we now see so clearly, are 'not made,' cannot be made, but 'grow.' Races, laws, arts, have their origins and end, are themselves ripples only on the great river of organic life; and language is changing on our very lips" (*Plato,* 20–21). The evolutionary theory—Hegelian and Darwinian—confirms the old Heracliteanism, the *panta rhei* (*Plato,* 19), Pater's fundamental experience of the flux of time. What to him personally was a tragic experience of the transience of all things he accepts as part of a cosmic scheme in which he, as a good Victorian, still sees "the dominant undercurrent of progress in things" (*Misc.,* 252).

Pater inherits from German historicism the belief and emphasis on *Zeitgeist.* The artist is "a child of his time" (*Ren.,* 199). There is a genius of an age, and art and literature "must follow the subtle movements of that nimbly shifting Time-Spirit or Zeitgeist" (*Appr.,* 256). In every age "there is a peculiar *ensemble* of conditions which determines a common character in every product of that age, in business and art, in fashion and speculation, in religion and manners, in men's very faces . . . nothing man has projected from himself is really intelligible except at its own date, and from its proper point of view in the never-resting 'secular process' " (*Plato,* 9–10). No wonder he can say of the historical spirit that "the scholar is nothing without it" (*Appr.,* 16).

At other times, however, Pater will argue against the purely "historical," antiquarian view in favor of an "individual," present-day relativism. Speaking of Du Bellay, he says that if a poet's work is to have "an aesthetic as distinct from an historical value, it is not enough for a poet to have been the true child of his age, to have conformed to its aesthetic conditions, and by so conforming to have charmed and stimulated that age; it is necessary that there should be perceptible in his work something individual, inventive, unique, the impress there of the writer's own temper and personality" (*Ren.,* 172) Here Pater does not appeal to any absolute standard; he rather abandons the criterion of historical success or representativeness in favor of personal impression and pleasure.

At other times it is with a somewhat different accent that he rejects the view that modern man can somehow transform himself in order to become an ancient in imagination. "Such an antiquarianism," he feels, "is a waste of power. The composite experience of all the ages is part of each of us; to deduct from that experience, to obliterate any part of it, to come face to face with the people of a past age, as if the Middle Ages, the Renaissance, the eighteenth century had not been, is as impossible as to become a little child, or enter again into the womb and be born" (*Sketches,* 14–15). What has been called historical reconstructionism is rejected in favor of a fuller, wider universal historicism.

In the early essay on Winckelmann, Pater had still accepted "a standard of taste, an element of permanence, fixed in Greece" (*Ren.,* 199). When in that essay he reproduced Hegel's scheme of evolution in the arts—the triad of symbolical, classical, and romantic art—he shared Hegel's (and Winckelmann's and Goethe's) view that classical art is exempt from time and sets an absolute standard. But the view that the classical tradition is "the orthodoxy of taste" (*Ren.,* 198) did not last. Pater's later Hellenism is a historical Hellenism, which sees Greece as a past stage of human culture that cannot be revived today. Though in his actual critical practice his preferences for the Greeks, for the Renaissance, and for the romantics are so strong that they exclude any interest in the genuinely medieval, the baroque, or the neoclassical, in his theorizing Pater accepts the full consequence of historicism. "All periods, types, schools of taste are in themselves equal" (*Ren.*, x). He proclaims for his own time the role of "eclecticism" (*Guardian,* 15) as he had, in *The Renaissance,* admired the syncretism of Christianity and paganism propounded by Pico della Mirandola. What Pater wants for himself and his time is humanism, "the belief that nothing which has ever interested living men and women can wholly lose its vitality" (*Ren.*, 49; cf. 35), a feeling for the totality of the past, which is still alive in us:

> For in truth we come into the world, each one of us, 'not in nakedness,' but by the natural course of organic development clothed far more completely than even Pythagoras supposed in a vesture of the past, nay, fatally shrouded, it might seem, in those laws or tricks of heredity which we mistake for our volitions; in the language which is more than one half of our thoughts; in the moral and mental habits, the customs, the literature, the very houses, which we did not make for ourselves; in the vesture of a past, which is (so science would assure us) not ours, but of the race, the species: that *Zeit-geist,* or abstract secular process.

Pater found another image in Bunyan's *Pilgrim's Progress* for this living past. He speaks of the *House Beautiful* "which the creative minds of all generations—the artists and those who have treated life in the spirit of art—are always building together." In it the oppositions between styles and types, classical and romantic, cease. "The Interpreter of the *House Beautiful,* the true aesthetic critic, uses these divisions, only so far as they enable him to enter into the peculiarities of the objects with which he has to do" (*Appr.*, 241). In our age "we must try to unite as many diverse elements as may be." "The individual writer or artist, certainly, is to be estimated by the number of graces he combines, and his power of interpenetrating them in a given work . . . The legitimate contention is, not of one age or school of literary art against another, but of all successive schools alike, against the stupidity which is dead to the substance, and the vulgarity which is dead to form" (*Appr.*, 261)

Ernst Robert Curtius has called these words

> a landmark in the history of literary criticism: they signify a breakthrough to a new freedom. The tyranny of Standard Classicism is surmounted. Obedience to the rules and imitation of model authors no longer bestows any right to a good grade. Only the creative minds count. The concept of tradition is not abandoned in consequence, it is transformed. A community of the great authors throughout the centuries must be maintaineed if a kingdom of the mind is to exist at all. But it can only be the community of creative minds. This is a new kind of selection—a canon if you like, but bound only by the idea of beauty, concerning which we know that its forms change and are renewed. That is why the House Beautiful is never finished and closed. It continues to be built, it remains open.[31]

But it seems to me that Pater's House Beautiful has not escaped, and none of Pater's work has escaped the limitations of 19th-century aestheticism, its hectic cult of Beauty (a very narrow and exclusive type of beauty), its Alexandrian eclecticism, which made it impossible for the age to create a style of its own and which encouraged a historical masquerade. Historicism had to be transcended, as it has been during more recent years in Eliot's concept of tradition or in Malraux's imaginary museum.

Notes

[1] "A Brief Treatise on the Criticism of Poetry," *Chapbook,* II, 9 (March, 1920), 2.

[2] *The Renaissance,* p. 125; in the Library Edition (London, 1910). All quotations from Pater's works, unless otherwise indicated, are from this edition.

[3] See Bernhard Fehr, "Walter Paters Beschreibung der Mona Lisa und Théophile Gautiers romantischer Orientalismus" in *Archiv für das Studium der neueren Sprachen,* CXXXV (917), 80–102 and Mario Praz, *The Romantic Agony* (London, 1933), pp. 239–42.

[4] Fehr, pp. 87–88.

[5] *Sketches and Reviews,* ed. Albert Mordell (New York, 1919), p. 3.

[6] See my *History of Modern Criticism,* II (New Haven, 1955), 191 ff.

[7] *Appreciations* (Library Edition), p. 122.

[8] *Greek Studies* (Library Edition), p. 59.

[9] Cf. *Dichtung und Wahrheit,* Part III, Book 12. Werke, *Jubiläumsausgabe,* XXIV, 76.

[10] *Essays from the Guardian* (Library Edition), p. 29.

[11] *Miscellaneous Studies* (Library Edition), p. 14.

[12] *Plato and Platonism* (Library Edition), pp. 73–74.

[13] I cannot see why Geoffrey Tillotson should call the Wordsworth of the "Appreciation" "a scented Wordsworth." See "Arnold and Pater," in *Criticism and the Nineteenth Century* (London, 1951), p. 119.

[14] See D. K. Ziegler, *In Distinguished and Divided Worlds* (Cambridge, Mass., 1943) and Austin Warren's "The Style of Sir Thomas Browne" in *The Kenyon Review,* XIII (1951), 674–87.

[15] In *Westminister Review,* 1866.

[16] Reprinted in *Sketches.*

[17] In Ward's *English Poets,* 1880.

[18] The first edition is called *Studies in the History of the Renaissance* (1873); the second edition *The Renaissance: Studies in Art and Poetry* (1877).

[19] In *Nouveaux Lundis,* XII (1867).

[20] *Gaston de Latour* (Library Edition), p. 60.

[21] *Marius the Epicurean,* I (Library Edition), 96–97.

[22] See *Biographische Aufsätze,* 1866. Cf. Wright, *The Life of Walter Pater,* I, 232. Pater did not yet know of Justi's great work.

[23] See Bernhard Fehr, "Walter Pater und Hegel," in *Englische Studien,* L (1916–1917), 300–308.

[24] Goetz dates from 1773, twenty-five years before the German Romantic Movement began.

[25] *Die Bernsteinhexe,* 1838–1843, and *Sidonie von Bork,* 1847.

[26] "Exposition universelle de 1855," in *Curiosités esthétiques,* ed. Crépet (Paris, 1923), p. 224.

[27] First serially in *Belgravia,* 1876.

[28] Pater quotes Heraclitus in the epigraph to the Conclusion, *Ren.* 233 and often elsewhere, e.g., *Plato,* 19

[29] "Le Byron de nos jours," from *Men and Women.*

[30] Cf. *Guardian,* pp. 15, 36–37.

[31] *European Literature and the Latin Middle Ages,* tr. W. R. Trask (New York, 1953), pp. 396–97.

PART VI Drama

30.

Arthur Ganz

The Divided Self in the Society Comedies of Oscar Wilde

It is usually said that Oscar Wilde's society comedies have foolish plots and brilliant dialogue, and as far as it goes this critical commonplace is true. *Lady Windermere's Fan, A Woman of No Importance,* and *An Ideal Husband* do in fact have foolish plots and brilliant dialogue. But the foolishness of these plots does not prevent them from expressing Wilde's personal and artistic positions, while the brilliance of this dialogue has often obscured both its value and its meaning. These are the things that I wish to demonstrate here.

This dichotomy between plot and dialogue which mars the society comedies does not appear in Wilde's masterpiece, *The Importance of Being Earnest.* But to achieve the unity of *The Importance* Wilde had to suppress half his nature. That suppression constitutes a kind of deception, for we are given only a part of Wilde's reaction to his world. If we wish to understand fully what Wilde put into *The Importance,* we must also understand what he left out.

But however useful the society comedies are as an explication of *The Importance,* their real significance lies in themselves. Each of these plays contains two worlds, not only contrasting but conflicting. One is the world of the sentimental plots, where ladies with mysterious pasts make passionate speeches and the fates of empires hang on intercepted letters and stolen bracelets.

Reprinted by permission of the author and the editor from *Modern Drama* Vol. 3 (1960), 16–23.

This is the world I will call Philistine. Opposed to it is the dandiacal world, where witty elegants lounge about tossing off Wildean epigrams and rarely condescend to notice, much less take part in, the impassioned actions going on about them. The tension between these two worlds gives to the society comedies their peculiar flavor, their strength, and unfortunately their weakness.

Our first impulse is to admire the charm and wit of Wilde's dandies but to insist that while the shabby mechanisms of his well-made plots might have been suitable for our grandfathers, they will not pass muster with us. In justice to late Victorian literary taste, it should be pointed out that this was precisely the attitude of our grandfathers. William Archer thought he had discerned an English Ibsen in the author of *A Woman of No Importance* and even Bernard Shaw felt that Sir Robert Chiltern of *An Ideal Husband* had struck "the modern note" in defending his wrongdoing, but these examples are exceptional. Most of the Victorian critics grudgingly admired Wilde's wit and pointed out that his plots were compounds of various well-worn devices.[1] What was said about the society comedies when they first appeared is, for the most part, what is said about them today.

Such judgments are true enough, but to deny the Philistine parts of the society comedies the highest literary merit is not to deny them meaning. If we look closely at these plays, we see that each of them repeats the same pattern of action. A writer of Wilde's obvious gifts is not likely to indulge himself in such a repetition unless it is, for him at least, a meaningful one.

In each play the central character is someone who has in his past a secret sin. Mrs. Erlynne, who has alienated herself from good society by running away from her husband, fills that role in *Lady Windermere's Fan*. The motive force in the play is Mrs. Erlynne's desire to re-enter that society and be accepted by it. Although she knows the weaknesses of Philistine society, Mrs. Erlynne suffers from her ostracism and warns her daughter against a similar fate:

> MRS. ERLYNNE: You don't know what it is to fall into the pit, to be despised, mocked, abandoned, sneered at—to be an out-cast! To find the door shut against one, to have to

> creep in by hideous by-ways, afraid every moment lest the mask should be stripped from one's face, and all the while to hear the laughter, the horrible laughter of the world, a thing more tragic than all the tears the world has ever shed. You don't know what it is. One pays for one's sin, and then one pays again, and all one's life one pays. You must never know that.

This speech is, of course, a piece of nineteenth-century stage rhetoric, and if it stood alone in Wilde's work, the reader might safely ignore it. But in every play there are passages, if not as unfortunate in their phraseology, at any rate comparable in their content. The outcast is always repentant and desires forgiveness.

Mrs. Erlynne is easily recognizable as that stock figure, the woman-with-a-past, one of the innumerable progeny of Marguerite Gautier, the lady of the camellias. But Wilde uses this figure for his own purposes. Played off against Mrs. Erlynne is a cold and unforgiving moralist, her daughter, Lady Windermere. The real action of the play is Lady Windermere's education. She learns that a single act is not a final indicator of character and that a sinner may be a very noble person indeed. At the end of the play Lord Windermere tells Lord Augustus, who is about to marry Mrs. Erlynne, that he is getting a very clever woman. Lady Windermere knows better now. "Ah," she says to Lord Augustus, "you're marrying a very good woman."

In *A Woman of No Importance* Mrs. Arbuthnot is the character who parallels Mrs. Erlynne. Like her predecessor, Mrs. Arbuthnot is a woman with a secret sin in her past. In this case it is the fact that her son, Gerald, is the product of an illegitimate liaison. Though Mrs. Erlynne has led a life of pleasure and wickedness and Mrs. Arbuthnot has devoted herself to good works, the essential point about each is that, though a sinner, she has remained pure in heart and therefore, according to Wilde, deserves to be pardoned. As Mrs. Erlynne was opposed by the inflexible Lady Windermere, so Mrs. Arbuthnot is by the young Puritan, Hester Worsley. Lady Windermere had said that women who had sinned should never be forgiven. As Mrs. Arbuthnot makes her first entrance, Hester exclaims, "Let all women who have sinned be punished." Hester's conversion is no less complete than Lady Windermere's. At the end of the play, when Mrs. Arbuthnot points out that she and Gerald are outcasts and that such is God's law, Hester rebukes her. "I was wrong," she says, "God's law is only love." Again the sinner has been proved noble at heart, and the Puritan has been converted.

The woman-with-a-past, in the person of Mrs. Cheveley, appears again in *An Ideal Husband,* but here it suits Wilde's convenience to make her the villainess. In *An Ideal Husband* the sinner who must be pardoned is Sir Robert Chiltern, and the Puritan who must be converted is his wife. Chiltern laid the basis of his personal fortune and thus of his political career by selling a state secret. When he is black-mailed, he fears not only the ruin of his career but the loss of his wife, who has always idealized him. Above all, he desires her pardon and her love. "It is not the perfect, but the imperfect who have need of love," he says. "All sins, except a sin against itself, Love should forgive." Even after the threat of blackmail has been removed, Lady Chiltern demands that her husband retire from public life, but finally she relents and comes to realize that, as Lord Goring says, "women are not meant to judge us, but to forgive us when we need forgiveness. Pardon, not punishment is their mission."

It is easy to see the concealed sin and the plea for acceptance and forgiveness as a reflection of the situation forced upon Wilde by his homosexuality. In his journals (26 June 1913) André Gide hints at a concealed meaning in Wilde's plays, presumably along these lines. Robert Merle in his excellent study of Wilde is more specific.[2] He suggests not only that Wilde, in demanding pardon for his sinners, in demanding pardon for himself but that Wilde makes this demand most strongly for Mrs. Arbuthnot because her sin, like his, is sexual.

What Merle says is true, but to see in Wilde's plays, or even in the Philistine sections of them, only a reflection of his sexual inversion is to limit them unnecessarily. Wilde, along with many others, had rejected the mores of the ordinary middle-class society of his time, and in his case the isolation of this position was undoubtedly intensified by his sexual eccentricity. But Wilde was far from being the only writer of that period who was torn between a distaste for the values of the society about him and a simultaneous desire to be accepted and praised by it. The exile can never finally free himself of the desire to see his home again.

The Philistine aspects of his plays invariably brought out the worst in Wilde as a stylist, but because the language in which he expresses himself rings false, we cannot assume that the emotion which produces it is also false. Behind the mechanical facades of their well-made plots the society comedies are deeply expressive of the isolation of an artist and an individual man. The Philistine parts of these plays, though of limited aesthetic value, are of the greatest interest, for they reveal that the dandiacal Wilde was not a casual pose nor the easy expression of an amusing impulse but the product of emotional and intellectual conflict.

This conflict is visible not only in the division of his plays but in the opposition of those divided parts. The Philistine and dandiacal points of view are more than different; they are contradictory. The Philistine my insist that his heart has remained pure, but he admits that he has sinned and asks society for pardon. The dandy, however, instead of acknowledging his sin, denies that sin exists and creates a set of dandiacal standards by which he indicts society itself. Where the Philistine is humble, the dandy is belligerent; and where the Philistine's defense is sentimental rhetoric, the dandy's weapon is wit.

But what is loosely called Wilde's wit is not all of a piece. Much, perhaps most, of it is truly dandiacal, and this is what we are concerned with. On the other hand, much of it is simple humor and is to be enjoyed as such. An example is the series of jokes associated with the Duchess of Berwick and her trisyllabic daughter, Agatha, whose lines consist entirely of the phrase "Yes, mamma," worked into increasingly elaborate and ingenious contexts. Further examples can be adduced indefinitely. Occasionally we find a piece of what may be called capsule wisdom, such as the celebrated remark about the cynic's being one who knows the price of everything and the value of nothing. A more striking example is one of Chiltern's comments in Act II of *An Ideal Husband*. "When the Gods wish to punish us," he exclaims, "they answer our prayers." In addition, Wilde's dialogue often contains touches of genuine satire. When Kelvil of *A Woman of No Importance* remarks that the East End is a very important problem, Lord Illingworth replies, "Quite so. It is the problem of slavery. And we are trying to solve it by amusing the slaves." Wilde can be penetrating, but the amount of true satire in his work is slight. The satirist accepts a certain social code and criticizes those who do not follow it, but the dandy is an alien and can never follow ordinary society. All of these elements, humor, wisdom, satire, are present in Wilde's dialogue, but none of them gives it its peculiar flavor; none of them is dandiacal.

Oscar Wilde did not invent dandyism. He inherited a dandiacal tradition in both life and literature, and to this tradition he added certain elements that make Wildean dandyism unique. But to be unique is not necessarily to be isolated. Wilde must have felt himself to be one of the great dandies of the line that included Sheridan, Byron, Brummel, and above all, Benjamin Disraeli.[3] Like Wilde, Disraeli was an artist who had used eccentric clothes and brilliant conversation to seize the attention of Victorian society. But for the true dandy clothes are incidental and wit has a purpose.

The theory of dandyism as a philosophy of life was developed in France by Jules Barbey D' Aurevilly and Charles Baudelaire.[4] In his long essay on Brummel, *Du Dandysme et de Georges Brummell,* Barbey stresses the idea of the dandy as individualist, as the element of caprice in a stratified and symmetrical society. The dandy uses his wit to shock and startle that society while he himself remains impassive. Baudelaire accepts the idea of dandyism as a philosophy. He sees it, in fact, as a kind of religion, a cult of the self. Baudelaire's dandy, like Barbey's, is an individualist in revolt against his society. He is the last burst of heroism in a decadent age.

All of these ideas were intensely sympathetic to Wilde. His dandies, like Baudelaire's and Barbey's, are aristocrats whose elegance is a symbol of the superiority of their spirits. They use their wit to shock the gross Philistines about them. Above all, they are individualists who demand absolute freedom. Wilde insisted on his own individualism and wrote that nothing seemed of any value "except what one gets out of oneself."[5] To Wilde anything that interfered with the untrammeled expression of the self was intolerable.

Yet the Wildean dandy, however much he owes to tradition, is not simply a composite of English and French models. Wilde took the figure of the dandy because it embodied much of what he wished to express, but he added to it the elements we recognize as peculiarly Wildean. One of these is the theory of sensation. Wilde was a lifelong disciple of Pater's *The Renaissance* with its famous conclusion stressing the desirability of experience itself rather than the fruit of experience. The dandiacal individualist, as Wilde sees him, revels in exquisite sensations. The more of them he can absorb, the richer and more nearly perfect will be his personality.

It is in this reverence for the exquisite that we find the center of the creed of the Wildean dandy. He is a kind of exalted art critic, a savorer of beautiful things. And for Wilde beauty always lay in perfection of form. The content of a work was irrelevant; what was important was "the satisfying beauty of the design."[6] Wilde said that an artist "gains his inspiration from form, and from form purely," and so does the dandy.[7] The essence of the Wildean dandy's code is the substitution of aesthetic values for moral values. The Philistine world is, above all, the world of Victorian morality, but the dandiacal world is the world of pure aestheticism. Dandyism has many aspects and many disguises, but its presence in the society comedies is unmistakable.

A glance at the plays will show how the characteristics I have described appear in Wilde's dialogue. In the opening pages of *Lady Windermere's Fan* we meet Lord Darlington, the first dandy to appear in one of Wilde's comedies. The fact that he is a lord is significant. If the dandy is to dominate his society, he should possess social as well as intellectual superiority, and Wildean dandies tend toward the upper reaches of the peerage. As soon as he enters, Darlington displays his taste by admiring Lady Windermere's roses and then her fan. But more important than his title or his elegance is the fact that he is wicked. "Dear Lord Darlington," exclaims the Duchess of Berwick, "how thoroughly depraved you are." Lord Illingworth, the chief dandy of *A Woman of No Importance,* is introduced in much the same way. Lady Stutfield says of him, "The world says that Lord Illingworth is very, very wicked." Even the likeable Lord Goring of *An Ideal Husband* boasts of his bad qualities. "When I think of them at night," he says, "I go to sleep at once." The villain in a Wilde comedy is invariably a dandy, for the dandy is inherently anti-social. Breaking a moral convention is, in itself, a pleasure for the dandy. Mrs. Allonby of *A Woman of No Importance,* pointing out that women have a better time than men, explains that, "there are far more things forbidden to us than are forbidden to them."

The dandy can accept no interference from society. His individualism demands absolute freedom. "Lord Illingworth says that all influence is bad," reports Mrs. Allonby, "but that a good influence is the worst in the world." Lord Goring has the same attitude. "I always pass on good advice. It is the only thing to do with it. It is never of any use to oneself." A Wildean dandy, in fact, desires to be not only individual, but unique. When Lord Augustus of *Lady Windermere's Fan* ventures to agree with Cecil Graham, the latter answers, "Sorry to hear it, Tuppy; whenever people agree with me I feel I must be wrong."

What the dandy seeks from life is a series of exquisite sensations to enjoy. "Moods don't last," says Mrs. Allonby. "It is their chief charm," Lord Illingworth replies. "One should always be in love," he explains later. "That is the reason one should never marry." Mrs. Allonby sums up the dandy's desire for sensation when she remarks, "Life, Lady Stutfield, is simply a *mauvais quart d'heure* made up of exquisite moments."

The dandy savors these exquisite moments as he savors any beautiful object, for the rules of aesthetic form are the rules of his life. To the dandy, an aesthetic flaw is a moral flaw. Mrs. Cheveley of *An Ideal Husband* explains that "a woman whose size in gloves is seven and three-quarters never knows much about anything. You know Gertrude has always worn seven and three-quarters? That is one of the reasons why there was never any moral sympathy between us." From this point of view it is only a step to the assumption that all bourgeois goodness is ugly. "A woman who moralizes," remarks Cecil Graham, "is invariably plain." Lady Markby of *An Ideal Husband* dislikes high intellectual pressure because "it makes the noses of the young girls so particularly large." She mentions that a friend who had an unhappy life "went into a convent, or on to the operatic stage, I forget which. No; I think it was decorative art-needlework she took up." These are phenomena of a very different order, but for the dandy there is no distinction. They are all breaches of form.

The exaltation of the artistic, and thus the artificial, leads to a denigration of the natural. In *Lady Windemere's Fan* Dumby mentions that young Hopper has bad manners. "Hopper is one of nature's gentlemen," replies Cecil Graham, "the worst type of gentleman I know." In the eyes of the dandy artifice is everything. "My dear fellow," Graham says to Lord Darlington, "what on earth should we men do going about with purity and innocence? A carefully thought-out buttonhole is much more effective."

The essential point of the dandy's creed is always the exaltation of form over content, of externals over internals. "My dear Windermere, manners before morals," says Mrs. Erlynne. In the dandiacal system morals hardly exist. "It is absurd to divide people into good and bad," Lord Darlington maintains, "People are either charming or tedious." (Wilde had used almost exactly these words in the preface to *Dorian Gray*: "A work of art is neither moral nor immoral, only well or poorly written.") The content of a statement is of no importance if its form is perfect, as Lord Goring implies in his reply to Mabel Chiltern's rebuke. "That is the first unkind thing you have ever said to me. How charmingly you said it." Lord Goring is so much a dandy that he even employs a dandiacal butler, and the description of this personage in Act III of *An Ideal Husband* is Wilde's best compact definition of dandyism. "The distinction of Phipps is his impassivity. . . . The Sphinx is not so incommunicable. He is a mask with a manner. Of his intellectual or emotional life history knows nothing. He represents the dominance of form." Here is the key to the dandiacal code. Above all, the Wildean dandy represents the dominance of aesthetic form.

We can see clearly now the nature of the divided self in the society comedies of Oscar Wilde. Speaking in the person of his Philistine self, Wilde, the exile artist, admits that he has sinned in rejecting the mores of society. He insists, however, that he has remained uncorrupted at heart and begs society for pardon and acceptance. Speaking in the person of his dandiacal self, Wilde disdains that society and demands absolute freedom for the expression of the self. He denies the existence of evil and good and maintains that the only realities are ugliness and beauty.

Wilde seems never to have realized the significance of this pattern of division, although it is a persistent one in his work. Only in *The Importance of Being Earnest* did Wilde overcome this pattern and produce a work of pure dandyism and a masterpiece. But *The Importance* does not show the conflict that generated the world of dandyism. We must turn to the society comedies to see that conflict and the nature of the divided self.

Notes

[1] In this contention they were, of course, entirely correct. Wilde found the plays of Dumas *fils* a particularly useful source-book. Mrs. Erlynne's entrance in the second act of *Lady Windermere's Fan* is an adaptation of a scene in *L'Etrangère; Le Fils naturel* provided Wilde with the situation of *A Woman of No Importance,* and the misunderstood letter at the end of *An Ideal Husband* in Dumas' *L'Ami des femmes.* It is worth noting, however, that Wilde's borrowings appear in the Philistine parts of his plays but not in the dandiacal.

[2] *Oscar Wilde: Appréciation d'une oeuvre et d'une destinée* (Rennes, 1948), p. 355.

[3] For a discussion of Wilde's admiration of Disraeli, see J. Joseph Renaud, "Oscar Wilde et son oeuvre," *La Grande revue,* XXX–XXXIV (1905), 403.

[4] See Barbey's *Oeuvres completes,* XI (Paris, 1927) and Baudelaire's "Le Dandy" in *L'Art romantique* (Paris, 1931).

[5] *De Profundis* (New York, 1950), p. 79.

[6] "L'Envoi" in Rennell Rodd, *Rose Leaf and Apple Leaf* (Philadelphia, 1882), p. 12.

[7] *Intentions* (London, 1947), p. 201.

Suggestions for Further Reading

Victorianism

Books

Charlesworth, Barbara. *Dark Passages: The Decadent Consciousness in Victorian Literature.* Madison, Wis., 1965.
Evans, Joan. *The Victorians.* London, 1966.
Houghton, Walter E. *The Victorian Frame of Mind, 1830–1870.* New Haven, 1957.

Articles and Essays

Buckler, William E. "A Dual Quest: The Victorian Search for Identity and Authority," *Arts and Sciences,* I, i (1963), 27–33.
Culler, Dwight A. "Aspects of Victorian Literature," *Yale Review,* XLI (1952), 303–308.
Goldfarb, Russell M. "Late Victorian Decadence," *Journal of Aesthetics and Art Criticism,* XX (1962), 369–73.
Johnson, Wendell Stacy. "The Fourth Dimension of Victorianism," *Victorian Newsletter,* No. 21 (1962), pp. 1–7.
Madden, William A. "The Victorian Sensibility," *Victorian Studies,* VII (1963), 69–97.

Victorian Poetry

Articles and Essays

Miller, J. Hillis. "The Theme of the Disappearance of God in Victorian Poetry," *Victorian Studies,* VI (March, 1963), 207–28.

Smidt, Kristian. "Points of View in Victorian Poetry," *English Studies,* XXXVIII (1957), 1–12.

Browning

Books

Bryson, John. *Browning.* London, 1959.
Duffin, Henry Carles. *Amphibian: A Reconsideration of Browning.* Cambridge, 1956.
Honan, Park. *Browning's Characters: A Study in Poetic Techniques.* New Haven, 1962.
Kenmare, Dallas. *An End to Darkness: A New Approach to Robert Browning and His Work.* London, 1962.
King, Roma A. *The Bow and the Lyre: The Art of Robert Browning.* Ann Arbor, Mich., 1957.
Whitla, William. *The Central Truth: The Incarnation in Browning's Poetry.* Toronto, 1963.

Articles and Essays

Clements, Clyde C. Jr. "Browning's Poetry: Four Aesthetic Problems Answered," *McNeese Review,* XVI (1965), 3–15.
Hitner, John M. "Browning's Grotesque Period," *Victorian Poetry,* IV (1966), 1–13.
Knickerbocker, Kenneth L. "Robert Browning: A Modern Appraisal," *Tennessee Studies in Literature,* IV (1959), 1–11.
Kroeber, Karl. "Touchstones for Browning's Victorian Complexity," *Victorian Poetry,* III, i (1964), 101–107.
Langbaum, Robert. "Browning and the Question of Myth," *PMLA,* LXXXI (1966), 575–84.
Lindsay, Norman. "The Mask of Robert Browning," *Southerly,* XX (1960), 182–200.
Timko, Michael. "Ah, Did You Once See Browning Plain?" *Studies in English Literature,* VI (1966), 731–42.

Tennyson

Books

Buckley, Jerome Hamilton. *Tennyson: The Growth of a Poet.* Cambridge, Mass., 1960.

Marshall, George O. *A Tennyson Handbook.* New York, 1963.
Pitt, Valerie. *Tennyson Laureate.* London, 1962.
Richardson, Joanna. *The Pre-eminent Victorian: A Study of Tennyson.* London, 1962.

Articles and Essays

Duncan, Edgar Hill. "Tennyson: A Modern Appraisal," *Tennessee Studies in Literature,* IV (1959), 13–30.
Esher, Viscount. "Tennyson's Influence on His Times," *Essays by Divers Hands,* XXVIII (1956), 35–47.
Golffing, Francis. "Tennyson's Last Phase: The Poet as Seer," *Southern Review,* II (1966), 264–85.
Johnson, W. Stacy. "The Theme of Marriage in Tennyson," *Victorian Newsletter,* No. 12 (1957), pp. 6–10.
Korg, Jacob. "The Pattern of Fatality in Tennyson's Poetry," *Victorian Newsletter,* No. 14 (1958), pp. 8–11.
Preyer, Robert. "Tennyson as an Oracular Poet," *Modern Philology,* LV (1958), 239–51.
Sonn, Carl Robinson. "Poetic Vision and Religious Certainty in Tennyson's Earlier Poetry," *Modern Philology,* LVII (1959), 83–93.

Arnold

Books

Duffin, Henry Charles. *Arnold the Poet.* London, 1962.
Eells, John S. Jr. *The Touchstones of Matthew Arnold.* New York, 1955.
Robbins, William. *The Ethical Idealism of Matthew Arnold: A Study of the Nature and Sources of His Moral and Religious Ideas.* Toronto, 1960.

Articles and Essays

Kato, Takashi. "The Quest for the Genuine Self: Matthew Arnold and the Modern World," *Studies in English Literature,* XXXVIII (1962), 29–43.
Plotinsky, Melvin L. "Help for Pain: The Narrative Verse of Matthew Arnold," *Victorian Poetry,* II (1964), 165–77.

Roper, Alan H. "The Moral Landscape of Arnold's Poetry," *PMLA*. LXXVII (1963), 289–96.

Ryals, Clyde De L. "The Two Desires: Ambivalence Towards Action in Arnold," *Lock Haven Review,* Ser. I, No. 2, pp. 58–68.

Stevenson, Lionel. "Matthew Arnold's Poetry: A Modern Appraisal," *Tennessee Studies in Literature,* IV (1959), 31–41.

Kipling

Books

Bodelson, C. A. *Aspects of Kipling's Art*. New York, 1964.

Tompkins, J. M. S. *The Art Of Rudyard Kipling*. London, 1960.

Articles and Essays

Annan, Noel. "Kipling's Place in the History of Ideas," *Victorian Studies,* III (1960), 323–48.

Cross, Thomas N. "Rudyard Kipling's Sense of Identity," *Michigan Quarterly Review,* IV (1965), 245–53.

Deutsch, Kail W., and Wiener, Norbeit. "The Lonely Nationalism of Rudyard Kipling," *Yale Review,* LII (1963), 499–517.

Eliot, T. S. "Rudyard Kipling," *Mercure de France,* CCCXXXV (1959), 5–15.

Swinburne

Books

Connolly, Thomas E. *Swinburne's Theory of Poetry*. Albany, New York, 1965.

Peters, Robert L. *The Crowns of Apollo: Swinburne's Principles of Literature and Art: A Study in Victorian Criticism and Aesthetics*. Detroit, Mich., 1965.

Articles and Essays

Peters, Robert L. "Algernon Charles Swinburne and the Use of Integral Detail," *Victorian Studies,* V (1962), 289–302.

———. "Swinburne's Idea of Form," *Criticism,* V (1963), 45–63.
———. "Swinburne and the Moral Design of Art," *Victorian Poetry,* II (1964), 139–54.

Hopkins

Books

Boyle, Robert, S. J. *Metaphor in Hopkins.* North Carolina, 1961.
Downes, David. *Gerard Manley Hopkins: A Study of his Ignation Spirit.* New York, 1959.
Pick, John. *Gerard Manley Hopkins: Poet and Priest.* London, 1966.

Articles and Essays

Boyle, Robert. "Hopkin's Imagery: The Thread for the Maze," *Thought, XXXV* (1960), 57–90.
Byrne, Virginia C. "The Creator and the Maker in the Aesthetics of Gerard Manley Hopkins." *McNeese Review,* XIV (1963), 60–73.
Cherigny, Bell Sale. "Instress and Devotion in the Poetry of Gerard Manley Hopkins," *Victorian Studies,* IX (1965), 141–53.
Donoghue, Denis. "Technique in Hopkins," *Studies,* XLIV (1955), 446–56.
Downes, David A. "The Hopkins Enigma," *Thought,* XXXVI (1961), 573–94.
Hines, Leo. "Pindaric Imagery in G. M. Hopkins," *The Month,* XXIV (1963), 294–307.
Litzinger, Boyd. "The Pattern of Ascent in Hopkins," *Victorian Poetry,* II (1964), 43–47.
Miller, J. Hillis. "The Creation of the Self in Gerard Manley Hopkins," *Journal of English Literary History,* XXII (1955), 293–319.
Onesto, P. A. "The Self in Hopkins," *English Studies in Africa,* IV (1961), 174–81.
Schoeck, R. J. "Influence and Originality in the Poetry of Hopkins," *Renascence,* IX (1956), 77–84.

Humiliata, Sister Mary. "Hopkins and the Prometheus Myth," *PMLA,* LXX (1955), 58–68.

Wooton, Carl. "The Terrible Fire of Gerard Manley Hopkins," *Texas Studies in Literature and Language,* IV (1962), 367–75.

Pre-Raphaelite Poetry: Rossetti

Books

Gyrlls, Rosalie Glynn. *Portrait of Rossetti.* London, 1965.

Hyder, Clyde K. "Rossetti's *Rose Mary*: A Study in the Occult," *Victorian Poetry,* I (1963), 197–207.

Johnson, Wendell Stacey. "D. G. Rossetti as Painter and Poet," *Victorian Poetry,* III (1965), 9–18.

Weatherby, Harold L. "Problems of Form and Content in the Poetry of Dante Gabriel Rossetti," *Victorian Poetry,* II (1964), 11–19.

Victorian Fiction

Books

Allott, Miriam. *Novelists on the Novel.* New York, 1959.

Praz, Mario. *The Hero in Eclipse in Victorian Fiction.* Translated by Angus Davidson. London, 1956.

Stang, Richard. *The Theory of the Novel in England, 1850–1870.* New York, 1959.

George Eliot

Books

Allen, Walter. *George Eliot.* New York, 1965.

Bennett, Joan. *George Eliot: Her Mind and Her Art.* Cambridge, Eng., 1962.

Hardy, Barbara. *The Novels of George Eliot: A Study in Form.* London, 1959.

Harvey, W. T. *The Art of George Eliot.* London, 1961.
Paris, Bernard J. *Experiments in Life: George Eliot's Quest for Values.* Detroit, 1965.
Stump, Reva. *Movement and Vision in George Eliot's Novels.* Seattle, 1959.

Articles and Essays

Adam, Ian. "Character and Destiny in George Eliot's Fiction," *Nineteenth-Century Fiction,* XX (1965), 127–47.
Carroll, O. R. "An Image of Disenchantment in the Novels of George Eliot," *Review of English Studies,* XI (1960), 29–41.
Feltes, N. N. "George Eliot and the Unified Sensibility," *PMLA,* LXXXIX (1964), 130–136.
Harvey, W. T. "George Eliot and the Omniscient Author Convention," *Nineteenth-Century Fiction,* XIII (1958), 81–108.
Hyde, William J. "George Eliot and the Climate of Realism," *PMLA,* LXXII (1956), 952–61.
Mansell, Darrel, Jr. "George Eliot's Conception of 'Form,'" *Studies in English Literature,* V (1965), 651–62.
Milner, Ian. "George Eliot and the Limits of Victorian Realism," *Philologica Pragensia,* VI (1963), 48–59.
Paris, Bernard J. "George Eliot's Religion of Humanity," *Journal of English Literary History,* XXIX (1962), 418–43.
Pinney, Thomas. "The Authority of the Past in George Eliot's Novels," *Nineteenth-Century Fiction,* XXI (1966), 131–47.
Welch, Alexander. "George Eliot and the Romance," *Nineteenth-Century Fiction,* XIV (1959), 241–54.

Dickens

Books

Cockshut, A. O. J. *The Imagination of Charles Dickens.* New York, 1962.
Davis, Earle Rosco. *The Flint and the Flame: the Artistry of Charles Dickens.* Columbia, 1964.
Engel, Monroe. *The Maturity of Dickens.* Cambridge, Mass., 1959.

Garis, Robert. *The Dickens Theatre: A Reassessment of the Novels*. Oxford, 1965.
Miller, J. Hillis. *Charles Dickens: The World of His Novels*. Cambridge, Mass., 1958.
Stoehr, Taylor. *Dickens: The Dreamer's Stance*. New York, 1966.
Wagenknecht, Edward. *The Man Charles Dickens: A Victorian Portrait*. Oklahoma, 1966.

Articles and Essays

Brook, G. L. "Dickens as a Literary Craftsman," *Bulletin of the John Rylands Library,* XLIX (1966), 47–68.
Coolidge, Archibald C., Jr. "Dickens' Use of Character as Novelty," *South Atlantic Quarterly,* LXI (1962), 405–10.
Coolidge, Archibald C., Jr. "The Unremoved Thorn: A Study of Dickens' Narrative Methods," *North Dakota Quarterly,* XXX (1962), 8–13.
Cox, C. B. "In Defence of Dickens," *Essays and Studies by Members of the English Association,* XI (1958), 86–100.
Raleigh, John Henry. "Dickens and the Sense of Time," *Nineteenth-Century Fiction,* XIII (1958), 127–37.
Rodrigues, Eusebio L. "The Dickens of Great Expectations," *Literary Criterion,* VII, ii (1966), 41–53.
Rosenberg, Marvin. "The Dramatist in Dickens," *Journal of English and Germanic Philology,* LIX (1961), 1–12.
Wilson, Arthur Herman. "The Great Theme in Charles Dickens," *Susquehanna University Studies,* VI, iii (1959), 422–57.

Thackeray

Books

Loofbourow, John. *Thackeray and the Form of Fiction*. Princeton, N. J., 1964.
Ray, Gordon N. *Thackeray: The Uses of Adversity*. New York, 1955.
Ray, Gordon N. *Thackeray: The Age of Wisdom, 1847–1863*. New York, 1958.

Articles and Essays

Davies, Phillips George. "The Miscegenation Theme in the Works of Thackeray," *Modern Language Notes,* LXXVI (1961), 326–31.

Fraser, Russell A. "Pernicious Casuistry: A Study of Character in *Vanity Fair,*" *Nineteenth-Century Fiction,* XII (1957), 137–47.

Sharp, Sister M. Corona. "Sympathetic Mockery: A Study of the Narrator's Character in *Vanity Fair,*" *Journal of English Literary History,* XXIX (1962), 324–36.

Taube, Myron. "The Character of Amelia in the Meaning of *Vanity Fair,*" *Victorian Newsletter,* No. 18 (1960), pp. 1–8.

Taube, Myron. "Thackeray and the Reminiscential Vision," *Nineteenth-Cenutry Fiction,* XVIII (1963), 247–59.

Tilford, John E., Jr. "The Degradation of Becky Sharp," *South Atlantic Quarterly,* LVIII (1959), 603–608.

Hardy

Books

Morell, Roy. *Thomas Hardy: The Will and the Way.* Malaya, 1965.

Sankey, Benjamin. *The Major Novels of Thomas Hardy.* Denver, 1965.

Articles and Essays

Bailey, J. O. "Hardy's Visions of the Self," *Studies in Philology,* LVI (1959), 74–101.

Beckman, Richard. "A Character Typology for Hardy's Novels," *Journal of English Literary History,* XXX (1963), 70–87.

Hyde, William J. "Hardy's View of Realism: A Key to the Rustic Characters," *Victorian Studies,* II (1958), 45–59.

Goldberg, M. A. "Hardy's Double-Visioned Universe," *Essays in Criticism,* VII (1957), 374–82.

Goodheart, Eugene. "Thomas Hardy and the Lyrical Novel," *Nineteenth-Century Fiction,* XII (1957), 215–25.

Gregor, Ian. "What Kind of Fiction Did Hardy Write?" *Essays in Criticism,* XVI (1966), 290–308.

Neiman, Gilbert. "Thomas Hardy, Existentialist," *Twentieth-Century Literature,* I (1955), 207-14.

Neiman, Gilbert. "Was Hardy Anthropomorphic?" *Twentieth-Century Literature,* II (1956), 86–91.

Scott, James F. "Spectacle and Symbol in Thomas Hardy's Fiction," *Philological Quarterly,* XLIV (1965), 526–44.

Scott, Nathan A., Jr. "The Literary Imagination and the Victorian Crisis of Faith; The Example of Thomas Hardy," *Journal of Religion,* XL, 267–81.

Spivey, Ted R. "Thomas Hardy's Tragic Hero," *Nineteenth-Century Fiction,* IX (1954), 179–91.

Charlotte Bronte

Books

Crompton, Margaret. *Passionate Search: A Life of Charlotte Bronte.* New York, 1955.

Martin, Robert Bernard. *The Accents of Persuasion: Charlotte Bronte's Novels.* London, 1966.

Articles and Essays

Blondel, Jacques. "*Jane Eyre:* A Romantic Exempliem with a Difference," *Studies in English Literature,* XXXVI (1959), 1–13.

Day, Martin S. "Central Concepts of *Jane Eyre,*" *The Personalist,* XLI (1960), 495–505.

Momberger, Philip. "Self and World in the Works of Charlotte Bronte," *Journal of English Literary History,* XXXII (1965), 349–69.

Moser, Lawrence E., S. J. "From Portrait to Person: A Note on the Surrealistic in *Jane Eyre,*" *Nineteenth-Century Fiction,* XX (1965), 275–81.

Emily Bronte

Books

Ewbank, Inga Stina. *Their Proper Sphere: A Study of the Bronte Sisters as Early Victorian Novelists.* Cambridge, Mass., 1966.

Articles and Essays

Gose, Elliot B., Jr., "*Wuthering Heights:* The Heath and the Hearth," *Nineteenth-Century Fiction,* XXI (1966), 1–19.

Jordon, John E. "The Ironic Vision of Emily Bronte," *Nineteenth-Century Fiction,* XX (1965), 1–18.

Moser, Thomas. "What is the Matter with Emily Jane? Conflicting Impulses in *Wuthering Heights,*" *Nineteenth-Century Fiction,* XVII (1962), 1–19.

McCaughey, G. S. "An Approach to *Wuthering Heights,*" *Humanities Association Bulletin,* XV, ii (1964), 28–34.

George Meredith

Books

Kelvin, Norman. *A Troubled Eden: Nature and Society in the Works of George Meredith.* Stanford, Calif., 1961.

Lindsay, Jack. *George Meredith: His Life and Work.* London, 1956.

Wright, Walter F. *Art and Substance in George Meredith: A Study in Narrative.* Lincoln, Neb., 1963.

Articles and Essays

Beer, Gillian. "Meredith's Idea of Comedy: 1876–1880," *Nineteenth-Century Fiction,* XX (1965), 165–76.

Fanger, Donald. "George Meredith as Novelist," *Nineteenth-Century Fiction,* XVI (1962), 317–28.

Sudrann, Jean. " 'The Linked Eye and Mind': A Concept of Action in the Novels of George Meredith," *Studies in English Literature,* IV (1964), 617–35.

Henry James

Books

Cargill, Oscar. *The Novels of Henry James.* New York: 1961.

Clair, John A. *The Ironic Dimension in the Fiction of Henry James.* Pittsburgh, 1965.

Krook, Dorothea. *The Ordeal of Consciousness in Henry James.* Cambridge, 1962.

Sharp, Sister M. Corona. *The Confidante in Henry James: Evolution and Moral Value of a Fictive Character.* Notre Dame, Ind., 1963.

Ward, Joseph A. *The Imagination of Disaster: Evil in the Fiction of Henry James.* Lincoln, Neb., 1961.

Wright, Walter F. *The Madness of Art: A Study of Henry James.* Lincoln, Neb., 1962.

Articles and Essays

Allot, Miriam. "Form versus Substance in Henry James," *Review of English Literature,* III (1962), 53–66.

Berland, Alwyn. "Henry James and the Aesthetic Tradition," *Journal of the History of Ideas,* XXIII (1962), 407–19.

Cambon, Glauco. "The Negative Gesture in Henry James," *Nineteenth-Century Fiction,* XV (1961), 335–43.

Dove, John R. "Tragic Consciousness in Henry James," *Texas Studies in Literature and Language,* II (1960), 303–14.

Emerson, Donald. "Henry James and the Limitations of Realism," *College English,* XXII (1960), 161–66.

Goldsmith, Arnold L. "Henry James's Reconciliation of Free Will and Fatalism," *Nineteenth-Century Fiction,* XIII (1958), 109–26.

Roberts, James L. "An Approach to Evil in Henry James," *Arizona Quarterly,* XVII (1961), 51–16.

Silverstein, Henry. "The Utopia of Henry James," *New England Quarterly,* XXXV (1962), 458–68.

Willey, Frederick. "The Free Spirit and the Clever Agent in Henry James," *Southern Review,* II (1966), 315–28.

Victorian Prose

Books

Klingopulos, G. D. "The Spirit of the Age in Prose," in *Pelican Guide to English Literature,* V (1958), 130–51.

Ruskin

Books

Rosenberg, John D. *The Darkening Glass: A Portrait of Ruskin's Genius.* New York, 1961.

Articles and Essays

Burd, Van Akin. "Ruskin's Quest for a Theory of Imagination," *Modern Language Quarterly,* XVII (1956), 60–72.

Smallwood, Osborn T. "John Ruskin and the Oxford Movement," *College Language Association Journal,* III (1959), 114–18.

Thomas, J. D. "Poetic Truth and Pathetic Faculty," *Texas Studies in Literature and Language,* III (1961), 342–47.

Carlyle

Articles and Essays

Marlin, Peter E. "Carlyle and Mill: The Anti-Self-Conscious Theory," *Thoth,* VI (1965), 20–34.

Metzger, Lou. "*Sartor Resartus:* A Victorian *Faust,*" *Comparative Literature,* XIII (1961), 316–31.

Moores, Carlisle. "The Persistence of Carlyle's Everlasting Yea!" *Modern Philology,* LIV (1957), 187–96.

Roellinger, Francis X., Jr. "The Early Development of Carlyle's Style," *PMLA,* LXXII (1957), 951–63.

Sanders, Richard. "Carlyle, Poetry, and the Music of Humanity," *Western Humanities Review,* XVI, 53–66.

Sharrock, Roger. "Carlyle and the Sense of History," *Essays and Studies by Members of the English Association,* XIX (1966), 74–91.

Newman

Books

Dibble, Romuald A. *John Henry Newman: The Concept of Infallible Doctrinal Authority.* Washington, 1956.

Kaiser, Brother F. James. *The Concept of Conscience According to John Henry Newman.* Washington, D.C., 1959.

Articles and Essays

Cameron, J. M. "The Night Battle: Newman and Empiricism," *Victorian Studies,* IV (1960), 99–117.

Dessain, C. Stephen. "Newman's First Conversion," *Studies,* XLVI (1958), 44–59.

Dooley, D. J. "The Newman Question," *Culture,* XX (1959), 41–47.

Abbot of Dawnside. "The Significance of Newman Today," *Dublin Review,* CCXXXIII (1959), 337–46.

Friedman, Norman. "Newman, Aristotle and the New Criticism: On the Modern Element in Newman's Poetics," *PMLA,* LXXXI (1966), 261–71.

Jost, Edward F. "Newman and Liberalism: The Later Phase," *Victorian Newsletter,* No. 20 (1963), pp. 1–6.

Pearsall, Ronald. "The Oxford Movement in Retrospect," *Quarterly Review,* CCIV (1966), 75–83.

Strachey

Books

Sanders, Carles R. *Lytton Strachey: His Mind and Art.* New Haven, Conn., 1957.

Articles and Essays

Kallich, Martin. "Psychoanalysis, Sexuality, and Lytton Strachey's Theory of Biography," *American Imago,* XV (1958), 331–70.

Victorian Criticism

Books

Tillotson, Geoffrey. *Criticism and the Nineteenth Century.* London, 1951.

Arnold

Books

Johnson, Wendell Stacy. *The Voices of Matthew Arnold: An Essay in Criticism.* New Haven, Conn., 1961.

Articles and Essays

Coulling, Sidney, M. B. "The Evolution of *Culture and Anarchy,*" *Studies in Philology,* LX (1963), 637–68.

Ebel, Henry. "Matthew Arnold and Classical Culture," *Arion,* IV (1965), 188–220.

Shumaker, Wayne. "Matthew Arnold's Humanism: Literature as a Criticism of Life," *Studies in English Literature,* II (1962), 385–402.

Pater

Books

Cecil, Lord David. *Walter Pater, the Scholar-Artist.* Cambridge, 1956.

Johnson, R. V. *Walter Pater: A Study of His Critical Outlook and Achievement.* Melbourne, 1961.

Articles and Essays

Bizenk, Eugene J. "The Unique Fictional World of Walter Pater," *Nineteenth-Century Fiction,* XIII (1958), 217–26.

Sudrann, Jean. "Victorian Compromise and Modern Revolution," *Journal of English Literary History,* XXVI (1959), 425–44.

Victorian Drama

Books

Rowell, George. *The Victorian Theatre: A Survey.* London, 1956.

Wilde

Books

Winivar, Frances. *Oscar Wilde and the Yellow Nineties.* New York, 1958.

Articles and Essays

Ellman, Richard. "Romantic Pantomime in Oscar Wilde," *Partisan Review,* XXX (1963), 342–55.

Ganz, Arthur. "The Meaning of *The Importance of Being Earnest*," *Modern Drama,* VI (1963), 42–52.

Gregor, Ian. "Comedy and Oscar Wilde," *Sewanee Review,* LXXIV (1963), 501–21.

Woodward, A. G. "Oscar Wilde," *English Studies in Africa,* II (1959), 218–31.